POWERS OF POSSIBILITY

In *The Meaning of Contemporary Realism* (1957) Georg Lukács discussed how the power struggle of the Cold War made it all the more pressing for literary writers to present 'concrete potentialities' of individual character in novel ways. *Powers of Possibility* explores how American experimental writers since the 1960s have set about presenting exactly that while engaging with specific issues of social power.

The book's five chapters cover a range of writers, literary genres, and political issues, including: Allen Ginsberg's anti-Vietnam War poems; LeRoi Jones/Amiri Baraka and Black Power theatre; William S. Burroughs's novels and the Space Programmes; Kathy Acker's fiction and Biopolitics; and Lyn Hejinian, Language poetry, and the Cold War.

Each chapter examines how relations of character and social power were widely discussed in terms of potentiality: Black Power groups, for example, debated the 'revolutionary potential' of African Americans, while advances in the space programmes led to speculation about the evolution of 'human potential' in space colonies. In considering how the literary writers engage with such debates, Alex Houen also shows how each writer's approach entails combining different meanings of 'potential': 'possible as opposed to actual'; 'a quantity of force'; a 'capacity' or 'faculty'; and 'potency'.

Such an approach can be characterized as a literary 'potentialism' that turns literary possibilities (including experiments with style and form) into an affective aesthetic force with which to combat or reorient the effects of social power on people. Potentialism is not a literary movement, Houen emphasizes, so much as a novel concept of literary practice—a concept that stands as a refreshing alternative to notions of 'postmodernism' and the 'postmodern avant-garde'.

Powers of Possibility

Experimental American Writing since the 1960s

ALEX HOUEN

OXFORD
UNIVERSITY PRESS

OXFORD
UNIVERSITY PRESS

Great Clarendon Street, Oxford, OX2 6DP,
United Kingdom

Oxford University Press is a department of the University of Oxford.
It furthers the University's objective of excellence in research, scholarship,
and education by publishing worldwide. Oxford is a registered trade mark of
Oxford University Press in the UK and in certain other countries

© Alex Houen 2012

The moral rights of the authors have been asserted

First published 2012
First published in paperback 2014

Impression: 1

All rights reserved. No part of this publication may be reproduced, stored in
a retrieval system, or transmitted, in any form or by any means, without the
prior permission in writing of Oxford University Press, or as expressly permitted
by law, by licence or under terms agreed with the appropriate reprographics
rights organization. Enquiries concerning reproduction outside the scope of the
above should be sent to the Rights Department, Oxford University Press, at the
address above

You must not circulate this work in any other form
and you must impose this same condition on any acquirer

Published in the United States of America by Oxford University Press
198 Madison Avenue, New York, NY 10016, United States of America

British Library Cataloguing in Publication Data
Data available

ISBN 978–0–19–960929–1 (Hbk.)
ISBN 978–0–19–871992–2 (Pbk.)

Links to third party websites are provided by Oxford in good faith and
for information only. Oxford disclaims any responsibility for the materials
contained in any third party website referenced in this work.

Acknowledgements

Most of this monograph was written while I was teaching in the School of English, University of Sheffield, during which time I benefited from three periods of sabbatical leave as well as an award of University Devolved Funds for research trips to the USA. The School's unique collegial geniality—long may it last—was a real boon. I am grateful also for a British Academy Small Grant that enabled me to undertake archival research at the following institutions: Duke University Library; Howard University Library; Mandeville Special Collections Library, University of California, San Diego; and Department of Special Collections, Stanford University Libraries. My thanks to the librarians there for their assistance. I should also acknowledge the sanctuary that was my former house, 79 Sandford Grove Road, Sheffield; thank you for having always been there for me. Thankfully, since moving to Cambridge I have benefited hugely from the collegiality and vibrant intellectual atmosphere nurtured by The Master and Fellows of Pembroke College, and by other colleagues in the Faculty of English.

Where would I be without the following individuals who have assisted me with this book in various ways? (On a park bench staring at an unfinished manuscript containing errors that this one doesn't contain, that's where.) I am very grateful for the editorial guidance of Jacqueline Baker and Andrew McNeillie at Oxford University Press, as well as the copy-editing of Charles Lauder, Jr, and the meticulous proofreading of Anne Halliday. My thanks to Matthew Campbell, Paul Faulkner, John Haffenden, Erica Sheen, Anne Stillman, Marcus Waithe, and Karla Zažirejova for their ideas and talk. My thanks to Tim Armstrong, Charles Bernstein, Bruce Gardiner, Daniel Matlin, Chris Nealon, Peter Nicholls, and two anonymous readers at the Press for having read drafts of chapters. My deepest gratitude to Adam Piette, Matt Bevis, and Geoff Gilbert for discussions, comments on drafts, and for their being so inspiring.

A version of sections of Chapter 1 first appeared as '"Back! Back! Back! Central Mind Machine Pentagon...": Allen Ginsberg and the Vietnam War', in *Cultural Politics*, 4:3 (Autumn 2008), 351–74; Berg Publishers, an imprint of A&C Black Publishers Ltd, have granted permission to adapt the material. Parts of Chapter 3 first appeared in 'William S. Burroughs's Cities of the Red Night Trilogy: Writing Outer Space', *Journal of American Studies*, 40:3 (Winter 2006), 523–46; permission to adapt the material has been granted by Cambridge University Press. Some of the ideas in Chapter 4 draw on my article 'Sovereignty, Biopolitics, and the Use of Literature: Michel Foucault and Kathy Acker', *Theory & Event*, 9:1 (Spring 2006), reprinted in Stephen Morton and Stephen Bygrave (eds), *Foucault in an Age of Terror: Essays on Biopolitics and the Defence of Society* (London: Palgrave Macmillan, 2008); permission to adapt the material has been granted by The Johns Hopkins University Press and Palgrave Macmillan. Some ideas in the Conclusion were first essayed in my 'Introduction: Affecting Words' published in a special issue on 'Affects, Text, and Performativity' of *Textual Practice*, 25:2 (March/April 2011). I have drawn from the latter with the permission of Taylor & Francis Publishers. I am grateful to all the publishers for their kind permission to adapt and reprint material.

A.H.
Pembroke College, Cambridge

Contents

Introduction   1

1. 'Back! Back! Back! Central Mind Machine Pentagon...':
   Allen Ginsberg and the Vietnam War   22
   - The possibility of the 1960s   22
   - The war's start and a change of heart   25
   - 'Wichita Vortex Sutra'   31
   - 'Miserable picnic, Police State or Garden of Eden?'   40
   - 'Bodies alert' and the war's end   50

2. 'This Black World of Purest Possibility':
   LeRoi Jones/Amiri Baraka   62
   - Black Power and black possibility   62
   - 'My poetry is whatever I think I am': from Beats to Black Arts   65
   - Performing Black Arts   78
   - From Pan-Africanism to Third-World Socialism   94

3. Writing Outer Space for 'Potential America':
   William S. Burroughs   103
   - 'We have lift-off...'   103
   - The space race, 1957–64   106
   - Cut-ups, fold-ins, and the Nova trilogy   109
   - From watershed to Watergate   116
   - Space exploration in the 1970s   120
   - The Cities of the Red Night trilogy   125
   - From 'Star Wars' to 'Critical Space'   135
   - *The Western Lands*   138

4. Novel Biopolitics: Kathy Acker and Michel Foucault   145
   - Introduction   145
   - Self-writing, dreams, and allobiography   149
   - *Blood and Guts in High School*: from sympathy to 'order words'   160
   - *Homo œconomicus* and Corporeality Inc.   165
   - 'This's no world for idealism': AIDS, abortion, and Reagan's body   170

Empire of the Senseless: cyberdrag and 'languages of the body'	178
Pussy, King of the Pirates: filthy myth and the 'language of abjection'	185

5. Making a Person Possible: Lyn Hejinian and Language Poetry — 193

Language Group beginnings: 'the 1960s by other means'? — 193
'Oneself is possible': *My Life* — 201
The Conspiracy of 'US': 1980s language politics — 209
Russia, estrangement, and the 'cold of poetry' — 213
Happily: from *amor fati* to *amor possibilis* — 223
A Border Comedy and *The Fatalist*: a critique of fatal judgement — 231

Conclusion: Potentialism and Practical Imagination — 241

Bibliography — 257
Index — 277

Introduction

In 2009 the financial services company American Express launched an advertising campaign around the central slogan 'Realise the Potential™'. Cashing in on this imperative is easy, as the company's website explains: every time you purchase something on your Amex card, you are rewarded with 'points' that can be 'redeemed' for a range of 'extraordinary treats'.[1] The implication is that owning such a card means possessing the ability to convert metaphor into real exchange—'What if last night's dinner could become an iPod?'—and this power of transmutation is supposedly the potential to change your life; a power to redeem the costs and tedium of your daily commute, for example, by turning them into a reward for yourself. In short, the world is full of 'untapped potential' for redemption; a human resource that lies latent in our 'experiences' no less than in 'things around us'. And the campaign is keen for people to realize the creative possibilities of what it is pushing: 'the pen that writes the humble shopping list can also write the next Pulitzer prize-winning novel'.[2] Well, surely that depends on the literary abilities of the person holding the pen? But the point is that the advertisement doesn't want you to think your abilities are fixed or limited, for its underlying suggestion is that even if the metamorphic potential you 'realise' is trademarked, it is still a potential for change that you, personally, are credited with. To the extent that it does mark individual agency and creativity with trade, the advertisement is grist to the mill of anyone who thinks, like Fredric Jameson, that we are living in an age of postmodernism characterized by predicaments such as the following: culture is now primarily conceived in terms of consuming commodities; the constant investment in new products and services means aesthetic innovation and experiment have lost their novelty; with cultural change turned into cycles of consumption, we have lost

---

[1] American Express website, http://www.AmericanExpress.com/Potential, accessed 4 September 2010.
[2] Ibid.

a 'practical sense of the future'.[3] Today the 'treat', tomorrow the commute. That is to say, we have also lost practical and aesthetic senses of potential other than those of late capitalism.

I'll return to the relation of postmodernism and aesthetics shortly; first, I want to outline a more particular view of potentiality as combining individual capacity, possibility, and power. That view has recently been theorized by a number of Italian political philosophers, including Massimo de Carolis, Paolo Virno, and Giorgio Agamben. In de Carolis's view, personal liberty in modern society is now perceived in terms of 'freedom as practical power (*potentia*, or possibility)' that entails 'having at one's disposal concrete possibilities'.[4] Consequently, he argues, the only rationale for one's actions is 'the accumulation of ever greater potential'.[5] Social life becomes a competition between those who have power and those who do not; or, in other words, between '*those who can* and *those who cannot*'— membership of the former clan being what the American Express advertisement implicitly extends. A main attraction of the 'practical power' described by de Carolis is the corollary that one can buy it freely, regardless of the faculties one might have inherited genetically. Against this idea of a free market of potential, though, Paolo Virno draws on Karl Marx's notion of 'labour-power' to point out that people's abilities are selected and valued as the '*potential* to produce': 'The living body [of an employee] becomes an object to be governed not for its intrinsic value, but because it is the substratum of what really matters: labor-power as the aggregate of the most diverse human faculties (the potential for speaking, for thinking, for remembering, for acting, etc.)'.[6] The faculties Virno lists there are clearly generic, but they are also shaped into specific skills and potentials that are subject to exigencies of supply and demand. The result is that although such labour-power as 'potential' is 'non-present, non-real' and 'quite distinct from its correspondent acts', it is nevertheless turned into a 'commodity'.

Going on strike is one way an employee can try to wrest some control over her or his labour-power. The efficacy of a strike lies not just in workers stopping production but in demonstrating that they retain the

---

[3] See Fredric Jameson, *Postmodernism, or, The Cultural Logic of Late Capitalism* (London: Verso, 1991), 3–6.
[4] Massimo de Carolis, 'Toward a Phenomenology of Opportunism', trans. Michael Turits, in Michael Hardt and Paolo Virno (eds), *Radical Thought in Italy: A Potential Politics* (Minneapolis: University of Minnesota Press, 1996), 38.
[5] Ibid. 39.
[6] Paolo Virno, *A Grammar of the Multitude*, trans. Isabella Bertoletti, James Cascaito, and Andrea Casson (New York: Semiotext(e), 2004), 83. See also Karl Marx, *Capital: A Critique of Political Economy*, Vol. 1: *The Process of Capitalist Production*, trans. Ben Fowkes (1867, repr.; London: Penguin, 1990), Chs 6 and 7.

potential to work again if their conditions of employment are improved. As Aristotle argued, if an individual capacity is a potential (*dunamis*) that has a latent existence even when it's not being exercised, then the potential to do or be something is also the capacity *not* to do or be it.[7] For Agamben, an awareness of that is what Herman Melville's character Bartleby the Scrivener forces on his employers when he starts responding to their repeated requests with the statement 'I would prefer not to'.[8] Imprisoned for not executing directives, Bartleby effectively executes himself in preferring not even to act on the urges of his bodily appetites: refusing food in prison he ends up dying of starvation. Despite that concluding sting to Melville's tale, Agamben upholds Bartleby as exemplifying the kind of 'inoperativeness' (*inoperosità*) whereby the capacity *not* to act guarantees individuals a degree of free will and autonomy: 'processes of living are never simply *facts* but always and above all *possibilities* of life, always and above all power (*potenza*)'.[9] In stating this, Agamben draws attention to the fact that the Italian word '*potere*' is both a noun for 'power' and the infinitive verb of 'being able'. The same kind of intimacy is evident in the Greek *dunamis*; that it can denote both 'power' and 'potentiality' is why it's also 'dynamic'.[10] The French words '*puissance*' and '*pouvoir*' similarly register a dynamic intimacy of power and capacity—an intimacy that's crucial for an understanding of how Michel Foucault develops his theory of power in terms of both politics and individuals. If, as Agamben argues, individuals always retain some power over how and whether they exercise their potential, in Foucault's view that is why political power (*pouvoir*) is founded on bringing the capacities of people under its sovereign rule. As he states in a 1976 lecture he gave at the Collège de France, power's sovereignty

assumes from the outset a multiplicity of powers [in its subjects] that are not powers in the political sense of the term; they are capacities, possibilities, and it can constitute them as powers in the political sense of the term only if it has in the

---

[7] Aristotle, *Metaphysics, I-IX*, trans. Hugh Tredennick (Cambridge, MA: Harvard University Press, 1980), 461 (IX, 1056 b 10).
[8] See Giorgio Agamben, 'Bartleby, or On Contingency', in *Potentialities: Collected Essays in Philosophy*, trans. Daniel Heller-Roazen (Stanford, CA: Stanford University Press, 1999), 245–61; also Herman Melville, 'Bartleby, the Scrivener' (1853), in *Billy Budd, Sailor, and Selected Tales*, ed. Robert Milder (Oxford: Oxford University Press, 2009), 3–41.
[9] Giorgio Agamben, 'Form-of-Life', trans. Cesare Cesarino, in Hardt and Virno (eds), *Radical Thought in Italy*, 150–1, Agamben's emphases. As Leland De la Durantaye points out in *Giorgio Agamben: A Critical Introduction* (Stanford, CA: Stanford University Press, 2009), 6–7, Agamben's notion of inoperativeness is inspired by the 'Refuse to Work!' slogans of radical Italian workers' groups in the sixties and seventies.
[10] See Paul Weiss, 'The Dunamis', *Review of Metaphysics* 40:4 (June 1987), 657–74.

meantime established a fundamental and foundational unity between possibilities and powers, namely the unity of power.[11]

Strictly speaking, the management of that 'foundational unity' is not purely political; as Foucault argues, from the eighteenth century onwards nation states have had to rely increasingly on administrative and economic networks to regulate individuals' capacities to procreate, work, and trade for the common good. Managing people's 'multiplicity of powers' has thus required a 'biopolitics' that draws politics and economics into a marriage of convenience. And in the lecture course he delivered between 1978 and 1979 at the Collège de France, Foucault discusses US neo-liberalism since World War II as the modern incarnation of biopolitics par excellence. (Many of the points he makes about it have clearly been influential for de Carolis, Virno, and Agamben when thinking about labour and 'practical power'.) In Foucault's view, neo-liberalism effectively promulgates the evolution of '*homo œconomicus*' by casting personal capability as 'capital ability' such that a person becomes 'an entrepreneur of himself'.[12]

The extent to which individual capacities and potentials have been politically and economically managed in America since the sixties is a particular concern of this book. My main aim, though, is to approach that issue by examining how a range of US writers addressed it through experiments in literature and performance. Given the slipperiness of potentiality as a concept it's perhaps not surprising that there's been very little attention given to how it has been an issue for different US writers and political movements over recent decades. As Martin Heidegger wrote, because 'the entire history of Western humanity' has been more comfortable 'thinking purely and simply in terms of actualities [...] we are still unprepared [...] when it comes to thinking *possibility*, a kind of thinking that is always creative'.[13] As I've shown above, a range of thinkers in recent years *have* made advances in thinking possibility in terms of a potentiality that draws power and individual capacity together. While I'm indebted to their work, I've been more interested in considering how various literary writers have themselves thought creatively about such matters. Accordingly, instead of adhering to one theory of either potentiality or power, I've sought to present in this book a genealogy of how

---

[11] Michel Foucault, '*Society Must Be Defended*': *Lectures at the Collège de France, 1975–76*, trans. David Macey (London: Lane, 2003), 44.
[12] Michel Foucault, *The Birth of Biopolitics: Lectures at the Collège de France, 1978–79*, trans. Graham Burchell (London: Palgrave Macmillan, 2008), 226.
[13] Martin Heidegger, *Nietzsche*, Vol. II: *The Eternal Recurrence of the Same*, trans. David Farrell Krell (San Francisco: Harper and Row, 1984), 130, Heidegger's emphasis.

concepts of both have been explicitly related and debated in America over recent decades. Rather than expand further here on theories of power like Foucault's, then (I'll return to him in Chapter 4 when considering how the novelist Kathy Acker engages with him), it'll serve the rationale and trajectory of the book's chapters better if I outline some of the ways in which relations of power and potentiality grew from the mid-1950s onwards as a pointedly US concern.

Responding to recent advances in technology, industry, and science—particularly confirmation of the role played by DNA in genetic heredity—the American social psychologist Gardner Murphy, for example, stated in his book *Human Potentialities* (1958) that 'Human nature remains largely undiscovered'.[14] On one hand, he argued, 'science' and the 'mass democratic movement' presage new possibilities for human evolution; on the other hand, those possibilities are hampered by Cold War 'power systems' that increasingly regulate people's lives while threatening total annihilation. Having emigrated from Germany to America in 1940, the social theorist Herbert Marcuse voiced similar concerns in *Eros and Civilization* (1955), arguing that the Cold War's invidious effects were exacerbated by the 'automatization of necessity and waste, of labor and entertainment, [that] precludes the realization of individual potentialities'.[15] One means of liberating those potentials, he suggested, lies with art, for while industrial civilization constantly requires people to subordinate dreams and desires to a reality principle rooted in work and consumption, art can provide ways of realizing alternative possibilities. It can also liberate the 'senses', he wrote, 'which, far from destroying civilization, would give it a firmer basis and [...] greatly enhance its potentialities'.[16]

Marcuse's writings were influential for numerous members of the New Left counter-culture that gathered momentum in America in the sixties. Inspired in part by a Hippie movement eager to explore the liberating benefits of the contraceptive pill, LSD, and rock 'n' roll, the counter-culture's vision of the personal as political was also one of realizing individual potential. The New Left organization Students for a Democratic Society (SDS), for example, announced in its 'Port Huron Statement' (1962) that it regarded individuals as 'infinitely precious and possessed of unfulfilled capacities for reason, freedom, and love'.[17] As I'll show in Chapter 1, for counter-cultural exponents like the poet Allen

---

[14] Gardner Murphy, *Human Potentialities* (New York: Basic Books, 1958), 14.
[15] Herbert Marcuse, *Eros and Civilization* (London: Sphere Books, 1970), 92.
[16] Ibid. 149.
[17] Quoted in Theodore Roszak, *The Making of a Counter Culture: Reflections on the Technocratic Society and its Youthful Opposition* (1968, repr.; Berkeley, CA: University of California Press, 1995), 58.

Ginsberg, the need for nurturing those capacities was made particularly pressing by the Vietnam War's industrial consumption of lives. Another manifestation of America's military–industrial complex was its space programmes, which prompted extensive discussion of 'human potential' in terms of evolutionary options. For Lewis Mumford the advent of the astronaut was just another small step towards turning man into an automaton controlled by a governing 'megamachine' that wants 'human potentialities [...] suppressed or completely eliminated'.[18] In contrast, Buckminster Fuller was sanguine about the prospect of turning the planet into a 'Spaceship Earth' on which 'our higher potentials' could be attained by modifying social environments through networked technology.[19] The anthropologist Roger Wescott was similarly positive, if more eccentrically so, in his study of human potentials. Musing on the possibilities of evolution in terms of future extraterrestrial life he wrote that his 'maximally human being would be a sort of furless and tailless but hooved and winged monkey with arthropod appendages'.[20] The absurdity of that statement diminishes if one considers, as I do in Chapter 3, the wider debates around space colonies and evolution, much of which clearly informed the novelist William S. Burroughs's 'space-age mythology' and his views on 'human potentialities'.

Whether such potentials were indeed available to all humanity wasn't without equivocation; they certainly didn't seem universal to revolutionary Black Power groups in the sixties. Disenchanted with the extent to which hard-won legislative changes to voting rights and segregation actually changed the daily injustices faced by many African Americans, these groups repeatedly accused 'white America' of trammelling their chances in life. Opposing what they perceived to be white power with Black Power, the groups frequently invoked their 'revolutionary potential' and called on the 'revolutionary possibilities' of black art and literature to bolster a cultural realization that African Americans could comprise a separate nation *within* the nation.[21] How this involved pairing cultural practice with political projects is what I examine in Chapter 2 in relation to Amiri Baraka's plays and poetry. What I want to emphasize here is the diversity of debate in sixties America around the terms I'm discussing. The references

---

[18] Lewis Mumford, *The Myth of the Machine: The Pentagon of Power* (1970, repr.; London: Secker and Warburg, 1971), 303.
[19] R. Buckminster Fuller, *Utopia or Oblivion: The Prospects for Humanity* (1969, repr.; London: Penguin, 1970), 395.
[20] Roger W. Wescott, *The Divine Animal: An Exploration of Human Potentiality* (New York: Funk and Wagnalls, 1969), 319.
[21] See, for example, Harold Cruse, *Rebellion or Revolution?* (New York: William Morris, 1968).

to potentiality that I've cited are not lone references; whether it was a question of Black Power, Flower Power, or Cold War 'power systems', what various intellectuals and writers emphasized is that these involved contests over individuals' potentials that pertain to a host of specific issues, including race, labour, creativity, gender, and sexuality.

If, then, one is to consider how power and possibility have variously been debated and conjoined in recent decades in America, one must consider the sixties as a watershed in the matter. The degree to which that decade's contestations have remained a live, influential legacy is another issue, and one that I take up at various points in this book. As various social commentators have pointed out, the groundswells of sixties liberations were met in the seventies with a growth of neo-conservatism that continued to consolidate itself over the next two decades.[22] The kind of ideology that Foucault identified as evolving *homo œconomicus* was also being advanced in America from the early seventies with initiatives like the corporate 'Quality of Working Life' (QWL) ethos, which, as Nikolas Rose points out, encouraged employees to see work not just as economically satisfying but even as the creative fulfilment of 'individual potential'.[23] If policies like QWL served to absorb people's lives and labour power more fully, such management was subsequently reinforced biopolitically during Ronald Reagan's presidency with legislation on issues such as abortion, drugs, and HIV/AIDS. In Chapter 4 I argue that those biopolitical measures, coupled with enhanced powers of policing and incarceration, were cast by various public figures, including Kathy Acker, as involving a new crisis in relations between power and potentiality—both social and individual. Growing interest in theories of power like Foucault's among US intellectuals in the eighties also enabled new insights into how the regulation of people's capacities extended right up to the structural dynamics of capitalism and the Cold War. The extent to which those dynamics had, by that decade, buried the legacy of the sixties under a pedestal of postmodernism is an issue that I explore in Chapter 5 when discussing how the Language poets addressed it with regards to literary powers of possibility.

Whether literary powers can indeed be politically affective—or can at least combat the effects of political power on oneself—is a central preoccupation for each of my chapters. I've already mentioned that the

---

[22] See, for example, Stephen Paul Miller, *The Seventies Now: Culture as Surveillance* (Durham, NC: Duke University Press, 1999), Ch. 1, and John Ehrman, *The Eighties; America in the Age of Reagan* (New Haven: Yale University Press, 2005), Ch. 5.

[23] Nikolas Rose, *Governing the Soul: The Shaping of the Private Self* (London: Routledge, 1989), 118.

burgeoning interest in human potential from the mid-1950s saw theorists like Marcuse argue that aesthetic practice is essential for fostering alternative civilizing possibilities. He wasn't alone in arguing along those lines; in *The Meaning of Contemporary Realism* (1957) the literary theorist György Lukács deliberates about potentiality when outlining bases for a 'new style' of literature that could bridge Cold War divisions. A crucial benefit of the novel approach he discusses would be 'a fuller understanding of the possibilities of human development, and of the laws underlying it'.[24] And in Lukács's view, the first step towards that understanding necessitates making a distinction between 'abstract' and 'concrete' potentials. The former he associates with the 'subjectivism' of Western modernism, which, he claims, unrealistically apportioned 'infinite' possibilities to individual character by figuring it as something that isn't rooted in social habitat. In contrast, concrete or 'real' potentiality is what arises from a 'dialectical' exchange between character and social environment.[25]

Lukács doesn't relate his theory of potentiality to those of other thinkers, but the distinction he makes in formulating it is not without precedent. Aristotle differentiates between potentials that are innate and those that are acquired by practice.[26] More pertinent to Lukács's distinction between the abstract and concrete is the contrast Avicenna makes in the eleventh century (CE) when outlining a tripartite hierarchy of potential that ranges from one's general capacity to learn a skill, to the partial acquisition of a skill through training, to the full potential of a skill that's been mastered.[27] The ability to train new capacities is also affirmed by the American theorists of human potential when claiming it can evolve and therefore isn't bound by the entelechy Aristotle outlined (in which potentiality is fundamentally a capacity to attain one's generic form, which is essentially fixed).[28] Similarly, other theorists like Gilles Deleuze and Félix Guattari advocate a fluid notion of individual power and potential by drawing on Spinoza's assertion that a person's singularity is primarily a capacity to affect and be affected—that capacity changing according to the

---

[24] György Lukács, *The Meaning of Contemporary Realism*, trans. John and Necke Mander (London: Merlin Press, 1969), 98.
[25] Ibid. 22–4.
[26] Aristotle, *Metaphysics I-IX*, 443 (IX, 1047 b 31).
[27] See Arthur Hyman, 'Aristotle, Algazali, and Avicenna on Necessity, Potentiality, and Possibility', in Karl-Ludwig Selig and Robert Somerville (eds), *Florilegium Columbianum: Essays in Honor of Paul Oskar Kristeller* (New York: Italica, 1987), 73–82.
[28] See, for example: Gardner, *Human Potentialities*, Ch. 17; Wescott, *The Divine Animal*, Ch. 12; and Israel Scheffler, *Of Human Potential: An Essay in the Philosophy of Education* (London: Routledge and Kegan Paul, 1985), Ch. 2. Regarding Aristotle's entelechy, see Charlotte Witt, *Ways of Being: Potentiality and Actuality in Aristotle's* Metaphysics (Ithaca, NY: Cornell University Press, 2003), 4–13.

environment and social relations in which the person is immured.[29] In light of these visions of flexible potential, whether one can distinguish rigidly between abstract (or general) capacity and concrete capacity is equivocal, and certainly an implicit issue of contention for the writers I discuss. If a person's potentials are not simply innate, are they reducible to the concrete manifestations of capacity that are in evidence through that person's interactions with an environment? Might the person not retain other *unrealized* capacities for thinking, feeling, and acting—capacities that can be extended and reoriented through being exposed to alternative worlds of possibility, for example? These aren't questions that Lukács considers when he valorizes concrete potential over the abstract—the concrete species having been, in his opinion, more the concern of socialist realism, to which his literary sensibilities incline. Nevertheless, his call for some new stylistic syncretism is in part an awareness that Stalin's advocacy of socialist art as an 'engineering of souls' was more dictatorial than dialectical.

In the chapters that follow I show how distinctions between abstract and real potentials of character are explored by the writers I discuss in terms of degrees to which new literary powers of possibility can be fashioned and turned into experience. This means realizing that there is a fundamental unity between literature and potentiality. Not all literature is characterized as fiction by genre, but there is an aspect of fictionality that is inherent to all literary genres as well as theatrical performance. Whether we are faced by a narrator in a novel, a character in a play, or a speaker in a poem, we realize that each pronounces its literary suspension from both the author and real world. With that suspension hangs the fictionality that gives the play or literary work licence to stand as an alternative world of possibility. However, when literary critics have considered the status of literary potential by making recourse to the 'possible worlds' theories of Saul Kripke and others, they've tended to hobble that potential on two counts. First, while the writers I examine explicitly figure plays *and* poems *and* novels in terms of possible worlds, the critics who relate such worlds to literature tend to focus solely on prose fiction. Second, the conclusion of these critics is that fictional worlds of possibility are essentially abstract. In Lubomír Doležel's view, for example, fictional worlds are 'nonactualized possible states of affairs',[30] and that ontological status is sealed by Ruth

---

[29] See Gilles Deleuze and Félix Guattari, *A Thousand Plateaus: Capitalism and Schizophrenia*, trans. Brian Massumi (Minneapolis: University of Minnesota Press, 1987), 256–7; also Deleuze's *Spinoza: Practical Philosophy*, trans. Robert Hurley (San Francisco: City Lights, 1988), 97–104.

[30] Lubomír Doležel, *Heterocosmica: Fiction and Possible Worlds* (Baltimore: Johns Hopkins University Press, 1998), 16.

Ronen with a further segregation: 'it is obvious that possible worlds are indeed non-actualized but *actualizable* [...] whereas fictional worlds are non-actualized in the world but also *non-actualizable*, belonging to a different sphere of possibility and impossibility altogether'.[31] Viewing fictive worlds from a twin perspective of ontology and epistemology, Ronen is clearly basing her argument on the conviction that the kind of fantasy world conjured by Lewis Carroll in his Alice adventures cannot be actualized as a factual state of affairs. Even if you suspend disbelief in watching film director Tim Burton's '3D' cinematic reprise of the Alice books, the sad fact is that the dimensions that appear to be dancing all around you are as phantasmal as the Cheshire cat's smile...

But what about the *aesthetic* aspect of literature's possible worlds, an aspect which, as the Greek etymon 'aesthesis' registers, touches on sensibility, feeling, and experience? Yes, it may be that a novel's narrator or a poem's speaker or a play's character is suspended from the world, but that doesn't prevent the text from eliciting thoughts, desires, and feelings that do take place in the real bodies and minds of readers and audiences. *Just because a literary work shapes worlds of possibility doesn't mean it's incapable of real affective potency*. Doreen Maitre acknowledges something of this in her work on literary worlds, thereby presenting a refreshing alternative to the blinkered vision of most other critics who have addressed the topic. Limiting her discussion to fictional worlds of possibility, Maitre argues that they afford an opportunity for 'imaginative identification' whereby readers' capacities for sympathy are roused to enable them to 'become (imaginatively) another'.[32] Fiction thus allows one to live through alternative 'states of consciousness' and thereby extend 'the range of one's experience'.[33] What about other literary genres or theatrical performance, though? And if performance and various genres can extend one's experience, can they also have enduring effects on one's capacities for thinking and feeling? Maitre doesn't consider individuals' capacities in terms of potentiality, nor does she relate literary worlds to political power, but if those worlds can turn potentials into lived experience then can they be an effective utopic force—perhaps not by way of changing political structures but at least by altering the way individuals feel, think, and interact with their social environment? Such questions subtend each chapter of this book. And in terms of the US context that I'm examining, they also bear

---

[31] Ruth Ronen, *Possible Worlds in Literary Theory* (Cambridge: Cambridge University Press, 1994), 51, Ronen's emphases.
[32] Doreen Maitre, *Literature and Possible Worlds* (London: Middlesex Polytechnic Press, 1983), 16.
[33] Ibid. 54.

on debates about literary and cultural postmodernism, particularly regarding whether the avant-garde should also be accorded the status of phantasmal Cheshire cat.

I cite avant-gardism as an important practice at stake here because the 'historical avant-garde' has traditionally been cast as attempting to turn new aesthetic possibilities into powers of social action. Basing his theory of the avant-garde mostly on the Italian Futurists, Renato Poggioli, for example, argues that modernist avant-garde movements had three main tendencies: turning art into praxis (agonism); opposing social conventions and mores (antagonism); and constantly overturning the movement's own beliefs (nihilism).[34] Those who argue that since the sixties all three of those characteristics have become moribund do so mostly on the basis of believing that postmodernism has made avant-gardism neither culturally nor stylistically viable. Matei Calinescu and Andreas Huyssen, for example, both assert that the demise of avant-garde practice, particularly in America, has resulted from the predominance of consumerism and popular culture.[35] For Huyssen, the development in the fifties of Pop Art bore testament to how avant-gardism was already being incorporated by consumer culture. That accords with Jameson's claim that from the early sixties aesthetic production in general—including the experiments of writers like Thomas Pynchon and John Cage—had become uncritically spongiform in absorbing elements of popular culture.[36] Along with Calinescu, Huyssen, and Jameson, Stuart Hobbs and Charles Russell similarly agree that the sixties marks the 'closing chapter' of avant-gardism in America.[37] For Calinescu, its 'novelty' by this period had simply 'lost any trace of heroic appeal'.[38] Once stylistic innovation is symptomatic of mass turnover in novel commodities, genuine stylistic innovation is no longer possible. And if literary writing has increasingly recycled and blended copies of cultural copies, that's because it reflects how our daily lives are already saturated with a stream of simulacra. From those arguments, Jameson draws several corollaries: real individual characters have

---

[34] Renato Poggioli, *The Theory of the Avant-Garde*, trans. Gerald Fitzgerald (Cambridge, MA: Harvard University Press, 1968), 23–7, 66–74.
[35] Matei Calinescu, *Five Faces of Modernity: Modernism, Avant-Garde, Decadence, Kitsch, Postmodernism* (Durham, NC: Duke University, 1987), 276–312, and Andreas Huyssen, *After the Great Divide: Modernism, Mass Culture, and Postmodernism* (Bloomington, IN: Indiana University Press, 1986), Ch. 9.
[36] Jameson, *Postmodernism*, 1–3.
[37] See Stuart D. Hobbs, *The End of the American Avant-Garde* (New York: New York University Press, 1997), and Charles Russell, *Poets, Prophets, and Revolutionaries: The Literary Avant-Garde from Rimbaud through Postmodernism* (Oxford: Oxford University Press, 1985), Ch. 8.
[38] Calinescu, *Five Faces of Modernity*, 148.

become no less a 'pastiche' than the literature they produce; and because everyday experience is largely of simulacra, the postmodern condition engenders an endemic 'waning of affect' as another of its symptoms.[39] In other words, the condition anaesthetizes individuals to the very loss of autonomy with which it infects them.

Those assertions don't make for positive answers to the questions I posed before them. In contradicting the view that literary works can pose genuinely alternative worlds of possibility—whether at the level of style or content—the arguments also deny the ability for such works to extend the range of a person's capacities for thinking and feeling. The affective force of literature is diminished along with a notion of potentiality—both social and individual. So when Jameson argues that we've lost a 'practical sense of the future', that supports his view that the collective ideals of an 'artistic or political avant-garde' expired along with the 'notion (or experience) of the so-called centred subject'.[40] Losing individual and aesthetic autonomy to postmodern culture is also why, in his opinion, literature can no longer be an affective utopic force. Hobbs comes to the same conclusion, and cites the growth of creative-writing courses in American universities since the sixties as evidence of how artistic vanguards have been assimilated not just by consumerism but by cultural institutions.[41] In Chapter 5 I take issue with this assumption that a poet, for example, teaching at a university is ineluctably compromised aesthetically and politically by that institution; what of the fact, for example, that the salary the university provides can enable a writer not to depend on the mainstream literary market for a living? As I'll demonstrate, these issues have also been carefully considered by Charles Bernstein and fellow Language poets, most of whom have some university affiliation. For Bernstein, rather than simply countermanding literary possibilities, teaching writing in a university can itself become a form of utopic agonism, and that conviction complements his view of postmodernism: '*We can act*: we are not trapped in the postmodern condition if we are willing to differentiate between works of art that suggest new ways of conceiving our present world and those that seek rather to debunk any possibilities for meaning.'[42]

Those who can versus those who cannot; that distinction, which de Carolis associates with divisions in earning capacity, is brought to bear by Bernstein on the opposed camps of opinion regarding whether

---

[39] Jameson, *Postmodernism*, 7–10, 17–18.
[40] Ibid. 15.
[41] Hobbs, *The End of the American Avant-Garde*, Ch. 7.
[42] Quoted in Marjorie Perloff, 'Avant-Garde or Endgame?', in *Radical Artifice: Writing Poetry in the Age of Media* (Chicago: University of Chicago Press, 1991), 14, Bernstein's emphasis.

postmodernism holds individuals' lives and potentials in a straitjacket. But their respective notions of capacity are not commensurate; while de Carolis suggests that 'those who can' are seen as those able to purchase possibilities as consumable commodities, the ability for aesthetic action Bernstein develops is more about using literary possibilities to build a capacity in oneself for *combating* particular patterns of thinking and feeling that consumer culture encourages. The literary critics and theorists who, like Bernstein, contest the existence of hegemonic postmodernism are numerous, and include Jean-François Lyotard, Marjorie Perloff, Henry Sayre, and Philip Nel. In defending literary vanguardism they also make recourse to notions of potentiality. Nel, for example, criticizes Jameson and others for eliding the 'oppositional potential of particular postmodernisms', which is why in Nel's eyes the 'adversarial potential' of the avant-garde remains feasible.[43] Similarly, Sayre argues that since the seventies a distinct avant-garde in art and literature has emerged in America, one that places an emphasis on performance and the kind of compositional 'indeterminacy' that Perloff associates with John Cage's work. Citing the performance-oriented poetry of David Antin and Jackson Mac Low (among other examples), Sayre suggests that an important feature of such work is that it 'becomes a situation, full of suggestive potentialities, rather than a self-contained whole'.[44] This belief in the continuing possibility of avant-gardism also leads Sayre and like-minded critics to contest the 'great divide' that Huyssen identifies as separating the era of modernism from that of postmodernism. For Perloff the division is 'more apparent than real',[45] while for Lyotard the 'modern', 'postmodern', and 'avant-garde' are equally implicated in writers' rejections of 'taste', 'form', and 'consensus'. The postmodern avant-garde artist or writer works 'without rules', he argues, 'in order to formulate the rules of what *will have been done*'—namely, something newly modern.[46]

Lyotard's argument implies not only that the modernist injunction to 'Make it New' continues to be honoured by writers, but also that they continue to innovate the kind of 'practical sense of the future' that Jameson thinks has been lost. This raises the distinction that some other

---

[43] Philip Nel, *The Avant-Garde and American Postmodernity: Small Incisive Shocks* (Jackson, MS: University Press of Mississippi, 2002), xxi.
[44] Henry M. Sayre, *The Object of Performance: The American Avant-Garde since 1970* (Chicago: University of Chicago Press, 1989), 7.
[45] Marjorie Perloff, *21st-Century Modernism: The 'New' Poetics* (Oxford: Blackwell, 2002), 164.
[46] Jean-François Lyotard, 'Answering the Question: What is Postmodernism', trans. Regis Durand, in *The Postmodern Condition: A Report on Knowledge* trans. Geoffrey Bennington and Brian Massumi (Minneapolis: Minneapolis University Press, 1984), 81, Lyotard's emphasis.

critics have posited regarding US writing since the sixties: that between the innovative and the experimental. In his book on American fiction of recent decades, Richard Walsh, for example, uses 'innovative' rather than 'experimental' to 'suggest the broadest of literary orientations' that can encompass work ranging from John Barth's metafictional explorations to the more mainstream 'New Realism' of Raymond Carver.[47] Marcel Cornis-Pope takes a similar tack in extending the moniker of 'innovative fiction' from the 'surfiction' of Raymond Federman to the 'midfiction' of a novel like William Gibson's *Neuromancer*, which in Cornis-Pope's view 'narrowed the boundary between experimentation and traditional fiction' (we shall see what Kathy Acker makes of *Neuromancer* in Chapter 4).[48] In terms of poetry, Jed Rasula finds 'innovative' more useful than 'experimental' for two reasons: first, because some poets who innovate at the level of form and content would not consider themselves to be 'experimental'; and second, because unlike experimentation, he argues, innovation isn't necessarily 'volitional' and can be 'circumstantial'.[49] Despite such distinctions, what these critics attribute to innovative literature no less than those who defend the persistence of avant-gardism is potentiality. Although he doesn't address Lukács's work on contemporary realism, Cornis-Pope, for example, argues that by questioning mimetic conventions with self-reflexive narration, novelists such as Federman and Ronald Sukenick opened up 'ignored possibilities' of fiction to contest official constructions of Cold War reality.[50] If Walsh also concludes that innovative novelists have given 'the creative imagination access to the full potential of its means', it's largely because such novelists have themselves emphasized the importance of that potential—as when Sukenick wrote of the need for 'repatriating' narrative techniques 'from the realm of determinism to that of potential', or when Federman stated the importance of imagining a history to-come in order to provide 'a potential point of view, preremembering the future rather than remembering the past'.[51]

I've offered this brief purview of stances on postmodernism, avant-gardism, and experimentation in part to highlight how little consensus

---

[47] Richard Walsh, *Novel Arguments: Reading Innovative American Fiction* (Cambridge: Cambridge University Press, 1995), ix–x.

[48] Marcel Cornis-Pope, *Narrative Innovation and Cultural Rewriting in the Cold War and After* (Basingstoke: Palgrave, 2001), xii–xiii, 19.

[49] Jed Rasula, *Syncopations: The Stress of Innovation in Contemporary American Poetry* (Tuscaloosa: University of Alabama Press, 2004), 1–2.

[50] Cornis-Pope, *Narrative Innovation and Cultural Rewriting*, 42.

[51] Walsh, *Novel Arguments*, 166; Ronald Sukenick, *Blown Away* (Los Angeles: Sun and Moon Press, 1986), 114; Raymond Federman, *The Twofold Vibration* (Bloomington, IN: Indiana University Press, 1982), 1–2.

there is about the valencies of those terms, even though they've been debated extensively over the past three decades. In my view, the division that supposedly separates modernism and postmodernism is as porous as that which purportedly divides the 'historical' avant-garde movements from more recent *soi-disant* vanguards like the Language poets. Those who claim that the sting of such groups has been blunted by mass-consumerism need to take into account that even the Italian Futurists—Poggioli's avatars of bellicose avant-gardism—were producing rather chichi advertisements for Campari by the 1930s and had become the quasi-official aesthetic movement of the Italian Fascists.[52] I make the point not to suggest, like Peter Bürger, that the avant-garde has *always* been uniformly overdetermined by institutions and commodification;[53] instead, I'm suggesting that modernist avant-garde movements *as well as* more recent ones have, with varying degrees of success, had to struggle to be culturally oppositional. Moreover, to consider the 'historical avant-garde' as a solidary practice is also problematic given that there have been so many disagreements between vanguard groups over how combative they really were—the Vorticists' charges that Italian Futurism embraced mass-modernization too readily is just one case in point.[54] Too frequently, the contestations of cultural assimilation advanced by groups such as the Vorticists have been ignored by theorists of the avant-garde, and that's also the case with responses like Jameson's to contemporary movements such as the Language poets, who have proffered their own critiques of postmodernism while putting them into poetic practice.[55] Such critiques have extended to reflecting on vanguardism itself, as when Hejinian claimed:

The Language [poetry] community has less in common with modernist avant-garde movements than with aesthetic tendencies grounded in marginalized cultural communities—the cultures, for example, of the so-called (racial) 'minorities' and of gay and lesbian communities.[56]

As Günther Berghaus has noted, affiliations with marginal political movements have also largely been ignored by theorists and critics when

---

[52] See Fortunato Depero (ed.), *Numero Unico Futurista Campari 1931* (repr.; Paris: Éditions Jean-Michel Place, 1979).
[53] See Peter Bürger, *Theory of the Avant-Garde*, trans. Michael Shaw (Minneapolis: University of Minnesota Press, 1984), 23–34.
[54] I discuss this particular quarrel more in my *Terrorism and Modern Literature: From Joseph Conrad to Ciaran Carson* (Oxford: Oxford University Press, 2002), Ch. 2.
[55] See Jameson, *Postmodernism*, 28–9.
[56] Lyn Hejinian, 'Materials' (1990), in *The Language of Inquiry* (Berkeley, CA: University of California Press, 2000), 171.

considering avant-gardism since the sixties.[57] Like Hejinian, though, he hesitates in aligning recent movements with modernist antecedents: 'the new avant-garde (or post-avant-garde, or whatever it may be called) must be the result of a *critique* of the old avant-garde'.[58]

So much equivocation about what is postmodern and what is avant-garde—even from someone like Hejinian whose fellow Language-group members *have* claimed vanguardist credentials! The lack of consensus surrounding the terms is one reason why I'm proposing with this book to offer an alternative approach by examining the work of experimental American writers in terms of their concern with powers of potentiality, both aesthetic and political. As I've stated, theorists of postmodernist and avant-garde literature make frequent reference to potentiality when discussing how (if at all) literature can still be utopic, affective, or innovative. It's rare, though, for those theorists to relate literary possibilities to philosophical concepts of potentiality, and even rarer for them to relate those possibilities to particular cultural debates about the concepts. In the chapters that follow I show how five US writers each engages with such debates and specific issues of political power while developing a literary practice that draws together the following *OED* definitions of 'potential': (1) possible as opposed to actual; capable of coming into being or action; latent; (2) possessing power (potency); (3) a quantity of energy or force; (4) the 'potential' or 'subjunctive mood' (grammar). To return to the points I made about possible worlds, the simplest way of characterizing this literary practice is to say that it builds a world of possibility that can act as an affective force to combat the effects of social and political power on individuals' capacities for thinking and feeling. Such an approach, *pace* Lukács, is not a revamped realism; I propose instead that it requires a new concept of literary practice to do it justice: *potentialism*.

One benefit of focusing on how potentialism has been developed in a US context since the sixties is that it provides a new basis for drawing connections between an array of writers who've never been discussed in relation to each other at length in any other literary study: namely, Allen Ginsberg, Amiri Baraka, William S. Burroughs, Kathy Acker, and Lyn Hejinian. It would be difficult to group these figures in terms of avant-gardism for the fact that Acker was never part of a literary movement, and although Burroughs (like Ginsberg) was associated with the Beat movement from its inception, he increasingly pursued his own interests from the early sixties. When critics have used avant-gardism as the basis for relating

---

[57] Günther Berghaus, *Avant-garde Performance: Live Events and Electronic Technologies* (Basingstoke: Palgrave Macmillan, 2005), 263.
[58] Ibid. 261.

some of these writers to others it's usually been by way of a single genre.[59] As I stated earlier, though, the literary interest in forging oppositional possible worlds hasn't been limited to novelists, and in the chapters that follow I show how the writers I examine variously experiment with different genres as well as performance. The generic correspondences I assemble have also mostly been missed by other critics who have focused on a single genre while adhering to postmodernism or the avant-garde as their hermeneutic term of choice. In adducing new similarities between the writers in question, I'm certainly not proposing that they form a movement that they didn't realize they were forming. Nor am I suggesting that the varied potentialist practices they develop are essentially identical. The following chapter outlines testify to some of the differences at stake in the writers' approaches.

In Chapter 1 I discuss Jameson's claims that the 'realm of freedom and voluntarist possibility' championed by the sixties counter-culture was illusory, and I consider how the matter was taken up in that decade by counter-culture exponents like Allen Ginsberg when protesting the US war effort in Vietnam. Seeking to counteract the spread of 'coldwar subjectivity', Ginsberg composed a number of what he called 'auto-poems' in which he experimented with dictating into an audio-tape recorder snippets of lyrical observation and, occasionally, material sampled from the radio. In anti-war auto-poems like 'Wichita Vortex Sutra' we are presented with combinations of the various senses of 'potentiality' that I cited above from the *OED*: the poem addresses specific matters of political power while posing alternative possible worlds that are given an affective force through various 'mantra'—mantra which Ginsberg claimed were intended to educe 'latent feeling' and 'bodily *potential* of feeling [...] in the *whole* body'.[60] I examine how he continues to develop that potentialist approach in the seventies, and I also consider how it was linked to counter-cultural demonstrations of the time that used performance when appealing to America as a democracy.

Faith in America's democratic vistas wasn't shared by most African Americans at the time. I've mentioned that various black intellectuals

---

[59] See, for example: Perloff, *Radical Artifice*; Susan Vanderborg, *Paratextual Communities: American Avant-Garde Poetry since 1950* (Carbondale and Edwardsville: Southern Illinois University Press, 2001); Nathaniel Mackey, *Discrepant Engagement: Dissonance, Cross-Culturality, and Experimental Writing* (Cambridge: Cambridge University Press, 1993); Christopher Beach, *Poetic Culture: Contemporary American Poetry between Community and Institution* (Evanston, IL: Northwestern University Press, 1999); Arnold Aronson, *American Avant-Garde Theatre: A History* (London: Routledge, 2000).
[60] Allen Ginsberg, 'Poet's Voice' (1966), in *Deliberate Prose: Selected Essays, 1952–95*, ed. Bill Morgan (New York: HarperCollins, 2000), 258, Ginsberg's emphases.

questioned how universally accessible the individual potentials extolled by New Left groups actually were. In Chapter 2 I pursue this when exploring how the black writer and dramatist Amiri Baraka (who changed his name from LeRoi Jones) became a key figure in the separatist Black Arts Movement as well as the politics of black Cultural Nationalism. Situating his work in relation to claims about African American 'revolutionary potential', I examine how Baraka experimented with poetic improvisation and performance 'rituals' to inculcate a sense in black Americans of being culturally distinct. That aesthetic programme is envisioned by him as fomenting an alternative social imaginary: 'The imagination is the projection of ourselves past our selves as "things". Imagination (image) is all possibility because from the image, the initial circumscribed energy, any use (idea) is possible. [...] Possibility is what moves us.'[61] Whereas Ginsberg appeals to the nation indiscriminately to *draw out* 'latent' anti-war sentiment, Baraka seeks to contest America's political system and *instil* new separatist racial potentials.

If Ginsberg's view of individual potential was broadly humanist, William S. Burroughs's was more about escaping humanity—preferably by leaving the planet. In Chapter 3 I discuss Burroughs's growing disenchantment with the space programmes and I examine how, from the sixties to the eighties, he fashioned an alternative literary 'space mythology'. Starting with his 'Nova' trilogy, I analyse his experiments with textual 'cut-ups', which entailed randomly splicing together fragments of different texts. Burroughs presented cut-ups as scrambling conventional lines of cognitive association and thereby opening new possibilities of experience. By the end of the Nova trilogy he also figured these possibilities as affecting 'biological potentials'. I consider how he cultivates that idea in subsequent novels which feature counter-cultural communities, 'retro-active utopia', and human-alien characters who are figured as 'blueprint hybrids' awaiting a 'Guardian' reader to 'realize their potential' through the experience of reading.[62] All of this is depicted by Burroughs as a quest for a new 'Potential America' ('P.A.').[63] Viewing that quest in patriotic terms is questionable, though, for ultimately he envisages his literary potentialism as an alternative space programme with which to foster capacities for astral travelling in readers, thereby enabling them to leave both America and their physical bodies behind.

---

[61] LeRoi Jones, 'The Revolutionary Theatre' (1965), in *Home: Social Essays* (1966, repr.; Hopewell, NJ: Ecco Press, 1998), 213.
[62] William S. Burroughs, *The Western Lands* (1987, repr.; London: Picador, 1988), 42.
[63] William S. Burroughs, *The Place of Dead Roads* (1983, repr.; London: Flamingo, 2001), 140.

Around the same time that Burroughs was plotting eccentric escape, Kathy Acker, who'd been much inspired by him, was decidedly pessimistic about the state of America, as is clear from her eighties novels. Some of her earlier writing was anarchically insouciant, particularly her experiments in splicing her own diary material with other authors' texts. By the late seventies, though, Acker was avowedly adopting a more diagnostic approach in trying to analyse social power. Believing that 'potentialities' are 'Models and paradigms for actions' as well as being 'politically kin to the imagination',[64] Acker by the eighties presents grim pictures of how such potentialities are economically and politically managed. I discuss this with particular reference to how she addresses biopolitical policies of the time on matters like abortion, HIV/AIDS, and incarceration. I then consider her subsequent turn: whereas Burroughs sought escape from the body, Acker develops what she calls 'languages of the body' that draw on taboo and abjection to generate alternative capacities of feeling in order to combat biopolitical management, particularly regarding gender and sexuality. She also employs those languages, I argue, to give affective force to the potentialism she plots in her later fiction that features a range of pirates and cyborgs.

Acker's change in approach is partly about contesting the effects of power on oneself rather than attempting, like Baraka, to instigate changes in political institutions. As I demonstrate in Chapter 5, the relative merits of both kinds of approach have been debated periodically by the Language poets since the early eighties. Informed, like Acker, by post-structuralist and postmodern theory, the Language group has written extensively about the legacy of sixties counter-cultural movements, as well as whether experimenting with poetic form and content can be a way of engaging power and potentiality. I show how this is evident in early exchanges about realism that Hejinian initiated in the group. It's also evident in her ideas about 'open text', and in Ron Silliman's experiments with the 'New Sentence' as a particular Language style. The point at which Hejinian's poetry takes on an overtly potentialist slant, though, is when she formulates her notion of a 'person' as a subject who constructs him/herself performatively within situations that demand an awareness of possibility: 'The recognition of these possibilities constitutes one's first exercise *of* possibility, and on that depends one's realization that oneself is possible.'[65] A poem, for Hejinian, can present such a situation and can

---

[64] Kathy Acker, 'Writing, Identity, and Copyright in the Net Age' (1995), in *Bodies of Work: Essays* (London: Serpent's Tail, 1997), 99.

[65] Lyn Hejinian, 'The Person and Description' (1991), in *The Language of Inquiry* (Berkeley, CA: University of California Press, 2000), 203, Hejinian's emphasis.

therefore train readers to exercise potential in their everyday lives. Like Acker, though, Hejinian is also aware of political and economic strictures that are placed on people's capacities, and I examine how she and other Language poets address those strictures not only in poems but in critical reflections on capitalism, socialism, and US–Soviet relations.

In gathering the five writers that I consider, I'm not suggesting that they're the only ones with potentialist tendencies in America during the period under consideration. John Cage, for example, is another figure I could have discussed at length, and I do make reference over the course of the chapters to various writers with whom the ones I discuss share an aesthetic affinity. My decision to offer a series of individual case-studies was taken because potentialism involves a complicated set of issues— literary and political—and I realized that case-studies would best enable me to analyse how the writers I consider have experimented with different techniques to address the particular issues of power that individually concern them. My choice of the five writers was made primarily because, more than most other US writers of this period, they offered explicit and protracted questioning of whether power and individual possibilities have become amalgamated into the kind of 'foundational unity' that Foucault posited. As I've intimated in my chapter outlines, the various literary experiments involved in their questioning are an important feature of the potentialism that each writer builds, for the experimentation is seen by each to be synonymous with establishing new possibilities of conjoining form, content, and affective power.

So: 'potentialism'. I realize it's not the most euphonic term. (One colleague suggested it has too many syllables for ears that have grown up on English—to which I replied that it has the same number as 'literature'.) But it sounds better than 'possibilism', which would have the added disadvantage of not doing justice to the various senses of 'potential' that I've cited ('possibility' being just one of them); senses that the writers I consider are certainly intent on correlating as an essential part of their aesthetic practices. Doing justice to those correlations is one justification for coining the neologism, then. Another is that the writers' experiments are also informed by the rich currency of discussion in America about 'human potentialities' that I've cited—discussion that has received scant regard from literary scholars, despite the fact that the province of potentiality makes up so much of the ground on which literature treads, and despite the fact that literary potentials have frequently been invoked by theorists of postmodernist, innovative, and avant-garde literature, even though those theorists rarely pause to consider the conceptual complexity of potentiality. While I do defend potentialism, then, as the most apposite term to ascribe to the complex literary practices I examine, I stand by its 'ism' with several caveats in hand. I've stated that I don't see the term as denoting a unified movement that has hitherto not been identified. I'm also not suggesting that all aspects of the entire oeuvre of each writer I consider should be redesignated 'potentialist'. As I'll show, the term is more appropriate for some texts and periods of work than others, and it also takes on a different tenor with each of the writers I discuss. The five case-studies are intended to present something of the variability of potentialism as a practice, and I'll reflect more on its ramifications, and on the benefits and limits to using the term, in my Conclusion.

1
'Back! Back! Back! Central Mind Machine Pentagon...'

Allen Ginsberg and the Vietnam War

THE POSSIBILITY OF THE 1960s

In a 1986 interview Allen Ginsberg summed up what he considered to be the legacy of sixties counter-culture in America:

There is a permanent change in civilized consciousness so that it includes [...] the awareness of the fragility of the planet as an ecological unity, the absorption of psychedelic styles in dress and music into the body politic, the sexual liberation movement, the black liberation movement, the women's liberation movement.[1]

For Ginsberg this 'change in civilized consciousness' is indicative of how a new cultural 'awareness' and new forms of 'liberation' movement evolved in tandem. As he proceeds to explain: 'I think there was a glimpse of possibility of survival of the planet, partly through spirit, partly through imagination and poetry, partly through psychedelic insight'.[2] In this chapter, I'll consider how Ginsberg presents 'glimpses' of various possibilities in his lengthy engagement with the Vietnam War. In doing so, his anti-war poems also establish a singular confluence of the various senses of 'potential' that I discussed in my Introduction—possibility, latency, capacity, power, and energy. In tracing the specific potentialism that Ginsberg thus develops, one overarching question I want to pose in this chapter is: Just how possible was counter-cultural poetry in the Vietnam War era? But the seriousness of that question can only be approached once we've considered another: How were the 1960s in America possible?

---

[1] Allen Ginsberg, untitled interview with Simon Albury (3 June 1986), in *Spontaneous Mind: Selected Interviews, 1958–96*, ed. David Carter (2001, repr.; New York: Perennial, 2002), 463.
[2] Ibid.

It's a question most commentators on the period struggle with, not least because the valency of possibility as a cultural or historical force is difficult to establish. Fredric Jameson made a notable attempt in his essay 'Periodizing the 60s' (1984), in which he relates 'an immense freeing or unbinding of social energies' in sixties America to 'the development of new and militant' forms of counter-cultural 'surplus consciousness'.[3] Jameson initially acknowledges that this would contradict traditional Marxist understandings of class politics to the extent that such consciousness appeared to be 'surplus' by virtue of being liberated from the economic base, thereby introducing a 'realm of freedom and voluntarist possibility'.[4] Theodore Roszak made a similar observation in *The Making of a Counter Culture* (1968). Commenting on the propensity of New Left groups like 'Students for a Democratic Society' (SDS) to posit the personal as political, Roszak argues that 'Class consciousness gives way [...] to *consciousness* consciousness', and he quotes the SDS's 'Port Huron Statement' (1962) as an example: 'We regard *men* as infinitely precious and possessed of unfulfilled capacities for reason, freedom, and love [...]. We oppose the depersonalization that reduces human beings to the status of things'.[5] These 'unfulfilled capacities' are clearly central to the 'surplus consciousness' and 'realm' of 'voluntarist possibility' that Jameson questions. In his opinion, though, the counter-culture's 'sense of freedom and possibility' was ultimately 'a historical illusion', for its 'unbinding of social energies' was in reality *symptomatic* of 'infrastructural' upheavals in capitalism that saw the growth of 'multinational corporations' and a culture of simulacra.[6] In other words, sixties voluntarism and surplus consciousness weren't really possible; rather, they were economic.

Citing 1967 as the start of this infrastructural shift, Jameson argues that 1973 marks its consolidation—the point at which the 'mass politics of the antiwar movement' became moribund.[7] Such a view is echoed by Stuart D. Hobbs in his account of sixties American avant-gardism. The culture of consumerism and mass production conspired to draw avant-garde practice into mainstream society, argues Hobbs, as did the government's decision to fund American art (such as Abstract Expressionism) as a

---

[3] Fredric Jameson, 'Periodizing the 60s', in Sohnya Sayres, Anders Stephenson, Stanley Aronowitz, and Fredric Jameson (eds), *The 60s without Apology* (Minneapolis: University of Minnesota Press, 1984), 208.
[4] Ibid.
[5] Theodore Roszak, *The Making of a Counter Culture: Reflections on the Technocratic Society and Its Youthful Opposition* (1968, repr.; Berkeley: University of California Press, 1995), 62, 58, Roszak's emphasis.
[6] Jameson, 'Periodizing the 60s', 205.
[7] Ibid. 204.

way of pursuing the Cold War on a cultural basis. The result, he states, was that 'the cultural politics of avant-gardists intersected at key points with the ideals of Cold War liberals'.[8] In terms of American vanguardism, Hobbs thus concludes that since the sixties 'to speak of a van leading the way to the future has ceased to be socially and culturally meaningful'.[9] Ginsberg would have disagreed. By 1966 when he was dictating his anti-Vietnam War poem 'Wichita Vortex Sutra' into an audio tape recorder while driving around Kansas in a Volkswagen campervan, the notion that you couldn't have a 'van leading the way to the future' is precisely what he was contesting. And by 1973 his faith in the avant-garde remained steadfast.

Ginsberg was by no means the only poet who wrote against the Vietnam War—Robert Bly, Robert Duncan, Diane di Prima, and Denise Levertov are just a few of his notable contemporaries who produced significant volumes of poetry protesting the war effort.[10] But as several critics have pointed out, no other US poet came to personify the spirit of sixties protest more than Ginsberg, and no other poet gained such media attention for redirecting the subcultural experiments of the Beats and Hippies towards counter-cultural politics.[11] As biographer Barry Miles writes, 'Throughout the 1960s, Allen's fame continued to grow, until by 1967 he was a national figure; featured on talk shows, interviewed by *Playboy*, the subject of personality posters, a celebrity, famous for being famous'.[12] As a protest poet who gained celebrity status through the media, Ginsberg's writing and career therefore present an excellent case for questioning the extent to which vanguardism was subsumed by mass culture in the sixties.[13] Indeed, the role of the mass media is a theme that Ginsberg continually confronts in his anti-war poems because opposing the war's mediation was, for him, related to the possibility of opposing its management. For this reason, the potentialism he develops is frequently concerned with looping together autobiography, autonomy, and automation into a novel circuit. But before examining how in 1966 Ginsberg

---

[8] Stuart D. Hobbs, *The End of the American Avant-Garde* (New York: New York University Press, 1997), 123.
[9] Ibid. 181.
[10] See, for example: Robert Bly (ed.), *Forty Poems Touching on Recent American History* (Boston: Beacon Press, 1970); Robert Duncan, *Bending the Bow* (1968, repr.; London: Jonathan Cape, 1971); Diane di Prima, *War Poems* (New York: The Poets' Press, 1968); Denise Levertov, *1968 Peace Calendar & Appointment Book: Out of the War Shadow* (New York: War Resisters' League, 1967).
[11] See, for example: Roszak, *The Making of a Counter Culture*, Ch. 4; also James J. Mersmann, *Out of the Vietnam Vortex: A Study of Poets and Poetry against the War* (Lawrence, KS: University of Kansas Press, 1974), Ch. 2.
[12] Barry Miles, *Ginsberg: A Biography* (1989; repr.; London: Virgin, 2000), 368.
[13] Subarno Chattarji, *Memories of a Lost War: American Poetic Responses to the Vietnam War* (Oxford: Clarendon, 2001), 43.

begins to drive all these autos together in his campervan, we need to consider some of the changes of heart he underwent earlier in the decade.

THE WAR'S START AND A CHANGE OF HEART

Ginsberg had already gained national notoriety in 1957 when the publication of *Howl and Other Poems* resulted in an obscenity trial. Judged not to be obscene because it couldn't be deemed to be devoid of 'redeeming social importance', the book's exposure led to it being sold in tens of thousands of copies.[14] And with the publication of Kerouac's *On the Road* later that year, Ginsberg and his fellow Beats were frequently cited by the press as being largely responsible for the burgeoning Beatnik subculture. Along with Kerouac, though, Ginsberg was careful to distance Beat individualism and spiritualism from popular Beatnik fashion. From the beginning of the sixties he expanded his interest in spiritualism and alternative culture in various ways. Visiting Chile in January 1960, for example, he attended a writers' conference, went on solitary explorations of Inca ruins, and, at the suggestion of William S. Burroughs, sampled the hallucinogenic drug ayahuasca. Convinced by Timothy Leary and Burroughs of the benefits the drugs could have for mental liberation, by 1961 Ginsberg was working with Leary to catalyse a psychedelic revolution through mass distribution of LSD. As he explained in a letter to Beat poet Gary Snyder: 'Harvard opinion is that "arbitrary conceptualization" is located in a specific brain area—cortex—and that drugs knock out cortex activity and leave open brain. Thus the present world psychic struggle is a war over control of the nervous system.'[15] Just what role poetry might play in this struggle was by no means clear to Ginsberg, though, as he went on to state: 'I see no way of writing at the moment since my original interest was something like mind transmission and present scientific techniques have [...] perhaps now obviated words. At least that's Burroughs's/Leary's opinion.'[16]

It is Burroughs's approach to this problem that had the most impact on Ginsberg, for it was Burroughs who most shook his faith in language as being primarily a medium of individual consciousness. If, as Burroughs believed, individuals were being brainwashed with linguistic manipulations of the media networks and institutions, then both language and conscious-

---

[14] See Miles, *Ginsberg*, 224–45, and Michael Schumacher, *Dharma Lion: A Biography of Allen Ginsberg* (1992, repr.; New York: St Martin's Press, 1994), 258–68.
[15] Quoted ibid. 289.
[16] Ibid.

ness needed to be altered in some way. In a 1962 article Ginsberg summed up the problem he considered Burroughs to have posed:

> How escape rigidification and stasis of consciousness when man's mind is only words and these words and their images are flashed on every brain continuously by the interconnected networks of radio television newspapers wire services speeches decrees laws telephone books manuscripts?[17]

For Burroughs, one solution to this was the 'cut-up' technique he developed with artist and companion Brion Gysin in the early sixties. (I discuss Burroughs's cut-ups in detail in Chapter 3.) The technique basically entailed slicing up at least two texts into fragments and then randomly recombining the pieces into new syntactical composites. The intention was thus to attack the orders of language and thereby create new voices, new scaffolds of 'third mind' consciousness.[18] But for a poet like Ginsberg who, like other Beats, had been so invested in spontaneous lyricism, the injunction to compose impersonal alien voices prompted a real crisis in faith: 'I've been wandering in the doldrums [...] uncertain if there is enough Me left to continue as some kind of Ginsberg. I can't write, except journals and dreams down'.[19] Deciding that he needed further spiritual guidance, he resolved to seek enlightenment in India.

Ginsberg's travels around India and Tibet from February 1962 to May 1963 with his partner, Peter Orlovsky, were largely about finding a guru, and they met with a range of Hindu and Buddhist holy men during their stay.[20] But the person who most encouraged a change of heart in the poet was Swami Shivananda. Ginsberg recounts part of their exchange to Kerouac by letter: '"Where can I get a guru?" [I asked,] and he smiles and touches his heart and says, "The only guru is your own heart, dearie" or words to that effect...'.[21] By July 1963 when he wrote his poem 'The Change', Ginsberg saw that Shivananda had helped to show him a way out of the 'doldrums' that Burroughs's cut-ups had provoked in him.[22] His reinvigoration of personal faith was also boosted when he left India in May 1963 to visit Vietnam and Cambodia. With the conflict intensifying in

---

[17] Allen Ginsberg, 'Prose Contribution to Cuban Revolution', in *Deliberate Prose: Selected Essays, 1952–95*, ed. Bill Morgan (New York: HarperCollins, 2000), 142.
[18] Brion Gysin, 'Cut-Ups: A Project for Disastrous Success', in *The Third Mind* (London: John Calder, 1979), 44.
[19] Ginsberg, 'Prose Contribution to Cuban Revolution', 141–2.
[20] See Miles, *Ginsberg*, Ch. 11, and Schumacher, *Dharma Lion*, Ch. 16.
[21] Quoted in Miles, *Ginsberg*, 297.
[22] As Ginsberg explained in 1965: 'It wasn't petites sensations defined as expansion of mental consciousness to include more data—as I was pursuing that line of thought, pursuing Burroughs's cut-up—the area that I was seeking was heart rather than mind' ('The Art of Poetry', interview with Tom Clark, in Ginsberg, *Spontaneous Mind*, 48–9).

Vietnam between northern and southern forces, the general commotion in Saigon brought Ginsberg's personal tribulations into perspective. As he informed Orlovsky: 'it's like walking around in a mescaline nightmare—I can arrange to fly inland and see "model hamlets", but decided no and am scairt [...]. The war is a fabulous anxiety bringdown. It's *awful*'.[23]

Perhaps feeling that he himself was playing a model Hamlet in his decision not to see the action inland, Ginsberg moved on to Cambodia where he visited Buddhist temples, taking photographs and extensive notes which he published in 1966 along with the poem 'Angkor Wat' that he wrote during his stay. While his sense of the war in Vietnam had diminished his personal worries, the predominant tone of 'Angkor Wat' is nevertheless one of anxiety about how to respond to such political conflicts. Recalling his stay in Vietnam, for example, Ginsberg wrote:

> I wish I could fly o'er the leaves of the jungle and not
> > get killed see the bamboo stakes
> > piercing the foot of the beefy Marine?
> > or the bodies Viet Cong piled on the tank
> > Vietnamese bosses at Ap Bac lost whodunit?[24]

Clearly, he was having trouble finding his footing with the particularities of events like the January 1963 Battle of Ap Bac in which the South Vietnamese Army (ARVN) suffered heavy losses to North Vietnamese forces. With the characteristic enjambement of his lines, it's uncertain in this extract whether the question marks are syntactically attributed to the details of the bodies he imagines or to his desire to fly over and see them.

The unambiguously 'ecstatic experience' that Ginsberg subsequently captured in his poem 'The Change' was thus an intense relief for him. Following his own heart as guru was a change in heart, he realized; one that meant 'getting *in* the body rather than getting out of the human form [...]. Which then goes back to Blake again, the human form divine'.[25] 'The Change' accordingly presents Ginsberg voicing a welcome acceptance of his body and desires:

> I am that I am I am the
> > man & the Adam of hair in
> > my loins This is my spirit and
> > physical shape I inhabit
> > [...]

---

[23] Quoted in Miles, *Ginsberg*, 318, Ginsberg's emphasis.
[24] Allen Ginsberg, 'Angkor Wat', in *Collected Poems* (1984, repr.; London: Penguin, 1987), 311. *Collected Poems* hereafter cited as *CP*.
[25] Ginsberg, 'The Art of Poetry', 48.

>   Who would deny his own shape's
>   Loveliness in his
>   Dream moment of bed
>   Who sees his desire to be
>   Horrible instead of Him (*CP*, 328)

As 'Yahweh', one of the Hebrew names for God, means 'I am', Ginsberg arrogates 'the human form divine' here and so brings the numinous down to his own bodily, earthy self ('Adam' also being Hebrew for 'earth'). Similarly, while his 'I am' becomes a metrical iamb, so the deictic slipperiness of the statement '*This* is my spirit and physical shape I inhabit' suggests that it is *this poem* as much as his body that houses him as 'spirit and physical shape'. It's a matter of putting oneself on the line. And that's increasingly what Ginsberg resolved to do by pitting his person and poetry against the conflict in Vietnam. On 28 October 1963, for example, he joined over 500 demonstrators outside the Sheraton Hotel in San Francisco to protest the visit of Madame Nhu, the sister-in-law of the South Vietnamese President Ngô Đình Diệm.[26]

Having been installed in 1955 as the first democratically elected president of the newly formed Republic of Vietnam, Diệm, a Catholic, had initially received US backing. It didn't last; America's approval of Diệm's presidency waned increasingly over subsequent years as his autocratic approach to rule became apparent. By October 1963 a number of Buddhist monks had immolated themselves in protest at Diệm's anti-Buddhist policies, and at the time of Madame Nhu's visit to America President John F. Kennedy had already given tacit approval for the *coup d'état* which, on 2 November 1963, would bring Diệm's reign to an end. While denouncing Madame Nhu's visit, Ginsberg would have been unaware of the plottings behind the imminent putsch. What he was sure of, though, was that Diệm's rule, the monks' self-immolations, and the growing political tensions in Indo-China more generally were all symptoms of the Cold War's invidious effects. 'This is the first time I've taken a political stand', he told Ernie Barry outside the Sheraton, and he went on to explain that in his view, 'Until the human universe of direct feeling returns [...] people [...] will be afflicted by impersonal, non-personal, coldwar subjectivity'.[27]

---

[26] See Schumacher, *Dharma Lion*, 399–400.
[27] Quoted in '*City Lights Journal* interview with Ernie Barrie', in Ginsberg, *Spontaneous Mind*, 11.

By August 1964 the necessity to do battle with this 'coldwar subjectivity' had, for Ginsberg, reached new heights. Before his assassination in November 1963, President Kennedy had violated the terms of the 1954 'Geneva Accords' on Vietnam by sending more than 16,000 US military personnel to South Vietnam. By 2 August 1964 American involvement looked inevitable after North Vietnamese boats allegedly fired on a US destroyer in the Gulf of Tonkin. President Lyndon Baines Johnson's response was to request immediately what became known as the 'Tonkin Gulf Resolution'—an agreement from the US Congress to grant support for 'all necessary action' to protect US forces in South East Asia. With the resolution passed later that month, America was thus set to wage war in Vietnam.[28] Speaking in an interview just after Johnson's resolution request, Ginsberg described the crisis as a failure of feeling on the part of the American people:

You DON'T have $60 billion military budget without the EMOTIONS being affected [...]. Actually the majority don't 'feel' anything at all personally, where it comes to politics, just like the Germans. Total indifference to the Vietnam War. I feel a little since I been there [sic]. But the war goes on.[29]

Over the next year, though, many Americans *did* 'feel' affected by the situation; indeed, anti-war sentiment began gathering momentum as America's war effort accelerated. After Vietcong attacks on a US air base in South Vietnam, the Johnson administration on 2 March 1965 put 'Operation Rolling Thunder' into effect—a sustained bombing of North Vietnam that was to continue until October 1968. In opposition, anti-war students and academics at the University of Michigan, Ann Arbor, organized the first 'teach-in'—a mix of festivity, war protest, and critical discussion. Similar forms of activism soon spread to other campuses, culminating in a protest weekend on 15–16 May 1965 when 122 colleges were connected by radio to hear a Washington discussion on the war organized by the 'Inter-University Committee for a Public Hearing on Vietnam'.[30] Ginsberg had already commented in 1962 that the 'vast feedback mechanism' of media networks was largely responsible for indoctrinating individuals.[31] The decision to stage debates through the radio was thus an instance of trying to short-circuit that feedback through the very

---

[28] For a general history of the conflict in Vietnam, see Phillip B. Davidson, *Vietnam at War: The History, 1946–1975* (Oxford: Oxford University Press, 1988).
[29] Ginsberg, 'Back to the Wall' (August 1964), in *Deliberate Prose*, 7.
[30] See Nancy Zaroulis and Gerald Sullivan, *Who Spoke Up?: American Protest against the War in Vietnam, 1963–1975* (New York: Doubleday, 1984), 37–8.
[31] Ginsberg, 'Prose Contribution to Cuban Revolution', 143.

channels that disseminated it. And this development didn't go unnoticed in the media and press: for example, after the SDS organized the first nation wide anti-war demonstration in April 1965, the group received regular attention from the media and national broadsheets.[32]

Ginsberg also was experimenting with new forms of protest. After an October 1965 demonstration organized in Berkeley, San Francisco, by the Vietnam Day Committee was disrupted by pro-war Hell's Angels bikers, Ginsberg, along with Beat muse Neal Cassady and Ken Kesey from the Merry Pranksters, organized a meeting between the two factions. With tensions rising at the meeting, Ginsberg began chanting the Buddhist 'Prajnaparamita Sutra' until everyone, including the Hell's Angels, joined in and calmed down. 'I knew it was history being made', he subsequently stated; 'It was the first time in a tense, tight, situation that I relied totally on pure mantric vocalisation, breath-chant, to alleviate my own paranoia and anxiety.'[33] With the Hell's Angels subsequently agreeing to stay away from the next war demonstration, mantras became increasingly central to Ginsberg's poetic activism, particularly as they seemed to him an exemplary performance of the vocal power of one's body. At the same time, the need to assert counter-cultural opposition was also increasingly apparent to him, as his suggestion for the next Berkeley demonstration that year shows: 'We have to use our *imagination*', he wrote; 'A spectacle can be made, an unmistakeable statement OUTSIDE the war psychology which is leading nowhere. Such statements would be heard around the world with relief.'[34] On procuring some wheels, Ginsberg literally put this drive for autonomy into practice. Having used a Guggenheim Foundation grant to buy a Volkswagen camper van (complete with radio), by September 1965 he was intent on commencing a personal road-trip survey of the US in order to write what he was provisionally titling 'A Poem of These States'. Then in December 1965, Bob Dylan, whom Ginsberg had recently befriended, gave the poet $600 to buy a state-of-the-art Uher 1000R tape recorder. Wired for sound, the stage was set for the poet to try and loop automation, autonomy, and autobiography into a new lyrical circuit.

---

[32] See Todd Gitlin, *The Whole World Is Watching: Mass Media in the Making and Unmaking of the New Left* (Berkeley, CA: University of California Press, 1980), 27–9.
[33] Quoted in Miles, *Ginsberg*, 374. See also Schumacher, *Dharma Lion*, 452–5.
[34] Ginsberg, 'Demonstration or Spectacle as Example, as Communication; or, How to Make a March/Spectacle' (November 1965), in *Deliberate Prose*, 10, Ginsberg's emphases.

'WICHITA VORTEX SUTRA'

On 15 December 1965, Ginsberg, Peter Orlovsky, Peter's brother Julius, and their friend Steven Bornstein left San Francisco in the campervan to commence a series of road trips around the USA. With Peter driving, Ginsberg experimented with dictating into the tape recorder, which he described to fellow Beat poet Gregory Corso as 'a new ax for composition.'[35] So began Ginsberg's foray into what he called 'auto-poetry'—flashes of lyrical observation spoken spontaneously and sporadically into the Uher while travelling in some kind of transport. Between 1966 and 1972, he produced auto-poems by campervan, coach, train, and aeroplane, the audio recordings subsequently being transcribed into written poems which were published in his two volumes *Planet News* (1968) and *The Fall of America* (1972). Discussing how the auto-poetry coheres, he commented: 'they naturally tie together; they're all done the same way, during the same time period...with the same preoccupations and obsessions, during the war.'[36] And in none of the auto-poems is this central preoccupation with the war so clear as in 'Wichita Vortex Sutra'.

From San Francisco, Ginsberg and his companions had driven through Los Angeles and headed towards America's rural heartland, the mid-west of Kansas and Nebraska, and on 4 February 1966 they stopped at Wichita in Kansas. Over the next two months, Ginsberg made a number of road trips and also gave poetry readings to sold-out audiences in Wichita, Kansas City, Topeka, and Lawrence.[37] As 'Wichita Vortex Sutra' testifies, one of his main concerns during this stay was to convince people that even seemingly bucolic Kansas was implicated in the Vietnam conflict. Consisting of two parts dictated from separate road trips, the poem includes numerous statements on the war recorded from discussions Ginsberg picked up on the campervan's radio. In Part I, the emphasis is on positioning snippets of autobiographical lyricism in relation to the networks of automated industry in evidence. The point is to offer the poem as voicing precisely the kinds of statement that might lead 'OUTSIDE the war psychology'. At the same time, Ginsberg also wants to emphasize that such statements must entail a return to bodily feeling. That was the poem's job—as he declared in 1964, poetry should elicit 'the renaissance of individual sensibility carried thru the vehicle of individualized

---

[35] Quoted in Miles, *Ginsberg*, 376.
[36] Ginsberg, 'Improvised Poetics' (1968), in Allen Ginsberg, *Composed on the Tongue*, ed. Donald Allen (Bolinas, CA: Grey Fox Press, 1980), 27.
[37] See Miles, *Ginsberg*, Ch. 14, and Schumacher, *Dharma Lion*, Ch. 19.

metrics—individually differentiating and not conforming.'[38] Just how this poetic 'vehicle' relates to the one in which he was driving around Kansas is an issue that the poet confronts early on in 'Wichita Vortex Sutra':

> What if I opened my soul to sing to my absolute self
>   Singing as the car crash chomped thru blood & muscle
>   tendon skull?
> What if I sang, and loosed the chords of fear brow?
>   What exquisite noise wd
>   shiver my car companions?
>   I am the Universe tonite
>   riding in all my Power riding
> chauffeured thru my self by a long haired saint with eyeglasses
> What if I sang till Students knew I was free
>   Of Vietnam, trousers, free of my own meat,
>   free to die in my thoughtful shivering Throne?
>   freer than Nebraska, freer than America— (*CP*, 397)

Can one pose a lyrical autonomy of self (*autos*) when driving in one's auto? Ginsberg seeks to answer this by imagining his own—albeit chauffeured—death-drive, at which point he hits a dead end. If singing his 'absolute self' is predicated on experiencing his own death, that death would simultaneously terminate his capacity for experience. Rather than voicing autonomy from the world, then, we have poet, poem, and campervan all crumpling into one mass; hence the confusion about poetic agency that arises through the use of the word 'as' in the second line. Does it denote simile or simultaneity? Is Ginsberg able to open his 'soul' to his 'absolute self' only if he can sing *like* the chomping car, or if he sings *at the same time* that the car has chomped through his skull? It is undecidable. The point is that if being wholly free of 'Vietnam' and his 'own meat' means attaining his death, then that event can become tangible for him only through imagining *an other world of possibility*; only through framing that world with a hypothetical 'What if...'.

Part I of the poem thus dramatizes the way in which 'self' is inescapably entangled in the very world of automation that has been driving Ginsberg crazy. And at that point the poem shifts gear. Rather than seek absolute transcendence from the war psychology and automation, he uses his tape recorder to loop samples of war talk into novel lyrical contexts. In doing so, he begins to consider ways of changing the performative effects of statements so they can act with a renewed force of 'sensibility':

---

[38] Ginsberg, 'Back to the Wall', 8.

>   McNamara made a "bad guess"
> "Bad Guess?" chorused the Reporters.
> Yes, no more than a Bad Guess, in 1962
>   "8000 American Troops handle the
>   Situation"
>   Bad Guess (*CP*, 398)

This extract is from near the start of Part II which opens with Ginsberg listening to Republican senator George Aiken being interviewed on the radio programme *Face the Nation*. As he explains in the poem's notes: 'Senator Aiken pronounced the entire Indochina war involvement a "bad guess" by policymakers who had predicted 1962 [*sic*] that "8,000 American troops could handle the situation"' (*CP*, 777). Aiken's euphemism is thus taken by Ginsberg to be a prime example of automated war psychology. And having taped the comment from the radio, he then proceeds to use it as a refrain throughout Part II, as in the following passage:

>   Language, language
> Ezra Pound the Chinese Written Character for truth
>   defined as man standing by his word
>   Word picture: forked creature
>   Man
>   standing by a box, birds flying out
>   representing mouth speech
>   Ham Steak please waitress, in the warm café.
>   Different from a bad guess. (*CP*, 400–1)

In contrast to Aiken's insensitive turn of phrase, Ginsberg is at pains to bring language back to a sound body of feeling. So we find Ezra Pound's poetic corpus making an entrance in the allusion to the Chinese ideogram for 'truth', which, along with other ideograms, Pound had been using increasingly in his later cantos. The ideogram is actually 信 (xin4) ('truth', 'trust', 'sincerity') which appears in Pound's cantos 'XXXIV' and 'LXXXVI'.[39] It's notable, though, that Ginsberg omits the actual ideogram even though he gives voice to its graphic components. In doing so, he effectively introduces Pound's poetics to a new sensibility, which is exactly what he said he wanted to do in interviews around this time. Rather than write a 'museum of literature' like Pound, Ginsberg announced that he wanted to take 'whatever float[s] into one's personal consciousness' and then weave a poetic basket 'out of those materials.'[40] His emphasis, then, is on showing how language and poetic composition

---

[39] Ezra Pound, *The Cantos* (London: Faber and Faber, 1994), 171, 578.
[40] Ginsberg, 'The Art of Poetry', 50.

are always open to the living present, which is precisely what he is asserting in the passage above: what words *stand for* relates specifically to how you *stand by* them, how you use them. And he is clearly using his poetic skills to foster that sensibility: 'mouth speech', 'Ham Steak', and 'bad guess' all echo each other rhythmically in being spondees. Yet these lines also suggest that an act of 'mouth speech' requires negotiating a particular statement with a particular context, which is why they are 'Different' from each other. Such attention to semantics and context is what Ginsberg thinks is missing in Aiken's statement; the senator uses 'bad guess' to describe the war as casually as one might ask for a ham steak in a café—as though the human lives sacrificed in war and the animal lives killed for food are of the same order.

By splicing Aiken's comment in with his own lyrical questioning, Ginsberg attempts to combat the 'vast feed-back mechanism' that he saw to be nurturing 'coldwar subjectivity' more generally. Offering the poem as a lyrical short-circuiting of this feedback, he also identifies language as both a terrain and victim of the war:

> The war is language,
> language abused
>   for Advertisement,
> language used
> like magic for power on the planet. (*CP*, 401)

Some critics have taken statements like 'The war is language' to suggest that Ginsberg is ultimately complicit in Aiken's euphemizing of the conflict.[41] But Ginsberg explicitly questions in Part II the extent to which people view the war's reality as merely a media reality: 'Have we seen but paper faces, Life Magazine?' (*CP*, 400). From his perspective, fighting for a language rooted in physical 'desire and tenderness' is necessary to cut through the media images and reportage in order to win back hearts and minds and make a sense of reality possible again. As Michael Bibby has argued, 'Winning hearts and minds' (WHAM) was often called 'the other war' by Johnson's administration.[42] It is on the level of this 'other war' that Ginsberg wages his own.

In 'Wichita Vortex Sutra' this endeavour reaches its climax in Part II just after the poet has called on a series of gurus, yogis, prophets, and Gods 'to [come to] my side in this auto':

---

[41] See, for example, Chattarji, *Memories of a Lost War*, 49.
[42] Michael Bibby, *Hearts and Minds: Bodies, Poetry, and Resistance in the Vietnam Era* (New Brunswick: Rutgers University Press, 1996), 1, 2.

> I lift my voice aloud,
> > make Mantra of American language now,
> > > I here declare the end of the War!
> > > > Ancient days' illusion!—
> > > > and pronounce words beginning my own millennium.
> Let the States tremble,
> > let the Nation weep,
> > > let Congress legislate its own delight
> > > > let the President execute his own desire—
> this Act done by my own voice,
> > nameless Mystery—
> published to my own senses,
> > blissfully received by my own form
> approved with pleasure by my sensations
> manifestation of my very thought
> > accomplished in my own imagination
> > > all realms within my consciousness fulfilled
> 60 miles from Wichita (*CP*, 407)

Again, some critics have viewed these lines as a flippantly messianic denial of reality. But if we read them in line with the preceding interrogations of autonomy and automation, the passage can be seen as the point where the poem reaches a poignant climax. Does the war in Vietnam suddenly end because of Ginsberg's statement? Of course not; like his death by car accident, the reality is that at this point he can *only* imagine the war's end as an other world of possibility. That is the passage's poignancy. Whereas the President and Congress can effectively execute citizens in wars by executing legislation—even if war has *not* been declared by Congress, as was the case with the Vietnam War—Ginsberg, as citizen, can only match the power of Federal Acts through flights of fancy. But the fragile illegitimacy of his own pronouncement is what dramatizes the limits of the nation's democratic vistas; namely, the extent to which the Federal government can represent, and lay claim to, each citizen's body. As a speech act, then, the lines are intended to perform a critical awareness and a separatist stance. As Ginsberg argues in an interview when explaining what he meant by 'mak[ing] Mantra of American language now':

Where [Johnson and the State Department] say 'I declare—We declare war' [. . .] their mantras are black mantras, so to speak. They pronounce these words, and then they sign a piece of paper, of other words, and a hundred thousand soldiers go across the ocean. So I pronounce *my* word, and so the point is how strong is *my* word?[43]

---

[43] Ginsberg, 'Improvised Poetics', 48, Ginsberg's emphases.

The strength of Ginsberg's mantric speech acting lies in the way it turns poetic potential into an affective, aesthetic power.[44] Let me explain this in relation to those forms of 'potential' I discussed in my Introduction. As we've seen, although Ginsberg cannot attain an autonomy of voice or body, he is nevertheless able to splice quotations of networked language into new contexts of lyric poetry and bodily feeling. Thus, the linguistic possibilities he employs are not 'opposed to the actual' in the sense of being abstract; rather, they are fed off automated networks to form a counter lyric that can be fed back *within it*. Moreover, even where the poem poses other worlds of possibility that appear hypothetical—as in the imagined car crash—these states are still presented as being voiced *by* a speaking body as much as they act aesthetically *on* the body. As Ginsberg states when discussing mantra: 'Feeling and rhythm, which is concomitant bodily potential of feeling take place in the *whole* body, not just the larynx. The voice cometh from the whole body [...] when feeling is full.'[45] And because all the poem's vocalized language is rooted in the physical energy of bodily affects, Ginsberg views even the seemingly abstract statements of possibility as potentiating feeling in other bodies: '"I hereby declare the end of the war" simply sets up an example that other people recognize in their own feeling, and brings that latent feeling up to the surface consciously.'[46]

By the end of 'Wichita Vortex Sutra' this new potentialism remains firmly aimed through the heartland of America at the hearts of its citizens. Driving back to Hotel Eaton in Wichita, Ginsberg declares that the temperance agitator Carry Nation (1846–1911) 'fifty years ago, by her violence | began a vortex of hatred that defoliated the Mekong Delta', and he then proceeds to remonstrate with Wichita itself:

> Proud Wichita! Vain Wichita
>   cast the first stone!—
>   That murdered my mother
>   who died of the communist anticommunist psychosis
>   in the madhouse one decade long ago
>   complaining about wires of masscommunication in her head
>   and phantom political voices in the air (*CP*, 410)

---

[44] I discuss this passage more in terms of J. L. Austin's notion of speech acts in my 'Introduction' to a special issue (on 'Affects, Text, and Performativity') of *Textual Practice* 25:2 (March/April 2011), 215–32. In particular, I argue that Ginsberg's poem shifts the 'illocutionary' aspect of speech acts so that they're aimed at instantiating states of feeling more than states of affairs.

[45] Ginsberg, 'Poet's Voice' (1966), in *Deliberate Prose*, 258.

[46] Ginsberg, 'Improvised Poetics', 49.

In his notes to the poem Ginsberg relates Carry Nation's 'hereditary paranoia' to 'the communist anticommunist psychosis' (*CP*, 780) of his mother, and so channels the war in the Mekong Delta into an American crisis that is domestic on both a personal and national level. For Subarno Chattarji, he thus lays himself open to charges of not doing justice to events on the ground in Vietnam.[47] But I'd argue that Ginsberg doesn't lose sight of the enormity of the crisis in Vietnam, he just realizes the extent to which cold war ideology and domestic media networks are responsible for maintaining it. If the war effort is predicated on the democratic, domestic support of individual Americans whose primary exposure to Vietnam is through the domestic press and media, then combating the effects of the war's mediation is necessary in order to make Americans aware of their responsibility for the situation. Bypassing that mediation and imagining oneself to have direct access to the events in Vietnam would itself be irresponsible, as Ginsberg suggests in a later interview:

I was recording my reaction to the *electronic war*, the electronic images of war. It would have been a fake to enter into the battle imaginatively, actually there in the mud (which I do a couple of times in a line like "sensitive yellow boy by a muddy wall" [in 'Wichita Vortex Sutra', *CP*, 408]), but mostly it's just a recording of the headlines or the TV thing.[48]

Aimed at the American hearts and minds that were also being targeted by the Johnson administration, Ginsberg's potentialism thus seeks to combat the war effort on the home front. And he wasn't alone in waging this kind of combat; Robert Duncan, for example, criticized Denise Levertov for becoming embroiled in anti-war activism, but like Ginsberg he stressed in his collection *Bending the Bow* (1968) the importance of having poems re-spiritualize the body politic into a state of dissent: 'this poetry, the ever forming of bodies in language in which breath moves, is a field ensouling.'[49] Similarly, Robert Bly in his introduction to *Forty Poems Touching on Recent American History* (1970)—which contains Ginsberg's 'America' (1957)—argues that 'television and advertising do their part in numbing sensibilities' regarding the war, and he concludes that 'Killing awareness is easier than killing [a] man.'[50] The necessity of combating the

---

[47] Chattarji, *Memories of a Lost War*, 48.
[48] Quoted in Paul Portugés, *The Visionary Poetics of Allen Ginsberg* (Santa Barbara: Ross-Erikson, 1978), 134, Ginsberg's emphasis.
[49] Duncan, *Bending the Bow*, ii. On the Duncan and Levertov disagreement, see Marjorie Perloff, *Poetry On and Off the Page: Essays for Emergent Occasions* (Evanston, IL: Northwestern University Press, 1998), Ch. 9.
[50] Bly, *Forty Poems Touching on Recent American History*, 9.

war on the domestic front was thus perceived by many poets to be a democratic responsibility at this time. As Walter Lowenfels stated in his introduction to *Where Is Vietnam? American Poets Respond* (1967): 'Today we are writing from a different battlefield—our resistance movement is at home.'[51] Including contributions from Bly, Creeley, Levertov, and Ferlinghetti, Lowenfels's anthology also featured an abridged version of 'Wichita Vortex Sutra'.

For Ginsberg, engaging the war through the media networks also meant putting avant-garde practice on a novel, potentialist footing. Despite using technology, for example, Ginsberg is clearly far from extolling the general agonism of mechanized modernization that was so dear to Filippo Tommaso Marinetti's Futurists.[52] Conversely, in looping automation and autobiography into a new lyrical circuit he also veers away from the kind of separatist abstractions that Pound and Wyndham Lewis developed in the Vorticism of their journal *Blast* (1914–15).[53] The course taken by what we might term Ginsberg's 'camper-vanguardism' is further evidenced in the publication of 'Wichita Vortex Sutra'. On one hand, Ginsberg published the poem through the burgeoning sixties underground press in a number of US little magazines—including *The Village Voice, LA Free Press, Berkeley Barb, Fifth Estate*, and *Ramparts*. It was also published as a pamphlet by Ferlinghetti's City Lights Press, and was performed by Ginsberg at a number of public readings throughout 1966. On the other hand, he fed the poem to the mass-media. With *Life* magazine reporter Barry Farrell covering some of the poet's Wichita stay, Ginsberg decided to ride his growing status as celebrity and allow *Life* to publish a section of 'Wichita Vortex Sutra' alongside Farrell's profile of him. Having already cited *Life* in the poem as aiding the war's derealization, Ginsberg restated his point in Farrell's interview: 'because of overpopulation and because of this highly centralized network of artificial communications it becomes necessary to have a breakthrough of more direct, satisfactory contact that is necessary to the organism.'[54] It's another example of him looping his poetry into the media in order to short-circuit its feedback. And in the other auto-poems he wrote in this period, the media remains a primary target.

---

[51] Walter Lowenfels, *Where is Vietnam?: American Poets Respond* (New York: Doubleday, 1967), viii.
[52] See, for example, Filippo Tommaso Marinetti, *Let's Murder the Moonshine: Selected Writings*, ed. R. W. Flint, trans. Arthur A. Copatelli (Los Angeles: Sun and Moon, 1991).
[53] For a comparison of Vorticist and Futurist performativity see my *Terrorism and Modern Literature: From Joseph Conrad to Ciaran Carson* (Oxford: Oxford University Press, 2002), Ch. 2.
[54] Ginsberg interview with Barry Farrell, in Ginsberg, *Spontaneous Mind*, 58.

In 1966 alone, Ginsberg wrote a number of notable auto-poems. His success in turning them into 'vehicles' of 'individual sensibility' was, however, mixed. 'Kansas City to Saint Louis' (March 1966), 'Wings Lifted over the Black Pit' (June 1966), and 'Autumn Gold' (October 1966), for example, each offers a personal response to the networked presence of the war in an American locale, though without the sustained poetic intensity of 'Wichita Vortex Sutra'. In contrast, the latter's musings on personal body and body politic are taken up again in the lengthy 'Iron Horse' (July 1966), but the lyrical engagement with the war is less convincing. Written on a train and then a coach, the poem opens with Ginsberg in his 'little roomette' masturbating against the backdrop of two soldiers discussing Cambodia, the scene literally climaxing with him wishing they would make him 'Come like I'm coming now' (*CP*, 432). Although he subsequently states that 'he hated their Cambodia gossip', Ginsberg effectively positions the war effort and his auto-eroticism in disturbingly close proximity. The poem subsequently steadies its critical stance towards the end when musing on the media's de-realizing effects:

> Television shows blood,
>   print broken arms burning skin photographs,
>   wounded bodies revealed on the screen (*CP*, 454)

The second line's syntax of agglomeration voices a networked confusion of agency: are the 'broken arms' *objects* of 'print' or metaphorized *as* print? Does the burning skin *produce* photographs or is it absorbed adjectively *as* a photograph? Ginsberg's answer is that the confusion is symptomatic of the electronic war of images: 'The war is Appearances, this poetry Appearances' (*CP*, 455). But rather than cut through the illusions, the poem then steers towards a pure solipsism of 'Self':

> 'understand that the Self is not a Void'
>   not this, not that,
>   Not my anger, not War Vietnam
>   Maha Yoga a phantom
>   Blue car swerves close to the bus
>   —not the Self (*CP*, 455)

Here Ginsberg expands on the quotation from Sri Ramana Maharshi's book *Maha Yoga* (1937) to assert that the reality of transcendent 'Self' stands against the reality of the war and even his own anger about it. Self thus appears to have attained an autonomy from both his own feelings and the auto that swerves 'close to the bus'—an autonomy that was figured as problematic in 'Wichita Vortex Sutra'.

Ginsberg's auto-poetry of this period can thus veer in two directions. To oppose the war, as 'Iron Horse' does, by claiming that the war's reality is ultimately insubstantial is no real opposition; rather, it's a spiritualism that depends on transcending bodily feeling. In contrast, the mantric potentialism of 'Wichita Vortex Sutra' fosters a novel form of poetic activism that seeks to *make bodies possible* by pronouncing spliced lyrical potentials as new powers of experience. As the crisis in Vietnam dragged on and expanded into other South East Asian countries, Ginsberg certainly became more intent on researching the reality of the situation and developing a potentialist practice in opposition to it. And although such potentialism is clearly weak in directly confronting structures of state-sponsored violence, Ginsberg did view his lyrical defiance as fomenting pockets of opposition outside *and* within the media networks that the Johnson and Nixon administrations relied on for popular support. The story of how he continued to do this is in many ways symptomatic of the US counter-culture's anti-war stance more generally. So I want to move now towards considering how Ginsberg's potentialism was at play in two counter-cultural events: the attempted levitation of the Pentagon in October 1967, and the demonstrations at the August 1968 Democrats' Convention in Chicago.

'MISERABLE PICNIC, POLICE STATE OR GARDEN OF EDEN?'

In April 1966 Ginsberg made another oppositional advance in setting up the Committee on Poetry, a charitable organization that, over subsequent years, donated thousands of dollars to small presses, little magazines, and impecunious poets. Continuing to be outspoken against the war in newspaper and television interviews, he was far from isolated in his stance.[55] With anti-war sentiment increasing as the war escalated, some media networks had begun broadcasting a limited range of oppositional voices. For example, Democrat senator William Fulbright, who was increasingly dismayed at the war and its ramifications, orchestrated an extended televised public hearing of the Senate Foreign Relations Committee on the US involvement in Vietnam. Ginsberg alludes to this event in 'Iron Horse': 'Fulbright sang on the Senate floor | Against the President's Asian War' (*CP*, 449). Commencing on 28 January 1966 and broadcast over a period of three weeks, the hearing included testimony

[55] See Miles, *Ginsberg*, 384.

from Secretary of State Dean Rusk and from General Maxwell Taylor who'd been the US ambassador to South Vietnam between 1964 and 1965. As Nancy Zaroulis and Gerald Sullivan argue: 'The importance of the [...] Fulbright hearings cannot be overstated. [...] What made the hearings eligible for the appellation "national teach-in" was the fact that millions watched the proceedings on the ABC and NBC television networks.'[56] Such broadcasting certainly helped bring mainstream opposition to the war closer to the more radical counter-cultural movements at this time. But it didn't prevent Johnson's administration from deciding in the month of Fulbright's hearing to add to the 180,000 US military personnel already in Vietnam.[57] And although newspapers and television networks were beginning to give some voice to opposition within the USA, the direct reportage from Vietnam was mostly filtered through official US army sources.[58]

Commonly described as 'the first television war', even when television reporters began sending back live footage from Vietnam, the amount of actual combat broadcast was limited.[59] So with 389,000 US troops stationed in Vietnam by the end of 1966, and over 6,600 combat dead, it's reasonable to surmise that the majority of American citizens still in favour of intensifying military pressure didn't appreciate the reality of the situation. This was certainly the position Ginsberg was maintaining in 1967, as his contribution to the anthology *Authors Take Sides on Vietnam* shows:

The way to end the war has less to do with the situation in Vietnam than it has to do with the situation of internal propaganda, attitudinizing, brainwash, image-manipulation, news control, etc., within the United States. How the entire communications and media apparatus have been able to sustain sympathetic Myth rationalization for [...] over a decade is a little mysterious.[60]

Again, Ginsberg isn't denying the reality of the situation in Vietnam here; rather, he is contending that the crisis has materialized precisely

---

[56] Zaroulis and Sullivan, *Who Spoke Up?*, 75.
[57] See Davidson, *Vietnam at War*, 395.
[58] For a detailed overview of media reportage from the war see William M. Hammond, *Reporting Vietnam: Media and Military at War* (Lawrence, KS: University Press of Kansas, 1998).
[59] On this point see Lawrence Lichty, 'Comments on the Influence of Television on Public Opinion', in Peter Braestrup (ed.), *Vietnam as History* (Washington, DC: Woodrow Wilson International Center for Scholars, 1984). According to Lichty, from August 1965 to August 1970 only 76 out of 2,300 television news reports sent from Vietnam showed heavy fighting (158).
[60] Ginsberg, untitled statement against the war, in Cecil Woolf and John Bagguley (eds), *Authors Take Sides on Vietnam* (London: Peter Owen, 1967), 141.

because of the anaesthetizing effects of networked 'coldwar subjectivity'. That is why he sees the necessity of combating the war at the level of its 'Myth rationalization', and in that respect he echoes other prominent social theorists of the time; notably, Herbert Marcuse, Hannah Arendt, and Lewis Mumford, all of whose ideas were gaining currency in the counter-culture.[61] In an interview of 1967, Ginsberg describes the relation between technological superstructure and ideology as one of 'circular feedback' that makes people's 'life consciousness [...] increasingly conditioned.'[62] Such feedback was particularly evident in the growing automation of the conflict in Vietnam. As General William Westmoreland proudly stated in 1967: 'Today, machines and technology are permitting an economy of manpower on the battlefield, as indeed they are in the factory [...] enemy forces will be located, tracked, and targeted almost instantaneously through the use of data links, computer assisted intelligence evaluation, and automated fire control.'[63] And that is exactly what came into being with the introduction of an electronic barrier just below the Demilitarized Zone (DMZ) separating North and South Vietnam. Consisting of a vast network of radar, infrared, seismic, magnetic, and acoustic sensors triggering mines and prompting assault aircraft and bombing sorties, America's war in Vietnam was increasingly being fought as a technologized reflex response.

In opposition to this twinning of technology and automated ideology—Mumford called it 'the myth of the machine'—Ginsberg and other counter-culture exponents pursued new forms of statement and public event that might undermine the war's Myth rationalization. By 1967 Ginsberg was frequently depicted as a leader of the Hippie 'flower power' movement that had been sprouting in communities like that of Haight-Ashbury in San Francisco. Along with friends like Timothy Leary, Gary Snyder, Gregory Corso, Jerry Rubin, Ed Sanders, and Abbie Hoffman, Ginsberg had also been active in helping the Hippie subculture join forces with New Left political organizations like SDS. One example of the growing confluence was the October 1967 March on the Pentagon organized by the National Mobilization Committee to End the War in

---

[61] See, in particular, Herbert Marcuse, *One Dimensional Man: Studies in the Ideology of Advanced Industrial Society* (1964, repr.; London: Routledge, 2002); Hannah Arendt, *The Human Condition* (1958; Chicago: University of Chicago Press, 1998); and Lewis Mumford, *The Myth of the Machine: The Pentagon of Power* (1970, repr.; London: Secker & Warburg, 1971).

[62] Ginsberg, 'Public Solitude' (1967), in *Deliberate Prose*, 132.

[63] Quoted in Kim McQuaid, *The Anxious Years: America in the Vietnam–Watergate Era* (London: HarperCollins, 1989), 75.

'Back! Back! Back! Central Mind Machine Pentagon' 43

Vietnam (popularly known as 'the Mobe').[64] Scheduled as part of three days' protest in Washington, DC, the estimated rally of around 100,000 people included an array of counter-culture groups, celebrities, intellectuals, and writers such as Robert Lowell, Noam Chomsky, and Norman Mailer who covered the event in his *Armies of the Night* (1968).

Divided into two parts—'History as Novel' and 'The Novel as History'—Mailer's New Journalist account of what happened is fascinating for the way it figures the protest as a demonstration of how to turn imagination into history. Mailer's first impression of the rally is of a kind of other world of electronic possibility: 'it is [...] electronics on the march. The public address system hisses, then rings in a random chorus of electronic music, sounds of cerebral mastication from some horror machine of Outer Space [...] we are in the penumbra of psychedelic netherworlds.'[65] With Ginsberg and other counter-culture leaders in attendance, their intention to put technology to more magical, spiritual devices soon became apparent. While Ginsberg chanted mantras, his friend Abbie Hoffman, leader of the 'Youth International Party' ('Yippies'), led a mass attempt to levitate the Pentagon, and Ed Sanders followed suit by performing Ginsberg's poem 'Pentagon Exorcism' (1967).[66] Originally titled 'No Taxation without Representation', the poem reflects on networked life and includes a Buddhist mantra for clearing a site for ceremony:

> [...] Pay my taxes? No *Westmoreland* wants
> To be Devil, others die for his General Power
> Sustaining hurt millions in house security
> Turning to images on TV's separate universe where
> Peasant manhoods burn in black & white forest
> Villages [...]
>
> [...] Om Raksa Raksa Raksa Hum Hum Hum Phat Svaha!
> Anger Control your Self feared Chaos, suffocation
> Body-death in Capitols caved with stone radar sentinels!
> Back! Back! Back! Central Mind-machine Pentagon reverse
> Consciousness! Hallucination manifest! [...]
>   (*CP*, 483, Ginsberg's emphasis)

Questioning the price he must pay for political representation, Ginsberg, by way of an answer, identifies a confusion of mass agency in the military–

---

[64] See Zaroulis and Sullivan, *Who Spoke Up?*, 133–7.
[65] Norman Mailer, *Armies of the Night: History as a Novel, The Novel as History* (1968, repr.; London: Harmondsworth, 1971), 43–4.
[66] Regarding the attempted levitation of the Pentagon see Roszak, *The Making of a Counter Culture*, 124–5; also Julie Stephens, *Anti-Disciplinary Protest: Sixties Radicalism and Postmodernism* (Cambridge: Cambridge University Press, 1998), 37–40.

industrial complex. With General Westmoreland's power being capitalized into a corporation of its own (like 'General Motors' or 'General Electric'), its relation to the domestic body politic becomes unclear. The clauses 'others die for his General Power | Sustaining hurt millions' suggest a vicious circular feedback whereby both the dying 'others' and the General Power can be read syntactically as 'sustaining' casualties of 'millions', and where these millions could be monetary as well as lives. If people are fighting for a power that puts themselves and others to death, they are also fighting for the death of that awareness to the extent that the 'hurt millions' are fed back, 'turned' into money and a 'separate universe' of 'black & white' televisual images. Ginsberg's mantric exorcism is thus intended to be a poetic *demonstration* in two senses: it both shows and parodies how the 'Central Mind-machine' transforms its material effects into an other televisual world. In other words, the 'exorcism' is absurd in order to demonstrate (against) the perceived absurdity of the Pentagon's 'Myth rationalization'. It must, ironically, make the General Power's 'Hallucination manifest' in order to reveal that the hallucination is, in part, contingent on being performative. By realizing that this 'General Power' is also an ideological role that people can refuse to invest in, the awareness performed by the ritual makes countering history possible. And for Ginsberg, the importance of such demonstrations shouldn't be underestimated. As he explained in a 1968 interview when discussing the 'fatal sickness' linked to the 'giant fantasies of the Cold War': 'The first step towards a cure for the sickness is to realize it's there.'[67]

Mailer, for one, was impressed with the March on the Pentagon despite his efforts to remain cynical. What the protestors had showed, he argued, was a national 'schizophrenia' that had become apparent in America as both Christian and corporate nation: 'For the center of Christianity was a mystery, a son of God, and the center of the corporation was a detestation of mystery, a worship of technology.'[68] Reinventing spiritual warfare, the protesters had converted an historical event into mystical experience, which, Mailer wrote, is what necessitated his New Journalist account featuring himself autobiographically as a novelistic 'character' narrated in the third person: 'an explanation of the mystery of the events at the Pentagon cannot be developed by the methods of history—only by the instincts of the novelist. [...] history is interior [...] the novel must replace history at precisely the point where experience is sufficiently emotional, spiritual, psychical, moral, existential, or supernatural.'[69] So

---

[67] Ginsberg, '*Playboy* Interview with Paul Carroll' (1969), in *Spontaneous Mind*, 191.
[68] Mailer, *Armies of the Night*, 200.
[69] Ibid. 268.

while Ginsberg's 'Wichita Vortex Sutra' weaved a poetic potentialism *out of* found discourse, Mailer acknowledges that events like the Pentagon exorcism were about making counter potentials *out of* history. In both instances possibility is not figured as an abstracted fancy or fiction, it is performed, *real*-ized, as lived experience.

The limits of such 'interior' history became evident, however, with Ginsberg's participation in the demonstrations surrounding the August 1968 Democrats' Convention in Chicago. The year was already proving a watershed for the Vietnam war and counter-culture alike. On 30 January, North Vietnamese forces had launched their massive surprise offensive during the usual ceasefire of the Tet annual holiday for the Vietnamese New Year. As the popular CBS reporter Mike Wallace commented, the Tet offensive 'demolished the myth'[70] that allied strength controlled South Vietnam. The media were turning. Visiting South Vietnam in February 1968, Walter Cronkite, another prominent CBS journalist, reported back that America's only hope was to negotiate a way out of the war. President Johnson's response to his advisors was: 'If I've lost Cronkite, I've lost middle America.'[71] On 31 March, Johnson publicly announced new invitations for negotiations with North Vietnam and also stated his intention not to stand for re-election later in the year. Sensing the fragility of the situation, counter-culture groups readied themselves for action. In March, Abbie Hoffman organized a nationally televised discussion with Ginsberg and Jerry Rubin to set out plans for a Yippie festival of protest at the Democratic Convention. Having followed with interest the left-wing student protests that had exploded nationally in France during May that year, Hoffman subsequently borrowed one of the French slogans: 'Be Realistic. Demand the Impossible.' But by the time of the Democratic Convention in August the Yippie's rhetoric had taken on a distinctly militant tone, as one of their leaflets distributed at the demonstrations shows. A deliberate parody of *The Communist Manifesto* (1848), the leaflet calls on youth to disobey all authority figures and to 'break down the family, church, nation, city, economy: turn your life into an art form, a theatre of the soul and a theatre of the future.'[72] By this stage they were also running their own presidential candidate, a pig named 'Pigasus the Immortal'. Taking all this into account, Chicago Mayor Richard Daley promptly refused the Yippies' application to sleep in Chicago's

---

[70] Quoted in Hammond, *Reporting Vietnam*, 111.
[71] Quoted in Davidson, *Vietnam at War*, 486.
[72] Quoted in Jonah Raskin, *For the Hell of It: The Life and Times of Abbie Hoffman* (1996, repr.; Berkeley, CA: University of California Press, 1998), 151.

parks, ordered a curfew, put the city's police on extended shift-work, and requested 6,000 national guard troops to be at hand.

With the likelihood of Hoffman's 'Festival of Light' turning into an incandescent fracas, Ginsberg, for one, was getting cold feet over the Yippies' plans: 'confusion of assassinations, resignations, changes of terminology, police violence, make the purpose of me or younger people going to Chicago unclear.'[73] Notably, he also distinguished the kind of potentialist programme that he had been pursuing from the Yippies' and others' 'Party politics':

Conceiving, blueprinting, imagining an alternative anarchistic humanistic spiritual yet technological and over-populated State or No-State [. . .] is a proposition now so gigantic I have little to offer except in tiny particularities wherein I'm experienced, like sexual *upaya* or language skills or narcotic-mystic-educational programs.[74]

I've already argued that the potentialism I'm ascribing to Ginsberg's poetic practice is a weak power in terms of confronting force with force. Ginsberg acknowledges that implicitly here, which is why he restates his investment in 'tiny particularities' of self-potentiation. Accordingly, his increasing divergence from the Yippies became apparent in the Chicago demonstrations. On 24 August 1968 Ginsberg joined Hoffman and others in a march to Lincoln Park, which culminated in minor scuffles with the police. The next day the demonstrators again gathered in the park where their defiance was roused by the rock group MC5. With police moving in to disperse the crowd, Ginsberg attempted mass mollification by repeatedly chanting 'Om', which in Tibetan Buddhist practice is done to elicit consciousness of the Supreme Being. Amidst the chaos of the Chicago protests, Ginsberg and around fifty others continued the chant for seven hours during which time he underwent something of an epiphany. As he reported in an interview, with the lights of the John Hancock skyscraper coming on opposite the park it felt like his breath began to take his body away:

I realised that I was going through some kind of weird trance [. . .]. But it wasn't mystical. It was the product of six continuous hours of chanting 'Om', regularised breathing and altering body chemistry. [. . .] I'd got to euphorias, ecstasies of pleasure, years before; but this was the first time I'd gotten neurological sensations, cellular extensions of some kind of cosmic consciousness within my body. I was able to look at the Hancock building and see it as a tiny little tower of electrical

---

[73] Ginsberg, '1968 Chicago Democratic Convention: Ginsberg's Answer to Claude Pélieu's Questionnaire', in *Deliberate Prose*, 47.
[74] Ibid. 48.

lights—a very superficial toy compared with the power, grandeur and immensity of one human body.[75]

On one hand, if this is an act of personal liberation it also seems a form of escapism, one that's clearly powerless to prevent the violence from taking place in Chicago, let alone Vietnam. But that is the point, for it is also a public demonstration of opposition to violence and power structures— whether of the Democrat Party, Hoffman's Yippies, or the John Hancock building. The mass chanting is offered as a way of taking over a public place in order to take place publicly as a living form of enlightened opposition, one that is built out of something as fragile as one's own breath.

Despite Ginsberg's efforts, though, the enduring image of the protests was one of violence. On 28 August tensions among police, national guardsmen, and the protesters exploded into serious clashes that were broadcast around the world. Ginsberg's bleak view of the events is evident in the concluding stanza of his short poem 'Grant Park: August 28, 1968':

> Miserable picnic, Police State or Garden of Eden?
> in the building walled against the sky
> magicians exchange images, Money vote
>   and handshakes—
> The teargas drifted up to the Vice
>   President naked in the bathroom
> —naked on the toilet taking a shit weeping?
> Who wants to be President of the
>   Garden of Eden? (*CP*, 507)

The bleakness pronounced is again one of 'circular feedback'; locked into a mutual escalation of violence, Police State and Garden of Eden are meshed in a common confusion. Similarly, the use of 'teargas' is figured as doubling back on the President of 'Vice' (emphasized through the line break) and is thus implicated in the exposed vulnerability of his 'weeping'. It's not the most sophisticated of Ginsberg's poems, but it does highlight the way in which control generally was out of control. Indeed, in Todd Gitlin's opinion the escalation of violence on 28 August was largely attributable to both sides being caught up in the amplifications of media feedback:

As floodlit demonstrators took up the rousing chant, 'The whole world is watching!' in front of the cameras, police clubs swung, blood flowed, cameras ground,

---

[75] Quoted in Miles, *Ginsberg*, 413.

image became reality, reality was doubled back as image, and accusation became self-fulfilling prophecy.[76]

I'd argue that what this feedback demonstrated was the extent to which the media, protesters, *and* state were not in control of events. As Gitlin points out, the counter-culture groups were publicly associated with the violence in Chicago and subsequently lost much media sympathy. But the decision to use such police violence at Chicago also elicited widespread condemnation. Moreover, after the Tet offensive the government, press, and media began to diverge in their views of the war's rationale. With Nixon subsequently defeating Hubert Humphrey (the presidential candidate whom the Democrats had chosen at the Chicago convention), Nixon soon realized the extent to which the press could become opposed to the war effort. In March 1969 the *New York Times* began to publish leaked, secret documents from the US Defense Department detailing decision-making behind the war's running. Nixon moved (unsuccessfully) to block the publication and then ordered the secret surveillance of those suspected of being involved in the leaks.[77] By 1974 this particular strand of history had culminated in the termination of Nixon's presidency after his role in the Watergate scandal was confirmed by the revelation of his own confidential conversations that he had kept on audio-tape. In contrast to Jameson's argument that the sense of 'freedom and possibility' in the sixties was ultimately an 'historical illusion' that belied the grip of late-capitalism, I'd argue that the sense of political and military *control* was an historical illusion—an illusion that was itself being powered by the kinds of corporate militarism that Ginsberg was decrying at the time. And on Ginsberg's part this contention was given a boost when the publication of his *Planet News* collection in Autumn 1968 was met with favourable reviews. Paul Zweig, for example, wrote that by being 'selectively reckless' Ginsberg had opened 'the marvel of endless possibility' in the volume.[78]

At this point, given that the 'endless possibility' Ginsberg publishes comes just after 1967—the year that Jameson considers to be the beginning of the end for sixties' possibilities—I want to consider further the relation between the counter-culture and postmodernism more generally. As Julie Stephens argues in *Anti-Disciplinary Protest* (1998), the idea that the sixties 'move[d] from emancipatory promises [...] to the apparent end of all possibility of a transformative politics' is the 'most familiar' of

---

[76] Gitlin, *The Whole World is Watching*, 187. See also Zaroulis and Sullivan, *Who Spoke Up?*, 178–200.
[77] See Hammond, *Reporting Vietnam*, 259.
[78] Paul Zweig, 'A Music of Angels', *The Nation* (10 March 1969), 313.

depictions.[79] One consequence of that, she writes, is that commentators have mostly sidelined the importance of the sixties' counter-culture, either 'exclud[ing] it from serious consideration' or seeing it as simply another manifestation of 'postmodernism.'[80] Against these views, Stephens argues that counter-cultural activism like the levitation of the Pentagon or the Yippie's 1968 Festival of Light amounted to a novel form of 'anti-disciplinary politics'. Such protest, she writes, has an affinity with Michel Foucault's assertion that 'disciplinary' power circulates throughout society through various channels and is generated even in individuals on levels of 'knowledge and desire.'[81] (I'll take up Foucault's notions of power more fully in Chapter 4.) Demonstrating against traditional institutions of disciplinary power, counter-culture groups also rejected traditional forms of protest, and thereby created a new 'parodic political language':

They did this by deliberately exploiting the idea of their own capacity to be assimilated as a means of distinguishing themselves from the old and New Left, especially through the parodic borrowing from and display of popular culture motifs.[82]

Stephens' point, then, is that the counter-culture has largely been discounted because it actively disrupted the critical and political frameworks that many commentators have used to appraise it.

In my view, such anti-disciplinary performance was politically oppositional to varying degrees. At the more psychedelic end of the spectrum, for example, the 'Acid Tests' of Ken Kesey's 'Merry Pranksters' were more about 'tuning out' of reality than engaging with it. Combining light shows, psychedelic rock bands, and the collective consumption of LSD, the participants' political awareness was questioned by Tom Wolfe in *Electric Kool-Aid Acid Test* (1968) when organizers of a Test in Watts, Los Angeles, proved oblivious to the race riots that had only recently taken place there.[83] In contrast, the San Francisco Diggers' 'Free Frame of Reference' programme in Haight-Ashbury was more pointedly political in instituting community initiatives. Setting up 'Free stores' distributing free food, clothes, and even money, the Diggers also published a magazine providing information on how to procure free shelter, education, legal services, and entertainment.[84] The programme thus envisioned personal

---

[79] Stephens, *Anti-Disciplinary Protest*, vii.
[80] Ibid. 4.
[81] Ibid. 23.
[82] Ibid. 94.
[83] See Tom Wolfe, *Electric Kool-Aid Acid Test* (1968, repr.; New York: Bantam, 1999), Ch. 20.
[84] See Stephens, *Anti-Disciplinary Protest*, 42–5.

liberation in part as being freed from capitalist economy. And even though anti-disciplinary tactics frequently blurred the distinction between popular culture and counter-culture in its parodies, the emancipatory drive of groups like the Diggers was patently running counter to processes of postmodernization. As Stephens argues:

> while it has become standard to associate the sixties with a retreat into the personal, mass political involvement and protest as a collective enterprise were repeatedly celebrated and brought into being. Few equivalents exist in the landscape of postmodernism of the collective effort which inspired countless underground newspapers, communes, alternative schools, health co-operatives, food coalitions and the like.[85]

For Jameson, writing in 1984, such 'freedom' appears an 'historical illusion' in hindsight because it failed on Marxist terms to prevent the consolidation of multinational corporate power that took place throughout the seventies and eighties. But as Stephens contends, departing from Marxist models of revolutionary change was precisely the point for many counter-cultural exponents.[86] As with Ginsberg's poetic activism, the Yippies, Diggers, and other groups were unable to fight the military industrial complex on its own terms. That being the case, such activists had to develop other forms of power and protest. Ginsberg used poetry and performance to do so, and in the next section I'll consider how he continued to build his oppositional potentialism right up to the end of the Vietnam War.

'BODIES ALERT' AND THE WAR'S END

It's certainly true that counter-culture movements began to splinter and fade after 1968. SDS disbanded in June 1969, riven with internal dissensions, and although that same year the Mobe organized the largest anti-war demonstrations to date, by May 1970 it, too, disbanded because of leadership problems.[87] But the anti-war movement, counter-culture, and growing antipathy to the war in the US media and Congress had already played their part in convincing the Nixon administration that America had to find some way of extricating itself from the worsening situation in Vietnam. At the same time, with Nixon making repeated announcements over the course of his presidency about pulling US forces out, turning over

---

[85] Stephens, *Anti-Disciplinary Protest*, 126.
[86] See ibid. 40.
[87] See Zaroulis and Sullivan, *Who Spoke Up?*, 253–5, 336–40.

the fighting to the South Vietnamese, negotiating cease-fires, and pushing for peace, the anti-war movement began to dissolve because opposition to the war had already become mainstream, and the mainstream perceived the war to be winding down. When US 'incursions' into Cambodia in 1970 and Laos in 1971 showed that Nixon wasn't necessarily practising what he was preaching, his popular support and influence over the media were further undermined.[88]

Admittedly, Nixon was able to keep the war effort going for the rest of his presidency because he was so adept at orchestrating an illusion of pacification. But an infrastructure of illusion was also what both the Johnson and Nixon administrations were controlled by to the extent that their investment in the war's bureaucratized automation ran out of control. In 1967, for example, the Secretary of Defense Robert McNamara had set up the Hamlet Evaluation System (HES) with the CIA to maintain a constant statistical survey of the effects of US pacification in South Vietnam. In 1970 this was supplemented by the Pentagon's 'Vietnam Task Force' to process Vietnam intelligence and statistics. As General Douglas Kinnard recounts, by 1970 'the gaps between HES numbers and actual conditions in [South Vietnamese] provinces had reached ludicrous proportions'; 'Before long the task force was living in its own statistical world.'[89] The very systems designed to manage the war's reality thus played an instrumental part in losing touch with that reality. As Kim McQuaid argues, then, '*Illusion* [...] is a key concept to keep in mind regarding all Vietnam War-related policy after the Tet offensive.'[90]

By the early seventies, the war's de-realization was intrinsic to the way it was being waged. Nixon's attempt to control the North Vietnamese supply lines along the Ho Chi Minh trail between 1969 and 1972 involved a massive investment in the automated warfare that General Westmoreland and others had advocated. Code-named 'Operation Igloo White', Vietnam veteran Erik Herter commented on its effects during a 1972 investigation by Vietnam Veterans against the War (VVAW): 'the people of villages have gone from being "gooks" [...] to being grid-coordinates, blips on scan screens [...]. The machine functions. The radar blip disappears. No village is destroyed. No humans die. For none existed.'[91] This is precisely the kind of systematic illusion-mongering that Ginsberg had been protesting throughout the sixties. And with the US

---

[88] See McQuaid, *The Anxious Years*, 112–26.
[89] Douglas Kinnard, *The War Managers* (Hanover, NH: University of Vermont Press, 1977), 107.
[90] McQuaid, *The Anxious Years*, 104, my emphasis.
[91] Quoted ibid. 77. On the 'automated' war, see also Philip Jones Griffiths's extended photo-essay, *Vietnam Inc.* (New York: Collier, 1971), 194.

incursions into Cambodia and Laos in the seventies, he continued to use poetry and activism mutually to reinforce his voice of dissent within the mainstream media. In early 1970, for example, Ginsberg along with Dr Benjamin Spock, Joan Baez, and Pete Seeger announced the formation of a War Tax Resistance organization for citizens wanting to withdraw support for the war effort by not paying taxes. It was, he said at a press conference, one way of helping to 'short circuit the nerve system of our electronic bureaucracy.'[92]

Later that year, Ginsberg carried out extensive research into the CIA's suspected support of opium production in Laos, and recovered a letter missing from a Senate operations committee file as evidence. His findings made the *New York Times*, which cited him in reporting that 'The CIA has raised a 10,000 man army from the Meo Tribesman. Without their opium trade, they might require massive US economic aid.'[93] In this way Ginsberg did his best to use mainstream press and media channels to help counter the circulation of illusions and secrets that he viewed as helping to maintain the war effort against the perceived threat of Communism. He also continually made reference in poems like 'Friday the Thirteenth' (March 1970) to the automated warfare being prepared in Laos. The date of the latter poem alludes to the accidental explosion in a house being used as a bomb factory by a group of young Weathermen terrorists—three of them died in the blast. That bombing was one of many that took place in 1970 as elements of the counter-culture turned more militant, and Ginsberg is at pains in the poem to voice his concern over the turn of events:

When Violence floods the State from above, flowery land razed for robot proliferation
metal rooted & asphalted down 6 feet below topsoil,
then when bombcarrying children graduate from Grammar-school's sex-drenched gymnasia
terrified of Army Finance Meatbones, busted by cops for grassy hair,
Who can prophesy Peace, or vow Futurity for any but armed insects . . . (*CP*, 539)

Like his 1968 'Grant Park' poem, in this extract Ginsberg adduces a spiral of violence and paranoia that sweeps up the 'State' and 'bombcarrying children' into a mutual escalation. And escalate they did; in response to the bombings, Nixon on 11 April publicly called for new surveillance powers that would involve wire-tapping, informers, and undercover

---

[92] Quoted in Schumacher, *Dharma Lion*, 540.
[93] Quoted in Miles, *Ginsberg*, 433.

agents. When he subsequently announced the invasion of Cambodia on 30 April, violent protests spread around numerous university campuses, one of the worst being at Kent State University, Ohio, where National Guards shot dead four students.[94]

Still being described in the press and media as a guru of American youth culture, Ginsberg's response to the escalation of violence was to continue advocating spiritual resistance through his poetry and in numerous interviews and public addresses. For example, visiting Kent State University in April 1971, just before the anniversary of the shootings, he declared that he thought the left-wing violence had been 'prolonging the war, prolonging the killing in Vietnam', and he spoke of mantra and 'massive demonstrations' as more viable alternatives.[95] Leading a poetry seminar at Wisconsin State University the following week, he expanded on the continued importance of mantra: 'its function is to be *only* magic speak, or mantra, or prayer [...] its function is only to be a physiological vehicle for feelings and understood as such.'[96] If the auto-poems were intended to pose new vehicles of sensibility, so Ginsberg remained adamant that poetry could offer *techniques* for feeling as an alternative to the kinds of ideology-driven *technology* that he detailed in another address at the University of California, Davis:

Ideology created Helios and STOLs (that is, Short Take-off and Landing Planes), specialized infrared sensory equipment to smell the heat of human bodies underneath green leaves—a whole technical scientific apparatus exfoliated out of Kennedy's liberal hipness.[97]

For Ginsberg, then, the war's 'Myth rationalization' that he'd declaimed in 1967 was still in operation. Consequently, in 1972 he began extensive research of 'Operation Igloo White', continued to denounce the war in press and television interviews, and was determined to help prevent Nixon's re-election at any cost.

For Nixon's part, 1972 saw him continue to adopt a public stance of pacification for Vietnam while maintaining the intensity of the military campaign. In January, for example, he announced that his National Security Advisor, Henry Kissinger, had been in secret peace talks with the North Vietnamese. 'Vietnamization', the policy of withdrawing

---

[94] See Zaroulis and Sullivan, *Who Spoke Up?*, 313–31.
[95] Allen Ginsberg, 'War and Peace: Vietnam and Kent State' (6 April 1971), in *Allen Verbatim: Lectures on Poetry, Politics, Consciousness by Allen Ginsberg*, ed. Gordon Ball (New York: McGraw-Hill, 1974), 207, 204.
[96] Ginsberg, 'Words and Consciousness' (13 April 1971), in *Allen Verbatim*, 25, Ginsberg's emphasis.
[97] Ginsberg, 'Myths Associated with Science' (27 April 1971), in *Allen Verbatim*, 213.

American troops and handing over the ground combat to the South Vietnamese, was also still proceeding. Moreover, Nixon publicly extended pacification towards America's main communist foes; in February he travelled to China to re-establish cordial relations, and in May he travelled to Moscow where he signed a 'Strategic Arms Limitation Treaty' (SALT 1).[98] Despite the setback of a massive North Vietnamese offensive at the end of March, Nixon's public gestures of peace ensured that he deflated the importance of the war and opposition to it even though he extended the US bombing ambit in North Vietnam, Laos, and Cambodia. With the media's attention on the war significantly diverted, Ginsberg undertook his own extensive research as his unpublished 'Vietnam War / 1972 Election Note & Copybook' testifies. Drawing on US Senate hearings, press clippings, and military journals, he recorded a range of statistics on war casualties and expenditures, wrote lists of armaments and sensors used in 'Operation Igloo White', and noted examples of how the latter operated:

TV Screen map moving lights truck caravans on [Ho Chi Minh] Trail
    picked up by seismic & Acoustic sensors.
    the 'worm' illuminated line of light crawls his
screen
AO [Assessment Officer] & Computer map pick a geographic box to trap the worm.
Fighter & Gunships: head plane is radioed info for
airborne computers
    [. . .]
        'We got the Ho Chi Minh trail wired
        like a pinball machine.'[99]

Just as Erik Herter commented that Igloo White had turned the enemy into 'blips on scan screens', so Ginsberg notes here that enemy vehicles have become 'worms' in a 'pinball machine' war (the quotations being drawn from a '1971 Military Aircraft journal').[100] Previously he'd noted the role of domestic media in doctoring the war's reality for the American public; here he notes that radio and 'TV' technology are actually involved in waging the war.

---

[98] See Robert D. Schulzinger, 'Richard Nixon, Congress, and the War in Vietnam, 1969–74', in Randall B. Woods (ed.), *Vietnam and the American Political Tradition: The Politics of Dissent* (Cambridge: Cambridge University Press, 2003), 291–3; also McQuaid, *The Anxious Years*, 115–19.
[99] Ginsberg, 'Vietnam War / 1972 Election Note & Copybook', Allen Ginsberg Papers (M0733), Department of Special Collections, Stanford University Libraries, Series 2 (Box 24, Folder 16), pp. 3–4.
[100] Ibid. 4, Ginsberg's emphasis.

Ginsberg's opposition to Igloo White and Nixon's running of the war came to a climax when he went to protest at the August 1972 Republican Convention held in Miami. Having taken formal vows as a Buddhist in May, he remained intent on developing mantric poetry as a vehicle for anti-war sentiments. While travelling to the convention by plane he wrote an auto-poem, 'These States: to Miami Presidential Convention', in which he declares 'Ah! Shall be my mantra—America's gasp of Awe' (*CP*, 583). An exclamation commonly used by Romantic poets like Blake and Whitman whom Ginsberg so admired, 'Ah' is also a 'seed syllable' in Hindu and Buddhist mantra that is linked with the heart chakra.[101] In Ginsberg's poem his sense of the syllable as both exclamation of bodily feeling is readily apparent:

> Ah! to the Heart from Heart ever Grateful
>   for mercy human understanding sigh—
> Ah! for our loves dead & gone
> Ah! for miseries we caused, youthful screaming
>   Pig Cop selves
>   Violence in other streets and nations (*CP*, 583)

Even within this passage the anaphora builds in complexity as 'Ah!' repeatedly emphasizes an awareness of different things and events—'our loves dead & gone', 'miseries we caused', 'Violence in other streets and nations'. And in being voiced 'to the Heart from Heart', this awareness of events is looped into a more pronounced emotional response at the same time that the emotion is expelled from the body through the syllable as exhalation.[102] So whereas in earlier auto-poems Ginsberg had sometimes veered towards a solipsistic denial of reality, 'These States' performs as a kind of affective filtration system. The impact of political events is registered in terms of collective emotions and responsibility—'our loves', 'miseries we caused'—where the lack of such emotion and responsibility is viewed by the poet as having been part of the problem in the first place. Voicing these affects back, the poetic vehicle of feeling is offered up as a kind of public transport in which the poem is both affectively purgative and potentiating in appealing to the body politic:

---

[101] Ginsberg discusses the importance of mantric seed syllables in 'Improvised Poetics', 33–4.

[102] At Chögyam Trungpa's suggestion, Ginsberg had been practising samatha meditation, which specifically concentrates on exhalation. Miles quotes Ginsberg describing it: 'Specifically, samatha—as distinct from Zen style—is paying attention to the breath leaving the nostril and dissolving into the space in front of the face... I've heard it described as touch and let go, touch and let go—or attention to the breath going out, and then dropping it as the breath ceases, and then attention again to the breath when it goes out' (*Ginsberg*, 450).

> Great Government Robot State
>   above us dominates our news,
> takes up our telephone time labor paper work
>   in Magic War,
> Ah! that we return to our Bodies alert
>   electric limb'd, lungs & heart
>   empty tingling, lightness
>   we all know Heaven on Earth
> Our Will Be Thine as we Say (*CP*, 585)

Ginsberg had first sung himself electric with mantra in front of Chicago's John Hancock building in 1968, but this is a more politically overt statement in opposing collective sentiments to the 'Great Government Robot State'.

A more pronounced democracy is also what Ginsberg called for at the Republican Convention. Meeting up with other counter-cultural friends like John Giorno, Rennie Davis, Hoffman, and Rubin, Ginsberg drafted a lengthy 'Public Statement signed by Poet Friends' to be read and distributed at protests outside the convention. The statement was written as a poem, includes war statistics he'd researched, and repeatedly alludes to Vietnam's electronic battlefield:

> Is this the Country of God?
> Are we the Nation under Christ?
> Automated Electronic Bombing
>   in the name of the Holy Ghost
>   the Sacred Heart
>   the crown of Thorns,
> <u>Igloo White</u> last bombs
>   in the Name of Jesus' Cross?
> In the Name of Jesus Christ
>   America Make up your mind.
> Don't Vote for Nixon to Continue War
>   murder.[103]

By adopting an evangelical tone in denouncing 'Igloo White', Ginsberg's 'Statement' appeals to the very 'schizophrenia' of America as corporate and Christian nation that Mailer had declared to be at stake in the levitation of the Pentagon. But the performance of the poem is also directed at persuading people to oust Nixon democratically by voting for the Democrats' presidential candidate, George McGovern, as we see in the closing lines:

---

[103] Ginsberg, 'Draft for Public Statement signed by Poet Friends', in 'Vietnam War / 1972 Election Note & Copybook', 20, Ginsberg's emphasis.

> Wake up! Don't be Crazy! Don't let Nixon in
> White House assassinate Cambodia Laos Vietnam
>   another 4 years with
> Automated Electronic Battlefield Bomb War!
> Make McGovern Win, everyone help DO IT,
> Pray ring doorbells all folk register
>   Vote McGovern, Ah![104]

The political appeal thus combines mantric seed syllables with slogans—'Make McGovern Win' and 'Don't let Nixon in' echoing each other with their trochees in addition to rhyming. Not that Ginsberg succeeded in getting what he called for, though. Having organized a small peace march outside the convention, the march was caught up in violence between police and members of VVAW.[105] Arrested for disturbing the peace, he was gaoled for three days, and by November that year Nixon was re-elected to office with more than 60 per cent of the vote.

Over the next two years, though, Ginsberg did have the pleasure of seeing his anti-war poetry gain in popularity and success while the war's 'Myth rationalization' and Nixon's power crumbled. The publication of *The Fall of America* in 1972 gathered more of the auto-poems he'd written since 1965 and was heralded as a landmark work by critics such as Helen Vendler and Lyman Andrews, the latter declaring that '*The Fall of America* confirms Ginsberg's status as the true successor to Whitman.'[106] Nixon's American fall was a different matter. As the bombing campaign continued in 1973 while publicized peace negotiations failed, the US Congress followed public opinion in maintaining that enough was finally enough. Passing a bill cutting off funds for the war effort, Congress also passed a 'War Powers Resolution' limiting the extent to which a president could involve US troops in conflicts without congressional support.[107] With the Watergate scandal brewing from March 1973 Nixon was thus increasingly backed into a corner, and by August he was forced to promise an end to the bombing in Cambodia.

I've argued already that Watergate is evidence of the extent to which the dominant US culture of control became subject to the industry of illusion it promulgated, and that's certainly the view that Ginsberg was taking at the time. Writing to his father on 9 May 1973, for example, he argued that Watergate was,

---

[104] Ibid. 23.
[105] See Miles, *Ginsberg*, 448, and Schumacher, *Dharma Lion*, 567–70.
[106] Quoted in Schumacher, *Dharma Lion*, 572.
[107] See Zaroulis and Sullivan, *Who Spoke Up?*, 407–12, and Schulzinger, 'Richard Nixon, Congress, and the War in Vietnam', 292–9.

like a woollen sweater. [...] If the thread keeps unravelling the whole fabric of 'mass hallucination' public imagery will fall—and what *should* be seen is that all of Vietnam, all the 'brainwash' imagery [...] was also a giant Watergate-type conspiracy.[108]

Contrary to the argument that after 1972 the potentials of the sixties could be seen as an 'historical illusion', Ginsberg in 1973 holds that it was the voice of the counter-culture that had made it possible to see how much Watergate and the electronic war had been running on 'mass hallucination'. (As we'll see in Chapters 3 and 4, Watergate was a matter that William Burroughs and Kathy Acker were also keen to address.) More recently, historian Stephen Paul Miller has been similarly critical of the extent to which the seventies marked a turn away from the 'new possibilities' of the sixties back towards 'reality':

> Because a sense of reality was so problematic in the sixties, it is not surprising that the seventies concerned a return to reality. But what reality? Was it possible to forget how political realities had been discredited by the Vietnam War, the string of sixties assassinations, and the electoral system's inability to run an antiwar presidential candidate in 1968?[109]

Ginsberg's answer in 1974 to such a question would have been a firm 'no'. As he stated that year: 'The insights we're getting from Watergate came from 1964–68.'[110]

* * *

'Gate, gate, paragate' (gone, gone, gone beyond) are the opening words of the Prajnaparamita sutra with which Ginsberg had calmed down the Hell's Angels in 1965. But by 1974 'Gate, gate, Watergate' is a mantra he could have coined with Nixon going, going, and then finally gone. It was also the year in which *The Fall of America* was awarded the National Book Award. As Ginsberg averred in his acceptance speech for the award, though, to focus on Nixon's downfall was to risk losing sight of the underlying issues: 'Watergate is a froth on the swamp: impeachment of a living president does not remove the hundred billion power of the military nor the secret billion power of the police state apparatus.'[111] In his opinion, the attention paid to the scandal by the media and public was symptomatic of a continuing investment in the very 'mass hallucination'

---

[108] Quoted in Schumacher, *Dharma Lion*, 572.
[109] Stephen Paul Miller, *The Seventies Now: Culture as Surveillance* (Durham, NC: Duke University Press, 1999), 16.
[110] Quoted in Schumacher, *Dharma Lion*, 583.
[111] Ginsberg, '*The Fall of America* Wins an Award' (17 April 1974), in *Deliberate Prose*, 20.

that had powered Nixon's downfall.[112] Accordingly, he persisted in using his celebrity in any way he could to criticize publicly the effects of the 'national media consciousness' that had helped to promote such mass illusions.

Admittedly, Ginsberg's seventies appeals through popular channels appeared at times to compromise the experimental drive of his earlier work. The last poem in *The Fall of America*, 'September on Jessore Road' is a case in point:

> Where are the helicopters of U.S. AID?
> Smuggling dope in Bangkok's green shade.
> Where is America's Air Force of Light?
> Bombing North Laos all day and all night? (*CP*, 573)

Written after a brief 1971 trip to India to witness the effects of recent floods, most of the poem is concerned, like this stanza, with contrasting America's continuing military presence in Indochina with its lack of aid for India. One could argue that despite the political opposition voiced in the poem, the couplets and predominantly dactylic rhythm sound a retreat from the poetic dynamism of the 'open form' versifying that Ginsberg had previously championed as a vehicle for liberated sensibility. On the other hand, one could maintain that even the stanza above stands as a fairly novel folk-poetic hybrid that combines a range of influences: Andrew Marvell's 'green shade' from his poem 'The Garden' (*c*.1650); Bob Dylan's abab song rhymes of the time; and the slogan chanting of counter-cultural demonstrations. Ginsberg admitted that he wanted to 'write a poem or song with words that are so inevitable that people will be able to use it all the time—like Dylan or Blake.'[113] And that's clearly what he intended when he and Dylan recorded musical versions of 'September on Jessore Road' and performed it, along with versions of the 'Vajra Mantra', and Blake's 'A Dream' and 'Nurse's Song', on public broadcast television in New York in November 1971. Ultimately, then, I'd argue that the poem is an example of Ginsberg experimenting with yet another form of mantric poetry in order to engage *with* 'media consciousness' *through* 'media consciousness'. Rather than viewing such pop collusion as

---

[112] In 1974, for example, Ginsberg argued that 'the Cambodian bombing was much more violent and illegal than any of the Watergate stuff. And yet everybody, the whole national consciousness—I should say, national media consciousness—is concerned with Watergate wire tapping on that slight level and has not yet been willing to confront this real heavier violence of the Cambodian bombing and the illegality of that which was just as illegal as the plumbers' activities—much more illegal!' (Ginsberg, 'Interview' with Ekbert Faas (27 March 1974), in Ekbert Faas (ed.), *Towards a New American Poetics: Essays and Interviews* (Santa Barbara: Black Sparrow Press, 1978), 279).

[113] Quoted in Schumacher, *Dharma Lion*, 559.

amounting simply to a postmodern loss of critical distance, Ginsberg clearly saw the possibility of fashioning for popular culture a kind of critical immanence. Indeed, asked in 1974 whether he thought that a mantric statement like 'I here declare the end of the war' was still viable, he cited Dylan's 'Even the President of the United States must someday stand naked' (from 'It's Alright Ma (I'm Only Bleeding)' (1965)) as an effective 'mantric phrase' for 'the kind of mentality that could go through Watergate.'[114]

With President Gerald Ford, Nixon's successor, having declared 7 May 1975 to be the end of the 'Vietnam Era', Ginsberg's participation in Dylan's 'Rolling Thunder Review' later that year could also appear to be politically questionable. But as the war had ended, the emphasis of the tour was on celebrating the seeds of sixties counter-culture that remained.[115] As Barry Miles points out, Ginsberg was more intent on making a tour film with conversations between himself and Dylan '"wrap [ping] up" questions on ecology, capitalism, communism, God, poetry, meditation, and America, "as best we can".'[116] Moreover, in no way had he turned his back on political activism, open-form poetry, little magazines, or alternative communities. In 1974, for example, he founded with Anne Waldman the Jack Kerouac School of Disembodied Poetics at the Naropa Institute in Boulder, Colorado, which still teaches and funds experimental poetry to this day. Continuing to be outspoken on US foreign policy Ginsberg also began researching and publicly protesting the production of nuclear energy and weapons.[117] In particular, his poem 'Plutonian Ode' (1978) shows that he was still invested in turning the mantric potentialism of poems like 'Wichita Vortex Sutra' into a form of 'apokatastasis': 'the transformation of satanic energy to celestial energy.'[118]

For Ginsberg, then, the possibilities of the sixties survived after the era. As he stated in 1986, that survival is 'not merely a few scattered institutions, in which I would include things like Naropa', for it also entails 'basic changes in attitude which have been adopted by the majority.'[119] Given that the eighties did see such a surge of corporatism, consumerism, and neo-conservatism in America, it's understandable that from Jameson's

---

[114] Ginsberg, 'A Conversation' (8 August 1974), an interview with Paul Geneson, in *Composed on the Tongue*, 100.
[115] See Schumacher, *Dharma Lion*, Ch. 25, and Miles, *Ginsberg*, 458–63.
[116] Miles, *Ginsberg*, 461.
[117] On Ginsberg's nuclear energy research and activism, see Schumacher, *Dharma Lion*, 624–32.
[118] Ginsberg, 'The New Consciousness' (1975), interview with Yves Le Pellec, in *Composed on the Tongue*, 89.
[119] Ginsberg, untitled interview with Simon Albury, in *Spontaneous Mind*, 466.

Marxist perspective the counter-cultural dreams of the sixties seem in hindsight a failure because they didn't succeed in preventing the growth of multinational corporatism. But such a wholesale revolution wasn't what Ginsberg had been fighting for. What he and other counter-culture proponents showed was that individuals could develop alternative possibilities of community and voice *within* the very culture they were protesting. In doing so, they also demonstrated how one can combat symptoms of a war's 'Myth rationalization' *in oneself*, even when the pervasiveness of those symptoms are at their zenith.

2
'This Black World of Purest Possibility'
LeRoi Jones/Amiri Baraka

BLACK POWER AND BLACK POSSIBILITY

In December 1964, the 30-year-old African American poet and dramatist LeRoi Jones declared that 'every black' in North America 'is a potential revolutionary'.[1] He wasn't alone in thinking this way, and with the rise of the Black Power and Black Arts movements over the next four years, cultural and political potentials of black Americans were widely debated. By 1968 Jones had already realized many of his own revolutionary potentials; having changed his name to Amiri Baraka he'd also established himself as one of the leading exponents of black Cultural Nationalism. That same year, Harold Cruse in *Rebellion or Revolution?* reaffirmed the necessity of such a separatist movement by raising again the issue of black potentiality:

If the realities of the American way of life lead us to rule out the possibilities of voluntary evolutionary social change along racially or ethnically democratic lines, we are then faced with the other alternative: revolutionary ideas and methods.[2]

To argue that social evolution for African Americans was only possible through revolution was, of course, contentious given the advances made by Civil Rights groups such as the Student Nonviolent Coordinating Committee (SNCC), the National Association for the Advancement of Colored People (NAACP), and Martin Luther King's Southern Christian Leadership Conference (SCLC). Not only had these groups fought for racial integration at a local level, they'd also helped bring about the Civil Rights Act (1964) and the Voting Rights Act (1965), both of which helped outlaw racial segregation and prejudicial voting practices. Yet as

---

[1] Quoted in Jack Newfield, 'LeRoi Jones at Arms: Blues for Mr Whitey', *Village Voice* (17 December 1964), 12.

[2] Harold Cruse, *Rebellion or Revolution?* (New York: William Morris, 1968), 107.

commentators have noted, racial integration was not the everyday experience of many African Americans in the wake of those Acts.[3] Continuing tensions between black communities and predominantly white authorities were seen by many people as primary causes of the race riots that subsequently shook various US cities in the latter part of the 1960s—particularly Los Angeles (1965), Newark, and Detroit (both 1967). For an increasing number of African American activists, seeking integration within a society that still appeared fundamentally racist was decidedly illogical. Consequently, by 1966 the SNCC was rejecting the Civil Rights chant of 'Freedom Now' in favour of a more militant call for 'Black Power', while in Oakland, California, Huey P. Newton and Bobby Seale established the 'Black Panther Party for Self Defense' to fight for separatist autonomy of the local black community.[4] Cruse's statement that social evolution for black Americans would only be possible with social revolution is thus precisely the position that Black Power organizations had already begun to champion.

'We do not want a Nation, we are a Nation'[5]—so LeRoi Jones summed up the message of the black nationalist leader Malcolm X after his assassination in February 1965. By this point, X's argument that black Americans could constitute a separate nation *within* America was drawing support as an alternative stance to Civil Rights, and that stance gained in popularity after X's death. For Jones, building such nationalism had to be predicated on recognizing that African Americans were culturally different: 'Nations are races', he argued, and 'Race is feeling. Where the body, and the organs come in.'[6] Asserting that it was the task of the arts to develop such racial feeling, Jones subsequently helped establish a Cultural Nationalist movement which maintained that the possibility of social evolution for black Americans was linked to possibilities of art and literature. Thus, when Cruse in *Rebellion or Revolution?* declared that because of cultural difference 'the American Negro is the only potentially revolutionary force in the United States today', he was effectively echoing Jones.[7]

---

[3] See, for example, Maurice Isserman and Michael Kazin, *America Divided: The Civil War of the 1960s* (Oxford: Oxford University Press, 2000), 177–8, and Allen Matusow, *The Unravelling of America: A History of Liberalism in the 1960s* (New York: Harper, 1984), 362–3.

[4] On these developments, see Komozi Woodard, *A Nation within a Nation: Amiri Baraka/LeRoi Jones and Black Power Politics* (Chapel Hill, NC: University of North Carolina Press, 1999), Ch. 1.

[5] LeRoi Jones, 'The Legacy of Malcolm X and the Coming of the Black Nation', in Amiri Baraka, *The LeRoi Jones/Amiri Baraka Reader*, ed. William J. Harris (New York: Thunder's Mouth Press, 2000), 161.

[6] Ibid. 166.

[7] Cruse, *Rebellion or Revolution?*, 96.

As Larry Neal stated the case in 1968: 'Afro-American life is full of creative possibilities, and the movement is just beginning to perceive them. [. . .] If art is the harbinger of future possibilities, what does the future of Black America portend?'[8]

From the statements I've quoted, it's evident that the faith Ginsberg and his fellow counter-culturalists placed in people's capacity to harness a *common* fund of potentiality is something that Jones and other Black Power figures were questioning at the time. As we saw in the last chapter, Theodore Roszak argued that the 'Port Huron Statement' (1962) of Students for a Democratic Society (SDS) ignored consciousness of class in favour of what he called 'consciousness consciousness' when it made sweeping humanist statements like 'we regard *men* as infinitely precious and possessed of unfulfilled capacities for reason, freedom, and love'.[9] One can also argue that such a statement doesn't account for the degree to which those 'capacities' might have been regulated along racial lines. Similarly, when Ginsberg appeals to America collectively in his poems on the basis of it being a democratic body-politic, one can question, like Cruse, the extent to which the democracy was capable of being wholly inclusive. In this chapter, then, I'll focus on how Jones/Baraka and the Black Arts Movement strove to develop racial potentials through a range of cultural practices. In examining this, one of my aims is to reconsider György Lukács's distinction between 'abstract' and 'concrete' potentialities that I discussed in my Introduction. As we saw, Lukács characterizes 'abstract potentiality' as the kind of infinite subjective possibility that the 'Port Huron Statement' advocates. In contrast, the 'concrete potentiality' he favours involves seeing individuals as having specific 'character' potentials drawn from 'inherited gifts and qualities', all of which evolve in a dialectical relation with 'objective reality'.[10] From the perspective of Cultural Nationalists like Baraka, though, the 'objective reality' of the USA is precisely what had prevented African Americans from realizing their potentials. In using art as a 'harbinger of future possibilities', nationalists like Baraka and Neal weren't simply drawing on 'inherited qualities', they were also trying to foster new cultural potentials that could help change objective reality. And in that sense, their project can be seen as

---

[8] Larry Neal, 'The Black Arts Movement' (1968), in Addison Gayle, Jr (ed.), *The Black Aesthetic* (New York: Doubleday, 1971), 290.
[9] Quoted in Theodore Roszak, *The Making of a Counter Culture: Reflections on the Technocratic Society and its Youthful Opposition* (1968, repr.; Berkeley, CA: University of California Press, 1995), 62, Roszak's emphasis.
[10] György Lukács, *The Meaning of Contemporary Realism*, trans. John and Necke Mander (1957, repr.; London: Merlin, 1969), 22, 24.

challenging the very distinction between 'abstract' and 'concrete' potentials that Lukács upholds. As I'll show, their Cultural Nationalism also entailed positing equivalences among 'possibility', 'spirituality', 'energy', and 'feeling'. The fusion amounts to a particular form of potentialism, and in order to outline its development in Baraka's work I'll trace it in relation to the three stances he adopted between 1957 and 1974: first, as a Beat aficionado; second, as a Cultural Nationalist; and third, as a Third-World Socialist who renounced his nationalist ideas.

'MY POETRY IS WHATEVER I THINK I AM': FROM BEATS TO BLACK ARTS

Having joined the US Air Force in 1954, Jones was given a dishonourable discharge in 1957 after he was accused (wrongly) of being a Communist when it was discovered that he owned a copy of the left-wing literary journal, *Partisan Review*.[11] He'd continued to write poetry since his undergraduate days at Howard University, and on moving to Greenwich Village after his discharge he soon decided to become a writer. Marrying a young Jewish woman Hettie Cohen in 1958 he also set up with her a literary magazine, *Yugen*, which ran until 1963. The first issue of *Yugen* included Beat writers such as Ginsberg, Philip Whalen, and Diane di Prima, and the journal became an effective vehicle through which Jones built up his literary contacts. *Floating Bear*, the journal he set up with di Prima, was another vehicle, and by 1960 he knew not just Beat writers but also Black Mountain and New York School poets, including Charles Olson, Robert Creeley, and Frank O'Hara.[12] 'I was sort of tight with all of them', he claimed in a 1978 interview; 'I hung out with all of them.'[13] Viewed primarily as a Beat-affiliated poet, though, the new connections Jones had made were, as he later stated, far from political: 'I used to make

---

[11] See Philip Uko Effiong, *In Search of a Model for African-American Drama: A Study of Selected Plays by Lorraine Hansberry, Amiri Baraka, and Ntozake Shange* (New York: University Press of America, 2000), 75. For extensive biographies see Jerry Gafio Watts, *Amiri Baraka: The Politics and Art of a Black Intellectual* (New York: New York University Press, 2001), and Amiri Baraka, *The Autobiography of LeRoi Jones/Amiri Baraka* (New York: Freundlich, 1984), hereafter cited as *Autobiography*.
[12] Jones had an affair with di Prima in 1960 and she subsequently had a daughter by him. See di Prima's *Recollections of My Life as a Woman: The New York Years* (New York: Viking, 2001), 220–1, 229–31.
[13] Quoted in Kimberley Benston, 'Amiri Baraka: An Interview', in *boundary 2* 6:2 (Winter 1978), 306.

statements that I was just a poet, I didn't care anything about politics.'[14] And nor did the poets he fraternized with, as far as he was concerned: 'the overwhelming line was always antipolitical. Or, when politics did emerge, as in Olson's work, I didn't agree with it.'[15]

At the start of the 1960s, though, two events in particular helped spark a political awakening in Jones. The first was a trip to Cuba in July 1960 with a delegation of artists, writers, and members of the Fair Play for Cuba Committee. Harold Cruse and Robert F. Williams—head of the militant NAACP chapter in Monroe, North Carolina—featured among the black delegates, and Jones also met a range of Cuban Socialist intellectuals who were critical of the USA and its writers.[16] As he stated in his 1960 essay 'Cuba Libre', 'The idea of a "revolution" had been foreign to me', and in opening his eyes to political issues the whole trip became for him a major turning point.[17] Inspired to become more politically active, on returning to Greenwich Village he became an enthusiastic member of the Fair Play For Cuba Committee, and in 1961 he was elected president of its New York chapter. The second event that became a watershed for him was the assassination in January 1961 of Patrice Lumumba, the first elected prime minister of the newly independent Republic of the Congo. With all kinds of speculation circulating about Belgian and US backing of the assassination, Lumumba's death immediately provoked angry debates about lingering intimacies between colonial and capitalist interests. Jones vented his own anger on 15 February that year; he was arrested for fighting police while protesting the assassination at the United Nations headquarters in Manhattan.[18] In addition to being an active poet, Jones was thus becoming increasingly involved in political activism. Yet neither Lumumba's murder nor the Cuba visit were enough to educe a clear perspective from Jones on the situation of black Americans. Soon after his return from Cuba he also set up an Organization of Young Men (OYM), which worked with another group, On Guard, in campaigning for a range of 'equality rights'. Cruse was one of the members of On Guard at this time, and in *The Crisis of the Negro Intellectual* (1967) he recounts that Jones and his Young Men 'did not understand their own social dynamic' and had no clear idea as to what the role of the 'Negro

---

[14] Quoted in Debra L. Edwards 'An Interview with Amiri Baraka' (1979), in *Conversations with Amiri Baraka*, ed. Charlie Reilly (Jackson: University Press of Mississippi, 1994), 152.
[15] Quoted in Benston, 'Amiri Baraka: An Interview', 306.
[16] See Baraka, *Autobiography*, 163–6; also Watts, *Amiri Baraka*, 51–5.
[17] LeRoi Jones, 'Cuba Libre', in *The LeRoi Jones/Amiri Baraka Reader*, 160.
[18] See Baraka, *Autobiography*, 181.

intellectual' should be.[19] Inexperienced in matters of activism, OYM soon faded away. As Cruse concludes, 'The Jones who could set up in Black Arts School in 1965 was not the Jones of 1961.'[20]

The fraught nature of the transitions Jones was undergoing is evident in his writings of this period. In his short essay 'How You Sound'—which appeared in Don Allen's landmark anthology, *The New American Poetry* (1960)—he declared, 'My poetry is whatever I think I am. [...] I CAN BE ANYTHING I CAN.'[21] Such a statement clearly equates unlimited possibilities of poetry with those of character, and in that respect it affirms the kind of infinite subjective potentiality that Lukács criticizes for being 'abstract'. In other publications of this time, though, Jones's stance on possibility is more 'concrete'. In the 'Cuba Libre' essay, for example, he asserts that any intellectual work in America is hampered by its social reality: 'The young intellectual living in the United States inhabits an ugly void. He cannot use what is around him, neither can he revolt against it.'[22] Suggesting implicitly that 'whatever I think I am' is trammelled by America, he also acknowledged elsewhere that his own identity as a poet was inexorably linked to being an African American: 'There are certain influences on me, as a Negro person, that certainly wouldn't apply to a poet like Allen Ginsberg'; 'I'm fully conscious all the time that I am an American Negro because it's part of my life.'[23]

These tensions between concrete and abstract potentialities are also manifest in his first published book of poetry, *Preface to a Twenty Volume Suicide Note* (1961). On the one hand, many of the poems echo the kinds of 'open form' poetry that Beat and Black Mountain writers were experimenting with at the time.[24] On the other hand, Jones's poetic freedom is frequently tempered by an uneasy sense of cultural stricture, as in the poem 'Look for You Yesterday, Here You Come Today'. He begins the poem with the statement: 'Part of my charm: | envious blues feeling', and the speaker proceeds to recount his daily gripes while making allusions to a range of white cultural figures, including 'Strindberg', 'Leonardo', 'Hogarth', 'Kline', and Baudelaire's 'Flowers of Evil'. In the final section of the poem, self censure suddenly draws this lyrical meandering to a halt: 'How dumb to be

---

[19] Harold Cruse, *The Crisis of the Negro Intellectual: A Historical Analysis of the Failure of Black Leadership* (1967, repr.; New York: New York Review of Books, 2005), 362.
[20] Ibid.
[21] LeRoi Jones, 'How You Sound', in *The LeRoi Jones/Amiri Baraka Reader*, 16.
[22] Jones, 'Cuba Libre', 145.
[23] Quoted in David Ossman, 'LeRoi Jones: An Interview on *Yugen*' (1960), in Reilly (ed.), *Conversations with Amiri Baraka*, 6.
[24] Jones quotes Olson's statement 'Who knows what a poem ought to sound like? Until it's thar' when discussing the poetry's possibilities in his 'How You Sound', 16.

sentimental about anything | To call it love & cry pathetically'.[25] With the next, fragmented stanza, though, the speaker realizes that to dismiss that 'maudlin nostalgia' is also to forget the charms of 'blues feeling', after which point he draws to a close by reflecting on the cultural sacrifices the poem has entailed:

> F. Scott Charon
> will soon be glad-handing me
> like a legionaire
>
> My silver bullets all gone
> My black mask trampled in the dust
>
> & Tonto way off in the hills
> moaning like Bessie Smith[26]

Having forsaken the Blues tradition to scorn melancholy in an open-form poem (complete with Creeley-esque short lines and enjambement), the speaker acknowledges that he's dangerously close to passing over to the 'other side'. Not only does he liken himself to a soldier in the French Foreign Legion (which played a considerable role in France's colonial expansions), he also imagines himself in the hands of F. Scott Fitzgerald who, as the mythical boatman, Charon, is presumably preparing to ferry him over to Hades. As the speaker recognizes, then, the 'black mask' he's been wearing in the poem isn't an African American one but that of the fictional television character The Lone Ranger (who came to be seen by Jones as representing everything execrable about US culture, as is clear from his later play *What Was the Relationship between the Lone Ranger and the Means of Production?* (1979)). Just as the brunt of The Lone Ranger's trials were frequently borne by Tonto, his faithful Native American 'assistant', so the cultural sacrifice that the poem's speaker has made is imagined as being borne by the Jazz and Blues singer, Bessie Smith. Whether or not 'F. Scott Charon' does actually ferry the speaker across is ultimately left in suspense. In contrast, Jones ensures that he gets the poem's point across by writing another blunter one entitled 'Notes for a Speech'. It begins by sounding a clear note of cultural estrangement: 'African blues | does not know me', and by the end of the poem the tone remains unchanged:

> My own
> dead souls, my, so called

---

[25] LeRoi Jones, 'Look for You Yesterday, Here You Come Today', in *Transbluesency: The Selected Poems of Amiri Baraka/LeRoi Jones (1961–1995)*, ed. Paul Vangelisti (New York: Marsilio, 1995), 20.
[26] Ibid.

> people. Africa
> is a foreign place. You are
> as any other sad man here
> american[27]

From 1962 onwards, Jones did everything in his power to counter that sense of being 'american' so he could identify himself as African American, and he did this largely by taking inspiration from the very thing that some of his poems suggest he had been neglecting: black American music. In his 1962 essay 'The Myth of a "Negro Literature"' he effectively offers a rejoinder to his 'Notes for a Speech' poem on two counts. First, he declares, as Malcolm X did, that black Americans shouldn't be thinking of returning to Africa so much as laying down foundations for their own culture within the USA: 'The traditions of Africa must be utilized within the culture of the American Negro where they *actually* exist, and not because of a defensive rationalization about the *worth* of one's ancestors.'[28] Second, he argues that it's primarily 'Negro music' that's been the driving cultural force in expressing the fraught 'paradox' of African Americans' 'experience'; namely, that it's 'a separate experience, but inseparable from the complete fabric of American life'.[29] This second assertion became controversial, for Jones also contended in the essay that the music's potency highlighted the general 'mediocrity' of African American literature. Only Jean Toomer, Richard Wright, Ralph Ellison, and James Baldwin, he claimed, had recently managed to produce 'serious' writing that could compare with the dizzying heights attained by musicians like Louis Armstrong or Charlie Parker.[30] This disparagement of literary precursors was clearly strategic for Jones: past failures could presage his own success. As I'll show, he certainly didn't think that developing a potent black literature was impossible; rather, he insisted that it still remained to be done. And over the next few years he laboured to develop a new black literary aesthetic partly through correlating poetry's compositional possibilities with those of recent Jazz.

In a number of essays that Jones published around this time, his engagement with music also betokens a concerted effort to refigure the Beat and Black Mountain poetics from which he had been drawing. With Ginsberg having taken inspiration from Bebop Jazz to launch his new 'bop prosody' in 'Howl' (1957), Jones sought to reassert the cultural under-

---

[27] Jones, 'Notes for a Speech', in *Transbluesency*, 48, 49.
[28] LeRoi Jones, 'The Myth of a "Negro Literature"', in *Home: Social Essays* (1966, repr.; Hopewell, NJ: Ecco Press, 1998), 111, Jones's emphases.
[29] Ibid. The 'paradox' of 'experience' is clearly intended to be an advance on W. E. B. Du Bois's notion of black Americans' 'Double-Consciousness' that he sets out in *The Souls of Black Folk* (1903, repr.; Oxford: Oxford University Press, 2008).
[30] Ibid. 107.

pinnings of African American music in a number of publications. In 'Jazz and the White Critic' (1963), for example, he argues that 'Negro music' wasn't a set of musical techniques so much as an aggregate of black experience: 'The notes *mean something*; and the something is [...] part of the black psyche'.[31] The innovation of Ginsberg's bop prosody was thus indebted, for Jones, to the dynamism of African American culture. Elsewhere, he specifically related this dynamism to matters of potentiality while engaging with the bases of Olson's poetics. In his essay 'Hunting is Not Those Heads on the Wall' (1964), for example, he rails against the underlying 'artifact worship' of Western art while advocating an alternative aesthetic based on valorizing 'process': 'the process itself is the most important quality because it can transform and create, and its only form is *possibility*'.[32] This alternative is nevertheless partly derived from Olson's essay 'Projective Verse' (1950), in which he emphasizes the importance of 'process' in 'shap[ing] the energies' of a poem: 'USE USE USE the process at all points, in any given poem always, always one perception must must must MOVE, INSTANTER ON ANOTHER'.[33] For Jones, though, nothing explored the 'possibility' of artistic 'process' so well as the kinds of improvisational Free Jazz that black musicians like Ornette Coleman, Sun Ra, Archie Shepp, and John Coltrane were developing in the 1960s.[34] With this 'New Black Music', Jones declared, black Americans 'are moved and directed by our total response to the possibility of all effects. We are bodies responding differently a (total) force'.[35] In contrast to the more abstract potentiality he'd acclaimed in 'How You Sound', then, Jones effectively replaced the possibilities of Black Mountain verse with those of 'New Black Music' in order to identify particular racialized potentials. This music, in his eyes, wasn't simply expressing inherited concrete potentials for it was also improvising new ones. And far from creating abstract potentiality in the process, Jones viewed such cultural improvisation as stimulating black 'bodies' to be a distinct cultural 'force'. What avowedly remained for him to do was to translate that suscitation into an equally energizing literature, and he made clear in the liner notes he wrote for Shepp's album *Four for Trane* (1964) that he was attempting to do just

---

[31] LeRoi Jones, 'Jazz and the White Critic', in *The LeRoi Jones/Amiri Baraka Reader*, 182, Jones's emphasis.

[32] LeRoi Jones, 'Hunting Is Not Those Heads on the Wall', in *Home*, 174, my emphasis.

[33] Charles Olson, 'Projective Verse', in Paul Hoover (ed.), *Postmodern American Poetry: A Norton Anthology* (New York: Norton, 1994), 614.

[34] William J. Harris explores at length the importance for Jones of Jazz and 'new black music' in *The Poetry and Poetics of Amiri Baraka: The Jazz Aesthetic* (Columbia, MO: University of Missouri Press, 1985).

[35] LeRoi Jones, 'The Changing Same (R&B and New Black Music)' (1966), in *The LeRoi Jones/Amiri Baraka Reader*, 187.

that. A track like Shepp's 'Rufus', stated Jones, 'makes its "changes" faster. *Changes* here meaning, as younger musicians use that word to mean, "modulation", what I mean when I say *image*.'[36] Again, Olson's processual shift of perceptions is replaced here with a 'modulation' of image, one that Jones proceeded to present in his poetry and plays as being fundamentally African American.

By associating black energy with aesthetic possibility, and in aiming to convert this possibility into racial force, the 'images' that Jones came to contribute to the Black Arts Movement amounted to a distinct form of literary potentialism. And if, as he argued in 1965, 'Race is feeling', and culture is the 'making' of feeling, then this potentialism is also intended to be a performative production of race. Unfortunately, in numerous poems and plays that Jones wrote around this time the performativity was less a matter of affirming African American images and more one of hate-speech against whites. 'Black Dada Nihilismus' is the most notorious example of this in Jones's 1964 collection of poems, *The Dead Lecturer*:

> [. . .] Come up, black dada
>
> nihilismus. Rape the white girls. Rape
> their fathers. Cut the mothers' throats.
> Black dada nihilismus, choke my friends
>
> in their bedrooms with their drinks spilling
> and restless for tilting hips or dark liver
> lips sucking splinters from the master's thigh.[37]

In an essay of the same year, Jones talked of 'American dada, Ornette Coleman style',[38] yet the extract above shows none of Coleman's improvisational verve in terms of its poetic imagery, rhythm, syntax, or stanza form. The intensity of aesthetic violence that the poem calls for seems more to indicate that 'dada nihilismus' lacks a positive black character of its own.[39] Initially, the poem's final stanza does seem to signal a change of heart in appealing to a 'lost god damballah' to 'rest or save us'—Damballah being the Voodoo serpent-god of creation. The subsequent lines, however,

---

[36] Quoted in Nathaniel Mackey, 'The Changing Same: Black Music in the Poetry of Amiri Baraka', *boundary 2* 6:2 (Winter 1978), 374, Jones's emphasis.
[37] LeRoi Jones, 'Black Dada Nihilismus', in *Transbluesency*, 98–9.
[38] LeRoi Jones, 'LeRoi Jones Talking', in *Home*, 183.
[39] Baraka's endorsement of machismo and sexual violence as incarnations of Black Power has not gone without criticism; see bell hooks, *Ain't I a Woman: Black Women and Feminism* (1981, repr.; London: Pluto Press, 1982), 106; and Michelle Wallace, *Black Macho and the Myth of the Superwoman* (1978, repr.; New York: Verso, 1999), 62.

make it clear that what the speaker needs to be saved from are 'the murders we intend' against the god's 'lost white children'.

Invoking spirituality effectively becomes an attack on it, then, and there's little evidence in *The Dead Lecturer*'s other poems that any god has been able to dissuade Jones from pursuing an aesthetic of murder. For example, in the five poems that comprise his 'Crow Jane' series Jones links the Crow Jane character of Blues songs to the 'Crazy Jane' series in W. B. Yeats's *The Winding Stair and Other Poems* (1933). Viewing his 'Crow Jane' as 'the Muse of Western poetry' 'transformed by the black experience',[40] his transformation of her also involves apostrophizing her as a corpse:

> Dead virgin
> of the mind's echo. Dead lady
> of thinking, back now, without
> the creak of memory.[41]

As he later clarified: 'I knew she has got to be killed off because there is no further use—I can't get anything else from her.'[42] Admittedly, the extract above does at least suggest that Crow Jane is a psychological figure of the speaker's mind, and in the poem '*An Agony. As Now*' the otherness of the 'mind's echo' is exchanged for a torturous narcissism:

> I am inside someone
> who hates me. I look
> out from his eyes. Smell
> what fouled tunes come in
> to his breath. Love his
> wretched women.[43]

Whereas Olson's 'Projective Verse' essay called for poems exploring new 'possibilities of the breath', here the speaker gives voice to a flat prosaic rhythm—perhaps because he's so attuned to the infective otherness he lives and breathes. With any hope of inspiration 'fouled' in advance, he can only relate how he is expiring in agony: 'It is a human love, I live inside. A bony skeleton';

> It burns the thing
> inside it.
> And that thing
> screams.[44]

---

[40] Quoted in William J. Harris, 'An Interview with Amiri Baraka' (1980), in Reilly (ed.), *Conversations with Amiri Baraka*, 174, 175.
[41] LeRoi Jones, 'Crow Jane's Manner', in *Transbluesency*, 88.
[42] Quoted in Harris, 'An Interview with Amiri Baraka', 175.
[43] LeRoi Jones, '*An Agony. As Now*', in *Transbluesency*, 60.
[44] Ibid. 61.

Far from offering new forms of 'process', the poem thus closes with an automatic rhyme and the image of a self that's been reified into the kind of 'artifact' that Jones elsewhere denounced for being antipathetic to black art. Even the cultural agency of suffering becomes equivocal in the poem for the fact that 'burns' can be either a transitive or intransitive verb.

Overall, the aesthetic of *The Dead Lecturer* is thus locked into a confused and viciously circular economy of sacrifice. Arriving at an intensity of black experience requires imagining suffering at the hands of a white other, which can only be exorcized by imagining that other's death. And this involves an attendant dilemma for the performative force of Jones's poetic. In calling for murder, his speakers adopt the very character that they imagine others accuse them of being:

> Yellow skin, black
> skin, or the formless calm of compromise. They will not come
> to see, or understand you. They will call you 'murderer',
> as new songs for their young.[45]

In this extract from 'A Poem for Neutrals', the accusation of being a 'murderer' is clearly linked to the speaker feeling estranged from people generally, whatever their skin colour. Yet much of Jones's incendiarism of this time was symptomatic of his increasing identification with the growing number of blacks who were renouncing Civil Rights for militant separatism. In his 1963 article 'What Does Nonviolence Mean?', for example, Jones argued that it was Civil Rights figures like Martin Luther King who were undermining the unity of black America by investing power in party leadership while appealing to a political system that remained opposed to racial inclusion. Like Malcolm X, Jones also criticized what he viewed to be the 'sham gesture' of the Civil Rights 'March on Washington' in August 1963 (at which King delivered his 'I have a dream' speech).[46] This radicalization of his views only intensified over the coming year as Jones increasingly embraced the black nationalism that Malcolm X was preaching. Thus, by the middle of 1964—the year in which three Civil Rights activists were murdered in Mississippi—Jones, along with Archie Shepp, was verbally assaulting whites at public events around Manhattan.[47] It was at the end of this year that he was declaring 'every black' to be 'a potential revolutionary', and that 'Guerrilla warfare by blacks is inevitable in the North and South'.[48] Any chance of a racial

---

[45] LeRoi Jones, 'A Poem for Neutrals', *Transbluesency*, 59.
[46] LeRoi Jones, 'What Does Nonviolence Mean?', in *Home*, 152.
[47] See Cruse, *The Crisis of the Negro Intellectual*, 486.
[48] Quoted in Watts, *Amiri Baraka*, 131.

rapprochement was, in his view, hopeless; instead, he argued, 'it is high time the black man began to make use of the Tonto-syndrome, *i.e.*, leave The Lone Ranger to his own devices, and his own kind of death'.[49]

How that death might be aided, and how the revolutionary 'potential' of blacks could be awakened—these were both things that Jones began to explore in a number of plays. Having taken a drama-writing workshop run by Edward Albee at the Cherry Lane Theater in New York, Jones's play *Dutchman* was selected to be produced in the Cherry Lane where it was given a year-long run commencing in March 1964. The week of its opening saw two more plays by Jones open at other theatres in Manhattan: *The Baptism* at The Writers' Stage, and *The Eighth Ditch*, which was double-billed with Frank O'Hara's play *The General Returns from One Place to Another*. As the *New York Post* drama reviewer Jerry Tallmer declared, it was 'LeRoi Jones week in the theater', and the triple debut was followed in December with a double-bill at St Mark's Playhouse of two other plays by Jones: *The Toilet* and *The Slave*.[50]

Winning an Obie award for Best Off-Broadway Play of the Year, *Dutchman* is particularly interesting in detailing the performativity of Jones's racial hate-speech. Split into two scenes, both of them are set within the same 'subway car' in which Clay, a 'twenty-year-old Negro', encounters the volatile Lula, a 'thirty-year-old white woman'.[51] After some awkward opening exchanges, it soon becomes apparent that the nature of Clay's character is of great interest to Lula, who increasingly laces her conversation with derogatory comments:

'You think I want to pick you up, get you to take me somewhere and screw me, huh?' (*D*, 79)
'You look like death eating a soda cracker.' (*D*, 79)
'You tried to make it with your sister when you were ten.' (*D*, 80)

The performative force of such statements is a matter of equating hypothesis with accusation, ascription with description, and possibility with fact. So, while she begins to make up character names for the two of them—calling herself 'Lena the Hyena' and him 'Morris the Hyena' (*D*, 83)—she also declares that he is 'a well-known type' and that she knows him 'like the palm of my hand' (*D*, 85). Veering as she does between cruelty and seduction, Clay rapidly grows unsure of how to read Lula's character. In

---

[49] LeRoi Jones, 'The Last Days of the American Empire (Including some Instructions for Black People)' (1964), in *Home*, 205.
[50] Jerry Tallmer, 'LeRoi Jones Strikes Again', *New York Post* (24 March 1964), 64.
[51] LeRoi Jones, *Dutchman*, in *The LeRoi Jones/Amiri Baraka Reader*, 76, hereafter cited as *D*.

contrast, she continues to confect absurdist possibilities for him while declaring them to be concrete dangers. And as threats can foreshadow the possibility of violence, by the end of Scene I Lula makes it clear to Clay that his threat and violence are already established: 'You're a murderer, Clay, and you know it' (*D*, 88).

In Scene II, however, exactly whom she thinks Clay might have murdered becomes unclear. After further heated exchanges, he then erupts with his own incandescent hate-speech, which suggests that the performative interpellation of Lula's insults has worked its magic:

'I could murder you now. Such a tiny ugly throat.' (*D*, 96)
'I'll rip your breasts off! Let me be who I feel like being. [...] And I sit here, in this buttoned-up suit, to keep myself from cutting all your throats. I mean wantonly. [...] If Bessie Smith had killed some white people she wouldn't have needed that music.' (*D*, 97)

Despite the vehemence of these statements, Clay's motivations for saying them are, by this stage, complex. Some of their intensity is clearly aimed at countermanding Lula's implicit accusation that it's not white people he's murdered so much as his own black identity (as when she tells him 'You ain't no nigger, you're just a dirty white man' (*D*, 94)). As with some of *The Dead Lecturer*'s poems, reasserting an intensity of black experience becomes a matter of expressing murderous feelings towards whites. Clay thus assumes the very character that Lula has accused him of being and so bears testament to the same circular economy of sacrifice that Jones's poems were outlining. And it's with an image of this sacrificial economy that the play draws to its conclusion: with Clay confirming Lula's flights of fancy to be true, she stabs him as he bends over her to retrieve his belongings. His death then engenders racist camaraderie between Lula and the other commuters who throw Clay's body off the subway car before they leave (*D*, 98–9).

Given the play's ending, one could argue that *Dutchman* identifies a racial inequity within this sacrificial economy: murder for Clay is at worst a fantasy and possibility, whereas Lulu as white racist is actually prepared to kill. Indeed, Jones defended himself along these lines in an interview of August 1964: 'The reason I'm not a violent man—that's what I'm trying to say in *Dutchman*—is that art is the most beautiful resolution of energies that in another context might be violent to myself or anyone else.'[52] In other words, a cathartic venting of rage reduces the possibility that the

---

[52] Quoted in Judy Stone, 'If it's Anger . . . Maybe that's Good: An Interview with LeRoi Jones', in Reilly (ed.), *Conversations with Amiri Baraka*, 10.

force of one's hatred might end up leading to actual murder. Understandably, not everyone saw Jones's play as a 'beautiful resolution of energies'. The *New York Times* reviewer Howard Tauberman, for example, wrote that *Dutchman* was 'an explosion of hatred rather than a play. [...] If this is the way even one Negro feels, there is ample cause for guilt as well as alarm and for a hastening of change.'[53] But the alarming timeliness of the piece was exactly what others felt to be its importance, and as a consequence Jones soon found himself being invited to write for a number of papers, including *The New York Times*. His aesthetic allegiances were soon tested, though, by two days of race riots that erupted in Harlem on 18 July 1964. Having accepted a guest lectureship that month at State University of New York, Buffalo, Jones decided to leave the position in order to be closer to what was happening. As he later claimed, the riots 'rang in me like the first shots of a war'.[54]

Although his statement that art could be a 'beautiful resolution of energies' was made after the riots, Jones's subsequent aesthetic stance turned increasingly confrontational. Whereas in *Dutchman* Clay's hate-speech becomes Lula's violence, this exchange is reversed in *The Slave*, one of the two plays that began running in December 1964 at St Mark's Playhouse. Set in the living room of a university professor, Bradford Easley, and his wife, Grace, Act I of the play opens with the couple discovering that lurking in the room's shadows is Walker Vessels, a middle-aged black man dressed as '*an old field slave*'.[55] Accompanied intermittently by the sound of black rioters outside, the dialogue swiftly descends into a melee of insults as a prelude to violence. With Bradford dismissing Walker's poetry, Walker being homophobic towards Bradford, and Grace calling Walker 'a nigger murderer', Jones finally resolves all this tension by having Walker shoot Bradford and tell Grace that her two daughters are also dead.[56] Rather than diminishing the likelihood of racial violence through catharsis, then, Jones now appeared intent on having his theatre perform its own cultural attack. And if there were any equivocation on this matter, his essay 'The Revolutionary Theatre' (1965) made it explicit. Jones used the essay to call for a new form of black theatre that must 'hate' white people 'for hating. For presuming with their technology to deny the supremacy of the Spirit'.[57] As he elaborates, the theatre he is

---

[53] Howard Tauberman, 'The Theater: *Dutchman*', *New York Times* (25 March 1964), Arts section, 3.
[54] Baraka, *Autobiography*, 192.
[55] LeRoi Jones, *The Slave: A Fable in a Prologue and Two Acts*, in *Selected Plays and Prose of Amiri Baraka/LeRoi Jones* (New York: William Morrow, 1979), 98.
[56] Ibid. 106, 129.
[57] LeRoi Jones, 'The Revolutionary Theatre', in *Home*, 210–11.

calling for is 'a weapon to help in the slaughter of these dim-witted fatbellied white guys', and its drama is essentially 'THE DESTRUCTION OF AMERICA'.[58] Was Jones turning his back on aesthetics in favour of political activism? Apparently not, for in the same essay he also expounds the importance of aesthetic possibility as a cultural power:

> What is called imagination (from magi, magic, magician, etc.) is a practical vector from the soul. It stores all data, and can be called on to solve all our 'problems'. The imagination is the projection of ourselves past our sense of ourselves as 'things'. Imagination (Image) is all possibility, because from the image, the initial circumscribed energy, any use (idea) is possible. And so begins that image's use in the world. Possibility is what moves us.[59]

The essay thus clearly outlines what amounts to a potentialist basis for the Black Arts that Jones, and others inspired by him, proceeded to develop. If art can explore unlimited possibilities of 'image', it can also turn them into concrete black potentials, and it can achieve this by fostering an anti-materialist aesthetic as a distinct 'energy' of 'soul'. As Jones emphasizes, the possibility of a black nation rests on drawing together 'Force. Spirit. Feeling'.[60]

With the assassination of Malcolm X in February 1965, Jones's convictions about the need for black Nationalism attained even greater heights. Writing a lengthy encomium for X in the form of his essay, 'The Legacy of Malcolm X and the Coming of the Black Nation', he reaffirmed that the possibility of separatist liberation depended on creating new black images: 'What a culture produces, is, and refers to is an image— a picture of a process, since it is a form of process.'[61] In light of that, he argued, the 'Black artist is desperately needed to change the images his people identify with, by asserting Black feeling, Black mind, Black judgement'.[62] And that's precisely what Jones resolved to do on a grander scale. Leaving his wife, Hettie, and their two children, he moved uptown to Harlem where he set up the Black Arts Repertory Theatre/School (BART/S), followed by the Spirit House theatre in Newark, New Jersey. Before considering the new potentialist directions his Black Arts plays and poems were taking, though, we need first to examine some wider cultural issues surrounding the founding of those theatres and the Black Arts Movement more generally.

---

[58] Ibid. 211, 215. [59] Ibid. 213. [60] Ibid. 212.
[61] Jones, 'The Legacy of Malcolm X', 166–7. [62] Ibid. 167.

PERFORMING BLACK ARTS

In an essay in the June 1965 issue of the journal *Liberator*, Larry Neal wrote about the opening weekend of BART/S and announced it to be a landmark event: 'The Black Arts officially opened their school on April 30th with an explosive evening of good poetry.'[63] The weekend also featured Jazz music and African dancing, and overall it convinced Neal 'of the potential for creative encounter existing in our community'.[64] For Jones and the other members of BART/S the organization was more than just a theatre. Jazz musicians including Sun Ra and Albert Ayler were, as he stated, 'always on the scene', and the School side of BART/S offered classes for the community, including history taught by Harold Cruse, as well as training in a range of arts, from the literary to the martial.[65] Jones in his autobiography states that the theatre put on a number of his recent plays as well as new ones he developed there, including *Jello* (1966) and *A Black Mass* (1966). But while the performances and classes were reportedly well attended, BART/S soon began to suffer from two main problems. The first was that its running was largely funded by a $200,000 grant from Harlem Youth Opportunities Unlimited (HARYOU), the money coming from the Federal government to nurture President Lyndon B. Johnson's 'Great Society' initiatives. As Jerry Gafio Watts points out, after BART/S's nationalist separatism became apparent, the fears voiced about it in the media were exacerbated by Jones when he responded with statements like: 'I don't see anything wrong with hating white people. Harlem must be taken from the beast and gain its sovereignty as a black nation.'[66] HARYOU's response was to cease making its payments, and this financial trouble was worsened by the second problem that BART/S faced: a growing division between members like Jones who were invested in cultural activism, and those whom he reports to have been more interested in militancy.[67] In Cruse's opinion, the chief problem was a failure in Jones's leadership, his inability 'to link up a cultural institution with political and economic organization'.[68] From Jones's perspective, the

---

[63] Quoted in Nilgun Anadolu-Okur, *Contemporary African American Theater: Afrocentricity in the Works of Larry Neal, Amiri Baraka, and Charles Fuller* (New York: Garland, 1997), 10.
[64] Ibid.
[65] Baraka, *Autobiography*, 204.
[66] Quoted in Watts, *Amiri Baraka*, 159.
[67] Baraka, *Autobiography*, 209.
[68] Cruse, *The Crisis of the Negro Intellectual*, 540.

problem was more the fractious membership that constituted BART/S, and as this predicament came to seem intractable he decided to make a fresh start. So, in 1966, he moved to Newark where he set about creating another cultural community centre in the shape of the Spirit House.

Along with his various writings of this period, Jones's work with BART/S helped extend his nationalist influence, particularly as a dramatist. Indeed, Watts asserts that judging from the frequency with which it was cited, Jones's 'The Revolutionary Theatre' essay was 'the most widely read' Black Arts essay of the time.[69] His collection *Home: Social Essays* (1966)—in which 'The Revolutionary Theatre' was reprinted—also became a canonical Black Arts text. Despite the institutional faltering of BART/S, then, the nationalist aesthetic it was seen to stand for helped galvanize the nascent Black Arts Movement, and from 1966 other Black Arts theatres began to open across the USA, including the Free Southern Theater in New Orleans, Concept East Theater in Detroit, and the New Lafayette Theater and the National Black Theater in Harlem. Such expansion was also aided by the succession of new black journals—notably, *Umbra, Soulbook, Liberator, Black World*, and *Journal of Black Poetry*—which together provided a vibrant new forum for Black Arts writing.[70] But the spread of Cultural Nationalism wasn't without complications. As Komozi Woodard has stated, Jones's Spirit House drew inspiration from other black Revolutionary Nationalists like the Black Panther Party.[71] During a stint as visiting lecturer at San Francisco State College early in 1967, Jones was particularly impressed by the Communications Project that the College's Black Student Union collaborated on with members of the Panthers.[72] As the sixties wore on, though, he and other Cultural Nationalists increasingly distanced themselves from the Revolutionary Nationalists' Marxist-Leninist beliefs, and disagreements between the two camps began to be violent. Yet by 1974 Jones himself was renouncing Cultural Nationalism in the name of Third-World Socialism. What paved the way for such a shift was his growing involvement in politics at both local and national levels.

As with BART/S, Jones intended the Spirit House to be not just a theatre but also a community centre. His published 'Work Notes' (1966) show that he was aiming to provide a mixture of classes and performance (including lectures, plays, and readings), which together would present

---

[69] Watts, *Amiri Baraka*, 172.
[70] See Abby Arthur and Ronald Maberry Johnson, *Propaganda and Aesthetics: The Literary Politics of Afro-American Magazines in the Twentieth Century* (Amherst: University of Massachusetts Press, 1979), Ch. 6.
[71] Woodard, *A Nation within a Nation*, 70–3.
[72] Baraka, *Autobiography*, 250–1.

live black 'images' to counteract the influence of the 'white' mass-media.[73] In addition, he also set up a publishing press, Jihad Publications, which he launched with a poetry anthology, *Black Art* (1966), the front cover of which showed a Spirit House habitué taking one of the theatre's martial arts classes. The name of the press—'*jihad*' means 'struggle' in Arabic—is also indicative of the spiritual metamorphosis that Jones was undergoing at the time. After the death of Malcolm X, he became interested in Sunni Islam, which X had followed, and he subsequently declared his publishing venture to be waging *jihad* as an Islamic 'Holy War'.[74] But he'd also cultivated an interest in the African Yoruba religion, in which Spirit House offered tuition along with classes in Yoruba dancing. For Jones the possibility of unifying these spiritual interests is what Maulana Karenga's syncretistic 'Kawaida' religion appeared to offer. A doctoral student in African history and languages, Karenga had set up the Cultural Nationalist 'US Organization' in September 1965 at the age of 24. By early 1967, when Jones first met him, he'd already built up Kawaida as an eclectic congeries of spiritual and political influences, including Nation of Islam, Malcolm X, Frantz Fanon, and a range of African religions.[75] The underlying precepts of both Kawaida and US were, however, summarized by the '*Nguzo Saba*', the seven principles that Karenga derived from Swahili words: '*umoja*', unity of race and community; '*kuchijagulia*', self-determination; '*ujima*', collective work and responsibility; '*ujamaa*', cooperative economics; '*nia*', purpose; '*kuumba*', creativity; and '*imani*', spiritual faith.[76] As Jones later stated in his autobiography, US's Cultural Nationalism thus seemed a 'higher stage of commitment and organization' than that of Spirit House, and he was also impressed by its male cadre of '*simba wachanga*'—the 'young lions' undertaking paramilitary training.[77] Consequently, it wasn't long before Jones was presenting himself as a Kawaida convert, and Spirit House was offering lessons based in Kawaida at the African Free School that he'd established as part of the theatre. Deeming that the spiritual war he was now waging called for a new *nom-de-guerre*, Jones decided early in 1967 to take the Arabic title Imamu

---

[73] LeRoi Jones, 'Work Notes—'66', in *Raise Race Rays Raze: Essays since 1965* (1971, repr.; New York: Vintage, 1972).
[74] Baraka, *Autobiography*, 244.
[75] See ibid. 253–4. On Karenga and US more generally, see Scot Brown, *Fighting for US: Maulana Karenga, the US Organization, and Black Cultural Nationalism* (New York: New York University Press, 2003).
[76] See Amiri Baraka, '7 Principles of US: Maulana Karenga & the Need for a Black Value System', in Baraka, *Raise Race Rays Raze*, 133–45.
[77] Baraka, *Autobiography*, 245.

('spiritual leader') and the Arabic names Amiri ('prince') and Baraka ('blessed'). His faith in Kawaida was thereby made official.

Having reoriented himself spiritually, Baraka's political mettle was soon put to the test by the race riots that erupted in Newark in July 1967. The city wasn't alone in witnessing such rebellions. Federal agencies registered 164 racial 'disorders' in 1967 across the USA, which collectively resulted in 89 deaths and millions of dollars worth of damage.[78] In Newark, racial relations were particularly strained because the city had no African American representatives in the municipal government, even though more than 60 per cent of the city's population was black. These tensions finally boiled over on 12 July that year after a black taxi driver was beaten by local police. With rioting and looting erupting over the next two days, the civil strife was only quelled after the city's mayor, Hugh Addonizio, called in the National Guard.[79] For Baraka's part, if the 1964 Harlem riots had been 'like the first shots of a war' then the Newark riots marked the point at which he became caught up in actual violence. Driving around the areas on 13 July where the disturbances were occurring, Baraka and some of his friends were soon arrested by police. Badly beaten in the process, he was charged with illegally possessing two revolvers and was made to pay $25,000 bail in order to secure his release.[80] His subsequent trial, in which he pleaded 'not guilty' to the charges, attracted a great deal of media publicity, partly because the presiding judge, Leon Kapp, used Baraka's poem 'Black People!' (1967) as evidence of an intention to agitate for the disturbances that had taken place.[81] Given the poem's various incitements, it's easy to see how it wouldn't have helped the poet's plea of innocence:

> All the stores will open if you will say the magic
> words. The magic words are: Up against the wall mother fucker
> this is a stick up! Or: smash the window at night (these are
> magic actions) smash the windows daytime, anytime, together
> [...] We
> must make our own World, man, our own world, and we can not
> do this unless the white man is dead. Let's get together and
> killhim my man [...][82]

---

[78] Robert L. Allen, *A Guide to Black Power in America: An Historical Analysis* (New York: Victor Gollancz, 1970), 108–9.
[79] Ibid. 111–12; see also Woodard, *A Nation within a Nation*, 74–80.
[80] See Baraka, *Autobiography*, 258–65; also Watts, *Amiri Baraka*, 295–9.
[81] See Theodore R. Hudson, 'The Trial of LeRoi Jones' (1973), in *Imamu Amiri Baraka (LeRoi Jones): A Collection of Critical Essays*, ed. Kimberley W. Benston (Englewood Cliffs, NJ: Prentice-Hall, 1978), 49–53.
[82] Amiri Baraka, 'Black People!', in *The LeRoi Jones/Amiri Baraka Reader*, 224.

Baraka clearly had great faith in poetic licence as a buttress for freedom of speech. But apart from the text's lineation there are no generic markers which indicate that it's a poem. Not only does it read more like a manifesto, it blatantly subordinates the possibility of its performative 'magic' to the performance of violent actions. In short, aesthetics has become looting and killing. And if Baraka wanted people to think of his art as a 'weapon', that is effectively what Judge Kapp confirmed in sentencing the poet to not less than two-and-a-half years in prison. With the *New York Times* reporting the outcome in an article headlined 'The Magic Word was "Prison"', a number of groups offered Baraka assistance.[83] The American Civil Liberties Union defended him on the grounds of his right to freedom of speech, and Allen Ginsberg's Committee On Poetry organized a public statement of support that was signed by a host of literary luminaries, including Creeley, Olson, di Prima, John Ashbery, Denise Levertov, and Gregory Corso.[84] The endorsement clearly aided Baraka's appeal against his sentence, and in a subsequent retrial the conviction was quashed. He was free to take the nationalist struggle to another level.

The controversy surrounding Baraka's conviction wasn't the only thing that confirmed his public status as a leading exponent of Black Arts. One week after the riots in Newark the city hosted the second national Black Power Conference, and the event helped propel Baraka to the forefront of nationalist political activism. At a press meeting he organized at the Spirit House, Baraka and other Black Power leaders—including Karenga, who was on the Conference's organizing committee—called on the United Nations to set up a permanent group of observers in the USA to monitor its 'terrorism' against black Americans.[85] At the same four-day Conference, Baraka founded the United Brotherhood, a local organization that would campaign for better political representation of African Americans in Newark. By the end of all the proceedings, preparations had also been made to inaugurate what became the Modern Black Convention Movement, which proved to be a significant national forum in which Black Power groups built allegiances and developed new political networks.[86]

---

[83] See Hudson, 'The Trial of LeRoi Jones', 52.
[84] Ibid. 53; see also Watts, *Amiri Baraka*, 300.
[85] See 'Petition of Africans (Descendants of African Nationals) Living in the United States of America' (August 1967), in Amiri Baraka Archive, Moorland-Spingarn Research Center, Howard University Library (Box 8, Folder: 'United Nations'). All materials in this archive subsequently cited as from 'Amiri Baraka Archive, Howard University Library', with parenthesized box and folder title, followed by page number.
[86] See Woodard, *A Nation within a Nation*, 70, 84–5.

After the Newark riots and his trial, Baraka's commitments thus turned increasingly to political activism. Consequently, the kind of cultural practice he'd called for in 'Revolutionary Theatre' began to split in two contradictory directions. On one hand, he continued to experiment with plays and poems to present a spiritual anti-materialism that fused 'energy' and 'possibility' into a distinctly aesthetic force. On the other hand, as with his poem 'Black People!', he often undermined the force of such spiritualism by placing it at the service of material violence while announcing such violence to be 'art'. In a 1966 interview, for example, Baraka stated that using his 'energies' to devise ways of blowing up the White House would have been 'more beneficial to the majority of mankind' than writing his books.[87] But in the same year, he also started writing *A Book of Life* in which he asserted that 'The nature of Black People is to value energy. Spiritual presence. [...] The totality of all possibility is God. The Perfect poem includes all possibility.'[88] Baraka intended the book to be a comprehensive 'philosophical stance'[89] on Black Arts, and despite failing to secure a publisher for the volume he continued to write it until 1970. But if, as he claimed, a poem's perfection included 'all possibility', then his 1969 poetry collection, *Black Magic*, was far from perfect. Consisting of poems that he'd written between 1961 and 1967, the collection as a whole testifies to the diverging tendencies of his aesthetics. While a number of the poems present interesting experiments with *mise-en-page* (e.g. 'The Success' and 'American Ecstasy'), rhythm (e.g. 'The World is Full of Beautiful Things'), and syntax (e.g. 'Tone Poem' and 'The People Burning'), other poems like the notorious 'Black Art' once again ignore expressions of spiritual energy in favour of hate-speech. As a result, the close of the predominantly tender poem 'Ka 'Ba'—'What will be the sacred words?'—finds its answer in the call to riot of 'Black People!', which is also featured in the volume.[90] There is, however, a new development in the collection with the use of chants and incantations in poems such as 'Trespass Into Spirit':

> dededededededededededededede aaaaaaaaaaaa
>   —A Chant to rise with all

---

[87] Quoted in Stewart Smith and Peter Thorn, 'An Interview with LeRoi Jones' (1966), in Reilly (ed.), *Conversations with Amiri Baraka*, 16.

[88] Amiri Baraka, 'Creation is Evolution' (1966), in Amiri Baraka Archive, Howard University Library (Box 16, Folder: '*Book of Life*'): 2.

[89] Amiri Baraka, 'Book of Life' [outline] (December 1966), in Amiri Baraka Archive, Howard University Library (Box 26, Folder: '*Book of Life*'): 1.

[90] Amiri Baraka, 'Ka 'Ba' and 'Black Art', in *The LeRoi Jones/Amiri Baraka Reader*, 222, 224.

>   with all rising thru and let the scope
>   diry jsolekks eoo fjoel fjkks ei OO dkkle;pspekl"mels;;a;;sll
>
>   [. . .]
>
>   the machines head is gone[91]

The freestyle typing of this extract's fourth line is in fact the closest Baraka comes to the improvisations of Free Jazz that he admired. Ironically, though, the typing is presented as the death throes that mechanized writing suffers after the 'Chant' of 'aaaaaaaaaaaaa' has inflicted on it a verbal *coup de grâce*. The poem thus presents its 'Trespass Into Spirit' as a 'live' voice's exorcism of technologized language. Appearing also in 'Vowels 2' and 'Black Art' in the collection, these onomatopoeic notations echo both the mantras that Ginsberg was using around this time and the voice experiments of avant-garde precursors such as Filippo Marinetti, Kurt Schwitters, and Antonin Artaud. Indeed, in his 'Revolutionary Theater' essay, Baraka cited Artaud's 'theater of cruelty' and its extemporized 'screams of joy' as a particular inspiration for the kind of black theatrical force he wanted to develop.[92] What poems like 'Trespass Into Spirit' show, then, is the degree to which Baraka had become less intent on crafting literary texts, and more interested in performing live. And by the third national Black Power Conference in 1968 it was apparent that theatre had become the favoured form of Black Arts literary practice, largely because it could incorporate arts like dance and music into its performance.[93]

As in Baraka's earlier work, the plays he was developing around this time provide the best examples of the kinds of possibility his aesthetics could perform. With his one-act play *Great Goodness of Life: A Coon Show* (1967), for example, he shows how his Black Art could be aimed less at inciting violence and more at offering a critical view of how the mass-media's 'electronic curtain' screened racial issues. Baraka wrote the play in anger in 1967 after his father told the Federal Bureau of Investigation (FBI) of his son's whereabouts, and the play's main character, Court Royal, is largely a depiction of his father as a naïve man who's become 'half-white' by not questioning his racial status. In the play's Kafkaesque opening, Court is accused by a 'Voice' of 'shielding' a 'murderer', and is

---

[91] Amiri Baraka, 'Trespass Into Spirit', in *Black Magic* (New York: Bobbs-Merrill, 1969), 151–2.
[92] Jones, 'The Revolutionary Theatre', 211.
[93] See Amiri Baraka, 'Creativity Workshop Report and Resolution' (September 1968), in Amiri Baraka Archive, Howard University Library (Box 20, Folder: 'Black Power Conference', 1968): 1.

then informed that he'll be facing trial for his crime.[94] Pleading 'not guilty', Court argues that all he's done is work as a supervisor in the Post Office for thirty-five years, but his confusion only grows when he's subsequently told that he's in 'HEAVEN' (*GGL*, 69). After this point the play presents a series of substitutions between image and reality, while suggesting that such substitutions are symptomatic of the kind of sacrificial economy that Baraka had depicted earlier in plays like *Dutchman*. First, the murderer that Court is accused of harbouring is shown to be a collection of images:

VOICE: Shut up, liar. Do you know this man?
An image is flashed on the screen behind him. It is a rapidly shifting series of faces. Malcolm [X]. *Patrice* [Lumumba]. *Rev King.* [Marcus] *Garvey. Dead nigger kids killed by police. Medgar Evers.* (*GGL*, 72, my bracketed additions)

The faces are those of political figures who in some way made sacrifices trying to advance black culture, from Marcus Garvey to the Civil Rights activist Medgar Evers, who in 1963 was murdered by a Ku Klux Klan member. In having these figures appear in court as images, Baraka is evidently putting on trial the statement he had made in his essay on Malcolm X's legacy: 'What a culture is, and refers to, is an image—a picture of a process, since it is a form of a process.'[95] For Court to deny, as he initially does, that he recognizes this 'murderer' is thus tantamount to a repudiation of black culture. But with his repeated denial being accompanied by the flashing faces' wailing and screaming, Court subsequently concedes '*Almost trance-like*' that he must be sentenced along with the 'murderer', at which point he's informed by the Voice that the murderer is in fact 'dead' (*GGL*, 74). This disorienting series of exchanges between image and life, life and death, is then further complicated when the accused is informed that he'll be spared death if he kills the dead murderer. Presented with a young black man who is very much alive, Court is told that the youth is merely 'the myth of the murderer' and that the killing will therefore be a 'cleansing rite' (*GGL*, 77). Readily convinced, Court obeys the order and shoots the youth, whose parting word is 'Papa' (*GGL*, 78)—the play thus concludes with the image of a culturally brainwashed father who is incapable of registering that he has just killed his own son. Unlike poems such as 'Black People!' or 'Black Art', *Great Goodness of Life* thus asserts that imagining violence to be an aesthetic ritual results from

---

[94] Amiri Baraka, *Great Goodness of Life: A Coon Show*, in *Four Black Revolutionary Plays* (New York: Marion Boyars, 1998), 62, hereafter cited as *GGL*.
[95] Jones, 'The Legacy of Malcolm X', 166.

the enemy's arguments. It also implicitly reaffirms Baraka's earlier valorization of 'images' (rather than violence) as being an essential 'possibility' and 'energy' of black culture. In that respect, the play suggests that instead of trying to turn theatre into actual violence, Black Arts performances could pose a cultural imaginary as a distinct critical force. Larry Neal was certainly of this view: the chief benefit of drama like Baraka's, he argued, was that it 'suck[ed] the audience into a unique and very precise universe' in order to encourage the audience's 'emotional and religious participation' in the play.[96] That's to say, the performances worked to turn alternative possible worlds into affective communion. The extent to which this meant spiritualizing the drama is clear from two other short plays that Baraka developed around this time: *A Black Mass* (1966) and *Madheart* (1967).

A Black Mass is a one-act dramatic ritual whose stage directions specify that the performance should be accompanied by Sun Ra's music, and that the stage should have 'signs in Arabic and Swahili on the wall'.[97] Ra had already composed a series of pieces based on his faith in the benefits of travelling to alternative worlds, and such music would have made a fitting accompaniment to the Nation of Islam myth of Yakub that Baraka's play dramatizes. The myth tells of the creation of white people as resulting around 6,000 years ago from a terrible experiment by Yakub, a black scientist, and in Baraka's play the horrifying error of the scientist (whose name is rendered as 'Jacoub') is to have made a life-form that lacks a soul. As the magician Nasafi sums up the crisis: 'I looked into the wet corridors of the thing's heart [. . .]. Where the soul's print should be, there is only a cellulose pouch of disgusting habits' (*BM*, 47). This 'cellulose' interior suggests that the white man's nature is akin to an accretion of mass-media imagery, and just as Baraka had earlier exorcized his typewriter with transcriptions of live chanting, so he levels '*screaming Sun Ra music of shattering dimension*' against Jacoub's white 'beast' (*BM*, 46). Presented as a kind of slobbering animal robot, the status of the white man is further cast in doubt at the end of the play when Nasafi declares the creature to be 'not ourselves' but 'the hatred of ourselves. Our wholeness' (*BM*, 54). Like Baraka's earlier poetry collection *The Dead Lecturer*, then, some of the play's vituperation against white people becomes not just a matter of hate-speech but also one of self-castigation.

---

[96] Quoted in Sandra Hollin Flowers, *African American Nationalist Literature of the 1960s: Pens of Fire* (New York: Garland, 1996), 102.
[97] Amiri Baraka, *A Black Mass*, in *Four Black Revolutionary Plays*, 37, hereafter cited as *BM*.

Madheart continues this struggle around black consciousness in depicting a white living-dead 'devil lady' and the various degrees to which several black characters identify with her.[98] While the play's lone black male repeatedly attempts to kill the devil once and for all by stabbing her and driving a stake into her heart, the man's sister, mother, and another black woman mourn the attacks as though they have been inflicted on themselves. But violence is not the real answer to their plight, for the power the devil has over them is the spectral influence she exerts on their imaginations. The only effective resistance entails staging an alternative imaginary, a new consciousness of self, which is precisely what the male protagonist declares: 'I've made a new meaning. Let the audience think about themselves, and about their lives when they leave this happening. This black world of purest possibility.'[99]

By 1968 these worlds of possibility were spreading around the USA as organizations like the National Black Theater, the Free Southern Theater, and New Lafayette Theater also produced Black Arts rituals by Baraka as well as dramatists like Barbara Ann Teer and Ed Bullins—both of whom encouraged a high degree of audience participation.[100] That year, the general expansion of the Black Arts Movement was also confirmed with the publication of various books, including Cruse's *Rebellion or Revolution*, Floyd Barbour's *The Black Power Revolt*, and an anthology of writing, *Black Fire*, edited by Baraka and Larry Neal. The latter is particularly interesting in showing the degree to which the Black Arts Movement was still vacillating between aesthetics and violence. While Neal's essay, for example, concentrates on aesthetic 'energy' and praises plays like Baraka's *Black Mass* for affirming 'our highest possibilities',[101] Calvin Hernton's contribution focuses mostly on forecasting explosions of black militancy: 'The violence will be spontaneous, without leadership, without control [...]. Everybody will be a guerrilla—men, women, teenagers, and some children.'[102]

Such possibilities—both aesthetic and revolutionary—were certainly being taken seriously by the Federal government, as is evident from the

---

[98] Amiri Baraka, *Madheart*, in *Four Black Revolutionary Plays*, 87.
[99] Ibid. 93.
[100] On wider developments in Black Arts theatre, see C. W. E. Bigsby, *A Critical Introduction to Twentieth-Century American Drama*, Vol. 3: *Beyond Broadway* (Cambridge: Cambridge University Press, 1985), Ch. 14; also Effiong, *In Search of a Model for African-American Drama*, Ch. 5.
[101] Larry Neal, 'And Shine Swam On', in Larry Neal and LeRoi Jones (eds), *Black Fire: An Anthology of Afro-American Writing* (1968, repr.; New York: William Morrow, 1973), 655.
[102] Calvin C. Hernton, 'Dynamite Growing out of Their Skulls', in Neal and Jones (eds), *Black Fire*, 103.

reports on Baraka that the FBI had begun to compile since 1966. With the writer reportedly claiming in a March 1968 appearance that 'Every Negro is a potential Rap Brown [Justice Minister for the Black Panther Party]',[103] the FBI was itself confirming the threat of such possibility in justifying surveillance of Baraka on the grounds that he fell into the category of having a 'background [that] is potentially dangerous'.[104] Indeed, many of the Secret Service Agent reports that his FBI files consist of specifically involve deliberating on whether abstract potentiality might be concrete, and whether aesthetic practice might in fact amount to political insurrection. Several reports include copies of Baraka's poetry and plays, and a March 1969 memo to FBI director J. Edgar Hoover presents a summary of the *Black Fire* anthology and states that 'A few of the assembled works tend to have an energy that succeeds in impressing one with the violence and passion of the author's emotions'.[105] Concern over the incendiary potential of aesthetic 'violence' is also particularly evident in a Secret Service report of 7 February 1969 that discusses an imminent performance of *Black Mass* to be given by Baraka and his Spirit House Movers at Petersburg Junior College, in Clearwater, Florida. The report cites an anonymous Secret Service source as stating that the play is 'violently anti-white' and that 'local authorities have been notified of the possibility that some disorder could occur as a result'.[106] As many of the files also testify, after the 1967 Newark riots Baraka and his Spirit House troupe maintained a steady rate of appearances at venues across America. These appearances usually included speeches by Baraka along with poetry reading, dancing, and performances of plays. And if the tours were largely about staging black worlds of possibility they also frequently involved agitating for actual racial violence. For example, a performance in January 1968 at Patrick Campbell Junior High School, in Roxbury, Massachusetts, featured readings of poems like 'Black People!' and was also reported to have included musically accompanied exhortations to 'Kill whitey, kill him, kill him'.[107] While these performances inevitably generated controversy, Baraka was nevertheless invited by the prestigious American Program Bureau (APB) to give a series of lectures and perfor-

[103] FBI Special Agent (Baltimore, MD) Report (21 March 1968), in Amiri Baraka Archive, Howard University Library (Box 9, Folder: 'FBI Files'): 3.
[104] See, for example, FBI File (25 July 1966), in Amiri Baraka Archive, Howard University Library (Box 9, Folder: 'FBI Files'): 1.
[105] FBI Special Agent Memo (25 March 1969), in Amiri Baraka Archive, Howard University Library (Box 9, Folder: 'FBI Files'): 3.
[106] FBI Special Agent (Tampa, FL) Report (7 February 1969), in Amiri Baraka Archive, Howard University Library (Box 9, Folder: 'FBI Files'): 1.
[107] FBI (Newark) File (17 June 1968), in Amiri Baraka Archive, Howard University Library, (Box 9, Folder: 'FBI Files'): 15.

mances at various universities between October 1968 and February 1969. Correspondence between the APB and Baraka shows that the appearances were volatile affairs, and a number of the universities complained either that Baraka behaved belligerently or that performances were late or cancelled.[108]

By this stage, Baraka's desire to combine aesthetics and politics had evidently taken another new turn, for an FBI memo of February 1969 to Hoover reports that Baraka had announced himself at Dillard University, New Orleans, to be the 'Minister of Culture' for the Republic of New Africa (RNA).[109] Having declared in his essay 'The Revolutionary Theatre' that 'Possibility is what moves us', by May 1970 Baraka was calling for 'even more dazzling possibilities' and asserting that 'Utopia' is what would 'fuel' them, for it is 'in motion, and combustible'.[110] Utopianism is certainly what was fuelling the RNA. The organization was officially launched by Gaidi Obadele and Imamu Abubakari Obadele in Detroit on 31 March 1968 with a 'Declaration of Independence' that was signed that day by hundreds of the supporters they'd gathered.[111] The utopian dimensions of the RNA were patently clear from its demand that the black 'urban communities of the North and West', together with the southern states of Alabama, Georgia, Mississippi, Louisiana and South Carolina, become an independent, autonomous black nation.[112] Announcing that 'Our Southland, especially, is rich in military possibilities', the RNA directives detailed how organizing this nation would require a range of ministries, from Defense to Culture.[113] With Baraka in charge of the Culture ministry, the movement was clearly pleased with his nationalist contributions, for in 1970 one of the directives of the RNA's 'Security Forces' was outlining the importance of unity in terms of 'umoja'—one of Kawaida's key *Nguzo Saba* that I discussed earlier.[114] Lacking political power and grassroots support, though, the RNA's utopian

---

[108] See Box 20, Folder: American Program Bureau, in Amiri Baraka Archive, Howard University Library (Box 9, Folder: 'FBI Files'): 1.

[109] FBI Special Agent Memo (27 February 1969), in Amiri Baraka Archive, Howard University Library (Box 9, Folder: 'FBI Files'): 1.

[110] Amiri Baraka, 'Mwalimu Texts (from *Book of Life*), Pt 2' (May 1970), in *Raise Race Rays Raze*, 166.

[111] See Alphonso Pinkney, *Red, Black, and Green: Black Nationalism in the United States* (Cambridge: Cambridge University Press, 1976), 125–6.

[112] See RNA, 'The Freedom Corps: For Service in the Revolution' (1969), in Amiri Baraka Archive, Howard University Library (Box 16, Folder: 'Republic of New Africa'): 3.

[113] Ibid; see also RNA, 'Working Papers: Projection of Problems & Solutions for Ocean Hill-Brownsville as Independent State' (7–8 December 1968), in Amiri Baraka Archive, Howard University Library, (Box 16, Folder: 'Republic of New Africa').

[114] See RNA Security Forces, 'Directive No. 2' (6 May 1970), in Amiri Baraka Archive, Howard University Library (Box 16, Folder: 'Republic of New Africa'): 1.

aspirations remained unrealized and the movement remained vulnerable to the Counter-Intelligence Program (COINTELPRO) measures that the FBI successfully used to undermine its influence.

In contrast, the political organizations that Baraka helped launch after the Newark riots had been enjoying increasing success. In 1968 United Brothers was renamed (at Karenga's suggestion) 'Committee for a United Newark' (CFUN), and this group proceeded to initiate an effective drive for the registration of black voters. Divided into 'Departments' covering a range of areas—including economics, communications, education, and security—CFUN also built strategic links with Newark's disaffected Puerto Rican community, and in May 1970 it was successful in getting the city's first black mayor, Kenneth Gibson, democratically elected.[115] These developments initially gave Baraka new-found faith in electoral politics, and as a result his agitation for militant action subsided. Thus, when black Americans in Newark began rioting in April 1968 after news broke of Martin Luther King's assassination, Baraka and the United Brothers helped quell the rebellion by distributing leaflets suggesting people 'Take this city by ballot' rather than force.[116] Disagreement over the efficacy of ballots versus bullets was, however, a source of friction not only between Karenga's US organization and the Black Panthers but also between Baraka and Karenga. While the Panthers were increasingly of the opinion that Cultural Nationalists were misguided in denouncing whites, Baraka and Karenga had started inveighing against the Panthers' Revolutionary Nationalism for being based in the socialism of white thinkers more than in African American culture. With Karenga denouncing the Panthers' adoption of an openly militant stance, relations between the two groups became irreparably damaged after US members (ironically) shot dead two Panthers in August 1969.[117] Although Baraka himself had been critical of the Panthers, the negative publicity that US generated with the shootings became a clear reason to distance himself from Karenga. And as street fights between US and the Panthers continued into the early 1970s, the cohesion and influence of both groups soon went into decline.

Such political tribulations were counterbalanced, for Baraka, by his growing prominence in the late sixties as a writer and playwright. A number of his plays showed that he was still making waves as a dramatist, and Gilbert Moses's 1969 production of Baraka's one-act play *Slave Ship: A Historical Pageant* at the Chelsea Theater, Brooklyn, made a particularly strong impression on the critics. Just as the male

[115] See Woodard, *A Nation within a Nation*, Ch. 4.
[116] See Watts, *Amiri Baraka*, 306.
[117] See Woodard, *A Nation within a Nation*, 117–22.

'This Black World of Purest Possibility' 91

protagonist in *Madheart* had referred to the performance as a 'happening', so Baraka's opening stage directions for *Slave Ship* specify that the performance should involve the kind of sensorial barrage that practitioners of performance 'Happenings' like John Cage and Richard Schechner were developing at the time:[118]

Whole *theater in darkness.* [...] *Occasional sound, like ship groaning, squeaking, rocking. Sea smells.* [...] *Burn incense, but make a significant, almost stifling smell come up. Pee. Shit.*
African drums like the worship of some Orisha. Obatala. [...] *BamBamBamBam-Boom BoomBoom BamBam*[119]

Having trained as a director under Paul Sills—who was influenced by Schechner—Moses paid particular attention to the synaesthetic aspect of the play in order to create 'an emotional space' that would envelop both the audience and the performers.[120] As most of the play is set on a slave ship, he turned the whole theatre into the ship's hold so that the audience, who were crammed together on benches, were also drawn into the performance space.[121] By eliminating the distance between the performers and audience, and by foregrounding sounds, music, smells, and gestures, Moses's production exemplified the kind of Artaudian theatre of cruelty that Baraka had invoked in his essay 'The Revolutionary Theatre'. But as is evident from Baraka's opening reference to Obatala—father of the Yoruba spirits, or 'orishas'—any such influence from Artaud or 'Happenings' was also being given a significant Black Arts inflection.

The first third of the play depicts the horrors of life for the human 'cargo' on a slave ship: terrified adult and child captives chant in Yoruba and call on their orishas, while the white slave traders taunt them, laugh at them, and whip them. With dialogue repeatedly giving way to drum beats, cries, and screams, the ship's crossing culminates in one of the female slaves, Dademi, strangling her child and herself with her chain (*SS*, 136). The next section opens with the stage lights flashing on and off to present various snapshots of life on a plantation, and it soon becomes apparent that there's disagreement among the slaves as to whether they should revolt. While one of them, Reverend Turner, suggests they should 'Cut [the] godless throat' (*SS*, 139) of their white master, another slave is

---

[118] For a fine selection of writings by Cage, Schechner, and others on 'Happenings', see Mariellen Sandford (ed.), *Happenings and Other Acts* (London: Routledge, 1995).
[119] Amiri Baraka, *Slave Ship: A Historical Pageant*, in *The Motion of History and Other Plays* (New York: William Morrow, 1978), 132, hereafter cited as *SS*.
[120] Quoted in Harry J. Elam, *Taking It to the Streets: The Social Protest Theater of Luis Valdez and Amiri Baraka* (1997, repr.; Ann Arbor: University of Michigan Press, 2001), 79.
[121] See ibid. 78.

depicted informing the master of their rebellious intent. When the lights go down again, the stage directions specify that the screams and gunshots that ensue are a 'combination of slave ship and break up of the revolt' (*SS*, 140). This transfusion of history continues when ghostly voices from the slave ship call out Yoruba names and then English slave names, at which point there's another historical shift to modern times which is accompanied by a segue from drum beats to Christian hymn singing. The scene then reveals a modern black 'Preacher' who is the previous slave informant in a different guise, and who is extolling the virtues of integration to his congregation: 'we understand the dignity of Pruty McBonk and the Greasy Ghost. Of course diddy rip to bink, of vout juice. And penguins would do the same. I have a trauma that the gold sewers won't integrate' (*SS*, 142). The preacher's discourse clearly reflects Baraka's view that the Christian integrationism of figures like King was nonsensical, but it's also a satirical depiction of both the bop prosody and surrealism that poets like Ginsberg and O'Hara had respectively been developing.

Two things serve to break the preacher's verbal flow: first, the spectacle of a 'wrapped-up bloody corpse of a dead burned baby' (*SS*, 142) with which one of the congregation confronts him; and second, the subsequent scream of a '*New-sound saxophone*' (*SS*, 142). As the lights go down again, renewed sounds of the slave ship and screaming voices build to a crescendo that breaks into the collective singing of a song, 'When We Gonna Rise':

> When we gonna rise up, brother
> When we gonna take our own place, brother
> Like the world had just begun
> I mean, when we gonna lift our heads and voices
> Show the world who we really are
> Warriors-Gods, and lovers, The First Men to walk this star (*SS*, 143)

The song's lyrics clearly aren't particularly innovative in terms of poetics. The use of couplets is at least symptomatic of the song being a call to arts, though, and while the call to 'rise up' is insurrectionary in tone, the song also suggests that rising up means building spiritual and aesthetic pride. To 'take our own place' means taking place as a culture no less than regaining control of territory, and the performance plays out this logic, for it's only after the song's been sung that the lights come back up to reveal the performers taking possession of the theatre as a space of festive movement:

all the people in the slave ship in Miracles'/Temptations' dancing line. Some doing African dance. Some doing new Boogaloo, but all moving toward preacher [...]. It is a new-old dance, Boogalooyoruba line, women, children all moving, popping fingers, all singing, and drummers, beating out old and new, and moving, all moving. (*SS*, 144)

This eruption also leads to the murder of the preacher; nevertheless, the play's ending places more emphasis on the subsequent exorcism of the white Christian voice that's been hounding the characters like an offstage superego. And as the voice screams its last, the play closes with the performers encouraging the audience members to join in the dancing so that the festivities can turn into a collective 'party'.

Ultimately, then, *Slave Ship* exemplifies much of the potentialist Black Arts that Baraka had previously called for. While the first part of the performance is aimed at giving an impression of real horrors faced on slave ships, the overarching concern of the play is the performance of spliced possibilities of history. By resuscitating ghostly sounds and voices from the slave ships, Baraka suggests that passions of this period still exist as charged spiritual energies that can be called on to form new cultural affects. The live images of performers 'moving, all moving' is thus an embodiment of the kind of image he declared a culture to be in his essay on Malcolm X's legacy: 'an image' that is 'a picture of a process, since it is a form of a process: movement seen'.[122] In synthesizing 'new-old' cultural performance, historical movement itself becomes the 'Possibility [that] moves us'. And as Moses emphasized in his 1969 production, such aesthetic possibility was indissociably a matter of staging dance, music, and voice in new theatrical fusions.

'Force. Spirit. Feeling'—if a combination of those things was what Baraka intended his Black Arts potentialism to present, then the critics responses to *Slave Ship* suggest that Moses had presented a performance that was so affecting they were unsure what to feel about it. A *Newsweek* review, for example, noted that the play 'was acted with overwhelming intensity, with fine jazz-rock-blues music by Moses and Archie Shepp', but it also criticized the historical fusions for creating 'a false and destructive continuity'.[123] Similarly, Clive Barnes's review in the *New York Times* declared the performance to be 'riveting', but stated he was horrified at the 'symbolic destruction of white America': 'Whitey is got [. . .]. I am whitey.'[124] As with the FBI's response to Baraka's writing, some critics clearly felt that the emotional intensity of the performance had to be seen in terms of real violence. So while John Lahr argued that the play created an 'emotional environment that makes the audience believe a new world has begun',[125] Edwin Newman on NBC's *Eleventh Hour News* declared

---

[122] LeRoi Jones, 'The Legacy of Malcolm X', 167.
[123] 'J.K.', 'Dark Voyage', *Newsweek* (1 December 1999), 46.
[124] Clive Barnes, 'The Theater: New LeRoi Jones Play', *New York Times* (22 November 1969), A2, 22.
[125] John Lahr, 'On-stage', *The Village Voice* (6 December 1969), 45.

that it 'is not a show to be judged by ordinary standards'; 'We see the slaves slung in [...]. We see a woman raped, another kill herself.'[126] Admittedly, blending aesthetic and racial agitation is precisely what the play's song 'When We Gonna Rise' encourages, and the agitational potential of *Slave Ship* certainly became evident when Moses toured the play in 1970 with the Free Southern Theater. As Harry J. Elam recounts, at a performance in Baton Rouge, Louisiana, the audience were ready to riot by the end of the play and had to be locked in the theatre until their excitement had waned.[127]

FROM PAN-AFRICANISM TO THIRD-WORLD SOCIALISM

By 1970 Baraka's Black Arts reached its spiritual apogee, yet his excitement about Cultural Nationalist aesthetics waned in subsequent years as his investment in political organizing grew. In that respect, *In Our Terribleness: Some Elements and Meaning in Black Style* (1970) stands as one of his last publications that maintains a primacy of Kawaida-based spiritualism over other political theory. The book is a lengthy reflection on black images, and many of its points are developed in relation to accompanying photographs of urban black Americans by Billy Abernathy. In many ways, it also attempts to illustrate Baraka's 'philosophical stance' that remained unpublished (apart from extracts) in the form of his *Book of Life*. Thus, we find him asserting that the African American is inherently 'holy' in being 'a definition of the wholly detached from material'.[128] This capacity to transcend actual states of affairs is also declared by Baraka to be synonymous with black spiritual 'energy', which is itself declared a power of unlimited potentiality: 'The energy is random all possibility'.[129] In this way, the book affirms that black Americans collectively have access to the kind of infinite potentiality that Lukács characterized as 'abstract'. Yet Baraka argues that such potentiality can always be drawn on to incarnate concrete capacities: 'The energy must be harnessed, so that *our forms* will be given power.'[130] And as all forms of social life are subsumed within this spiritual 'Being' that makes 'all of us [...] one

---

[126] Edwin Newman, 'NBC 11th Hour News' [transcript] (19 November 1969), in Amiri Baraka Archive, Howard University Library (Box 39, Folder: '*Slave Ship*'): 1.
[127] See Elam, *Taking It to the Streets*, 122.
[128] Amiri Baraka and Billy Abernathy, *In Our Terribleness: Some Elements and Meaning in Black Style* (New York: Bobbs-Merrill, 1970), 6.
[129] Ibid. 106.
[130] Ibid. Baraka's emphasis.

body', the philosophical stance Baraka ultimately posits with this book amounts to a black monism.[131]

Ascribing racial boundaries to monism is inherently paradoxical, though, and harbours a logical vulnerability that also lurks in Baraka's earlier Black Arts writings. If, as he suggests, the vital energy of black life and identity are rooted not in materiality but in infinite spiritual Being, then how can that Being be limited biologically by race? Alternatively, if 'race is feeling' and cultural 'image', as he argues in his essay on Malcolm X's legacy, then there's nothing logically preventing someone who's genetically white from being 'black' if s/he identifies emotionally with black images. The latter is a possibility that Baraka never confronts directly in his Black Arts writings. As I've shown, he chooses instead to denounce integrationist black Americans for being, effectively, white. To be sure, prizing ethnicity over genetics also had some positive effects in terms of racial inclusion. It meant, for example, that the Black Arts Movement helped undermine any hierarchy among African Americans that might be based on some people being deemed genetically 'blacker' or 'browner' than others. That this racial inclusion had to be exclusively African American, though, only confirms the fraught nature of Black Arts monism, and nowhere is this more apparent than in the volume of poetry that Baraka published in 1970, *It's Nation Time*.

Comprised of three long poems, the first of them, 'Sermon for Our Maturity', sets out a black aesthetic as cosmology:

> Yes, you grown Blood
> Your Afro dealin w/ images in outter space
> Soft million tipped antenna
> Bring back and feed on the new images
> [...]
> feed the planes of feeling
> you growin blood
> and space in ecstasy to receive you[132]

With 'blood' also being slang for a fellow African American, this extract proceeds to build an ambiguity around the word. If the addressee is growing racial blood-lines by 'dealin w/ images in outter space', it also appears that the addressee has grown through consuming these images. The poem thus nourishes a slippage in agency (is 'grown' transitive or intransitive?) such that it becomes unclear as to whether race is generated

---

[131] Ibid. 136.
[132] Amiri Baraka, 'Sermon for Our Maturity', in *It's Nation Time* (Chicago: Third World Press, 1970), 18.

by biology or a cultural imaginary, for the difference between the two appears undecidable. That aporia feeds into a further slippage between cosmological 'outter space' and volumes of ecstatic bodily 'feeling'. Baraka thus struggles to portray relations between race and culture as anything other than a conflation of the two, but he also needs to conflate them in order to racialize spiritual Being. In the eponymous poem of the collection we thus find him identifying a host of spiritual figures as black: 'Shango buddha black | hermes rasis black | moses krishna | black'.[133] Similarly, 'Sermon for Our Maturity' ends with a black reprise of the kind of pantheistic invocation that Ginsberg had recently offered in poems like 'Wichita Vortex Sutra' (1966):

> Ommmm Mane Padme Hummmmmmm
> Ooshoobee doo bee
> Ashadu an la Illaha Illala
> Ooshoobee doo bee
> Tuna Jaribu Kuwa Weusi Tu
> Ooshoobee doo bee
> Kiss Venus for me while you up there man[134]

Moving from the Buddhist mantra of line one here, to the Islamic *Shahadah* ('I testify there is no Allah but Allah') in line three, to a Swahili injunction ('Strive to be only black') in line five, before closing with an allusion to the Roman love goddess Venus, Baraka builds a black poetic pantheon that he fuses together with his Doo Wop/Rhythm and Blues chorus line—'Ooshoobee doo bee'. *It's Nation Time* thereby strives to maintain a line in the Cultural Nationalism that Baraka and Karenga had consistently presented as being fundamentally African American. But as the inclusion of figures like Venus, Hermes, and Krishna shows, the limits of this nationalism were now expanding to breaking point. This crisis was indicative of an incipient change of heart in Baraka, and as he came to acknowledge this himself he began to adopt an alternative stance: Pan-Africanism.

The fundamental aim of Pan-Africanism is to establish cultural and political unity between people with African heritage in countries around the world, and by the end of 1970 Baraka was already playing a leading role in founding Pan-Africanism as an international movement. By broadening his nationalist horizons, he also began to widen his views on racial politics. Consequently, his engagement with Pan-Africanism became a prelude to his rejection in 1974 of race-based thinking in favour

---

[133] Amiri Baraka, 'It's Nation Time', ibid. 23.
[134] Baraka, 'Sermon for Our Maturity', 18–19.

of Third-World Socialism. Some of these shifts in Baraka's outlook were already manifest at the first International Assembly of the Congress of Afrikan People (CAP) that he helped organize in Atlanta, Georgia, in September 1970. Attracting around 2,700 political and cultural delegates from around the world, these included representatives of Australian Aborigines as well as people of African descent from South America and the Caribbean.[135] As coordinator of the Congress's 'Political Liberation Workshop', Baraka also invited Black Panthers and other left-wing black representatives in order to heal the rift between Cultural Nationalists and Revolutionary Nationalists that had worsened since the incident in which US members shot dead two Panthers.[136] This gesture of reconciliation was nevertheless symptomatic of Baraka's growing disenchantment with both Karenga and Cultural Nationalism, and the subsequent establishment of CAP cadres in cities around North America became yet another factor in the weakening influence of US.

These successes in linking national and international politics through the CAP were offset for Baraka by local politics back in Newark. Kenneth Gibson, the new black mayor, proved to be not so willing to adopt the kinds of CFUN policies that Baraka and his organization had said Gibson would advance.[137] It was another reason for Baraka to focus on his Pan-African activism, and he subsequently turned CFUN into the Newark chapter of the CAP. In September 1971 Newark also hosted the eastern regional CAP conference at which delegates agreed to help black Americans running for office in the lead-up to the 1972 American political elections. By this point, Karenga and two other US members had been convicted (in June 1971) for torturing two black women, and Karenga spent the next four years in prison.[138] Although Baraka tried to canvass support for Karenga's release, the conviction became yet another reason for him to distance himself from US and its leader.[139] Other black Americans felt similarly disenchanted, and by 1971 most of those who'd been involved in the political side of Cultural Nationalism were now identifying themselves as Pan-Africanists.[140] For his part, Baraka was also becoming increasingly interested in the forms of socialism that several African leaders had recently fostered while gaining independence from colonial rule—in particular, Kwame Nkrumah in Ghana, Sékou Touré in

---

[135] See Pinkney, *Red, Black, and Green*, 132–3.
[136] See Woodard, *A Nation within a Nation*, 169.
[137] See Watts, *Amiri Baraka*, 364–6.
[138] See Pinkney, *Red, Black, and Green*, 143.
[139] A number of letters from Baraka calling for Karenga's release are contained in the Amiri Baraka Archive, Howard University Library (Box 3, Folder: 'Maulana Karenga').
[140] See Watts, *Amiri Baraka*, 381.

the Republic of Guinea, Julius Nyerere in Tanzania, and Amílcar Cabral in Guinea-Bissau. The radical shift in outlook that these leaders' examples provoked in Baraka was later summed up by him in his autobiography: 'For Nkrumah and Cabral the enemy of Africa was imperialism, not just white people.'[141]

That Baraka's own political ideas were gaining influence was confirmed in 1972 with his elevation in both the National Black Political movement in America and the Pan-Africanist movement. The National Black Political Convention held at Gary, Indiana in March that year drew more than 8,000 black American delegates, including 1,800 elected officials.[142] Like the regional CAP gathering in Newark the previous September, the Convention focused on issues of black voter registration as well as strategies for unifying black political organizations within America. The latter also involved creating a new National Black Assembly (NBA), which would coordinate black activism at local and national level. With Baraka being elected the NBA's Secretary General, one of his first initiatives in the role was to launch a National Black Agenda, some of which featured the kind of utopian aspirations that the RNA had been advocating. Emphasizing the importance of a black-controlled media, the Agenda also called for free education for African Americans, reparation payments for slavery, and black political autonomy in the District of Columbia.[143] The fact that the Gary Convention was given endorsement by the Congressional Black Caucus clearly inspired confidence in Baraka regarding the NBA's ability to have an impact on party politics in America more generally. Not only did he try that year to canvass support for the Agenda among black delegates at the Democratic National Convention, he also did the same at the Republican Convention. The utopianism of the Agenda was a prime reason why delegates chose not to support it, though, and the result was that Baraka's cynicism about American democracy was swiftly restored. By the time the second CAP International Assembly took place on 1 September in San Diego, this cynicism was exacerbated by the Congressional Black Caucus's decision to boycott the CAP Assembly on the grounds of its separatism.[144] Despite these setbacks, Baraka continued to enjoy support within the Pan-African movement, and the extent of his support was shown by his election that year to national Chairman of the CAP.

All of these upheavals in his political views and commitments had major consequences for his cultural endeavours. At the 1970 CAP Assembly in

---

[141] Baraka, *Autobiography*, 298.
[142] See Woodard, *A Nation within a Nation*, 186.
[143] See Watts, *Amiri Baraka*, 409.
[144] See Pinkney, *Red, Black, and Green*, 134–5.

1970 his continuing dedication to cultural activism was apparent from the CAP 'Ideological Statement' that he issued: 'We must *separate the mind*, win the mind'; 'wage the revolution to win the Black man's mind so we will begin to move *together* conscious that we are a people'.[145] But by the 1972 Convention in Gary, he was denouncing struggles for cultural consciousness in order to emphasize the paramount importance of political activism:

> We should not make any statements that we cannot back up, in ways that our community can see and understand. Words are not immediate change. Crackers [whites] killed in revolutionary sentences are walking around killing us in the real streets.[146]

This vacillation between cultural and political activism was, of course, not without precedent. As I've argued, numerous plays and writings that Baraka wrote in the aftermath of the 1967 Newark riots show how he was torn between advocating cultural forces of possibility on the one hand and actual violence on the other. But from 1972 Baraka initiated a wholesale rejection of the spiritual potentialism he'd previously promoted. In its place, he came to uphold an aesthetics that would not only be subordinate to materialism, but would also largely eschew formal experimentation so that its political message could be more readily understood. This momentous volte-face meant that by 1971 Baraka was no longer committed to the Spirit House, and it soon began to dissolve as a consequence. Ironically, Cultural Nationalist aesthetics were simultaneously gaining exposure with the publication of essay collections like Woodie King's and Earl Anthony's *Black Poets and Prophets* (1972) and Baraka's own *Raise Race Rays Raze: Essays since 1965* (1971). But although such publications were also seen as supporting the new Pan-Africanist aesthetics, the truth was that the collections' essays had almost exclusively been previously published in the latter part of the sixties.

The extent to which Baraka's turn to socialism meant transforming his aesthetics is evident from two collections of poetry he published during this period, *Spirit Reach* (1972) and *Hard Facts: 1973–5* (1975). Following *It's Nation Time*'s example, *Spirit Reach* is the last gasp of Baraka's spiritual potentialism. With references to a range of black musicians, including John Coltrane and James Brown, the volume incorporates a range of rhythms, cries, and chants in order to present another fresh fusion

---

[145] Quoted in Watts, *Amiri Baraka*, 382, Baraka's emphasis.
[146] Amiri Baraka, *Strategy and Tactics of a Pan-African Nationalist Party* (Newark, NJ: CFUN, 1971), 13.

of spiritual and cultural energies. The penultimate poem, 'The Spirit of Creation is Blackness', is a good example:

> Yo head be all our heads and it's risen like it was the sun drawn you up
> with it, and we are drawn around in tune like motion, plane you plane me
> are plane we, a crowd of us, swahili black weusi jua, and there are words
> with this melody, and words and melody, tune, rhythm, the harmony, are all
> the same.[147]

Solar energy is linked in this extract to black musical energy in order to affirm a gathering movement of celestial racial monism. The 'crowd of us' is thus imagined to radiate as a black sun ('weusi jua') whose spiritual planes are implicitly plain to see. Some of these planes' binding energy are also linked to aspects of the poetics, particularly the sudden burst of spondees and rhymes—'plane you | plane me | are plane we'—along with the semantic possibilities that 'plane' relates in punning on its homonym. If 'Possibility is what moves us', as Baraka had previously argued, then this poem suggests that poetry is an exemplary source of that possibility and movement. In contrast, *Hard Facts* opens with Baraka calling for a socialist poetry that 'reflects the material life and values of a society' and that 'serves [...] the working masses of people'.[148] In light of that, the majority of the collection's poems proceed to reject exploration of poetic possibility in favour of clunking ideological declaratives like the following:

> from the tactical to the strategic, build the whole structure that will change the century, change the social system, change the way we live,
> change the peoples
> lives and the future of the world[149]

But history fills us completely
History stretches us out of old shape
into new shape
to be in the future
with[150]

---

[147] Amiri Baraka, 'The Spirit of Creation is Blackness', in *Spirit Reach* (Newark, NJ: Jihad, 1972), 24.
[148] Amiri Baraka, 'Introduction', in *Hard Facts* (Newark, NJ: CAP, 1975), ii.
[149] Amiri Baraka, 'Red Autumn', ibid. 23.
[150] Amiri Baraka, 'For the Revolutionary Outburst by Black People', ibid. 39.

If the lineation is the only thing preventing such poetry from collapsing into political manifesto, the same can admittedly be said of Baraka's earlier poems like 'Black People!' In his Black Arts period, though, the instances in which his aesthetic performance was muted with ideology were countervailed by the potentialism of works like *Black Mass* which, as we've seen, posed alternative historical potentials while performing new artistic syntheses. Such potentialism almost entirely disappears in Baraka's work after *Hard Facts*. Rather than creating aesthetic possibilities with which to move people, he sought instead to present writing that confirms the kind of view I cited from Fredric Jameson in the previous chapter; namely, that social possibility in the wake of the sixties was fundamentally a matter of economic infrastructure.

Baraka announced his socialist shift to be official in a number of articles and appearances in 1974, and in 1975 he resigned as Secretary General of the NBA and changed the CAP's name to the Revolutionary Communist League (RCL). As Sandra Hollin Flowers has stated, his defection was a major blow to what remained of the Black Arts Movement and to those who had been inspired by his 'Revolutionary Theatre'.[151] In 1972 the New Lafayette Theater folded, and by 1973 Barbara Ann Teer was describing black theatre as being riven by factions: 'The Negroes, The Niggers, The Militants, The Nationalists, The Revolutionaries and so on... Everybody's got their clique, their clan and we're very tribalistic people.'[152] With support diminishing as a result of these divisions, many black theatres subsequently either became less radical or cultivated a more multi-ethnic outlook. Barbara Ann Teer's National Black Theater was one notable exception that continued to draw large audiences with innovative African American plays. And although Baraka's socialist shift helped precipitate the demise of Black Arts in the 1970s, both he and the Black Arts Movement have continued to be significant influences. As Nilgun Anadolu-Okur has argued, along with fellow Black Arts theatre figures such as Larry Neal, Ron Milner, Ed Bullins, and Ben Caldwell, Baraka certainly played a major role in laying the foundations for more recent African American experimental drama.[153] The establishment in 1989 of a biannual National Black Theater Festival has also helped rekindle the kind of cultural solidarity that he and the Black Arts Movement had generated.

Unfortunately for Baraka, though, his withdrawal from Cultural Nationalism and Pan-Africanism led to a weakening of his influence

---

[151] Flowers, *African American Nationalist Literature of the 1960s*, 125.
[152] Quoted in Effiong, *In Search of a Model for African-American Drama*, 203.
[153] See Okur, *Contemporary African American Theater*, 99; also, Elam, *Taking It to the Streets*, 135–9.

both as a writer and as a political activist. Viewing art increasingly as a superstructural 'expression' of economic life, the vast majority of his literary writings since 1975 have been hampered by the weight of ideological content for which they've had to efface themselves. Admittedly, there have been exceptions. His long poem 'AM/TRAK' (1979), for example, offers interesting rhythmic experiences in engaging with John Coltrane's music and in reflecting back on Black Arts.[154] A number of poems in *Wise, Whys, Yz* (1995) also mark a return to interests in African American culture more generally and echo some of the stylistic innovations of his earlier poetry. But his plays, in particular, have been weakened as a result of his political turn. Rejecting the aesthetic fusions and energy of his previous rituals, socialist plays like *What Was the Relationship of the Lone Ranger to the Means of Production?* have been much more focused on staging undramatic declamations of capitalism.[155] No longer making cultural waves with formal or stylistic experiments and syntheses, it is the content of Baraka's work that has again made the headlines more recently—the most notorious example being his poem 'Somebody Blew Up America' (2001), which, as he later acknowledged, suggests that a 'coven' of 'politicians, capitalists [and] monopoly capitalists' were behind the terrorist attacks of 11 September 2001.[156] Since his shift to Third-World Socialism, critical responses to Baraka's literary writings have thus been largely unfavourable.[157] For that reason, the main studies of his literary and political career say little about his activities after his socialist turn, and even Baraka's autobiography comes to a close at 1975. From having upheld art in the sixties as something that could create new concrete potentials, 1975 marks the point at which Baraka committed himself to concrete reality. If in his eyes the potentialist aesthetics he'd called for were ultimately not adequate as political activism, the literary writing he has subsequently produced has frequently struggled to find acceptance as a literature that can move.

---

[154] See Amiri Baraka, 'AM/TRAK', in Hoover, *Postmodern American Poetry*, 269–72.
[155] See Amiri Baraka, *What was the Relationship of the Lone Ranger to the Means of Production?*, in *The LeRoi Jones/Amiri Baraka Reader*, 273–301.
[156] Amiri Baraka, 'Postscript: No Black Ink in Fax', in *Somebody Blew Up America, & Other Poems* (2001; Philipsburg: House of Nehesi, 2007), 52.
[157] See, for example, Watts, *Amiri Baraka*, Ch. 15; Bigsby, *A Critical Introduction to Twentieth-Century American Drama*, 395–402; and Werner Sollors, *Amiri Baraka/LeRoi Jones: The Quest for a 'Populist Modernism'* (New York: Columbia University Press, 1978), Ch. 10.

3
Writing Outer Space for 'Potential America'
William S. Burroughs

'WE HAVE LIFT-OFF...'

In August 1962 the American novelist Mary McCarthy surprised everyone by extolling the virtues of William S. Burroughs's *Naked Lunch* (1959), thereby raising the public profile of both the novel and novelist. The occasion was an Edinburgh conference on writing and censorship organized by the publisher John Calder, and attended by literary luminaries such as Norman Mailer and Henry Miller. For McCarthy the virtue of *Naked Lunch* was its timeliness, the way it appeared 'sort of speeded up like jet travel'; 'it has that somewhat supersonic quality'.[1] Addressing the conference audience, Burroughs went a step further, heralding a new epoch of space writing: 'I feel that a new mythology is now possible in the space age and that we can again have heroes and villains, with respect to the planet, and in closing I would say that the future of writing is in space and not in time.'[2] Norman Mailer disagreed with Burroughs at the conference, though, arguing that 'the future of writing is in time precisely, and never in space, and one of us is going to be right'.[3] Undeterred, Burroughs stuck to his guns—often literally—over the next three decades, and reaffirmed his position in his 1991 'Afterword' to a collection of critical essays on him:

Space travel involves time travel, seeing the dimension of time from outside time, as a landscape spread out before the observer, where a number of things are going on simultaneously—as in the Djemalfnaa in Marrakech: Gnaoua drummers, snake charmers, trick bicycle riders. The image of a market occurs repeatedly in [my] later work.

---

[1] Quoted in Ted Morgan, *Literary Outlaw: The Life and Times of William S. Burroughs* (1988, repr.; London: Pimlico, 2002), 333.
[2] Quoted ibid. 340.
[3] Quoted ibid. 340.

[...]

My purpose in writing has always been to express human potentials and purposes relevant to the Space Age.[4]

From these statements, it's clear that Burroughs is concerned with relating 'human potentials' to at least two kinds of 'outer' space: the first being one of interplanetary space programmes; the second being a space of alternative perception that entails 'seeing time from outside time'. This latter form, which Burroughs likens to the simultaneity of a 'market', is the launching pad from which he proceeds to explore space and potentiality in conjunction. Unlike Amiri Baraka's potentialism, then, Burroughs's aesthetic approach to possibility is more akin to that of his fellow Beat, Allen Ginsberg; far from seeking to turn infinite potentiality into concrete forms of racial possibility, Burroughs seeks to extend the possibilities of the human *as a species*. And as we shall see, the link between that extension and space exploration increasingly leads Burroughs to an embrace of what is alien...

It isn't just in Burroughs's later works that space, possibility, and markets are linked; the connection is already evident in *Naked Lunch* in a section describing the 'City of Interzone': 'The Composite City where all human potentials are spread out in a vast silent market.'[5] The most notable feature of this market is its hybridity, presenting as it does a bewildering agglomeration of cuisines, music, and architecture from different races and ages—for example: 'High mountain flutes, jazz and bebop, one-stringed Mongol instruments, gypsy xylophones, African drums, Arab bagpipes...' (*NL*, 98).[6] For Burroughs, the market displays a form of extra-temporal simultaneity that *is* the space of writing; a space that, like Eliot's *The Waste Land* or Pound's *Cantos*, can assemble textual artifacts from different eras in one textual volume. In setting his Interzone in a market, though, Burroughs clearly lays himself open to the charges Fredric Jameson makes against 'postmodern' writers. Regarding the question of who turned out to be right between Mailer and Burroughs, Jameson would doubtless nominate Burroughs, for as far as Jameson is concerned the era of postmodernism is indeed characterized by a

---

[4] William S. Burroughs, 'Afterword: My Purpose is to Write for the Space Age', in Jennie Skerl and Robin Lydenberg (eds), *William S. Burroughs at the Front: Critical Reception, 1959–89* (Carbondale: Southern Illinois Press, 1991), 266, 268, my emphasis.
[5] William S. Burroughs, *Naked Lunch* (New York: Grove Weidenfeld, 1990), 96, hereafter cited as *NL*.
[6] Burroughs's experiments with the hallucinogenic *yage* produced similarly disorienting effects, and in his *Yage Letters* to Allen Ginsberg he compares the disorientation to a kind of 'space-time' travel. An instance of this is replicated in 'The Market' section of *NL*, 99–100.

predominance of globally networked space over time. But with 'aesthetic production' having 'become integrated into commodity production generally', he writes, contemporary writers no longer benefit from the cultural 'semi-autonomy' enjoyed by modernists such as Pound and Eliot.[7] Consequently, literary postmodernists—Burroughs is cited as exemplary— have lost their 'critical distance' from consumer culture.[8] And to compare this 'alarming' disorientation of postmodern writing to the 'initial bewilderment of the older modernism', argues Jameson, is analogous to comparing 'the velocities of spacecraft to those of the automobile'.[9] Thus, what McCarthy identifies in *Naked Lunch* as a timely intervention is what Jameson would see as being too much *of* its time; too determined by postmodern consumerism. Yet *Naked Lunch* also describes American consumer culture as engendering interstitial spaces that undermine it. As Dr Benway argues:

there's always a space *between*, in popular songs and Grade B movies, giving away the basic American rottenness, spurting out like breaking boils, throwing out globs of un-D.T. ['un-Differentiated Tissue'] to fall anywhere and grow into some degenerate cancerous life-form, reproducing a hideous random image. (*NL*, 121, Burroughs's emphasis)

Wholesale exchange might be culturally entropic, but the degeneration also creates rogue hybrids and potentials that undermine any stability of the system. Consequently, the market throws up zones of indeterminacy '*between*' things—a cultural surplus that amounts to a form of alien 'interzone'. Contrary to Jameson, then, Burroughs gains purchase on the bizarre through the bazaar, discovering forms of 'outer space' as interzones that can lurk *within* a market.

Considering Burroughs's repeated avowals of being fascinated by space exploration, it's surprising that there's been no substantial critical attention paid to his engagement with the US or Soviet space programmes of the time. There's even been denial of the connection—Kathryn Hume, for example, asserting that Burroughs's writings 'have nothing to do with NASA and little to do with science fiction'.[10] Other critics have recently discussed his fascination with space travel as a literary endeavour, but the ways in which Burroughs might be tackling particular space programme

---

[7] Fredric Jameson, *Postmodernism, or The Cultural Logic of Late Capitalism* (London: Verso, 1991), 4, 48.
[8] Ibid. 48–9.
[9] Ibid. 44.
[10] Kathryn Hume, 'William S. Burroughs's Phantasmic Geography', in *Contemporary Literature* 40:1 (1999), 127.

developments remain unaddressed.[11] Admittedly, the 'space mythology' that Burroughs writes often appears to bear little surface resemblance to historical facts, but consideration of the debates surrounding the space programmes shows that his fiction does offer pointed engagement with them. Moreover, the fact that the historical links sometimes appear askew is often the point. Far from offering realist interventions, Burroughs became increasingly intent on fashioning his space-age mythology as an alternative form of space exploration.

In this chapter, then, I'll examine in detail how, as a foil to the space programmes, Burroughs develops his space mythology in two trilogies that comprise his major works: the 1960s 'Nova' trilogy, and the 'Cities of the Red Night' trilogy, which stretches from the mid-1970s to the mid-1980s. In tracing this development, I'll also show how Burroughs turns his own space programme into a sophisticated literary potentialism. As I'll show, that potentialism has a distinct trajectory. Starting with the Nova trilogy, Burroughs develops disorienting 'cut-up' and 'fold-in' techniques to explore new possibilities of textual 'outer space'. In the second trilogy, he sets about populating such space with more defined possible worlds as well as with hybrid, alien life-forms that are explicitly presented as textual 'potentials'; 'latent' bodies of 'energy'. Ultimately—and in clear opposition to the space programmes—Burroughs's potentialism aims to make encounters between his texts and readers elicit an outer space of lived experience. By outlining the trajectory of this potentialism in relation to historical developments in the space programmes, I have two attendant aims: first, to offer a more adequate account of Burroughs's engagement with space exploration; and second, to examine how his potentialism offers a rejoinder not just to the historical space programmes but also to claims about the postmodernization of global space that I've discussed above. Before we consider how Burroughs's launches his mythology with the Nova trilogy, though, we need to look in more detail at the cultural impact that the space race was having at the time.

THE SPACE RACE, 1957–64

By the time of *Naked Lunch*'s initial publication in 1959, the space race between the United States and the Soviet Union was really starting to take

---

[11] While they don't address relations between Burroughs's writing and the space race at any length, see the discussions of space travel in Burroughs's fiction by Eric Mottram, *William Burroughs: The Algebra of Need* (London: Boyars, 1977), 85–90, 269–71; also Jennie Skerl, *William S. Burroughs* (Boston: Twayne, 1985), Ch. 5.

off. In 1957, the USA had been stunned when the Soviets successfully launched the first satellite, *Sputnik I*, into orbit. It was swiftly followed in November that year by *Sputnik II*, which carried the first living organism into space; a dog named Laika. In response, President Eisenhower's administration passed a 'National Aeronautics and Space Act' in April 1958, and set up a new 'National Aeronautics and Space Administration' (NASA).[12] Successfully launching its own satellite for the first time in January 1958, the USA went on to increase the funding of its space programme dramatically over subsequent years while maintaining a high public profile for it. Having campaigned for the presidency under a banner of 'A New Frontier' in 1960, John F. Kennedy made it clear on taking up office that this frontier largely lay in outer space. It was clearly a question of keeping abreast of the Soviet Union. While the USA botched its *coup d'état* in Cuba with the Bay of Pigs fiasco in April 1961, the Soviets successfully sent the first man into orbit, Yuri Gagarin in *Vostok I*. America countered with Alan Shepard's sub-orbital flight in a *Mercury* capsule in May, and later that month President Kennedy famously declared his intention to push the US manned space programme towards a lunar landing: 'In a very real sense, it will not be one man going to the moon ... it will be an entire nation.'[13] Beating the Soviets in the space race wasn't simply governmental grandstanding for the benefit of the American public. The US space programme had already been instrumental in developing technology for intercontinental ballistic missiles (ICBMs) and supersonic flight in the 1950s, and the need for satellite reconnaissance seemed increasingly necessary, as the Cuban missile crisis in October 1962 made apparent. To a great extent, then, the space programmes were already a matter of taking the Cold War to new heights politically, technologically, and militarily.

The cultural impact was no small part of the space race, either. A central irony of the US programme was that undertaking interplanetary exploration was wholly linked to the terrestrial meshing of media and communications networks that Jameson and others have characterized as being quintessentially postmodern. Televised launches, in particular, ensured that mass awareness of the space race was symptomatic of the growing impact of mass media. Six months before Burroughs announced his intention to write a 'new mythology' for the 'space age' at the Edinburgh

---

[12] For detailed histories of the space programmes, see Dale Carter, *The Final Frontier: The Rise and Fall of the American Rocket State* (London: Verso, 1988); Walter A. McDougall, *The Heavens and the Earth: A Political History of the Space Age* (Baltimore: Johns Hopkins University Press, 1985); and Arthur L. Levine, *The Future of the U.S. Space Program* (New York: Prager, 1975), Chs 1–6.

[13] Quoted in Levine, *The Future of the U.S. Space Program*, 75.

conference, the US launch of John Glenn's orbital flight on 20 February 1962 was watched on television by an estimated television audience of 100 million. As the political scientist Jodi Dean asserts in *Aliens in America*, 'The space program was always in part a television program produced for audiences at home and abroad'; 'If it wasn't public, a spaceflight didn't happen.'[14] Accordingly, for William D. Atwill, the space programmes of the sixties must be viewed as a central factor in the consolidation of postmodernization:

> the space program had already become what we call postmodern. The rise of television as a global force was linked to the space program's ability to orbit geosynchronous relay satellites, and, just as the astronauts were almost never out of contact with ground control, no writer living through those times could avoid the media saturation of the launches.[15]

The media coverage clearly made an impact on Burroughs, despite his preference for watching television with the volume turned down and a random soundtrack played over it. There was also plenty of coverage aside from the televisual that was providing exposure. Popular news magazines such as *Life, Time, Fortune*, and *Newsweek* frequently reported on the personal lives of the astronauts and their families, thereby melding 'outer', 'public', and 'domestic' spaces into a packaged constellation. And while such media circulation emphasized a domesticated image of space exploration, NASA's selection process largely figured space travel as a decidedly middle-American pursuit. Astronauts were standardized individuals in so far as they had limits on their height, weight, and age. And as Dean argues,

> Not only did all the astronauts have military and test pilot experience, but all had been raised in small towns; all had been reared under a traditional ethos of effort and success. NASA's requirements, in short, produced astronauts as America's ideal citizens: strong, ambitious, white, middle-class men.[16]

Ironically, then, the alien novelties of space exploration were being promoted and experienced as the height of the homely.[17]

By the end of the sixties, such space race ironies were leading numerous writers and commentators to suggest that the 'giant leap for mankind' that Neil Armstrong announced in July 1969 on the moon was indicative of many steps backwards on earth. Hannah Arendt had argued as early as

---

[14] Jodi Dean, *Aliens in America: Conspiracy Cultures from Outerspace to Cyberspace* (Ithaca: Cornell University Press, 1998), 74.
[15] William D. Atwill, *Fire and Power: The American Space Program as Postmodern Narrative* (Athens: University of Georgia Press, 1994), 11–12.
[16] Dean, *Aliens in America*, 85.
[17] Carter, *The Final Frontier*, 3.

1958 that the Soviet launch of *Sputnik* seemed to presage an era in which space exploration would contribute to the impairment of the terrestrial 'human condition'. She expanded the argument in a 1963 essay, stating that the space programmes, with their massive investment in technological standardization, could bring about a situation whereby 'speech and everyday language' may as well be replaced by the 'meaningless formalism of mathematical signs'.[18] In view of such comments, Burroughs's new space-age mythology takes on a real seriousness (if not 'gravity'). Burroughs was himself aware of the regulative tendencies of the space programmes; indeed, he viewed these as making alternative narratives about space all the more necessary, as his Nova trilogy shows.

CUT-UPS, FOLD-INS, AND THE NOVA TRILOGY

The trilogy consists of *The Soft Machine* (1961), *The Ticket that Exploded* (1962), and *Nova Express* (1964), and in terms of deploying Burroughs's new 'cut-up' techniques, *The Soft Machine* is the most relentless. He had already published cut-ups in two prior texts: first with 'Minutes to Go' (1960), a pamphlet he collaborated on with Brion Gysin, Sinclair Beiles, and Beat poet Gregory Corso; and secondly with *Exterminator!* (1960), which included non-cut-up pieces he'd published in various magazines. Burroughs always declared Brion Gysin, the artist and long-term companion of Burroughs, to be the progenitor of cut-ups, although both of them acknowledged that the method was indebted to the Dadaist Tristan Tzara as well as the experiments in 'chance' composition carried out by John Cage and Earl Brown.[19] The fullest explanation of cut-ups is contained in *The Third Mind*, a series of essays compiled by Gysin and Burroughs between 1964 and 1965 that remained unpublished until 1976. The basic cut-up method is simple: sentences from at least two texts are literally cut into fragments and then recombined (usually randomly) into new syntactical composites.[20] As Gérard-Georges Lemaire states in his contribution to *The Third Mind*:

---

[18] Hannah Arendt, 'Man's Conquest of Space', *American Scholar* 32 (Autumn 1963), 540.

[19] See Burroughs's 1984 interview with Tom H. Corso and Paul Dickerson, 'Attack Anything Moving', and his 1996 interview with Kristin McKenna, both in Sylvère Lotringer (ed.), *Burroughs Live: The Collected Interviews of William S. Burroughs, 1960–97* (New York: Semiotext(e), 2001), 606 and 777, respectively.

[20] Oliver Harris rightly warns against the dangers of generalizing about cut-ups given the 'great range of cut-up procedures' ('Cutting Up Politics', in Davis Schneiderman and Philip Walsh (eds), *Retaking the Universe: William S. Burroughs in the Age of Globalization* (London: Pluto, 2004), 175–200). For other notable discussions of the cut-ups, see

Initially cut-ups were used only with short texts taken from newspapers or letters [...] [while] the business of disarming and redistributing the meaning of the message was left to chance. All possibilities of this message were explored. Two—or more—messages, once assembled according to this strategy on the page, revealed another message, which its components were careful not to communicate.[21]

These early cut-ups are thus viewed as a kind of deracinated method of exposure, then; a way of decoding links between cultural networks and discourses that Jameson sees the postmodern subject as being increasingly unable to 'map'.[22] Burroughs himself confirms the cartographic aspect of cut-ups in one of his contributions to *The Third Mind*: 'In my writing I am acting as a map maker, an explorer of psychic areas [...] as a cosmonaut of inner space, and I see no point in exploring ideas that have already been thoroughly surveyed.'[23] The cartography of the cut-ups is thus offered as potentiating new compounds of inner, outer, and textual space. Far from being realist representations of the world, the cut-ups map new psychic and communicational regions only insofar as they simultaneously establish them.

That inherent performativity of cut-ups is foregrounded by Gysin when he states that they create new interstitial voices: 'Shuffle the pieces and put them together at random. Cut through the word lines to hear a new voice off the page. A dialogue often breaks out. "It" speaks.'[24] The 'it' is a new, impersonal 'third mind', the concept of which is acknowledged as being derived, in part, from Eliot's *The Waste Land*—'who is the third who walks beside you'. Such interstitial voices are a further advance on the market interzones depicted in *Naked Lunch*. And as Gysin argues, the third mind is not intended to manifest textual abstraction but rather a rewriting of experiential and spatial coordinates:

One of the easy ways the human mind, probably owing to its structure, can best conceive Space is in the limitless projection of a multidimensional grid through which progressive movement can be plotted, an infinite variety of form conceived. It makes, in fact, a space picture rather like a cellular scaffolding—the bright jungle of gym mathematics; an exercise for controlling matter and knowing space.

Timothy S. Murphy, *Wising Up the Marks: The Amodern William Burroughs* (Berkeley, CA: University of California Press, 1997), Ch. 4; also Jamie Russell, *Queer Burroughs* (London: Palgrave, 2001), Ch. 2.

[21] Gérard-Georges Lemaire, '23 Stitches Taken by Gérard-Georges Lemaire and 2 Points of Order by Brion Gysin', in William S. Burroughs and Brion Gysin, *The Third Mind* (London: Calder, 1979), 15.
[22] Jameson, *Postmodernism*, 44.
[23] William S. Burroughs, 'Fold-Ins', in *The Third Mind*, 95.
[24] Brion Gysin, 'Cut-Ups: A Project for Disastrous Success', in *The Third Mind*, 44.

[...]
I roll you out a bright, new cellular framework of Space and, in it, I write your Script anew.[25]

The allusion here to the usual conception of space as a mathematical 'grid' is clearly close to Arendt's view of the space programmes' mathematical standardizations. Instead of predicting a turn towards 'mathematical signs', though, as Arendt does, Gysin and Burroughs offer the cut-ups as liberating new possibilities of space travel. Burroughs's 'fold-in' technique is another example of this. An extension of the cut-ups, Burroughs describes the fold-in as a process whereby half a page from one text is laid beside half a page from another; 'The composite text is then read across' the two.[26] Alternatively, one can use pages of the same novel to produce space-time travel within it:

The fold-in method extends to writing the flashback used in films, enabling the writer to move backward and forward on his time track—for example I take page one and fold it into page one hundred—I insert the resulting composite as page ten—When the reader reads page ten he is flashing forward in time to page one hundred and back in time to page one—the *déjà vu* phenomenon can so be produced to order.[27]

In place of the linearity that Burroughs regards as being time's chief characteristic, the fold-in opens a fluid, textual volume that can send the reader off in more than one direction at any given point. The narrative space is thus made up of 'composite' interzones that operate like black holes and resist being plotted textually or experientially. And it's in his Nova trilogy that Burroughs first offers the exploration of such interzones as facilitating an alternative form of space travel.

Burroughs stated on several occasions that he considered each of his novels to be part of one 'continual' book, and we certainly find characters and themes from the Nova books reappearing in his later works.[28] Each novel in the trilogy consists of a series of 'routines' deliberately arranged without linear progression, although the trilogy does have an overarching theme, as Burroughs explained to Allen Ginsberg: 'the planet has been invaded by Venutians and the book attempts to cope with the invasion'.[29]

---

[25] Ibid. 47, 51.
[26] Burroughs, 'Fold-Ins', 96.
[27] Ibid.
[28] See, for example, his 1974 interview with Philippe Mikriamos, 'The Last European Interview', in *Burroughs Live*, 279.
[29] Burroughs's interview with Allen Ginsberg, 'Spiritual Conspiracies', in *Burroughs Live*, 129.

These invading beings are, in fact, only one manifestation of the invidious 'Nova Mob' that has spread itself on Earth and elsewhere as a form of virus with the intention of 'always aggravat[ing] existing conflicts'.[30] Featuring viral characters such as Sammy the Butcher, Green Tony, and the Mob's leader, Mr Bradly Mr Martin, the trilogy's non-sequential 'routines' splice aspects of science fiction and crime writing into a Mob that Burroughs views to be a real 'power' behind Cold War hostilities:

> The Soviet Union and United States will eventually consist of interchangeable social parts and neither nation is morally 'right' [...]. One's ally today is an enemy tomorrow. I have postulated this power—the Nova Mob—which forces us to play musical chairs.[31]

Just as Lemaire stated that cut-ups confected a third, revelatory 'message' out of their textual 'components', so Burroughs presents his Nova mythology as fiction *and* historical exposé. Indeed, 'exposure' of the Mob's conspiracy is the stated aim of the 'Nova Police' who are introduced in *The Soft Machine*. That the Mob and Police share the Nova appellation suggests that they're in a state of symbiosis, which is precisely why the main Police agents—Bradly Martin, Inspector Lee, the District Supervisor, Agent K-9, and Uranian Willy—are eager to hasten the Mob's end. If photographic negatives can be ruined by exposing them to light, so the Police hope to destroy the Mob with a 'total exposure' plan that Uranian Willy succinctly outlines in *Nova Express*: 'Show them the rigged wheel of Life-Time-Fortune. Storm The Reality Studio' (*NE*, 59). With *Life*, *Time*, and *Fortune* magazines being, as I've mentioned, all invested in providing a domestic angle on the American space programme, the implication here is that the Nova Mob and the American mass media are part of the same virus.[32]

Little wonder, then, that one of the prime instances of the Police trying to sabotage the 'Life-Time-Fortune' wheel involves Bradly Martin creating a cut-up of a newspaper article about space travel:

WAS WEIGHTLESS—NEW YORK HERALD TRIBUNE PARIS APRIL 17, 1961—'One's arms and legs in and out through the crowd weigh nothing—grey

---

[30] William S. Burroughs, *Nova Express* (New York: Grove, 1992), 53, hereafter cited as *NE*.
[31] Burroughs's interview with Conrad Knickerbocker, 'White Junk' (1965), in *Burroughs Live*, 80. On his use of science fiction texts, see Burroughs's 1965 interview with *Science Fiction Horizons* magazine, 'The Hallucinatory Operators are Real', in *Burroughs Live*, 84–7.
[32] As Atwill argues in *Fire and Power*, 71, Henry Luce's *Life*, in particular, was a kind of 'aristocratic patron' of the US space programme in the sixties, offering exclusive contracts to astronauts and their wives for interviews.

dust of broom in old cabin—Mr. Bradly Mr. I Myself sit in the chair as i subways and basements did before that—but hung in dust and pain wind—My hand writing leaning to a boy's grey flannel pants did no change although vapor trails fading in hand does not weigh anything now—Gagarin said grey junk yesterdays trailing the earth was quite plain and past the American he could easily see the shores of continents—islands and great rivers'.

Captain Clark welcomes you aboard.

Glad to have you aboard reader, but remember there is only one captain of this subway...[33]

The quoted section (added to the 1966 edition) is supposedly from an article reporting Yuri Gagarin's successful voyage as the first man in orbit, but it's clearly not an actual quotation. Gagarin's statements on being liberated from gravity are cut up with fragments of Bradly Martin's own writing to produce a congeries of mangled images and phrases. The disorienting syntax also creates bizarre spatial conjunctions, as in 'Mr. Bradly Mr. I Myself sit in the chair as i subways and basements did before that'. The first clause of that sentence describes fairly straightforwardly Bradly's action of sitting, but the second clause takes a turn. Rather than qualifying the action of sitting with an adverb by saying, for example, 'as I *always* did before that', the 'I' falls to lower case as its agency is cut into a strange nounal compound: 'as i subways and basements did before that'. Suddenly the act of sitting floats into a nebulous network of underground spaces. The cut-up thus interferes with the usual syntactic lines of association by building alien compounds, and with the interruptive use of dashes the referentiality of phrases like 'grey dust of broom in old cabin' remains paratactically suspended. Crafting new 'outer' space for itself, the text also becomes a form of hybrid explorative vehicle (part 'subway', part spaceship)—'Glad to have you aboard, reader...'

With the introduction of the Nova Police's 'Operation Rewrite', *The Ticket that Exploded* and *Nova Express* further develop the importance of exposing the Nova conspiracy to its own negation. They also flesh out the viral nature of the Nova Mob, the '*Technical Deposition of the Virus Power*' in *Nova Express* presenting this straight from the virus's mouth:

We first took our image and put it into code [...]. This code was written at the molecular level to save space, when it was found that the image material was not dead matter, but exhibited the same life cycle as the virus. This virus released upon the world would infect the entire population and turn them into replicas [...]. (*NE*, 49)

---

[33] William S. Burroughs, *The Soft Machine* (1961; repr.; London: Flamingo, 1995), 118, hereafter cited as *SM*.

Burroughs argued in interview that 'We should distinguish the genre of science fiction in literature from the scientific fact from which one starts in a novel.'[34] and having declared the Nova Mob to be behind the Cold War, he repeatedly proffered his notion of the word/image virus as a literal depiction of contemporary linguistic control. The 'virus power manifests itself in many ways', he told Eric Mottram in 1964; 'In the construction of nuclear weapons, in practically all the existing political systems which are aimed at curtailing inner freedom.'[35] Drawing his ideas from an array of scientific works on virology and evolution, Burroughs's portrayal of the virus clearly invokes genetic DNA as a form of encoded biological message. So, in *The Ticket that Exploded*, we discover that the Mob's viral 'recordings' have rescripted the genetic make-up of its human hosts. Consisting of 'thin transparent sheets on which is written the action from birth to death',[36] the 'soft machine' of the human body has become a kind of *tabula errata* caught in what the District Supervisor calls a 'birth-death cycle' (*TE*, 10). The Nova Police's 'Operation Rewrite' is an attempt to place this cycle under 'arrest' by exposing the virus as an 'Other Half':

The realization that something as familiar to you as the movement of your intestines the sound of your breathing the beating of your heart is also alien and hostile does make one a bit insecure at first. Remember that you can separate yourself from the 'Other Half' from the word. The word is spliced in with the sound of your intestines and start splicing them in yourself. Splice in your body sounds with the body sounds of your best friend and see how familiar he gets. Splice your body sounds in with air hammers. Blast jolt vibrate the 'Other Half' right out into the street. (*TE*, 50)

Burroughs had in fact already begun to experiment with audio tape recordings like this with his friend Ian Somerville, to whom *The Ticket that Exploded* is dedicated.[37] We've already seen how, for Burroughs and Gysin, cut-ups and fold-ins can voice an interstitial 'third mind'; here we're faced with a kind of 'third body' spliced together from 'body sounds'. As we're told in the final section of *The Ticket that Exploded*, the techniques of 'Operation Rewrite' also involve possibilities for an alternative body politic: 'the physiological liberation achieved as word lines of association are cut will make you more efficient in reaching your

---

[34] Burroughs's interview with Nina Zivancevic, 'Life in Space' (1981), in *Burroughs Live*, 525.
[35] Burroughs's interview with Eric Mottram, 'Rencontre Avec William Burroughs', in Allen Hibberd (ed.), *Conversations with William S. Burroughs* (Jackson, MS: University Press of Mississippi, 1999), 12.
[36] William S. Burroughs, *The Ticket that Exploded*, 1966 rev. edn (New York: Grove, 1967), 160, hereafter cited as *TE*.
[37] See Barry Miles, *William Burroughs: El Hombre Invisible* (1992; London: Virgin, 2002), Ch. 9. Also Morgan, *Literary Outlaw*, Ch. 17.

objectives' (*TE*, 208); 'everybody splice himself in with everybody else yes boys that's me there by the cement mixer' (*TE*, 212). By the end of the novel, though, there is no defeat of the Nova Mob at what level there is of story line. *The Ticket that Exploded* follows Bradly Martin's adventures with fellow astronaut Lykin on the Venusian-run planet Minraud, but it closes with the exhortations to experiment with audio recordings.

'Operation Rewrite' is thus left to *Nova Express*, with Inspector Lee ordering 'total resistance [...] against the Nova Conspiracy and all those engaged in it' (*NE*, 7). This develops over the novel's eight chapters, with excursions into Minraud and the Nova conspiracy more generally. Again, though, the final denouement is not a revolutionary coup; rather, the novel ends with a legal case in which The Heavy Metal Kid takes the Nova Mob to 'The Biologic Courts'. What the Kid seeks to challenge is the right of any organism to occupy a host organism on the grounds of biological necessity. The verdict of the case is left 'suspended', but the point of the episode is not to wrap up plot so much as outline new powers for cut-ups. All counsellors in the Biologic Courts 'must be writers', we're told, 'since the function of a counsellor is to *create* facts that will tend to open biological potentials for his client' (*NE*, 137, Burroughs's emphasis). Models of literary and legal representation are altered alike, then; rather than build a case of established evidence, the writer-counsellor fabricates new facts and 'biological potentials', thereby breaking the 'body-prison contradictions of biologic law' (*NE*, 137). The precise methodology is revealed in a description of legal training: 'One of the great early counsellors was Franz Kafka and his briefs are still standard—The student first writes his own brief then folds his pages down the middle and lays it on pages of Kafka relevant to the case in hand' (*NE*, 137–8). In terms of both syntax and legal judgement, the 'sentence' that proceeds from such a fold-in clearly cannot adhere to precedents. Instead, both syntax and judgment derive from the chance procedure of the fold-in technique. In this sense, the cut-up counsellor is advocating a methodology similar to the one Jean-François Lyotard describes: 'The [postmodern] artist and the writer [...] are working without rules in order to formulate the rules of what *will have been done*.'[38] For Burroughs, such investments in the future-anterior don't culminate in abstraction. Closing with its own critique of judgment, *Nova Express* emphasizes that it's presenting a case for new human potentials. Like the 'third body' of the audio experiments, the 'biological potentials' that the writer-counsellor produces are literally conceived by

---

[38] Jean-François Lyotard, *The Postmodern Condition: A Report on Knowledge*, trans. Geoffrey Bennington and Brian Massumi (Manchester: Manchester University Press, 1984), 81.

Burroughs as being *latent living organisms*. Cut-up characters and interzones are forces waiting to become active, and as 'externalized section[s] of the human nervous system' (*TE*, 163) the spliced recordings are thus presented as new 'virus forms' (*TE*, 164). In using cut-ups and fold-ins to fashion a textual 'outer space', Burroughs thus begins to evolve a Nova potentialism with the intention of drawing biological and textual potentials into novel compounds.

FROM WATERSHED TO WATERGATE

A new 'outer space', a new form of 'space-time travel', and new alien beings—all from cut-ups and fold-ins. Why, then, does Burroughs's potentialism turn to more straightforward forms of syntax and narration after the Nova trilogy? In the opinion of some critics it's because his experiments reached an impasse.[39] Even Ginsberg voiced reservations about the hermeticism of the Nova novels, asking Burroughs 'how can you expect anybody to read through all this if you don't make big categorical distinctions? It's like reading a series of prose poems that have no end.'[40] In his defence, Burroughs argued that people were 'demanding less and less in the way of plot and structure', and that the trilogy was as 'accessible as any book you pick up at the airport'.[41] But this belies the fact that reviews of the Nova books had been mixed, sales had been low, and his US publishers, Grove Press, were concerned about the experimental direction he had taken.[42] Elsewhere Burroughs admits that he reached a saturation point with cut-ups: 'by 1967 [...] I had such an overrun on tape-recorders, cameras and scrapbooks that I couldn't look at them, and started writing straight narrative and essays'.[43] Having become absorbed with different cut-up applications using film, photomontage, and tape-recordings, by 1966 his actual literary output had almost come to a standstill. It wasn't until seven years after publishing *Nova Express* that a set of the 'straight' narratives he began writing in 1967 were published as his next major novel, *The Wild Boys* (1971)—some of the 'straight' essays and some interviews were published the previous year as *The Job*. In fact, *The Job*'s essays weren't so straight; they may not have been cut-ups themselves, but they were very

---

[39] See, for example, Murphy, *Wising Up the Marks*, 140; and Harris, *William Burroughs and the Secret of Fascination*, 38.
[40] Burroughs and Ginsberg, 'Spiritual Conspiracies', 129.
[41] Ibid.
[42] See Morgan, *Literary Outlaw*, 422–5.
[43] Quoted in Oliver Harris, 'Cut-Up Closure: The Return to Narrative' in Skerl and Lydenberg (eds), *William S. Burroughs at the Front*, 256.

much concerned with advocating cut-ups as means of fomenting political resistance. It was another attempt by Burroughs at making a timely intervention.

William H. Chafe has described 1968 as a 'watershed' in US political history, and Burroughs gained first-hand experience of what was at stake when he reported on the August 1968 Democrats' Convention in Chicago for *Esquire* magazine.[44] Over four days, tensions rose between the police and the assortment of New Left, Hippie, Yippie, Black Panther, and anti-Vietnam war demonstrators who gathered outside the convention building. On 28 August, the counter-culture demonstrators called a rally which saw Burroughs marching alongside Ginsberg and Jean Genet. (I discuss these demonstrations and counter-cultural protests in more detail in Chapter 1.) Disappointingly for Burroughs, though, the march ended peacefully and the destruction of the 'police machine' remained something to call for in *The Job*:

> the underground is agreed on basic objectives [...]. We intend to march on police everywhere. We intend to destroy the police machine and all its records. We intend to destroy the house organ of the world police that goes under the name of conservative press. We intend to destroy all dogmatic verbal systems.[45]

Elsewhere in *The Job* Burroughs upholds Black Power and Hippie communities as presenting viable alternatives to nationalized power. A host of other communities could be set up, he argues, that 'would become international and break down national borders'.[46] By 1975, though, Burroughs himself stated in an interview that 'The political hopes that many of us held proved to be unfounded. We have to face the fact that a leftist revolution is out of the question in this country.'[47] Nevertheless, in the same interview he also cites two events as having catalysed 'a terrific cultural revolution': 'the breakup of censorship and the phenomenon of Watergate'.[48] For the former, Burroughs could claim a fair share of responsibility. In 1965 a Boston trial ruled *Naked Lunch* to be obscene, despite statements from Ginsberg and Norman Mailer attesting to its social value. The case went to appeal at the Massachusetts Supreme Court, which delayed its ruling pending a review of obscenity law by the US

---

[44] William H. Chafe, *The Unfinished Journey: America Since World War II* (Oxford: Oxford University Press, 1991), 378. Chafe also discusses the importance of the Democrats' Convention, 374–5. On Burroughs's coverage of it, see Morgan, *Literary Outlaw*, 444–8.
[45] Burroughs's interview with Daniel Odier, 'Prisoners of the Earth Come Out', in Burroughs and Daniel Odier, *The Job*, (rev. edn; London: Calder, 1984), 83.
[46] Ibid. 99.
[47] Burroughs's interview with Angelo Lewis, 'The White Threat', in *Burroughs Live*, 324.
[48] Ibid.

Supreme Court. When the latter declared that a book could be ruled obscene only if it were deemed 'utterly without redeeming social value', the Massachusetts Supreme Court overturned the obscenity ruling on Burroughs's novel. Like the work of the writer-counsellor in *Nova Express*, then, *Naked Lunch* paved the way for new legal and literary judgments, for as Ted Morgan points out, the ruling on the novel effectively 'marked the end of literary censorship in the United States'.[49]

As for Watergate, Burroughs's 1975 opinion was that history would enshrine Nixon as 'one of the great folk heroes of America' because he 'destroyed the whole diseased concept of the revered image of the Presidency'.[50] Prior to this back-handed compliment, Burroughs had struck a more critical tone. The 'real scandal of Watergate', he declared, 'is the use of recordings'.[51] Having tried to broadcast the benefits of doing cut-ups of audio-recordings, it was clearly galling for Burroughs to see tape-recordings having been used for state surveillance. So, in response, he advocated forms of counter-surveillance that anyone could produce; a taped 'virus' being his favoured example:

On tape recorder one we will record speeches and conversations, carefully editing in stammers, mis-pronunciations, inept phrases—the worst number one we can assemble. Now, on tape recorder two we will make a love tape by bugging his bedroom. We can potentiate this tape by splicing it with a sexual object that is inadmissable or unacceptable or both, say, the Senator's teenage daughter. On tape three we will record hateful, disapproving voices. We'll splice the three recordings in together at very short intervals and play them back to the Senator and his constituents [...]. Once the association lines are established, they are activated every time the Senator's speech centers are activated.[52]

Burroughs elsewhere reported his own successes with such experiments, claiming to have provoked both a Scientology office and a rude café owner to move premises after he'd played back to them site recordings that he'd taken from around their buildings.[53] But the eccentricity of these audio experiments did little to endear his cause to people. In short, do-it-yourself cut-up surveillance didn't catch on.

Over-production of cut-ups wasn't Burroughs's only reason for turning away from them after 1967. He was also concerned about being regarded

---

[49] Morgan, *Literary Outlaw*, 347.
[50] Burroughs and Lewis, 'The White Threat', 324.
[51] William S. Burroughs, 'Playback from Eden to Watergate' (1973), in Burroughs and Odier, *The Job*, 17.
[52] Ibid. 15.
[53] See Miles, *William Burroughs*, 182.

as 'purely experimental', as he explained in a 1978 interview: 'If your objective is to have people read your books, then there has to be at least a line of narrative they can follow. Take the case of Joyce who spent 20 or 30 years writing *Finnegans Wake*, a book no one can really read. I can't let that happen.'[54] It wasn't the case that Burroughs simply decided to stop experimenting—in subsequent years he continued to publish a range of cut-ups and fold-ins in little magazines—but the Nova trilogy showed him that honing a cutting-edge narrative technique could blunt the point of his new space-age mythology if people didn't read it. Consequently, his later novels seek to potentiate his experiments in space-time travel, interzones, and viral characters by underpinning them with more regular forms of syntax and narrative consistency. What didn't change was Burroughs's fascination with space, as is clear from a 1974 interview: 'I feel that I am still working along the line of a myth for the Space Age and that all my books are essentially one book.'[55] But the space age had itself been mutating, having reached a climax with the lunar landing in July 1969, and in his foreword to *The Job* Burroughs was already decrying the directions that the space programmes were taking. What he took particular umbrage at is the sort of view he quotes Thomas Paine to be voicing about a 1968 NASA flight: 'This flight was a triumph of the squares of this world who aren't Hippies and work with slide rules and aren't ashamed to say a prayer now and then.'[56] 'Is this the great adventure of space?' Burroughs rejoined;

Are these men going to take the step into regions literally unthinkable in verbal terms? To travel in space you must leave the old verbal garbage behind: God talk, country talk, mother talk, love talk, [political] party talk [. . .]. Anyone who prays in space is not there.

The last frontier is being closed to youth. However there are many roads to space. Techniques exist for achieving such freedom.[57]

Before examining how Burroughs in his second trilogy turns his own 'Techniques' into a more developed and oppositional potentialism, we need to consider some of the trajectories being taken by the US and Soviet space programmes around this time.

---

[54] Burroughs's interview with Gérard-Georges Lemaire, 'Terrorism, Utopia and Fiction', in *Burroughs Live*, 401.
[55] Burroughs and Mikriamos, 'The Last European Interview', 279.
[56] Burroughs, 'Navigare necesse es. Vivare no es necesse', in Burroughs and Odier, *The Job*, 21.
[57] Ibid.

SPACE EXPLORATION IN THE 1970s

With US and Soviet satellites increasingly occupying orbital space in the sixties, the fact that it was still uncharted territory in international law was clearly a problem. So, in 1967, the United Nations (UN) established some ground rules with its Outer Space Treaty. Signed by sixty-two nations, the signatories agreed that outer space (including the planets) was international territory, thereby bestowing on it the same legal status as Antarctica.[58] Crucially, the treaty also banned weapons in space and on all celestial bodies. As Walter McDougall points out, though, when the treaty was ratified, the USA stipulated that only 'weapons of mass destruction' were banned from the earth's orbit.[59] The peaceful intentions behind the treaty thus gave way to Cold War tensions, as McDougall argues: 'the treaty effectively demilitarized the moon but specifically *sanctioned* the militarization of orbital space'.[60] And because the treaty didn't make allowance for governments to inspect foreign orbital space vehicles, there was no real way of verifying the vehicles' non-military status. Moreover, the distinction between offensive and defensive was already being undermined by satellites, indispensable as they were for developing an effective nuclear 'first-strike'. Spurred on by the Vietnam War, the USA in 1967 launched a major 'Defense Satellite Communication System' (DCSC) programme, and by the time of Jimmy Carter's presidency in the late seventies it could boast a fully fledged Global Positioning System (GPS) in its network of 'Navstar' satellites that could help pinpoint targets for nuclear strikes.[61] The more that science and military technology explored new frontiers in outer space, the more space on Earth became plotted by interweaving Cold War networks. Thus, the entanglement of space race and Cold War tensions evident from the late fifties through to the sixties proceeded unabated for the next two decades.

Earlier I argued that the sixties space programmes were instrumental in consolidating postmodern networks. The seventies, then, saw a tightening of this postmodernization, for as Atwill has argued, the escalation of US satellite programmes was 'the most visible evidence of an emerging American postmodern culture':[62]

---

[58] See Loring Wirbel, *Star Wars: US Tools of Space Supremacy* (London: Pluto, 2004), 4–6, 23–4, and McDougall, *The Heavens and the Earth*, 413, 415–18.
[59] McDougall, *The Heavens and the Earth*, 418.
[60] Ibid.
[61] Wirbel, *Star Wars*, 34, 46.
[62] Atwill, *Fire and Power*, 22.

It required very real grid space across the world to link up its communication network—conjuring up the most bizarre disjunctive architecture—concrete block tracking stations with huge parabolic dish antennae and barbed-wire perimeters carved out of the poverty of some remote jungle.[63]

So whereas Brion Gysin had argued that through cut-ups he and Burroughs would rewrite the usual 'grid' of space to create a 'new cellular framework', by the seventies US satellites networks were establishing their own form of geographical cut-ups to service the organization of 'real grid space'. For Burroughs the need for a counter space programme was thus all the more clear. It wasn't that he was against government-funded space projects per se; even at the start of the eighties he was bemoaning that 'they're cutting back on space programs everywhere'.[64] But as far as he was concerned the programmes were simply moving in the wrong directions, and he became increasingly determined to build his own alternatives.

The first lunar landing and its cultural impact were another watershed for Burroughs. 'For one priceless moment in the whole history of man, all the people of this earth are truly one'[65]—so Nixon indirectly paid tribute to the tightening global network involved in *Apollo II*'s success. In response, prominent commentators like Lewis Mumford chose to focus on the problems they saw to be resulting from space exploration. Echoing Arendt's concern over the space programmes' effects on the human condition, Mumford argued in *The Myth of the Machine* (1970) that investment in interplanetary travel is symptomatic of a global 'megamachine' of technological dehumanization:

just as the static physical structures supported the worshipper's belief in the validity of the Pharaoh's claims to divinity and immortality, so the new dynamic forms of the pyramid-complex—the skyscrapers, the atomic reactors, the nuclear weapons, the superhighways, the space rockets, the underground control centers, the collective nuclear shelters (tombs)—seem equally to validate and exalt the new religion.[66]

For Mumford this 'new religion' is powered by the megamachine's 'myth'—an ideology of automation. And in his opinion, nothing testifies more to the hold of this myth on people's minds than the 'acceptance' of space exploration as the 'laudable "next step" in man's de-natured

---

[63] Ibid.
[64] Burroughs addressing the Institute of Ecotechnics (1980), transcribed as 'Viral Theory', in *Burroughs Live*, 466.
[65] Nixon quoted in Chafe, *The Unfinished Journey*, 387.
[66] Lewis Mumford, *The Myth of the Machine: The Pentagon of Power* (London: Secker and Warburg, 1971), 300.

command of nature'.[67] Novelist Norman Mailer expressed similar concerns about space technocracy in his New Journalist account of it, *Of a Fire on the Moon* (1970). Based on three articles he wrote for *Life* magazine on the lunar landing, Mailer's book also echoes Arendt's anxieties about the space race when his narrator 'Aquarius' states that 'The heart of astronaut talk, like the heart of bureaucratic talk, was a jargon that could easily be converted to computer programming.'[68] In the text's final section, Aquarius fantasizes about space exploration leading the way to a new poetics: 'yes, we might have to go into space until the mystery of new discovery would force us to regard the world once again as poets'.[69] But the degree to which the space programmes entailed 'mystery' and 'new discovery' was highly questionable, as Tom Wolfe was at pains to show in his New Journalist study, *The Right Stuff* (1979). Wolfe's text expands on a series of articles he wrote for *Rolling Stone* magazine in 1973 that ponder the difference between the pioneer heroism of America's jet pilots in the fifties and the automatism of astronauts in the sixties. The shift is evident as early as Alan Shepard's 1961 orbital flight, Wolfe argues, for it had been rehearsed so many times that Shepard could only experience the flight *as* a simulation: 'The idea was to decondition the beast completely, so that there would not be a single novel sensation of the day itself.'[70] For Wolfe, Shepard's flight thus is instrumental in 'introduc[ing] the era of pre-created experience'.[71]

Such negative views of space exploration were, however, decidedly in the minority in the press and media. Three days after *Apollo II*'s lunar success, the rocket scientist Werner von Braun wrote in the *New York Times* that the moon landing was 'equal in importance to that moment in evolution when aquatic life came crawling up on land'.[72] The popular scientist Carl Sagan similarly opined in *The Cosmic Connection* (1973) that the possibilities of space exploration meant that 'There is no reason to think that the evolutionary process has stopped.'[73] Alluding to the analogy Harold Urey had drawn between the space programme and pyramid building, Sagan offers a different parallel:

---

[67] Mumford, *The Myth of the Machine*, 307. For an account of other literary engagements with the US space programmes, see Ronald Weber, *Seeing Earth: Literary Responses to Space Exploration* (Athens, OH: Ohio University Press, 1985).
[68] Norman Mailer, *Of a Fire on the Moon* (Boston: Little, Brown, 1970), 84.
[69] Ibid. 141.
[70] Tom Wolfe, *The Right Stuff* (London: Picador, 1990), 232.
[71] Ibid. 256.
[72] *New York Times* (20 July 1969), sec. 4, p. 12.
[73] Carl Sagan, *The Cosmic Connection: An Extraterrestrial Perspective* (London: Hodder, 1975), 5.

the pyramids are monumental and, we today believe, futile efforts to ensure the survival after death of one man, the Pharaoh. Perhaps a better analogy is with the ziggurats, the terraced towers of the Sumerians and Babylonians—the places where the gods came down to earth and the population as a whole transcended everyday life. There is no doubt a little of the pyramid in the great rocket boosters; but I think their ultimate significance is likely to be as contemporary ziggurats.[74]

As we'll see, there is a lot of the pyramids in Burroughs's later space writing too—largely because of his growing obsession with turning celestial travel into a quest for immortality. Unlike Sagan, Burroughs affirms the analogy with Egyptian beliefs, though in returning to them he also seeks to perform another 'Operation Rewrite'. So when Mumford declares the modern astronaut to be 'a kind of faceless ambulatory mummy',[75] Burroughs would have agreed, seeing this as all the more reason to evolve new forms of space travel and human astral beings:

Astronauts are just going up in aqualungs, which I think is the wrong way. In one sense, it's an accomplishment, but it's not the way to go. There have to be certain biologic changes, permutations. So one has to look at the organism, to consider how it can be altered. For one thing, it's too heavy. We have a model of a much lighter body that's almost weightless, the dream body. That would be the place to start.[76]

This 1981 statement shows the extent to which Burroughs was still intent on pursuing real alternatives to astronautical endeavours. It might appear that his space-age mythology has gone further into the realms of science fiction, but once again it's important, as Burroughs says, to distinguish 'science fiction' from 'scientific fact', for both the biological mutations and the astral travelling he speaks of had reportedly been pursued by scientists working on the US and Soviet space programmes.

For example, one popular science book that Burroughs cites as being of interest to him is David M. Rorvik's *As Man Becomes Machine* (1973), in which Rorvik discusses the benefits that biological modification, genetic grafting, and cyborg development could have for extraterrestrial journeys. Instead of travelling in a space ship, man could actually become one, argues Rorvik—the photosynthetic cyborg proposed by former NASA scientist Michael Del Luca being just one possible example. Able to convert energy out of sunlight for itself, the photosynthetic cyborg 'will not need any food at all', Rorvik writes, 'and will be free to spend his entire

---

[74] Ibid. 67.
[75] Mumford, *The Myth of the Machine*, note to illustrations 14–15 [no page no.].
[76] Burroughs's interview with Arthur Shingles, 'Mutation, Utopia and Magic' (1981), in *Burroughs Live*, 518.

life exploring the depths of the ocean or the far reaches of space'.[77] J. B. S. Haldane's suggestion of breeding astronauts without legs (gravity making the limbs obsolete) is another possibility Rorvik countenances—he even cites scientists' experiments with 'special viruses' that could provide the necessary genetic alterations. Such experiments would doubtless have fascinated Burroughs, even though they didn't bear on the astral body that he was becoming so enthused about. Other books in which Burroughs expresses interest do examine astral bodies, though, including Dion Fortune's *Psychic Self-Defence* (1930), Sheila Ostrander's and Lynn Schroeder's *Psychic Discoveries behind the Iron Curtain* (1971), and Robert Monroe's *Journeys out of the Body* (1972).[78] Ostrander's and Schroeder's text is particularly fascinating, being compiled from interviews with Communist scientists undertaking experiments in psychic research. Two chapters are dedicated to astral body experiments carried out 'near Soviet space centers in far-off Kazakhstan'. Basically, the astral body is an 'energy body' that is supplementary to the physical body, write Ostrander and Schroeder: 'It acts as a unit [...] and as a unit the energy body gives off its own electromagnetic fields and is the basis of biological fields.'[79] With the Soviet scientists using high-frequency 'Kirlian' photography (first developed in 1939) to document energy bodies, the book features a selection of such photographs showing energy bodies to be intact after the physical body has been damaged. 'The implications are awesome', declare Ostrander and Schroeder, who go on to claim that the Communist scientists were also working to determine whether the astral travelling that Indian yogis claim to practise is in fact undertaken by the energy body.[80]

Remarkably, then, the sort of alternative space programme Burroughs invokes in 1981 was seemingly rooted in real scientific considerations. But how could astral travelling, astral bodies, and evolutionary mutation be turned into a *literary* space programme? How could those things be linked to the kinds of textual interzones, viruses, and space travel featured in the Nova novels? These are matters that Burroughs seeks to resolve in his Cities of the Red Night trilogy.

---

[77] David M. Rorvik, *As Man Becomes Machine: Evolution of the Cyborg* (London: Sphere, 1979), 129.
[78] See Dion Fortune, *Psychic Self-Defence: A Study in Occult Pathology and Criminality* (London: Aquarian, 1952), Ch. 4; Robert A. Monroe, *Journeys Out of the Body* (London: Corgi, 1974), Ch. 13; and Sheila Ostrander and Lynn Schroeder, *Psychic Discoveries behind the Iron Curtain* (London: Souvenir, 1997), Chs 17 and 18.
[79] Ostrander and Schroeder, *Psychic Discoveries behind the Iron Curtain*, 177.
[80] Ibid. 177, 180.

THE CITIES OF THE RED NIGHT TRILOGY

The second trilogy consists of *Cities of the Red Night* (1981), *The Place of Dead Roads* (1983), and *The Western Lands* (1987), and it stands as Burroughs's last major literary endeavour, his final years being taken up primarily with painting. Having commenced work on *Cities* in 1975, his sustained engagement with the space race ironically culminates in the demise of manned space flights, the US investment in them suffering a serious blow with the 1986 *Challenger* shuttle disaster. Commitment to manned space travel was already being curtailed by Nixon at the start of the 1970s, though. With the USA having won the race to the Moon, subsequent public interest in interplanetary ventures rapidly waned. But Burroughs was never daunted by the prospect of proceeding alone, and Nixon's initial space cutbacks coincided with Burroughs's publication of *The Wild Boys*, in which a new approach to his space mythology is first evident. As several critics have noted, the novel is a major turning point for the writer.[81] Instead of having repeated and extended passages of cut-ups that deliberately scramble character and plot, the cut-ups in *The Wild Boys* are less frequent and more readily identifiable as expressing a particular character's state of mind. The cut-ups' disorientations are also diverted from basic syntax and applied to larger narrative blocks, even though the novel as a whole still consists of sequentially dislocated 'routines'. Thematically there is also a shift; instead of the Nova Police we're presented with the 'Wild Boys', a nomadic group of young homosexual partisans. Clearly, Burroughs was still hoping for a counter-cultural revolution, for the combativeness towards the 'police machine' that he stated in *The Job*—'We will destroy the police machine everywhere'—is also voiced verbatim by the wild boys in the novel.[82] If 'what might have been' no longer seemed possible historically, this didn't prevent Burroughs from filling his novelistic outer spaces with worlds of alternative possibility.

Cities is a strange textual beast whose genetic strands are spliced and mutated increasingly as the narrative proceeds. Divided into three 'books' like a nineteenth-century novel, there are three main narrative strands throughout, one about eighteenth-century pirates, one about Clem Snide, a private detective, and one involving six mythical cities of the Red Night in the Gobi desert: Tamaghis, Ba'dan, Yass-Waddah, Waghdas, Naufana,

---

[81] See, for example, Skerl, *William S. Burroughs*, 77–80, and Murphy, *Wising up the Marks*, Ch. 5.
[82] William S. Burroughs, *The Wild Boys: A Book of the Dead* (New York: Grove, 1971), 140.

and Ghadis. Burroughs introduces the pirate plot first with his foreword, 'Fore!', in which he expounds the importance of pirate communities such as the 'Libertatia' that 'Captain Mission' founded off the Madagascar Coast in the early eighteenth century. Quoting Don C. Seitz's *Under the Black Flag* (1971) as authoritative evidence, the importance of Mission's multi-racial community for Burroughs is that it eschewed any form of sovereign power and abided by its own 'Articles' of anarchic liberalism. 'Imagine such a movement on a world-wide scale', he writes:

I cite this example of retroactive Utopia since it could actually have happened in terms of the techniques and human resources available at the time. Had Captain Mission lived long enough to set an example for others to follow, mankind might have stepped free from the deadly impasse of insoluble problems in which we now find ourselves.[83]

What neither Seitz nor Burroughs mentions is that this utopia really was a 'no-place'; Captain Mission is in fact the 'Captain Misson' whose only recorded existence is in Daniel Defoe's quasi-historical work, *A General History of the Pyrates* (1728).[84] But historical veracity is decidedly not the point, for Burroughs is more concerned with producing different historical potentials. Having witnessed the demise of US counter-culture groups, by 1978 he was still hoping he could inspire other alternative communities.[85] In *Cities* then, he's seeking to pose counter-historical possibilities for the future. '[W]hat happened with Mission was another possibility', he stated in interview; 'if it had spread it could have been a whole different ball game for people...'.[86] For Burroughs, building these narratives of outlaw communes also means exploring narrative as an anarchic 'outlaw' space in its own right. So, by the end of the prefatory 'Invocation' we're left with words from the twelfth-century Ishmaelite assassin, Hassan i Sabbah: 'NOTHING IS TRUE. EVERYTHING IS PERMITTED' (*CRN*, 13).[87] And as the novel progresses it becomes clear that the need

---

[83] William S. Burroughs, *Cities of the Red Night* (London: Picador, 1981), 11, hereafter cited as *CRN*.

[84] See David Mitchell, *Pirates* (London: Thames and Hudson, 1976), 190–1, and Marcus Rediker, 'Hydrarchy and Libertalia: The Utopian Dimensions of Atlantic Piracy in the Early Eighteenth Century', in David J. Starkey, E. S. van Eyck van Heslinga, and J. A. de Moor (eds), *Pirates and Privateers: New Perspectives on the War on Trade in the Eighteenth and Nineteenth Centuries* (Exeter: University of Exeter Press, 1997), 31, 34.

[85] See, for example Burroughs's discussion with Richard Goldstein at 'The Nova Convention' (1978), transcribed as 'The Nova Convention', in *Burroughs Live*, 436.

[86] Burroughs's interview with Larry McCaffery and Jim McMenamin, 'An Interview with William Burroughs' (1987), in *Burroughs Live*, 178.

[87] For an extensive discussion of Hassan i Sabbah, resistance, and the Nova trilogy, see Murphy, *Wising Up the Marks*, Ch. 4.

to suspend disbelief is very much linked to the idea of counter-history as its own outer space.

Book One of the novel opens with the cities of the Red Night narrative strand and introduces the mysterious 'B-23 virus' that originated in them. Linked somehow to nuclear fallout, as the character Dr Pierson explains, B-23 caused widespread 'biological mutation' in the cities' inhabitants and became endemic by causing 'sexual frenzies that facilitated its communication' (*CRN*, 32). The story thus echoes Brion Gysin's 'legend' of the white race that Burroughs first presented in *Exterminator!* (1966):

According to [Gysin's] ancient legend, the white race results from a nuclear explosion in what is now the Gobi desert some 30,000 years ago. The only survivors were slaves marginal to the area who had no knowledge of science or techniques. They became albinos as a result of radiation and scattered in different directions.[88]

In *Exterminator!* the radioactive virus remains dormant, its 'metal sickness' only recurring again with the bombing of Hiroshima. In *Cities*, though, there is debate between Dr Pierson and Dr Peterson as to whether the virus was produced by radiation or potentiated by it after lying dormant in human hosts. As Dr Peterson explains: 'The whole quality of human consciousness, as expressed in male and female, is basically a virus mechanism. I suggest that this virus, known as the "other half", turned malignant as a result of the radiation' (*CRN*, 36). B-23 is thus presented as fallout from an ancient nuclear catastrophe, and like the Nova Mob it has a real historical valency for Burroughs: 'My view is that [nuclear war] has happened a number of times before. Just when the possibility of space exploration is there, it's blocked, often by a nuclear disaster.'[89] By rewriting Gysin's Gobi desert myth in *Cities*, he intended to clear a launching pad for his own revamped potentialism.

In Book Two we're given more detail about the consequences of the B-23 virus in a 'pamphlet'. The Red Night virus is revealed to have spread after a radioactive 'meteor or blackhole' hit the area near Tamaghis, but prior to this the cities' dwellers were already divided into two types of people: Transmigrants and Receptacles. Together they maintained a controlled system of codependent reincarnation—evidence that Dr Peterson's argument is correct in saying that the 'other half' virus was a 'human virus' that mutated. Two factors made this economy unstable, though, we're told. First, the development of 'artificial insemin-

---

[88] William S. Burroughs, *Exterminator!* (London: Calder, 1984), 23.
[89] Burroughs's interview with Arthur Shingles, 'Mutation, Utopia, and Magic' (1981), in *Burroughs Live*, 518.

ation' meant that the established economy of 'one death and one rebirth' was disrupted, as 'now hundreds of women could be impregnated from a single sperm collection' (*CRN*, 142). Second, the effects of the Red Night virus caused many biological mutations in the people and their procreative practices. So while the Council of Transmigrants in Waghdas had initially 'set out to produce a race of supermen for the exploration of space', after the virus took hold 'They produced instead races of ravening idiot vampires' (*CRN*, 144).

The task of rewriting the historical and biological script of B-23 falls to Clem Snide. The detective story opens in the eighth 'routine' of Book One, in which we find Snide employed to find Mr and Mrs Green's missing son, Jerry. It isn't necessary to go into all the subsequent twists of plot here; suffice to say that by the end of Book One, Snide has discovered that Jerry was suffering from a mysterious virus, and he is informed by the 'Iguana Twins' that both Jerry and another missing boy, John Everson, were being used for 'identity transfer'—Everson's being successful. The detective plot thus mutates into the Cities of the Red Night narrative at this point, for what lies behind Jerry's murder is the whole history of the B-23 virus, as the Iguana Twins reveal. Providing Snide with an eponymous 'Cities of the Red Night' pamphlet, a fragmented 'copy' of the 'original', the Twins employ Snide to recover the original, explaining to him that 'The only thing not prerecorded in a prerecorded universe are the prerecordings themselves. The copies can repeat themselves word for word. *A virus is a copy.* You can pretty it up, scramble it—it will reassemble in the same form' (*CRN*, 151, Burroughs's emphasis). Obviously, though, such an original could itself only exist as a record—a textual 'prerecording' not being something that could ever materialize. Wise to this, Snide proceeds to *forge* his own prerecording 'originals'. The effectiveness of his 'rewrites' lies not in scrambling found texts through cut-ups, then, but in fabricating a record that undermines the very difference between original and copy, history and fiction, reality and possibility.

This ontological blurring implicit in Snide's forgeries is also a new kind of potentialist interzone for Burroughs. The Nova trilogy pushed the interzones of *Naked Lunch* in the direction of cut-ups and fold-ins that voiced new expressions as forms of 'third mind' out of the spliced textual composites. Yet, as I've argued, such scramblings also prevented Burroughs's textual 'outer space' from forming choate narrative 'worlds'. We could say, then, that in the Nova trilogy he founds a literary Big Bang out of his anti-narrative techniques, and it's with the Cities of the Red Night trilogy that he begins to form more distinct worlds. In *Cities* the interzone *is* the ontological blurring of narrative frames, whereby history and fiction are forged into distinct hybrids as counter-worlds of possibility. And the extent to which this also entails establishing the novel as an ontological 'outer space' becomes clear in the pirate narrative.

One of *Cities*' dedicatees is Steven Lowe, who helped research the history of piracy for the novel, and it is clear from the opening statements on Captain Mission that Burroughs was indebted to Lowe's research. Like the cut-ups and fold-ins plundering new potentials from found materials, Burroughs's pirate(d) storyline charts new waters in terms of creative plagiarizing—he also acknowledges that the Snide narrative is written in the style of Graham Greene.[90] And while Captain Mission doesn't feature in the main body of the text, Burroughs's pirate leaders Captain Nordenholz and Captain Strobe are intent on founding similarly libertarian colonies. The fact that they operate outside sovereign territory in international waters is one way in which they can be linked to interplanetary exploration—the Outer Space Treaty (1967) having established space in general as international territory—and this marriage of outlaw space and outer space is consummated in Book Three of *Cities*.[91] Up to this point the pirate plot has mostly been maintained around 1702, although occasionally characters from the other two narrative strands are also grafted in. But things take a turn in Snide's narrative when he meets 'Blum & Krup', who inform him that they are the money behind the Iguana Twins, and thus his real employers. Confiscating Snide's 'originals', they then take him to a 'launching pad' for 'a space capsule that will also be a communications satellite' (*CRN*, 181). Once Snide is aboard the craft, the situation is explained to him by Jimmy Lee; the spaceship belongs to Krup, who is an 'intergalactically known space-swindler', also known as 'Opium Jones'. It is, we are told, 'a kook project with simulated space conditions and the old C.O. can't adjust. So they have called in Krup van Nordenholz, a nazi war criminal [...] but a space expert' (*CRN*, 188). Things are further complicated by Jimmy telling Snide who else is on board:

'All the boys from your scripts: Audrey, Jerry, all the Jims and Johns and Alis and Kikis and Strobe, Kelley, and Dahlfar. One foot in a navy mess and the other on some kooky spaceship. You see there is a pretense this is just a naval station and you never know which is the pretense: spaceship or navy. One minute you are getting popped in Tamaghis, the next you're [...] swabbing the deck.' (*CRN*, 186)

---

[90] Burroughs's interview with Michael White, 'Astral Evolution' (1981), in *Burroughs Live*, 490.
[91] On the 1967 Outer Space Treaty, see McDougall, *The Heavens and the Earth*, 413, 415–18.

Despite the passage's bizarre quality, it contains a number of pointed historical allusions. The confusing status of Krup's craft has a parallel in the system of Navstar/GPS that was developed by the late-1970s. Just as the USA had built this system for its navy to introduce orbital surveillance of international waters, so we find Burroughs figuring a confusing circuitry of 'spaceship' and 'navy'. The project's conjunction of space travel and 'simulated space conditions' thus echoes the simulated flight rehearsals for US astronauts noted by Wolfe in *The Right Stuff*. More sinisterly, the mutated Krup von Nordenholz bears a skewed resemblance to Werner von Braun, the scientist who had helped develop Germany's V-2 rockets in World War II before agreeing to work on the development of ICBMs for America.[92] Whether Krup's spacecraft is an offensive or defensive vehicle is thus questionable, just as the Navstar/GPS system was later dubbed a form of 'Navwar'. With all these resonances, the passage can be seen as a pointed historical critique satirizing the kind of 'bizarre disjunctive architecture' that Atwill argues arose from the communications networks that the space programmes were developing. Even the confusion over whether Krup is a commercial swindler or military commander has satirical overtones of the growing *mélange* of private and governmental finances invested in satellite networks from the start of the 1980s.[93] In forming his own pirate version of the space age, then, Burroughs also travesties it while drawing attention to his text's fictionality by referring to 'All the boys from [Snide's] scripts'. The narrative interzone that emerges is this switching between spaceship and navy, flight and simulation, real person and fictional character, such that Burroughs can construct an interstitial 'outer space' for his narrative by splicing and disfiguring the historical content with which it engages.

If the condensations and displacements of this new narrative interzone appear to exude the logic of a dream, that's because it is one. This is revealed at the end of *Cities* after the three plot strands have become increasingly miscegenated. With Snide having been blended into 'Audrey' for some time in Book Three, Audrey wakes up, along with Jerry and John Everson, to find himself in a Greek hospital that seems more like an 'American embassy' (*CRN*, 271). An American 'consul' Mr Pierson explains to Audrey that the three of them were admitted suffering delirium, probably due to 'a virus'—he then reveals to an anonymous other on

---

[92] On America's post-war assimilation of Nazi scientists ('Operation Paperclip'), see, for example: Dean, *Aliens in America*, 74–5; and Levine, *The Future of the U.S. Space Program*, 33. 'Krupp' was also the name of a major munitions manufacturer in Germany during WWI and WWII.
[93] See Carter, *The Final Frontier*, 244–6, and Dean, *Aliens in America*, 11–19.

the phone that the virus is B-23. The denouement is in fact a further knotting of plot, with neither the mystery of the B-23 virus nor the distinction between dream and reality being resolved by the novel's conclusion. What has emerged, though, is that Burroughs's space travel has taken a new turn. The novel as form of dream work is now intended to set up explorative capacities of dream bodies, as when the character Yen Lee astral travels to survey the Red Night cities (*CRN*, 25–7).

The astral dimension is developed further in *The Place of Dead Roads*, 'a sequel' to *Cities*, states Burroughs, that 'clarif[ies] and reiterat[es] similar themes'.[94] As I've stated, Burroughs's interest in the dream body was fuelled by a number of quasi-scientific books, and a copy of one of those mentioned, Monroe's *Journeys Out of the Body*, is owned by Mrs Green in *Cities*. For Monroe, the astral body is an entity that embodies a 'second state': 'this second body has weight as we understand it. It is subject to gravitational attraction, although much less than the physical body.'[95] He also argues that the experiences people have reported of sexual encounters with 'incubi' and 'succubi' spirits are in fact encounters with salacious, roaming 'second bodies'. Burroughs explained the potential benefits of such encounters to Victor Bockris:

We can only speculate as to what further relations with these beings might lead to, my dear. You see, the bodies of incubi and succubi are much less dense than the human body, and this is greatly to their advantage in space travel. Don't forget, it is our bodies which must be weightless to go into space. Now, we make the connections with incubi and succubi in some form of dream state. So I postulate that dreams may be a form of preparation, and in fact training, for travel in space.[96]

Crucially, there's no metaphor involved here in the notion of astral travelling for Burroughs: 'you're out of your body all the time, and particularly in dreams. Dreams are an intimation of what space is like [. . .]. I'm talking in factual terms, about actual space travel, not about mysticism.'[97] Writing his new space mythology thus increasingly meant working towards communion with alien life-forms.[98]

---

[94] Burroughs, 'Afterword', 267.
[95] Monroe, *Journeys Out of the Body*, 169.
[96] Quoted in Victor Bockris, *With William Burroughs: Private Conversations with a Modern Genius* (London: Fourth Estate, 1996), 189.
[97] Burroughs's interview with Nicholas Zurbrugg, 'Any Writing is Experimental' (1983), in *Burroughs Live*, 594.
[98] Russell in his *Queer Burroughs* (155–9, 180–7) relates Burroughs's fascination with astral bodies to Aleister Crowley's notion of the 'body of light'. Ron Roberts also discusses the link to Crowley and similarities between astral bodies, incubi, and succubi in 'The High Priest and the Great Beast', in Schneiderman and Walsh, *Retaking the Universe*, 225–40.

Burroughs describes *The Place of Dead Roads* as a work of abduction when he explains that the novel is indebted to one of his favourite novelists, Denton Welch: 'I sort of kidnapped him to be my hero. And so much of it is written in the style of Denton Welch. It's table tapping [...]. He's writing beyond the grave.'[99] The statement also reveals a further development in Burroughs's space programme: exploration of an afterlife. Having already subtitled *The Wild Boys* 'A Book of the Dead', *The Place of Dead Roads* follows suit when we're introduced to the main character, William Seward Hall, who goes by the 'pen name' of 'Kim Carsons'.[100] Divided into three books, like *Cities*, the opening paragraph of the novel is a newspaper cutting dated 'September 17, 1889' reporting that Hall and Mike Chase appeared to kill each other in a shoot-out at Boulder, Colorado, though it was later revealed that 'both men were killed by single rifle shots fired from a distance' (*PDR*, 13).[101] Rather than becoming a detective story about the mysterious killer of the men, the main body of the narrative proceeds to piece together different episodes from Kim's life prior to the shoot-out. However, determining any temporal sequence before the killings is complicated by repeated instances of time travel; for example, Carson's shoot-out recurs in a variety of dates and locations: Manhattan in 1920, Manhattan in 1894, and Boulder again, but in 1899. Furthermore, like Krup's spaceship hovering between flight and simulation, the shoot-out takes place in an interzone between fight and simulation, for Kim's death is repeatedly followed by reactions from a film 'Director'. In this way, Burroughs consolidates the ontological shift for his fiction. Instead of presenting us with a realist account whereby events and characters are portrayed as if they took place in reality, Burroughs's potentialism is more a matter of simultaneously fashioning and exploring other possible worlds.[102] Thus, characters and events are not offered as

---

Neither Russell nor Roberts discuss the wider research into astral and 'second' bodies being undertaken in the seventies.

[99] Burroughs's interview with *Talk Talk* magazine, 'Table Tapping, My Dear' (1981), in *Burroughs Live*, 497. In 'The Cut-Up Method of Brion Gysin' in *The Third Mind*, Burroughs also suggested that cut-ups could be a form of 'table-tapping' (30).

[100] William S. Burroughs, *The Place of Dead Roads* (1983, repr.; London: Flamingo, 2001), 13, hereafter cited as *PDR*.

[101] The date 'September 17, 1889' is also a mutation of the 'September 17, 1899' with which *NE* closes. Permutations of these years—1988, 1889, 1898—are also scattered throughout *The Wild Boys*.

[102] Brian McHale discusses possible worlds theory and narrative in his *Postmodernist Fiction* (London: Methuen, 1987). For McHale, Burroughs's possible worlds 'fail' because 'the instability of his world blocks our efforts to establish an integrated allegorical interpretation' (144). But Burroughs is not interested in making his worlds 'allegorical' or 'integrated'. He wants his possible worlds to have disintegrative effects on the real world.

representations of the real so much as presentations of potential—a potentiality that derives from the fiction.

The link between narrative space and astral bodies develops as the novel progresses. Kim's project is relatively straightforward; his 'Big Picture' is to orchestrate a wholesale takeover of America by building revolutionary 'Johnson' communities—the 'Johnson Family' being a 'cooperative' that realizes 'our biologic and spiritual destiny in space' (*PDR*, 140).[103] As one of the Johnsons explains, what they 'represent' is 'Potential America. P.A. we call it' (*PDR*, 140). In other words, they are undertaking a potentialist programme with both national and sidereal dimensions. The narrative plotting of all this is complex, but the importance of astral travel is foregrounded in a number of places, as when Kim's flights of fancy are discussed:

Kim considers these imaginary space trips to other worlds as practice for the real thing, like target shooting. As a prisoner serving a life sentence can only think of escape, so Kim takes for granted that the only purpose of his life is space travel. He knows that this will involve not just a change of locale, but basic *biologic* alterations, like the swim from water to land. There has to be the air-breathing potential *first*. (*PDR*, 43, Burroughs's emphases)

Burroughs thus implicitly presents his novel as involving a potentiation of biological changes in the human organism. That this is implicated in fostering an alternative evolutionary enterprise for the space programmes is emphasized by Burroughs in a speech he delivered at the Institute of Ecotechnics' 'Planet Earth Conference' in 1980:

The astronaut is not looking for Space, he's looking for more Time to do exactly the same things. He's equating Space with Time and the Space Program is simply an attempt to transport all our insoluble programs, our impasses, and take them somewhere else where exactly the same thing is bound to occur. However, like the walking fish, looking for more Time he may find Space instead, and then find that there is no way back.[104]

Critiquing the space programmes, Burroughs proceeds to explain his ideas on astral travelling by reading the passage on Kim's 'imaginary space trips' quoted above. The evolution of his writing is thus offered as a way of rescripting evolution, for the second state that his characters and narrative

---

[103] Burroughs explains the significance of the cooperative's name earlier: 'The original title of this book was *The Johnson Family*. "The Johnson Family" was a turn-of-the-century expression to designate good bums and thieves. It was elaborated into a code of conduct. A Johnson honors his obligations. His word is good...' (*PDR*, 7).
[104] William S. Burroughs, *The Four Horsemen of the Apocalypse* (Bonn: Expanded Media Editions, 1984), 22.

space embody is envisaged as acting not on the physical body of the reader, but on the 'second', astral body. Moreover, this development is also related to Burroughs's growing interest in turning his space programme into a bid for immortality.

The new quest for an afterlife is introduced in the second book of *The Place of Dead Roads* when Kim's interest in Egyptian mythology and the Ishmaelite assassin Hassan i Sabbah is explained:

What Hassan i Sabbah learned in Egypt was that *paradise actually exists and that it can be reached*. The Egyptians called it the Western Lands. This is the Garden that the Old Man *showed* his assassins [...]. This is no vague eternal heaven for the righteous. This is *an actual place* at the end of a very dangerous road.

The Garden of Eden was a space station, from which we were banished to the surface of the planet to live by the sweat of mortal brows in a constant losing fight with gravity. (*PDR*, 154, Burroughs's emphases)

Again, Burroughs creates a compound of history and mythology here in mixing contemporary debates on space stations with the legend of Hassan i Sabbah in addition to religious mythology gleaned from *The Bible* and *The Egyptian Book of the Dead*. It's also a spatial compound, for space station, 'Garden of Eden', and the Egyptian 'Western Lands' are all figured as the one 'actual place'. In this new space mythology, the Gods are seen as living beings responsible for monopolizing immortality by allowing only 'favored mortals' the keys to the paradisal Garden. The discovery of this, we're told, is what prompted Hassan i Sabbah to establish his own 'Garden of Alamut' 'station' on Earth, where, 'Free from harassment, the human artifact can evolve into an organism for space conditions and space travel' (*PDR*, 155). This 'Garden' is the secret one that Marco Polo recorded Hassan i Sabbah as having built for his assassin disciples in Persia's Alamut valley. Depicting it as a space station is Burroughs's own embellishment, the point being to develop another counter-history like his pirate stories in *Cities*. So while prominent commentators like Sagan and Mumford were making historical analogies between the space programmes and the Egyptian pyramids, Burroughs was forging his own counter-history figuring the pyramids as portals to space. If some scientists' were also interested in developing space colonies as an alternative to habitation on Earth, those colonies remained a distant prospect in the eighties.[105] Similarly, by the end of *The Place of Dead Roads* the garden of immortality is nowhere in sight. The journey to it is

---

[105] For a detailed overview of interest in space colonies up to the mid-eighties, see Ben R. Finney and Eric M. Jones (eds), *Interstellar Migration and the Human Experience* (Berkeley, CA: University of California Press, 1985).

left to *The Western Lands*, by which time Burroughs had become further critical of the space race. Before we turn to the final novel of the Red Night trilogy, then, let's look at those developments in more detail.

FROM 'STAR WARS' TO 'CRITICAL SPACE'

Despite government cutbacks to interplanetary exploration in the seventies, there'd been significant developments, notably with US and Soviet space stations and with the USA's space-shuttle programme.[106] Nixon endorsed initial investment in the reusable space shuttle in 1972, though the first successful shuttle flight didn't take place until April 1981 with *Columbia*. By this time, the USA had already seen major successes with mini space stations, starting with the 'Skylab' flights in 1973 and 1974—the final flight putting its astronauts into space for eighty-four days. By the mid-1970s, the establishment of permanent space communities was viewed as a real possibility. Princeton physicist Gerald O'Neill was largely responsible for this, publishing scientific papers on space 'colonies' and presenting detailed plans for them to the US House of Representatives in 1975. The wider cultural impact of these proposals is evident from publications like Stewart Brand's *Space Colonies* (1977), an edited collection of responses to O'Neill's ideas gathered from the popular Californian little magazine *CoEvolution Quarterly*. Featuring articles and interviews with O'Neill, the respondents include Mumford and Sagan, along with counter-culture acquaintances of Burroughs such as Ken Kesey, Gary Snyder, Michael McClure, and Timothy Leary. What's particularly interesting about the responses is how they present variations on Burroughs's later contention that the space race amounted to 'transport[ing] all our insoluble programs, our impasses, and tak[ing] them somewhere else'. As far as Mumford is concerned, for example, the 'colonies' are 'another pathological manifestation of the culture that has spent all its resources on expanding the nuclear means for exterminating the human race'.[107] Poet and novelist Wendell Berry concurred, stating that 'if [the colonies are] implemented, it will be the rebirth of the idea of Progress with all its old lust for [. . .] totalitarian concentrations of energy and wealth'.[108] In contrast, Stewart Brand and Carl Sagan declared the

---

[106] See McDougall, *The Heavens and the Earth*, Ch. 20, and Carter, *The Final Frontier*, 'Conclusion'.
[107] Quoted in 'Debate Section', in Stewart Brand (ed.), *Space Colonies* (Harmondsworth: Penguin, 1977), 34.
[108] Ibid. 36.

new 'High Frontier' to be an escape route from the Cold War's impasse. Such debates on space communities thus helped turn space exploration and evolution into pressing issues. That Burroughs was aware of this is clear from a comment he made in 1980:

> I agree with Timothy Leary—the only possibilities are in space. In a recent talk he gave about space stations, he said, 'When a place gets full to this extent, that is a sign that it's been successful and it's time to move'. He said, consider these space stations. We'll have the longevity pill; you can live 500, 600, 700 years.
> He's offering, it seems to me, the two most important things—immortality and space [...]. It seems to be a possibility within the range of modern technology.[109]

While this might suggest that, like the ventures he criticizes, Burroughs's own space enterprise involves buying more time, *The Western Lands* as we'll see offers a very different investment of capital. By the time of the novel's publication, scientific interest in developing space colonies was undiminished. But as with the space programmes of the sixties and seventies, hopes in the eighties for establishing celestial settlements were paralleled with a tightening of Cold War space on Earth.

We've already seen that by the end of the seventies a striation of global space was being facilitated by satellite systems like Navstar/GPS. With Ronald Reagan's presidential inauguration in 1980, though, two factors made the Cold War stand-off of 'mutually assured destruction' (MAD) unstable: first, Reagan's 1981 pledge of $1.2 trillion dollars for defence over a period of five years; and second, his announcement in March 1983 that the USA would be developing a 'Strategic Defense Initiative' (SDI) in the form of an orbital network of anti-missile weapons.[110] Popularly known as 'Star Wars', a number of commentators have viewed Reagan's defence spending and SDI proposals as undermining the progress of the Partial Test Ban Treaty (1963) and the US–USSR Strategic Arms Limitation Treaties (SALT) of 1972 and 1979.[111] The Soviets were certainly convinced that 'Star Wars' amounted to offensive militarization—particularly given that, at the time Reagan announced SDI, his administration was developing a new 'Space Command' for each of its armed forces.[112] For theorists Jean Baudrillard and Paul Virilio, the 'Star Wars' project was thus instrumental in catalysing a critical shift in the Cold War and in space generally. In Virilio's opinion SDI produced a 'critical space' in which the difference between 'imposed war' and 'preventative war' collapsed: 'the

---

[109] Quoted in Bockris, *With William Burroughs*, 179.
[110] For extensive accounts of SDI, see Wirbel, *Star Wars*, and Edward Reiss, *The Strategic Defense Initiative* (Cambridge: Cambridge University Press, 1992).
[111] See, for example, McDougall, *The Heavens and the Earth*, 434.
[112] Carter, *The Final Frontier*, 246.

defensive has become "offensive" since strategic deterrence has, as its principal consequence, provoked the "tactical" arms race, the incessant scientific and technological perfection of conventional and nuclear vectors of delivery, the acceleration of their speed, the multiplication of explosive charges'.[113] With US and Soviet orbital communications networks capable of triggering instantaneous responses to attack, the result, argues Virilio, was a free-floating, technologized 'pure war'.[114] And just as Atwill contends that the 'real grid' of satellite systems produced a 'disjunctive architecture' on Earth, so Virilio posits global, spatial consequences for this 'pure war'. In particular, classical 'space-time' was replaced by a new 'space-speed', he argues, so that strategy/action, before/after, attack/counter-attack became 'fused and confused' through networks of instantaneity. Traditional temporal and spatial distinctions were thus replaced with a relayed 'space beyond' [*outre espace*] of orbital-global simultaneity.[115] For Baudrillard, this means that the identity and value of things in general became subject to escalation. If one nation's defensive satellite is another country's offensive weapon, and that indistinction precipitates escalation on both sides, then one is faced with military inflation:

The only revolution in things is today no longer in their dialectical transcendence (*Aufhebung*), but in their potentialization, in their elevation to the second power, in their elevation to the nth power [...]. It seems that things [...] can only redouble themselves in their exacerbated and transparent form, as in Virilio's 'pure war' [...]. Spatial exploration likewise is a *mise en abyme* of this world. Everywhere the virus of potentialization and *mise en abyme* carries the day, carries us towards an ecstasy which is also that of indifference.[116]

Viruses, 'potentialization', abolition of space-time—is Burroughs's later space mythology simply a symptom of this 'pure war' that Virilio and Baudrillard describe?

I want to argue that Burroughs's approach to relating 'outer space' and 'potentials' develops counter to Baudrillard's and Virilio's depiction of Cold War and celestial space in general. By 1987, Burroughs was still stating in interview that 'Outer space is the only place that's going to create new roles', but he was also acknowledging that '[it's] monopolized

---

[113] Paul Virilio, 'Critical Space' (1984), in *The Virilio Reader*, ed. and trans. James Der Derian (Oxford: Blackwell, 1998), 66.
[114] Ibid. 67. See also Paul Virilio, *Pure War*, trans. Mark Polizzotti and Brian O'Keefe (New York: Semiotext(e), 1997).
[115] Virilio, 'Critical Space', 69.
[116] Jean Baudrillard, *Fatal Strategies*, trans. Philip Beitchman and W. G. J. Niesluchowski (1983, repr.; London: Pluto, 1990), 41.

by very, very few people in the military'.[117] In contrast, his own space programme was, he declared, open 'to *anyone* who has the courage and know how to enter'.[118] Furthermore, contrary to the 'second power' that Baudrillard sees as escalating in things to an 'nth power' beyond our control, Burroughs seeks to enhance the second state and astral body as a means of escaping control. And the final blueprint for his space-age potentialization is interred in *The Western Lands*...

THE WESTERN LANDS

Like many of the ancient pyramids, *The Western Lands* contains numerous dead ends and diversions, but there are key passages that lead straight to the central subject: space travel and immortality. Divided into ten chapters, the novel opens with the figure of the writer William Seward Hall, who was killed at the outset of *Place*. Like the latter, the novel thus draws attention to its status as 'Book of the Dead', for not only has Hall/Kim Carsons already died, he is 'set[ting] out to write his way out of death. Death, he reflects, is equivalent to a declaration of spiritual bankruptcy.'[119] From here, the narrative proceeds to reaffirm the move from physical body to second body with a disquisition on the 'seven souls' the Egyptians believed each individual possesses. *The Egyptian Book of the Dead* names these souls as 'Ren, Sekem, Khu, Ba, Ka, Khaibit, and Sekhu', each one having a specific role.[120] Outlining each soul's role in his narrative, Burroughs also translates them into his own syncretic cast—for example, Ren 'corresponds to my Director. He directs the film of your life from conception to death' (*WL*, 4). Not only do these 'souls' possess a level of physicality, as 'the Egyptians recognized' they also have 'many degrees of immortality': 'Can any soul survive the searing blast of an atomic blast? If human souls are seen as electromagnetic force fields, such fields could be totally disrupted by a nuclear explosion' (*WL*, 7). The reference to 'electromagnetic force fields' is straight out of the books by Monroe, Schroeder, and Ostrander that so interested Burroughs. Whereas in *Cities* and the Nova trilogy atomic radiation was linked to viruses and viral characters, *The Western Lands* cements a shift to

---

[117] Burroughs's interview with Jim McMenamin and Larry McCaffery, 'The Non-Body Route' (1987), in *Burroughs Live*, 682, my emphasis.
[118] Burroughs, *The Soft Machine*, 50, my emphasis.
[119] William S. Burroughs, *The Western Lands* (London: Picador, 1988), 3, hereafter cited as *WL*.
[120] See E. A. Wallis Budge, *The Egyptian Book of the Dead: The Papyrus of Ani—Egyptian Text, Transliteration and Translation* (1895, repr.; New York: Seager, 1967).

second-state characters from the start, which also explains the curious purgatorial limbo in which Hall appears to be held. In Chapter 4 this limbo is further clarified when Hall materializes again as 'Kim Lee': 'Kim knows he is dead. But he isn't in the Western Lands or any approximation' (*WL*, 74). So the quest commences; Kim/Hall is instructed by the 'District Supervisor' (a revenant from the Nova trilogy) to 'Find out how the Western Lands are created. Where the Egyptians went wrong and bogged down in their stinking mummies. Why they needed to preserve the body' (*WL*, 74).

Another important character is introduced in Chapter 2; 'Joe the Dead', who's revealed to be the mystery person who shot both Kim and Mike Chase in *Place*. Described as 'the Master of Light and Sound, the Technician' Joe is a 'Sekhem' soul and is intent on communicating with Hassan i Sabbah: '[Joe] knew there was only one man who could effect the basic changes dictated by the human impasse: Hassan i Sabbah: HIS. The Old Man of the Mountain. And HIS was cut off by a blockade that made the Gates of Anubis look like a dimestore lock' (*WL*, 28–9). The legend of HIS and the Western Lands that Burroughs developed in *Place* is thus reintroduced, the reference to Anubis also reappearing later in Kim's narrative: 'Ancient Egypt is the only period in history when the gates to Immortality were open, the Gates of Anubis. But the gates were occupied and monopolized by unfortunate elements [...] rather low vampires' (*WL*, 190). Reiterating the discussion of the Gods' monopolization of space and immortality from *The Place of Dead Roads*, this extract also echoes Burroughs's 1987 comment about the monopolization of space by 'very, very few people in the military'. Kim's quest for the Western Lands and Joe's search for 'HIS' are thus melded by Burroughs into a final push for a counter space mythology. In parallel with these quests, he also develops a familiar storyline in having both characters establish 'outlaw' communities. Just as the pirate plot in *Cities* blended aspects of 'outlaw space' and 'outer space', so we find Kim belonging to 'a secret service without a country' named 'Margaras Unlimited',[121] whose policy is 'SPACE'; 'Anything that favors or enhances space programs, space exploration, simulation of space conditions, exploration of inner space, expanding awareness [...]. Anything going in the other direction we will extirpate' (*WL*, 25). This is complemented by the group of 'Natural Outlaws' (NOs) that Joe the Dead is stockpiling. Specializing in 'evolutionary biology', Joe aims to break biological laws 'by bringing into

---

[121] 'MU' is also the acronym Burroughs uses to denote 'Magical Universe' inspired by Carlos Castañeda's writings on the 'nagual' (the unknown, unpredictable). See, for example, Burroughs's discussion of the Magical Universe quoted in Miles, *William Burroughs*, 249.

contact species that had never been in contact before' and 'open[ing] new potentials for hybridization' (*WL*, 37). With evolutionary change being intrinsic to Burroughs's plans for space travel, Joe carries out a number of genetic experiments, including a brain transplant from chimp to human. And in another important passage, Burroughs underlines the status of the hybrids as 'potentials':

> The hybrid concept underlies all relations between man and animals, since only a being partaking of both man and animal can mediate between two species. These are blueprint hybrids, potentials rather than actual separate beings, capable of reproduction.
> It is the task of the Guardian to nurture these half-formed creatures and to realize their potential. (*WL*, 42)

Burroughs offers a new model of potentialist inter-being here.[122] In a self-reflexive move, the hybrids are acknowledged as forms of textual 'blueprint' that are also potential life-forms. Just as Joe and Kim are offered to us as forms of inter-being—semi-physical souls that exist as textual after-lives—so Joe's experiments conjoin biology and text. And like the incubi and succubi that Burroughs explained to Victor Bockris may be 'dependent on contact with the denser form in order to exist', so we find Joe's 'half-formed creatures' needing a 'Guardian' 'to realize their potential'. In a later authorial aside in the novel, Burroughs expands on this desire for second-body reproduction: 'The point of contact with demons, elementals and succubi, incubi, radiant boys, Shining Ones, is to mate with them and produce desirable offspring by which I mean offspring with long-range survival potential' (*WL*, 202). For Burroughs, conceiving second-state offspring is thus an essential goal for writing and reading. Having offered cut-up viral characters in the Nova trilogy that exist 'as a potential like the spheres and crystals that show up under an electron microscope',[123] Burroughs presents *The Western Lands*' characters as ghostly, astral bodies that exist outside time. The latent state they embody is directly related to the narrative space in which they are interred. Existing extra-temporally as forms of text, they can nevertheless have their potential realized through any number of reader 'Guardians'.

The phenomenological implications that Burroughs's potentialist programme holds for the act of reading are complex. Effectively, acts of writing and reading are being offered by him as ways of precipitating alien

---

[122] I would argue that the emphasis here on non-human, inter-species procreation undermines Russell's claims in *Queer Burroughs* that the bodily 'becoming' that Burroughs explores in the later novels is resolutely 'the establishment of one fixed identity, the queer masculine' (180).
[123] Burroughs, *The Ticket that Exploded*, 19.

invasion. Burroughs explained to Bockris that just as a dreamer could be possessed by a succubus, so a person could be possessed by a voice: 'If you are listening to someone, that person's voice is inside your head. It has to some extent invaded and occupied your brain.'[124] In *The Western Lands*, this model of abduction attains its fullest expression. With his narrative exploring distinct, *ontological* interzones—hybridized worlds of other possibility—Burroughs gives the final touches to a *phenomenological* aspect of the interzones in so far as they're offered as taking place between the text and its writer or reader.

The interzonal blend of ontology and phenomenology is given its clearest exposition in Chapter 7 of *The Western Lands*. By this stage Joe's and Kim's quests have continued to merge, and with the action shifting between Egypt and Waghdas (the Red Night 'city of knowledge' introduced in *Cities*) we find Kim appearing as a newly spliced character, 'Neferti Kim Carsons', an Egyptian scribe searching for the Western Lands' 'blueprints'. The extent of the Gods' monopoly has been developed further in Chapter 5, the whole enterprise of immortality and paradise being shown to live off the life-force of mortal '*fellaheen*' workers: 'Obviously the mummies serve as receptacles to collect and store the plasma of the *fellaheen* needed to preserve their masters. In return the sucking mummies are given conditional immortality, as vampires to be milked like aphids' (*WL*, 111). This issue is taken up again in Chapter 7, at which point the narrative takes a critical turn:

We can make our own Western Lands.

We know that the Western Lands are made solid by *fellaheen* blood and energy, siphoned off by vampire mummies, just as water is siphoned off to form an oasis. Such an oasis lasts only so long as the water does, and the technology for its diversion. However, an oasis that is self-sustaining, recreated by the inhabitants, does not need such an inglorious vampire lifeline.

We can create a life of dreams.

'But how can we make it solid?'

'We don't. That is precisely the error of the mummies. They made spirit solid. When you do this it ceases to be spirit. We will make ourselves less solid'.

Well, that's what art is all about, isn't it? All creative thought, actually. A bid for immortality. So long as sloppy, stupid, so-called democracies live, the ghosts of various boring people who escape my mind still stalk about in the mess they have made.

We poets and writers are tidier, fade out in firefly evenings, a Prom and a distant train whistle, we live in a maid opening a boiled egg for a long-ago convalescent, we live in the snow on Michael's grave falling softly like the descent

---

[124] Quoted in Bockris, *With William Burroughs*, 188.

of their last end on all the living and the dead, we live in the green light at the end of Daisy's dock, in the last and greatest of human dreams... (*WL*, 165)

With three chapters still to come, this passage is nevertheless the text's real conclusion, for it *is* a blueprint of the Western Lands. Like the Chapel Perilous at the end of Eliot's *The Waste Land*, the Western Lands are never actually entered in Burroughs's novel, Joe and Neferti failing to complete their quests. Instead, the novel's final paragraph returns us to the figure of the writer that the novel opened with—'The old writer couldn't write anymore because he had reached the end of words...' (*WL*, 258)—before concluding with an allusion to *The Waste Land*: 'Hurry up, please. It's time' (*WL*, 258). But this is like one of the false passages in a pyramid that leads to a dead end, for Burroughs has already indicated the way to the Western Lands. The passage from Chapter 7 quoted above is the clearest expression of the novel as form of Western Land in itself. Rather than being a 'real' place, the Western Lands take place as a potentiality that is the novelistic space; a potentiality that embodies its own second state as 'a life of dreams'. This potentiality is a ghostly immortality to the extent that it secures, for example, an experience of 'firefly evenings' as a textual afterlife that remains open to various encounters. On one hand, such after-lives can enter into new textual arrangements, as when Burroughs juxtaposes Michael Furey's grave scene at the end of James Joyce's *Dubliners* ('he heard the snow falling [...] like the descent of their last end, upon all the living and the dead') with the 'green light [...] of Daisy's dock' at the end of F. Scott Fitzgerald's *The Great Gatsby*. On the other hand, these afterlives remain open to being blended with lived experience in the act of writing and reading. Indeed, this spectral textuality is the basis on which Burroughs suggests that the living and dead can continue to mix in a present continuous—'we live...'; 'we live...'; 'we live....'.[125]

For Burroughs, 'poets and writers' must develop techniques of 'fad[ing] into' the ephemeral and offering up their lives to it in order to give life to the immortal. In doing so, they can create an alternative 'oasis' of immortality to that of the 'vampire mummies' and their *fellaheen*, for the second-state beings Burroughs writes into existence are intended to be 'recreated' through any number of reader 'Guardians'. The second-state characters of *The Western Lands* thus call for a two-way labour. If Burroughs hopes his

---

[125] When William Triplett asked Burroughs about writers' immortality, Burroughs replied: 'If your books are around, then you are too. When the Zen master says "When your arrow hits the target in the dark, I'll be there", he means that quite literally' ('William Burroughs, International Gunman' (1984), in *Burroughs Live*, 611). Given the compound nature of Burroughs's characters, though, this lurking 'I' would surely also figure as a new hybrid form.

aesthetic beings can 'step out of the book' with the help of a Guardian, he also sees *The Western Lands* as showing readers how to step *into* the astral: 'I see that dreams are the lifeline to our possible biological and spiritual destiny. That's what *The Western Lands* is about.'[126] The passage from Chapter 7 quoted above isn't simply 'about' this astral lifeline, it *is* an astral lifeline. As a counter-narrative to the vampiric monopoly of the Western Lands, Burroughs's text calls for an intermingling of second-state characters and readers' lived experience so that readers can 'realize' and give life to the text's hybrid beings, while simultaneously being opened to the possibility of alien experiences. The exchange is the taking place of an interzone, and its mutually nourishing circuit is the 'self-sustaining' 'oasis' that doesn't need the 'inglorious vampire lifeline' or its mass of 'technology'.

In that respect the interzone Burroughs leaves as a legacy for the space-age is markedly opposed to the Cold War 'space beyond' that Virilio posits, as well as to the 'hyperspace' that Jameson figures as 'postmodern'. Rather than an automated orbital-global network that looms threateningly distanced from individuals' bodily experience—despite holding their lives in balance—Burroughs's interzones gather narrative potentials and the reader's experience into a new compound being, a synthesized 'affect' that takes place between the two. Consequently, these interzones cannot be seen as symptomatic of the networked, postmodern space that Baudrillard and Virilio describe, for they emerge as a 'space beyond' that is an interstitial event. Instead of depending on energy consumption, like the monopolies of the space programmes and the Egyptian Western Lands, the interzones exist latently in the narrative, and then take place in the act of reading as a mutual potentialization of reader and text. Thus, just as Gilles Deleuze and Félix Guattari see aesthetic 'affects' as synthesized 'bloc[s] of sensations', '*beings* whose validity [...] exceeds any lived', so Burroughs's interzones are manifested as a new ontological and phenomenological surplus that emerges from readers encountering the novel.[127]

To return to the aims I stated at the end of my Introduction, then, we can see that the space mythology Burroughs creates does indeed amount to offering a specific literary alternative to the space programmes and to wider cultural tendencies that commentators like Jameson have deemed to

---

[126] Burroughs's interview with James Fox, 'Return of the Invisible' (1987), in *Burroughs Live*, 646.
[127] Gilles Deleuze and Félix Guattari, *What is Philosophy?*, trans. Hugh Tomlinson and Graham Burchell (1991, repr.; New York: Columbia University Press, 1994), 164, their emphasis. Such affects also involve the viewer or reader, they state, for artists and writers 'not only create [affects] in their work, they give them to us and make us become with them, they draw us into the compound' (175).

be postmodern. And while Burroughs aligns his labours with 'poets and writers' in general, we need to recognize that his own alternative literary programme is ultimately made up of a complex blend of particular literary techniques honed over decades in relation to a specific set of interests. As Mary McCarthy realized as far back as 1962, Burroughs's writing was a timely intervention in space-age issues, and it continued to be so in posing alternatives to the space race. But ultimately his space mythology isn't simply of its time; rather, it provides continual access to *untimely* events as an 'outer space' on Earth.

4

Novel Biopolitics

Kathy Acker and Michel Foucault

INTRODUCTION

When Kathy Acker began experimenting with prose and fiction in the early seventies, William Burroughs was one of her main guiding stars. He remained so for the rest of her writing life. On first hearing of his death in 1997—the year in which breast cancer eventually made her a mortality too—Acker recounted in an obituary essay that 'All I could say was "William is the greatest living writer in the United States. I couldn't say "was".'[1] Explaining his greatness by way of his main ideas, she made reference to another major influence on her: 'The word is virus. In other words, language controls virally. [...] I don't know if Michel Foucault ever read William Burroughs: I do know he must have sucked Williams's books up through his navel.'[2] As we'll see, Acker's literary 'appropriations' of writers she admired—particularly male ones—were usually far from unquestioning, and that certainly holds for her engagement with Burroughs and Foucault. Experimenting with cut-ups in her early writing, Acker later questioned Burroughs's attitudes to women, and while she similarly nurtured an interest in piracy in her later work she worked with very different goals in mind. Whereas Burroughs sought to escape the body through his astral writings, Acker wanted her fiction to revive the body by potentiating new forms of gender and sexuality. This is where her interest in Foucault plays a substantial role. As the quotation above suggests, Foucault was important to her view of discourse as being intrinsic to power and social control, and several critics have noted this along with the influence on Acker of Foucault's writings about sexuality.[3]

---

[1] Kathy Acker, 'William Burroughs' (1997), in The Kathy Acker Papers, Duke University Library (Box 4, Folder: 'William Burroughs/J. G. Ballard'): 1.
[2] Ibid. 2.
[3] See Barrett Watten, 'Foucault Reads Acker and Rewrites the History of the Novel', in Amy Scholder, Carla Harryman, and Avital Ronell (eds), *Lust for Life: On the Writings of Kathy Acker* (New York: Verso, 2006), 58–77, and Carol Siegel, 'The Madness Outside

In this chapter I'll relate her literary interests more fully to Foucault's work by developing two linked lines of inquiry.

The first of these involves their shared conception of political power as bearing on individual potentiality. An active member of Students for a Democratic Society (SDS) when a student in the sixties, Acker throughout her writing career proceeded to question the 'unfulfilled capacities for reason, freedom and love' that the SDS 'Port Huron Statement' had so fervently invoked. In 1981 she was probing 'laws of possibility'[4] in relation to fiction, and by 1990 she was contending that Ronald Reagan, George Bush, and Margaret Thatcher had together caused 'a reduction in people's lives [...] of the possibilities of living through and by means of dreams, imaginings and desires'.[5] Yet that was all the more reason, she argued, for writers to promote the imagination as 'a world of expanding possibilities'.[6] Indeed, elsewhere she went so far as to claim that this was tantamount to waging a form of militant campaign against society; the 'only possible chance for change', she wrote, lay 'in the tactics of guerrilla warfare, in the use of fictions, of language'.[7] Just how metaphorical the relations between fiction and actual militancy were, continued to be a main concern for Acker. What she remained convinced of was that fiction could defend powers of imagination which, in turn, could draw on historical material and forge from it new ways of exercising power. As she stated in one of her last essays: 'If we throw history away, we are depriving ourselves of potentialities, potentialities for action. Models and paradigms for action. Potentiality is kin, and I am talking politically, kin to the imagination.'[8]

Foucault also repeatedly affirmed a coupling of politics and potentiality in his later work. One of the lectures he gave at the Collège de France in 1976 provides a prime example:

sovereignty assumes from the outset the existence of a multiplicity of powers that are not powers in the political sense of the term; they are capacities, possibilities, potentials, and it can constitute them as powers in the political sense of the term

---

Gender: Travels with Don Quixote and Saint Foucault', *rhizomes* 1 (Fall 2000): available at http://www.rhizomes.net/issue1/mad/quixote.html, accessed 5 August 2009.

[4] Kathy Acker, 'Peter Gordon: Ambiguity' (1981), in The Kathy Acker Papers, Duke University Library (Box 4, Folder: 'Peter Gordon: Ambiguity'): 18.

[5] Kathy Acker, 'Opening Speech for the Lahti Writers' Reunion' (1990), in The Kathy Acker Papers, Duke University Library (Box 4, Folder: 'Magazine Articles'): 4.

[6] Ibid.

[7] Kathy Acker, 'Postmodernism' (no date), in *Bodies of Work: Essays* (London: Serpent's Tail, 1997), 5.

[8] Kathy Acker, 'Writing, Identity, and Copyright in the Net Age' (1995), in *Bodies of Work*, 99.

only if it has in the meantime established a fundamental and foundational unity between possibilities and power, namely the unity of power.[9]

Power's political character is thus predicated on an ability to harness human capacities while managing them as a regulated 'field of possibilities'.[10] To ensure this, sovereignty has traditionally relied on disciplining individuals through various institutions—for example, the army, schools, and judiciary—but from the eighteenth century onwards, argues Foucault, both sovereign and disciplinary powers have needed supplementing with larger administrative networks of regulation. This is largely owing to the livelihood of states being tied increasingly to bourgeois mercantilism. As a state's prosperity becomes its population's capacities for consumption and production, governing it requires a new kind of power that regulates things such as wealth, resources, and rates of birth and mortality. This new power Foucault names 'biopolitics', for essentially it is 'a matter of taking control of life and the biological processes of man-as-species'.[11]

The unity of power and possibilities that Foucault posits is thus a primary concern for biopolitics, which is the second line of inquiry around which I'll relate his work to Acker's. For Foucault, there are several ways in which biopolitics can formalize particular forms of potential for people. Allowing political economy to regulate them as 'human capital' is one option. As I stated in my Introduction, Foucault cites US neo-liberalism as a prime example of such regulation, and he argues that it conceives of labour more in terms of people being 'abilities machines' that must offer their capabilities as 'capital ability'.[12] Individuals' capacities are thus selected, trained, valued, and managed within an economic market. In addition, ensuring people's willingness to become a kind of '*homo œconomicus*' means regulating as a 'collective interest' their 'desire' to invest themselves in social production. For Foucault, the growing economic importance of population also meant that from the eighteenth century sex became 'a thing one administered' as 'a public potential'.[13] Subject also to disciplinary measures of various institutions—scholastic,

---

[9] Michel Foucault, *'Society Must Be Defended': Lectures at the Collège de France, 1975–76*, eds Mauro Bertani and Alessandro Fontana, trans. David Macey (London: Allen Lane, 2003), 44.

[10] Michel Foucault, 'The Subject and Power' (1982), in *Essential Works of Foucault, 1954–84*, Vol. 3: *Power*, ed. James Faubion, trans. Robert Hurley et al. (London: Penguin, 2002), 342.

[11] Foucault, *'Society Must Be Defended'*, 247.

[12] Michel Foucault, *The Birth of Biopolitics: Lectures at the Collège de France, 1978–79*, ed. Michel Senellart, trans. Graham Burchell (London: Palgrave Macmillan, 2008), 225.

[13] Michel Foucault, *The History of Sexuality*, Vol. 1: *An Introduction*, trans. Robert Hurley (1976, repr.; London: Vintage, 1990), 24.

religious, medical, and legal—sexuality became inextricably bound to politics, he argues, such that power and sexual 'pleasure' 'seek out, overlap, and reinforce one another'.[14] The kinds of human potentials imbricated in biopolitical governance are thus diverse. In places, Foucault suggests that this diversity can be summarized as a people's 'possibilities of action'.[15] As I've pointed out, though, he also acknowledges that capacities for acting and working involve 'pleasures' and 'desires', and with his final writings he extends his notion of biopolitics to a wider one of 'governmentality'. The latter includes not only the management of its population, but also a family's management of its children and livelihood, and even the 'relationship of the self to itself'.[16] With this final move, then, biopolitical regulation extends from political affairs of state to ethical states of feeling.

How biopolitics and self-governance relate will be the comparative focus of this chapter, for a number of reasons. First, while Foucault examines a 'government of the self' in *The History of Sexuality* volumes, his discussion there is limited to practices in ancient Greece and Rome, and he never considers how these might pertain to contemporary contexts such as that of American neo-liberalism. Acker, in contrast, employs similar writing practices to those Foucault discusses, yet she puts them to very different purposes in addressing biopolitical issues around sexuality. Second, in outlining the importance of self-governance in classical writing exercises, Foucault identifies an 'aesthetics of existence' at the heart of them. The importance of this aesthetics also remains undeveloped in his writings. When relating his ideas on biopolitics to contemporary contexts, other theorists like Michael Hardt, Antonio Negri, and Éric Alliez have recently suggested that aesthetic practices would be useful for tempering effects of biopolitics.[17] But these theorists have at best provided only sketchy understandings of what shape that aesthetics would take, and how it would work. For Acker, in contrast, fostering an aesthetics of existence is crucial for negotiating degrees to which one's life is governed, particularly through language. This raises a third point of contrast: Foucault outlines the importance of social discourse for disciplinary power, but not for biopolitics, which he addresses more in terms of political economy. For Negri and Hardt, this is something of an oversight for they

---

[14] Foucault, *The History of Sexuality*, Vol. 1, 49.
[15] Foucault, 'The Subject and Power', 341.
[16] Michel Foucault, 'Ethics of the Concern for Self' (1984), in *Foucault Live: Collected Interviews, 1961–84*, ed. Sylvère Lotringer, trans. Lysa Hochroth and John Johnston (New York: Semiotext(e), 1989), 448.
[17] See Michael Hardt and Antonio Negri, *Empire* (Cambridge, MA: Harvard University Press, 2000), 209–10, and Éric Alliez and Antonio Negri, 'Peace and War', *Theory, Culture & Society* 20:2 (2003), 109–18.

see communications as having 'assumed a central position' in contemporary regulated life:

> Language, as it communicates, produces commodities but moreover creates subjectivities, puts them in relation, and orders them. The communications industries integrate the imaginary and the symbolic within the biopolitical fabric, not merely putting them at the service of power but actually integrating them into its very functioning.[18]

That Acker links Foucault and Burroughs on the basis that 'language controls virally' indicates that she does regard Foucault as suggesting that linguistic power and biopolitics are conjoined. Yet as I'll show, it's Acker who affords us a clearer idea of how language and an aesthetics of existence are implicated in contemporary governmentality. To that effect, in the next section I shall compare Foucault's accounts of classical 'self-governance' to Acker's early experiments with combining diary material, plagiarism, and fiction. I'll then consider how in her novels of the eighties she questions the use of this self-governance when confronted by unities of biopolitics and possibility. Discussing that in terms of her engagement with issues such as incest, abortion, HIV/AIDS, and biotechnology, I'll then examine how in the novels she published in the nineties she combines her own form of piracy along with 'languages of the body' into a more positive literary potentialism.

SELF-WRITING, DREAMS, AND ALLOBIOGRAPHY

When Foucault discusses Greco-Roman self-governance it's in terms of a mastery of self. In *The Use of Pleasure* (1984), for example, he examines the notion of *enkrateia* (self-control) propounded by Xenophon, Plato, and Aristotle. Essentially, *enkrateia* required regulating one's pleasures and desires, which were viewed by such ancients as 'enemy force[s]': 'The battle to be fought, the victory to be won, the defeat that one risked suffering—these were processes and events that took place between oneself and oneself.'[19] Attaining *enkrateia* called for an *askesis* (asceticism) that amounted to a kind of martial 'art of living' (*tekhnē tou bio*), which comprised specific techniques. Foucault gives the Stoics' 'self-writing' as a particular example of these techniques. There were two main forms of

---

[18] Hardt and Negri, *Empire*, 33.
[19] Michel Foucault, *The Use of Pleasure: The History of Sexuality*, Vol. 2, trans. Robert Hurley (1984, repr.; London: Penguin, 1992), 67.

such writing: notebooks (*hupomnēmata*), in which one collated one's own pearls of reason with useful quotations from others; and correspondence, in which one reflected on one's daily thoughts and activities. For Foucault, such writing didn't simply embellish a self that was already formed; rather, it involved 'nothing less than the shaping of the self'.[20] Epistolary accounts of one's life meant seeing oneself in terms of the addressee's perspective and so were aimed at a 'congruence' of gazes. The notebooks, too, involved absorbing others' precepts so that constituting selfhood meant assembling and embodying a social corpus. As Foucault argues in relation to Seneca:

> The role of writing is to constitute, along with all that reading has constituted, a 'body' [...]. And this body should be understood not as a body of doctrine but, rather—following an often-evoked metaphor of digestion—as the very body of the one who, by transcribing his readings, has appropriated them and made their truth his own: writing transforms the thing seen or heard into 'tissue and blood' [...]. It becomes a principle of rational action in the writer himself.[21]

Although he points out that this equates to a bioethical form of writing (*logos bioēthikos*), Foucault doesn't address how it might relate to contemporary biopolitics. Just how useful it could be in that context seems questionable when one considers the statements he makes in 'The Subject and Power' (1982):

> Maybe the target nowadays is not to discover what we are but to refuse what we are. We have to imagine and to build up what we could be to get rid of this kind of political 'double bind', which is the simultaneous individualization and totalization of modern power structures.[22]

That is certainly Acker's opinion even in the early stages of her work. First reading Foucault in the late 1970s, her fiction prior to this gives the impression that she somehow absorbed him through her navel, though her initial interest in relating writing, sexuality, and politics was more the consequence of directions in which her life had taken her since her adolescence. Born in New York City in 1944 to Jewish parents, Acker spent most of her childhood with her mother, Clare, after her father walked out on the family while Clare was still pregnant with Acker. Having considered aborting her, Clare proceeded to bring up her daughter resentfully, blaming her for the father's departure. Consequently Acker

---

[20] Michel Foucault, 'Self Writing' (1983), in *The Essential Works of Foucault, 1954–84*, Vol. 1: *Ethics, Subjectivity and Truth*, ed. Paul Rabinow, trans. Robert Hurley et al. (London: Penguin, 2000), 211.
[21] Ibid. 213.
[22] Foucault, 'The Subject and Power', 336.

rebelled, particularly in her teenage years when she started a relationship with P. Adams Sitney, who introduced her to a range of experimental filmmakers, artists, and writers. As she later stated in interview, her early literary inspirations were primarily poets such as Robert Kelly, Jackson Mac Low, and Charles Olson.[23] Developing a passion for Latin at school, though, Acker in 1963 decided to take up a place at Brandeis to study Classics, and around this time she also married Robert Acker, changing her 'maiden' surname to his. Then in 1965 she moved to the University of California, San Diego, where she worked with the social theorist Herbert Marcuse. His writings would certainly have prepared her for an interest in Foucault; for example, in the 'Political Preface' Marcuse wrote for the 1966 edition of his *Eros and Civilization* (1955), he announced that 'mass democracy', 'scientific management', and 'administered society' were combining to shape individuals' 'Life instincts' and 'libido'.[24] Addressing the 'work-world' of labour, he also foreshadowed the kinds of argument Foucault later made about regulated life: 'The automatization of necessity and waste, of labor and entertainment, precludes the realization of individual potentialities in this realm.'[25] For Marcuse, the etiolation of possibilities makes the roles of the imagination and aesthetics all the more crucial. If the imagination can envision a 'reconciliation' of 'desire with realization, of happiness with reason', so aesthetics can help liberate desire and sensuousness, which 'far from destroying civilization, would [...] greatly enhance its potentialities'.[26]

Returning to Manhattan after her studies at Brandeis, Acker gained first-hand experience of how labour can absorb desire when she commenced work in a sex show on 42nd Street.[27] It was a short-lived venture, like her marriage to Robert Acker, and by the early 1970s she was in a relationship with musician Peter Gordon and focusing on her writing. An *habituée* of the St Mark's Poetry Project, Acker later commented that the poetry performed there at this time was 'very autobiographical' and largely inspired by New York School poetry.[28] Rather than continue writing in that vein she turned to prose, mainly inspired by Jack Kerouac and Burroughs. Her early work differs from theirs, though, for the fact that it juxtaposes unexpurgated diary material with text plagiarized from

---

[23] Kathy Acker, 'Devoured by Myths' (1989–90), interview with Sylvère Lotringer, in *Hannibal Lecter, My Father* (New York: Semiotext(e), 1991), 3–4.
[24] Herbert Marcuse, *Eros and Civilization* (1955, repr.; London: Sphere, 1970), 11–12.
[25] Ibid. 92.
[26] Ibid. 121, 149.
[27] See Acker, 'Devoured by Myths', 5.
[28] Ibid.

others. As she states regarding her novel *The Childlike Life of the Black Tarantula by the Black Tarantula* (1973):

> I wanted to explore the use of the word I, that's the only thing I wanted to do. So I placed very direct autobiographical, just diary material, right next to fake diary material. I tried to figure out who I wasn't and I went to texts of murderesses. I just changed them into the first person [...].[29]

Although Acker had not yet read Foucault, *Childlike Life* is thus methodologically comparable to the Stoics' 'art of living' techniques. It also amounts to a departure from the Stoics' 'self-writing' in two ways. First, far from viewing desire as an 'enemy force' to be regulated, Acker is more intent on freeing it from stricture. Second, rather than attempt to shape a 'true' self, she's more intent on writing herself as a series of different characters. Autobiography is thereby transformed into what we might call *allobiography*—the writing of one's life *as other*. For example, the first chapter of *Childlike Life* is prefaced with the statement '*Intention: I become a murderess by repeating in words the lives of other murderesses*'.[30] Whose 'I' this is soon becomes questionable, though, when the narrator, initially identifying herself as 'Charlotte Wood', undergoes metamorphoses like the following: 'My name is Laura Lane. I'm born in Holly Springs, Mississippi, in 1837. My name is Adelaide Blanche de la Tremouille. I, K A, fall in love with D; D burns me' (*CLBT*, 17). As an end-note makes clear, the chapter is mostly an episodic pageant of appropriated voices; all its 'events' are taken from 'myself' and books on eighteenth- and nineteenth-century murder and adventuresses by E. H. Bierstadt, W. Bolitho, D. Dunbar, and C. Kingston (*CLBT*, 22). The rest of the novels' chapters are similarly based on varying mixtures of diary material and adulterated 'found' texts. And with each chapter presenting episodic switches internally, there's also little continuity between the chapters; the fourth, for example, is drawn largely from erotic novels by Alexander Trocchi and Lesley Branch, while the fifth uses material from W. B. Yeats's *Autobiography* (1938).

Childlike Life's switching of times, places, and narratorial identity is clearly redolent of Burroughs's work, but Acker's reliance on plagiarized material—often altered simply by changing pronouns from third- to first-person—makes for a different kind of fictionality. As Robert Macfarlane has argued, literary plagiarism has frequently challenged the originality of

---

[29] Acker, 'Devoured by Myths', 7.
[30] Kathy Acker, *The Childlike Life of the Black Tarantula by the Black Tarantula*, in *Portrait of an Eye: Three Novels* (New York: Grove, 2000), 2, hereafter cited in the text as *CLBT*.

'creativity' with an alternative notion of 'invention' that involves using 'what is already there' and subjecting it to a 'rearrangement'.[31] Using invention to that effect was avowedly important for Acker—'Creativity presupposes ownership'—and in *Childlike Life* dispossessing herself of an I was a pointed strategy: 'I really didn't want any creativity' (8); 'the I became a dead issue because I realised that you make the I and what makes the I are texts' (11). At this stage, then, Acker's allobiography is less a matter of creating fictions than of inventing fake autobiography from others' writings. And in the novel's final chapter, which reprises material from the Marquis de Sade, the narrator states that her inventions are also aimed at liberating herself from social control: 'I'm simply exploring other ways of dealing with events than ways my lousy habits—mainly installed by parents and institutions—have forced me to act' (*CLBT*, 86). This exploration bears additionally on sexuality and desire, as is evident from the following paragraph in which Acker blends her autobiography with some based on Yeats's:

I travel to Sligo where I'm living with my uncle George Ally who's taken over my grandfather's tall lonely house. [...] My grandmother lifts up my pink organdie dress shows the headwaiter my new panty girdle. My first true bloodstained kotex. I fuck D, A, stop for a year, when one boyfriend asks me how far I've gone I tell him only as far as I have with you thinking all the time he's a fool and stupid, then? P, B, then I become a nymphomaniac. [...] I think that having conquered body desire, lust, my physical inclination toward women and love, which I haven't done yet, I will live in ecstacy, seeking wisdom. O.K. (*CLBT*, 70)

The savage irreverence of the passage intimates a bond between form and content: with Yeats's childhood bleeding textually into her own, the narrative segues into Acker's account of her first menstruation. The subsequent statements about her sexual promiscuity then satirically undermine those based on Yeats aspiring to vanquish 'body desire, lust', which he struggled with in poems like 'Adam's Curse' (1904) and 'The Tower' (1928). Indeed, stating in the final chapter that she lusts not only after 'women' but 'hamsters, trains, criminals, black leather' (*CLBT*, 89), Acker's narrator is anything but invested in the kind of *enkrateia* advocated by the Stoics. And whereas for Foucault the Stoics sought to

---

[31] Robert Macfarlane, *Plagiarism and Originality in Nineteenth-Century Literature* (Oxford: Oxford University Press, 2006), 1. Given Acker's training in Classics she would doubtless have been familiar with the importance of 'invention' for classical rhetoric (see, for example, Cicero's *De Inventione* and Books I and II of Aristotle's *Rhetoric*). For an account of the historical development of rhetorical invention, see Rita Copeland's *Rhetorics, Hermeneutics, and Translation in the Middle Ages: Academic Traditions and Vernacular Texts* (Cambridge: Cambridge University Press, 1991).

incorporate others' writing into their 'tissue and blood' by making it a principle of 'rational action', in Acker's novels of this time introjecting text is more a matter of constituting a feeling body for oneself on the basis of drag.

Relations between drag and social control arise explicitly in Chapter 4:

> I'm sick of this society. 'Earn a living' as if I'm not yet living; lobotomized and robotized from birth, they tell me I can't do anything I want to do in the subtlest and sneakiest ways possible. [. . .] All forms of love are drag. How little do I have to do to survive except for passion, my desire to open and exist as I can only depend for existence on my surroundings, and if I have to do more, if I again have to prostitute by becoming straight, is life—fakery of living—that necessary to me? (*CLBT*, 58)

The sentence here on having to 'earn a living' echoes Marcuse's argument that the 'automatization' of social life precludes realization of 'individual potentialities'. In addition, the sentence's syntax makes it unclear as to whether the 'subtlest and sneakiest ways possible' are attributable to 'they' or 'I'—thus Acker intimates the kind of 'unity' that Foucault was later to ascribe to relations between biopolitics and human possibilities. Just as Ginsberg addressed the mechanization of sentiment in his 'auto-poems', Acker identifies a problem of what we could call *autopathy*: self-feeling regulated as automated feeling, which is what she parodies through drag. In asserting that 'All forms of love are drag', and that 'becoming straight' is a convention one is obliged to perform, Acker effectively foreshadows Judith Butler's argument in *Gender Trouble* (1990) about how drag highlights the constructedness of 'straight' sexuality as being made up of 'words, acts, gestures, and desire': '[Drag's] replication of heterosexual constructs in non-heterosexual frames brings into relief the utterly constructed status of the so-called heterosexual original. Thus, gay is to straight *not* as copy is to original, but, rather, as copy is to copy.'[32] So if Acker's allobiography presents techniques for faking life, it also suggests that 'straight' life and social life are *already* a 'fakery of living'. Whether the 'desire' and 'passion' the narrator speaks of can be free from 'robotized' 'fakery' is therefore equivocal, as she acknowledges when ventriloquizing Yeats: 'If everything is drag, there is no such thing as real love or friendship. I am drag too' (*CLBT*, 67).

In another novel of this period, *I Dreamt I was a Nymphomaniac: Imagining* (1974), Acker delves further into this problem when within a single chapter she presents four times the same two-page passage that begins:

---

[32] Judith Butler, *Gender Trouble* (1990, repr.; London: Routledge, 2008), 43, Butler's emphasis.

Last night I dreamt I was standing on a low rise of grassy ground; Dan was standing next to me facing me. He put his arms around my neck kissed me, said 'I love you'. I said 'I love you'. Two years later I'm riding through a forest with my four young sisters, green and wet, leaves in our eyes and skin; we push leaves out of the way the brown horse's neck lowered.[33]

The autopathic movement of this passage again links text and bodies: incorporating and repeating Dan's 'I love you' in order to formalize their romance, the narrator then dreams that the skin and eyes of herself and her sisters have absorbed the nature through which they ride. As Robert Glück has commented on reading the passage, its verbatim reiterations produce a 'strange doubling': 'I saw how artificial the emotions were—or were made to be—even as I fell into them.'[34] Instead of encouraging the reader to will suspension of disbelief in the world of the characters' sentiments, such writing actively suspends the nature of emotion by emphasizing its fabrication. In identifying *how* feeling can be autopathic, it also neutralizes that autopathy by encouraging readers not to identify *with* it but to view it ironically.

That work of neutralization is what Acker's writing has in common with dream-work (another link to Burroughs), which she increasingly came to explore in her novels. As the reiterated passage from *I Dreamt* suggests, not even dreams are free from autopathic convention. Indeed, in Freud's treatise *The Interpretation of Dreams* (1900) whether oneiric fabulation is really a 'free play' of the unconscious is a point with which he himself struggles. Dreams condense and displace repressed affects, he argues, thereby fashioning new images for them so they can slip through 'the censorship of endopsychic defence'.[35] Consequently, such affects make their appearance in the dream only to the extent that it precipitates their '*transformation*' and '*suppression*'.[36] A dream's formation thus depends on its evasion of the psyche's censorship. Yet by the end of his treatise this appears doubtful, for Freud also suggests that forms of psychic censorship are *intrinsic* to dream formation and 'operate by selecting from the broad mass of material in the dream thoughts, enabling them to enter the dream'.[37] As is clear from his subsequent writings, the structure of that psychic censorship is, for him, largely consequent upon navigating one's

---

[33] Kathy Acker, *I Dreamt I Was a Nymphomaniac: Imagining*, in *Portrait of an Eye*, 101, 103, 105–6, 107–8.
[34] Robert Glück, 'The Greatness of Kathy Acker', in Scholder, Harryman, and Ronell (eds), *Lust for Life*, 46.
[35] Sigmund Freud, *The Interpretation of Dreams*, trans. Joyce Crick (Oxford: Oxford University Press, 1999), 235.
[36] Ibid. 308, Freud's emphases.
[37] Ibid. 326.

way through the Oedipus complex—success in this demanding that a child repress any desires to eliminate its parent of the same sex and to possess its parent of the opposite sex. As resolution of the complex supposedly results from the child's identification with its same-sex parent, healthy psychic life is therefore rooted in a repression that subordinates desire and erotogenic pleasure to structures of psychic censorship that encode the body and also police oneiric labour.

One cannot simply rely on unadulterated accounts of dreams as guaranteeing escape from libidinal regulation, then, which is why Acker transforms them when incorporating them into her novels. In addition to refiguring them with techniques like the reiterations of *I Dreamt*, she also repeatedly exposes Oedipal and other taboos in order to militate against their role in censorship. The novels thus reverse the kind of dream dynamic that Freud theorizes: rather than suppressing and transforming repressed affects to enable them to slip through psychic defences, Acker suppresses the defences so as to provoke a fluid intensity of desire. The latent turns into the blatant. Much of this work also includes reworking conventional 'constructs' of gender, and in that respect Acker's writing can be compared to Baraka's. Whereas Baraka strove to galvanize new African American potentials through Black Arts cultural practice— thereby making ethnicity drive race—Acker's experiments with drag and gender constructs are aimed at establishing different sexual matrices. And as her other novels of the seventies show, her allobiography and exploration of taboos increasingly address the kinds of biopolitics that came to interest Foucault.

For example, in Acker's *Rip-Off Red, Girl Detective* (completed in 1973, published posthumously in 2002) the eponymous narrator presents a series of diary entries and dream sequences while embarking on a detective quest in which family intrigue transmutes into political conspiracy. The first chapter draws on Acker's relationship with Peter Gordon, whom she married in 1976 and separated from in the early eighties. After pages of graphic pornography, the narrator decides she is bored with sex, which is why they must undertake a role-playing quest: 'You're my brother and you're going to have to go along with everything I do. [. . .] From now on you're Peter Peter and I'm Rip-Off Red the famous detective. [. . .] This is a dream. We're going to New York to rip off the money.'[38] The quest is therefore framed as a journey into incest—the name 'Peter Peter' also echoes Humbert Humbert, the protagonist who preys on his step-

---

[38] Kathy Acker, *Rip-Off Red, Girl Detective*, in *Rip-Off Red, Girl Detective and The Burning Bombing of America* (New York: Grove, 2002), 8–9, hereafter cited in the text as *ROR*.

daughter in Vladimir Nabokov's *Lolita* (1955). Exploration of this taboo then proceeds through parallel strands of Rip-Off Red's fictive adventure and her childhood memories, which are drawn from Acker's life and touch on her bisexuality. In Rip-Off's 'first vision of New York' she meets a Sally Spitz, and after having sex with her—during which Sally appears to have a penis—Rip-Off decides that she is her 'sister' (*ROR*, 18). Telling Rip-Off that she wants to solve the mystery of her father's nightly absences, Sally is subsequently murdered and Rip-Off realizes she has her first detective case on her hands: 'I swear to dedicate my life to solving the mystery of Spitz's father [...] and to avenging my love for Spitz' (*ROR*, 26).

In Part 2, the detective romance is interrupted when Rip-Off recounts scenes from her childhood that also include paternal mystery and incest: 'My mother and I play together. She tells me she's my sister' (*ROR*, 63); 'My mother tells me my "father" isn't my real father' (*ROR*, 64). The latter is 'ripped off' from Acker's own childhood experience of her mother telling her that the man she regarded as her father was in fact her stepfather. Moreover, around the time of writing *Rip-Off Red* Acker unsuccessfully undertook her own detective quest to contact her natural father—he remained unknown to her.[39] Once her own life comes into the text, Acker immediately subjects it to Rip-Off's dream revisions while undermining the Oedipal taboo. Stating that her stepfather 'tries to rape me' (*ROR*, 66), Rip-Off also dreams of having sex with her mother:

Up down up down white rivers white fields white narcotics she lays above me she moves slowly into me she moves slowly into me her hands working rapidly maniacally I can feel them below me I can barely feel her body above me, thrashing I can hardly hear her hoarse whispers I want her to enter me and come in me. I love my mother. [...] She puts her arms around me I around her; we separate our bodies and she leaves. (*ROR*, 62)

Whereas her stepfather's advance is experienced as rape, the sexual contact with her mother is dreamed as being polymorphously pleasurable. The syntactic flow from white rivers, fields, and narcotics to her mother connotes a stream of milk that is then imagined more as semen when the narrator declares 'I want her to [...] come in me.' Undoing the Oedipal ban is thus experienced as unleashing repressed libido; both familial and sexual, the narrator's 'love' for her mother is no less fluid than her sense of their merging bodies. Rather than aiming to sublimate libido, the initial metaphorization—'white rivers white fields'—is channelled into blatant expressions of sexual desire.

---

[39] See Kathy Acker, 'On Narrative' (1993), in The Kathy Acker Papers, Duke University Library (Box 4, Folder: 'Reading the Lack of the Body'): 1–2.

If dreams for Freud are the 'royal road' to the unconscious, for Rip-Off they're a yellow-brick road to political revolution:

> I have to disintegrate my mind to the point my mind is inseparable from the common mind or my 'unconscious'. By thinking: dreaming, following sexual and other desires, and by inflaming you with sensuous images, we can get rid of the universities, the crowded towns, the bureaucracies. (*ROR*, 67)

But, by the end of the novel, her chances of realizing wholesale anarchy are dashed by her encounter with Sally Spitz's father, who confesses to being part of 'UNUN, the Universal Nuggets of the United Nations' (*ROR*, 129), a 'conspiracy' fighting against the infiltration of the United Nations by 'a deadly organization, CREEP' (*ROR*, 130). This organization, he states, is split into subsidiaries mired in a range of nefarious enterprises, including 'The Organization of Money [...] Electronic Bugging [...] and Political Espionage' (*ROR*, 130). The plot's convoluted nature is compounded by the fact that CREEP is also the acronym that was popularly given to President Nixon's 'Campaign for the Re-Election of the President' (CRP), whose money-laundering helped fund the legal costs of contesting Watergate scandal charges.[40] In the novel, Spitz accuses CREEP of institutional misogyny, though the appeal of his denunciation is diminished for Rip-Off by the revelation that he murdered Sally in pursuing his politics. Rip-Off's dream of collective liberation is thus blocked not only by CREEP but also by Spitz's conspiratorial patriarchy. That his own dream sounds strikingly similar to hers is also disturbing:

> I have a dream of morality that is no morality of people who are murderers the streets and buildings of New York turn yellow, the sun and piss, the sky reappears to our sightless eyes. The buildings of New York crumble; [...]. Children begin to have sex with each other at the age of two. People do their own minimal work. (*ROR*, 132)

Just as UNUN doubles more than it negates the CREEP-ridden UN, so Spitz as father repeats the same desire to undo sexual and social structures as Rip-Off, who promptly brings the novel to a close by declining the invitation to join his organization: 'I'm no longer a detective. I'll decide to become someone else' (*ROR*, 134).

For all its gestures towards anarchic liberation, such allobiography is cynically analytical more than it is utopic. As Rip-Off's encounter with Spitz suggests, taboo and repressed desire have the potential to be

---

[40] See Bruce J. Schulman, *The Seventies: The Great Shift in American Culture, Society, and Politics* (Cambridge, MA: Da Capo, 2002), 45–6.

transgressive, but their potential can also be forged by the very censorship that bans them. Foucault concurs on this point when linking biopolitics to his 'repressive hypothesis': desire isn't simply 'repressed', for the power that regulates it is 'what constitutes both desire and the lack on which it is predicated'.[41] This hypothesis, states Foucault, bears particularly on incest. Indeed, in a society where 'the family is the most active site of sexuality', sexuality is inherently 'incestuous':

> It is manifested as a thing that is strictly forbidden in the family insofar as the latter functions as a deployment of [social] alliance; but it is also a thing that is constantly demanded in order for the family to be a hotbed of constant sexual incitement.[42]

In relating this paradox to powers of biopolitical control, Acker's writing continues a lineage of US novel writing that conjoins familial love and social alliance through incest. As Elizabeth Barnes has argued, in the wake of American independence a series of novels suggested that 'familial feeling proves the foundation for sympathy, and sympathy the foundation for democracy'.[43] While a novel like Nathaniel Hawthorne's *The Scarlet Letter* (1850) obsessively explores sympathy in relation to adultery, others like William Hill Brown's *The Power of Sympathy* (1789), Herman Melville's *Pierre; or The Ambiguities* (1852), and Maria Cummins's *The Lamplighter* (1854) introduce incest into narratives when social alliance and family love become confused as 'domestic' affairs. Underpinning social cohesion, the power of sympathy, argues Barnes, frequently leads characters to desire marriage with those who are revealed to be family relations. And although novelists were not advocating incest, sentimental novels of the period were certainly aimed at fostering sympathy in a readership. In terms of Foucault's ideas on biopolitics of this period, then, the sentimental novel can be seen as exploring the unity between power and individual possibilities by nurturing intimacies between the state of democracy and states of feeling. In Acker's writing, though, because biopolitical bonding is largely viewed to be 'robotizing', she frequently replaces sympathy with autopathy, which she responds to with antipathy. *Blood and Guts in High School* (1984), which gained her both recognition and notoriety as a writer, is a case in point.

---

[41] Foucault, *The History of Sexuality*, Vol. 1, 81.
[42] Ibid. 109.
[43] Elizabeth Barnes, *States of Sympathy: Seduction and Democracy in the American Novel* (New York: Columbia University Press, 1997), 2.

BLOOD AND GUTS IN HIGH SCHOOL: FROM SYMPATHY TO 'ORDER WORDS'

Acker wrote *Blood and Guts* in the late seventies and had it copyrighted in 1978, though it wasn't until 1984 that she managed to get it published. Much of its taboo sexuality is in common with that of her other writings, but the focus on incest and sexual violence is certainly more brutal and unrelenting than in her previous work. Another feature that literally makes the novel more graphic is Acker's inclusion of her own illustrations, several of which are detailed drawings of genitals. As she later commented, it was the one book she wrote deliberately to 'shock', and she certainly succeeded; West Germany and South Africa banned it for being harmful to minors and obscene, respectively.[44] Around the time Acker was writing the novel her mother committed suicide (when Acker was thirty), and this event was doubtless a factor that contributed to the novel's blacker humours. The opening sentence draws on the event while writing it other: 'Never having known a mother, her mother had died when Janey was a year old, Janey depended on her father for everything and regarded her father as boyfriend, brother, sister, money, amusement, and father.'[45] Janey's story thus begins by reversing Acker's own parental upbringing, though the exploration of incest between Janey and her father soon turns to paternal abandonment. In *Rip-Off Red*, maternal incest was a matter of dream-work and libidinal fluidity; in *Blood and Guts* Janey's sex with her father, Johnny, is figured more as her attempt to gain his love. With Johnny ignoring her in favour of another girl, Sally, Janey's attempts become increasingly desperate and painful: 'He fucked [Janey] in her asshole because the infection made her cunt hurt too much to fuck there, though she didn't tell him it hurt badly there, too, cause she wanted to fuck love more than she felt pain' (*BGHS*, 21). Rather than presenting libidinal liberation, such scenes are devoid of dreams and depict her sexuality more as an addiction over which she has little control.

Despite Janey's willingness to succumb to his desires, Johnny sends her away to school in New York where she soon falls into old habits. Joining a gang called The Scorpions, she has sex with a number of boys which results in two abortions and the following assertion:

---

[44] See West German Federal Inspection Office for Publications Harmful to Minors, 'Immoral' (1986), in Kathy Acker, *Eurydice in the Underworld* (London: Arcadia, 1997), 144–50.
[45] Kathy Acker, *Blood and Guts in High School* (New York: Grove, 1984), 7, hereafter cited in the text as *BGHS*.

I'm not trying to tell you about the rotgut weird parts of my life. Abortions are the symbol, the outer image, of sexual relations in the world. Describing my abortions is the only real way I can tell you about pain and fear... my unstopppable drive for sexual love made me know. (*BGHS*, 34)

As Acker's mother considered aborting her daughter, the narrative here clearly bears on Acker's life story, but it also registers the fact that abortion had indeed become a major biopolitical issue of the time. In 1973 the US Supreme Court ruled in *Roe* v. *Wade* that women had a legal right to abortion, and in the wake of this the official figures for terminations rose dramatically. So did right-to-life activism, and in 1976 the US Congress passed an amendment that barred the use of Federal Medicaid money to fund abortions.[46] That same year, Gerald Ford and Jimmy Carter also placed abortion issues at the heart of their campaigns for the presidency. If, as Foucault argues, biopolitics 'is the power to "make" live and "let" die', then abortion in America was showing how biopolitics can intertwine money, bureaucracy, institutions, and bodies simultaneously. And while many feminists celebrated the *Roe* v. *Wade* decision, it also led conservatives in many states to refuse to ratify the Equal Rights Amendment (ERA), which would have decreed for the first time in America that equal rights could not legally be 'denied or abridged' 'on account of sex'.[47] The rights over one's body that *Roe* v. *Wade* made provision for thus became indicative of how women's sexuality continued to be regulated. Accordingly, in Acker's *Blood and Guts* abortion, as Janey suggests, is less about personal freedom of choice and more a sign of how even one's sex drive might be subject to power relations beyond one's control.

Janey's awareness of that becomes particularly acute when, aged thirteen, she is raped by two boys who then sell her to Mr Linker, an Iranian businessman who trades in 'white slavery', lobotomies, and summer resorts (*BGHS*, 65). When he imprisons her in a room she decides to kill time by appropriating Hawthorne's *The Scarlet Letter* (1850) for her own life story. As the etymology of plagiarism links kidnapping and literary thieving (the Latin '*plagiarius*' can denote either), it also connects the narrative's content and form. At the same time, the narrative relates Janey's life to Hawthorne's novel in terms of intimacy between sexual desire and biopolitical powers of language. *The Scarlet Letter* is set in seventeenth-century puritan Boston and opens with its female protagonist Hester Prynne being pilloried in public before being gaoled for adultery. Having borne her lover a child, Pearl, on release from prison Hester insists

---

[46] See Stephanie Slocum-Schaffer, *America in the Seventies* (Syracuse, NY: Syracuse University Press, 2003), 158–63.
[47] See Schulman, *The Seventies*, 164–70.

on wearing at all times a scarlet letter 'A' that she's embroidered as a token of her adultery and shame. As a result she becomes a stock 'type of sin', the textual character marking her own character 'type' in her eyes and those of others: 'When strangers looked curiously at the scarlet letter,—and none ever failed to do so,—they branded it afresh into Hester's soul.'[48] Continuing to see herself through others' moral perspective, the intensity of her shame is thus rooted in her continuing capacity for sympathy. Yet this sympathy also gives her insight into others' predicaments, which enables her to offer them moral succour. Consequently, many of the townsfolk begin to view her scarlet letter more sympathetically: 'as the token not of that one sin [...] but of her many good deeds since'.[49] In this way, Hawthorne's novel is, in part, a tale of linguistic performativity. Not only does it stress that a sign's significance is tied to what it does— 'typing' character, for example—it also suggests that the significance of these linguistic actions are contingent upon social convention.

Acker's appropriation of *The Scarlet Letter* similarly links language and character but places no such faith in sympathy. For Janey, the 'materialism' Mr Linker embraces is also what makes it difficult for her to feel anything: 'it's sooo easy to be a robot it's sooo easy not to feel. Sex in America is S & M' (*BGHS*, 99). The sexual is the political, as she states a little later on: 'At this point in *The Scarlet Letter* and in my life politics don't disappear but take place inside my body' (*BGHS*, 97). Suggesting that biopolitical life turns sex sadomasochistic, Janey's comment adheres to Marcuse's view of libido as utterly saturated by the 'work-world'. For Foucault, on the other hand, while sadomasochism is 'the eroticization of power', the point of its pleasure lies in turning power relations between people into a contractual 'game'.[50] Sadomasochism is effectively power in drag, and it invents 'new possibilities of pleasure' on that basis.[51] While a social contract of power also underlies the performative fragility of shame in Hawthorne's novel, Janey's predicament is clearly more one of being dominated without consent. The robotization of her life and sexuality is consequently seen by her in terms of society's carceral nature—'We all live in prison' (*BGHS*, 65)—her kidnapping being an objective correlative of that. Like Foucault at the time, then, Acker's novel suggests that sexuality is a matter of both disciplinary institutions (including that of the family) and biopolitical management. Unlike Foucault, though, Acker in this

---

[48] Nathaniel Hawthorne, *The Scarlet Letter* (Oxford: Oxford University Press, 2007), 69.
[49] Ibid. 127.
[50] Michel Foucault, 'Sex, Power, and the Politics of Identity' (1984), in *Foucault Live*, 387, 388.
[51] Ibid. 384.

novel portrays a rigidity of power more than possibilities of exercising it differently. She does that in part by suggesting that biopolitics becomes carceral through language.

As I mentioned earlier, although Foucault stresses the role institutional discourse plays in promulgating disciplinary power, his work on biopolitics tends more to political economy. However, when Janey decides to learn Persian, the intimacy of language and regulated life is made patently clear from the sentences she translates:

Janey is a peasant.
Janey is expensive,
but cheap.
[...]
to have Janey
to buy Janey
to want Janey
to see Janey (*BGHS*, 76, 84)

Each of these sentences exemplify how Janey needs to order herself as a subject according to rules of syntax and vocabulary. While the initial declaratives posit her as a person subject to social value, the subsequent list of infinitive clauses positions her more as an object akin to money. It's not Foucault's notion of institutional discourse that Acker is drawing on here so much as Burroughs's notion of 'the Word' as viral control. As she later stated the argument: 'All aspects of language—denotation, sound, style, syntax, grammar, etc.—are politically, economically and morally coded.'[52] Such a view also accords with Deleuze and Guattari's notion of linguistic power, Acker having read their *Anti-Oedipus* (1972) in the late seventies around the same time she first read Foucault. As Deleuze and Guattari contend in *A Thousand Plateaus* (1980), learning language is fundamentally a matter of learning social regulations; thus, the education system 'imposes upon the child semiotic coordinates possessing all of the dual foundations of grammar (masculine-feminine, singular-plural, noun-verb [...]). The elementary unit of language—the statement—is the order word.'[53] *Every* statement is an 'order word' (*mot d'ordre*) that involves social power, they argue. In using language, one is socially obliged (an implicit order) to employ established 'semiotic coordinates'. Descriptions of states of affairs are always *ascriptions* of linguistic structure. As in *The Scarlet Letter*, the significance of language for Deleuze and Guattari is

---

[52] Acker, 'Postmodernism', 4.
[53] Gilles Deleuze and Félix Guattari, *A Thousand Plateaus*, trans. Brian Massumi (Minneapolis: University of Minnesota Press, 1987), 76.

largely what it does performatively in constituting orders of things. Yet because order words are regulated by institution and social convention they also tend to enforce reiteration as linguistic 'redundancy'.[54] For Acker's Janey, such repetition is linked to the way social order seems propagated robotically through language, such that even feeling becomes autopathically redundant. In contrast, Deleuze and Guattari are closer to Hawthorne in asserting that the performative power of order words depends on social conventions and contexts of usage which are not essentially fixed. Order words therefore always bear a 'power (*puissance*) of variation' as a 'potentiality' within them.[55] Using them doesn't simply mean being *subject to* social power, then; it also involves exercising power and having the possibility of re-ordering it. Hence the importance of literary writers, argue Deleuze and Guattari; by experimenting with language they also establish new performative powers for it.[56]

In *Blood and Guts*, though, Janey uses language predominantly to establish the extent of her slavery. The autopathy she struggles with is also what prevents Mr Linker from having any sympathy for her. Preparing to force her into prostitution on the streets of Tangier he abandons her when he learns she has cancer. The narrative then confirms the extent to which biopolitics and desire are locked together when Janey writes of having sexual relations with President Jimmy Carter that swiftly deteriorate into the same kind of abusive relationship she had with her father. The same thing happens when she encounters the writer Jean Genet in Tangier, at which point the narrative turns into a play script. Appropriating Genet's play about North African revolution, *The Screens* (first performed in 1961), Janey takes on the role of Leila, who in the original play is purchased by Said, a thief who becomes a heroic rebel. As Susan E. Hawkins has pointed out, the revolutionary politics of Genet's play thus ignores the male economic subjection of Leila and the prostitutes that it figures.[57] This background subjection is what Acker brings to the fore when she depicts Janey having a relationship with Genet, who soon holds her in misogynistic abhorrence: 'The closer you get to me, the more I hate you' (*BGHS*, 138). Genet is thus another form of Johnny, as the similarity of their names suggests, and Janey remains subject to domination. With Genet giving her money to 'take care of herself', she promptly dies from the cancer at which point her story ends. Two short postscript sections

---

[54] Deleuze and Guattari, *A Thousand Plateaus*, 79.
[55] Ibid. 101, 99.
[56] Ibid. 98.
[57] Susan E. Hawkins, 'All in the Family: Kathy Acker's *Blood and Guts in High School*', *Contemporary Literature* 45:4 (2004), 653.

follow, 'The World' and 'The Journey', both of which consist of a series of annotated drawings and collages by Acker. These sections echo the graphic 'dream-maps' that appear briefly earlier in the text (*BGHS*, 46–51), but coming as they do after Janey's death they don't restore faith in dreams so much as emphasize how dream-work couldn't alter the course of Janey's story. To be sure, Acker doesn't leave Janey languishing passively in a state of autopathy; as Janey says, 'every howl of pain is a howl of defiance' (*BGHS*, 112)—and there are plenty of those in the text. It's not until after the mid-eighties, though, that Acker's novels draw dream-work, allobiography, and bodily desire together and work them into more positive biopolitical potentials. Before turning to those novels, though, we need to consider some of the main developments in biopolitics that took place under Reagan's presidency.

HOMO ŒCONOMICUS AND CORPOREALITY INC.

In Marcuse's epilogue to his *Eros and Civilization* he cites an objection to Freud, stating that the founder of psychoanalysis 'grossly underrated' the extent to which 'the individual and his neurosis are determined by conflicts with his environment'.[58] At one point in *The Interpretation of Dreams*, though, Freud admits economics into the dynamics of the unconscious—albeit metaphorically—when he likens the 'wish-fulfilment' of dream-work to that of an 'entrepreneur' drawing on reserves of 'capital'.[59] A series of economic initiatives in America during the seventies rendered relations between capital and wish-fulfilment less metaphorical. In 1971 Nixon detached the dollar from the gold standard, thereby allowing the currency's value to be regulated by the money market. Soon after, growing numbers of Americans began turning from traditional forms of savings to investment in money market mutual funds (MMMF).[60] If, for Foucault, neo-liberal biopolitics encourages the individual to become '*homo œconomicus*', an 'entrepreneur of himself',[61] that's precisely what MMMFs did. The introduction of the Visa credit card in 1973 also helped individuals to inflate their wishes and fulfil them. By 1979, though, the national inflation rate had reached double figures and was seriously undermining President Carter's chances of being re-elected. As communications adviser Jerry Rafshoon counselled him: 'It is impossible to overestimate the importance

[58] Marcuse, *Eros and Civilization*, 196.
[59] Freud, *The Interpretation of Dreams*, 366.
[60] See Schulman, *The Seventies*, 136–8.
[61] Foucault, *The Birth of Biopolitics*, 226.

of the inflation issue for your presidency. [...] It affects every American in a palpable way. [...] It affects the American Dream.'[62]

Such sentiments clearly bear on Foucault's and Acker's suggestions that managed life and individual desires have become invidiously yoked together. Drawing heavily on Foucault's work on biopolitics, Nikolas Rose in his study *Governing the Soul* (1989) also discusses how large American companies in the seventies encouraged workers to internalize corporatism. In collaboration with governmental and non-governmental bodies—including the left-leaning International Labour Organization—many corporations sought to enhance productivity by promoting worker well-being under the banner of 'Quality of Working Life' (QWL). Benefits to workers were part of a QWL ideology that encouraged them to value their labour and employer *as* their well-being. From this perspective, writes Rose,

work is no longer necessarily a constraint upon the freedom of the individual to fulfil his or her potential through the strivings of the psychic economy for autonomy, creativity, and responsibility. There is no longer any barrier between the economic, the psychological, and the social.[63]

This individual 'autonomy' derives from what Marcuse would consider to be its 'automatization'. As Foucault suggests when discussing *homo œconomicus*, such management works in tandem with neo-liberal economics to motivate individuals to regulate their own lives.[64] Corporate governance becomes incorporated; or, as Acker's Janey puts it, 'politics [...] take place inside my body'.

With Reagan's accession to the Presidency in 1981, the advocacy of self-regulation grew dramatically. Within weeks of taking office, he announced plans that would effectively reverse fifty years of social welfare policy rooted in Roosevelt's New Deal.[65] His introduction of 'Supply-Side' economic policy was initially beneficial—by stemming the supply of money and raising interest rates, he brought individual borrowing and the inflation problem under control.[66] What it didn't banish was recession. As Christian Parenti has argued, though, for the Reagan administration recession brought its own benefits. High unemployment kept labour

---

[62] Quoted in Schulman, *The Seventies*, 133.
[63] Nikolas Rose, *Governing the Soul: The Shaping of the Private Self* (London: Routledge, 1989), 118.
[64] Foucault, *The Birth of Biopolitics*, Chs 10 and 11.
[65] See Michael Foley, 'Presidential Leadership and the Presidency', in *The Reagan Years: The Record in Presidential Leadership* (Manchester: Manchester University Press, 1990), 32–7.
[66] See Gil Troy, *Morning in America: How Ronald Reagan Invented the 1980s* (Princeton: Princeton University Press, 2005), 65–7.

costs low, eroded union power, and thereby boosted companies' ability to make jobs a matter of markets.[67] The policy of deregulating financial markets and services also gave them greater freedoms. The Reagan administration's *raison d'état* was thus largely one of turning government over to businesses—as was evident from the decision to privatize aspects of public services, particularly health care and prisons. That there were estimated to be two million people homeless by 1987, and thirty-seven million people without health insurance by 1988, is indicative of the extent to which people were left to manage their own welfare.[68] Two other issues turned self-regulation into a biopolitical issue: drugs and the spread of HIV/AIDS.

Reagan's sustained campaign against drugs sought to turn use of them into a moral issue that citizens themselves would police. Federal funding for drug treatment was cut, while the budget for advertising the drug-war campaign grew—most of the advertisements drawing attention to individuals' responsibility to avoid a life of addiction. While encouraging citizens to judge their own lives, the administration also expanded disciplinary measures for the guilty. The Comprehensive Crime Control Act (1984) and the Anti-Drug Abuse Act (1988) together made provision for increased fines, new mandatory gaol sentences, and extension of the Federal death penalty for those involved in 'continuing criminal enterprise drug offenses'.[69] Just as Acker had suggested that sexual drives were caught between biopolitics and disciplinary institutions, so Reagan's war on drugs was waged against the production of aberrant addictions and affects through a mixture of advertising, prisons, and extended sovereign powers. For Foucault, biopolitics comprises strategies to 'make live' and 'let die', while sovereignty traditionally 'took life and let live'. As Reagan's policies on drugs and abortion show, biopolitical and sovereign powers were entwined in his role as president.

The spread of the AIDS epidemic from the early eighties also saw liberalism and biopolitics join forces. On one hand, the Reagan administration ultimately allocated more funds to finding a biomedical solution for the virus than all other countries put together. On the other hand, in the early years of the epidemic, as Peter Baldwin states, 'it was widely thought that everyone could be his own quarantine officer, taking the

---

[67] Christian Parenti, *Lockdown America: Police and Prisons in the Age of Crisis* (New York: Verso, 2000), 38–41.
[68] See Parenti, *Lockdown America*, 44; also Foley, 'Presidential Leadership and the Presidency', 35.
[69] See Parenti, *Lockdown America*, Ch. 3.

precautions required to avoid transmission'.[70] The fact that health care by this time was widely privatized made it all the more necessary for individuals to take sexual health matters into their own hands. For Baldwin, this promotion of self-control as a way of regulating the epidemic is also symptomatic of the biopolitical governmentality that Foucault writes of: 'Citizens govern themselves not just in terms of politics, but also in their own moral, instinctual, and emotional economy. [...] The modern state no longer instructs, commands, and punishes. It educates, informs, persuades, and discourages.'[71] For Foucault, though, the story of modern power is not one of serial usurpation whereby sovereignty is eventually replaced wholesale by governmentality. Instead, he argues, we need to think of continuing compounds of power, a flexible 'triangle' of 'sovereignty-discipline-government'.[72] Reagan's war on drugs is a particular example of that triangulated power. Measures employed in the eighties to control the spread of AIDS amounted to a similarly complex synthesis. For example, America passed more legislation protecting AIDS victims from discrimination than most of Europe. Yet as Baldwin points out, America was also 'particularly active in using the penal code against potentially transmissive behavior'.[73] Many states made it a criminal offence for someone infected with HIV not to inform his/her partner. Foreigners entering the country were screened for infection and excluded for having the virus. Some states required screening of couples before marriage, and by 1987 the Federal Bureau of Prisons began testing the serostatus of new inmates biannually.[74]

Under Reagan, mergers of biopolitical, disciplinary, and sovereign powers were thus galvanized and extended. But does this mean that the life of every individual came to be wholly dominated and determined by state power? No, it doesn't. If some people were empowered as entrepreneurs of themselves, the rises in homelessness, drugs use, and the prison population show that the extent to which people were enfranchised and regulated varied greatly, and factors such as race, class, and sexuality continued to play a role in those divergences. This doesn't mean that some people's lives were freer of power than others. As Foucault argues, 'there is no point where you are free from all power relations. But you can

---

[70] Peter Baldwin, *Disease and Democracy: The Industrialized World Faces AIDS* (Berkeley, CA: University of California Press, 2005), 129.
[71] Ibid. 160.
[72] Michel Foucault, 'Governmentality', in Faubion (ed.), *Essential Works of Foucault*, Vol. 3, 219.
[73] Baldwin, *Disease and Democracy*, 155.
[74] Ibid. 70, 121.

always change it.'[75] As for Deleuze and Guattari, power for Foucault is contingent upon how individuals use it. Consequently, people aren't simply subjugated by power networks; rather, they 'are in a position to both submit to and exercise this power'[76]—which is why 'there are always possibilities of changing the situation'.[77] These possibilities won't be the same for every circumstance and individual, nor will the types of change. Indeed, the variety of approaches is also evident in the differing stances of the writers I've discussed in the previous chapters: where Burroughs was intent on combating the effects of power on himself and individual readers, both Baraka and Ginsberg sought to link such combat to political activism.

Acker lies somewhere between those two positions. She declared allegiance to feminism and also associated with various subculture groups throughout her life, including motorcycle clubs and the San Francisco lesbian S/M collective, SAMOIS. Agreeing with Burroughs about the viral control of language, though, she also explored ways of resisting its effects, and after the mid-eighties that also entailed developing new 'myths' and alternative 'languages of the body'. As I'll show, Acker repeatedly presents these endeavours in terms of intimacies between power and individual possibilities. And as is evident from the novels, taking possession of power continued to be less about Stoical *enkrateia* and more about liberating bodily desire. *Blood and Guts* had marked a turning point, she said; the point at which her earlier interest in the 'I' and identity turned more to plagiarism.[78] As the titles *Great Expectations* (1982) and *Don Quixote* (1986) suggest, her novels of the first half of the eighties continued to invest in that plagiarism. *Don Quixote* marks another watershed, though:

By the end of [it] I was doing what I had always done, taking stuff and looking at context, seeing how they worked next to passages that had a lot of political meaning in them and seeing what society meant, but the meaning wasn't clear. [. . .] So I thought I should work toward a reformation of what would be sense.[79]

The title of Acker's next novel, *Empire of the Senseless* (1988), might seem to suggest otherwise. But the novel does turn away from the analytical work that Acker ascribes above to *Don Quixote* and her previous texts—work which she describes elsewhere as 'deconstruction'.[80] Rather than

---

[75] Foucault, 'Sex, Power, and the Politics of Identity', 167.
[76] Foucault, *'Society Must Be Defended'*, 29.
[77] Foucault, 'Sex, Power, and the Politics of Identity', 167.
[78] Acker, 'Devoured by Myth', 10.
[79] Ibid. 17.
[80] See, for example, Kathy Acker, 'Kathy Acker Interviewed by Rebecca Deaton', *Textual Practice* 6:2 (February 1991), 278–9.

focus on looking at found material in new contexts, *Empire* is more concerned with constructing new 'myths' of power. Bearing in mind Acker's statement about writing in a similar vein up to *Don Quixote*, in turning to her novels of the eighties I'll discuss those before *Empire* only briefly, focusing on how they relate biopolitical and presidential powers.

'THIS'S NO WORLD FOR IDEALISM': AIDS, ABORTION, AND REAGAN'S BODY

In 1981, while still writing *Great Expectations*, Acker wrote an essay that muses at length on possibility. By the end of it she concludes that 'the tools I use to observe are shaping what I see. My uses turn possibilities into actualities. In the realm of possibility, chaos and indeterminacy exist alongside of order and determinacy.'[81] This seems to herald a promising turn: like Deleuze and Guattari's view of order words, Acker declares her use of language to be a performative realization of 'possibilities'—fiction being the particular 'realm' in which to foster them. Having suggested that, though, she then asks 'What are the laws of possibility?'[82] This question subtends her novels of the first half of the eighties; in terms of the biopolitical 'unity of power and possibility' that Foucault asserts, they examine rigidities of power more than its potentials.

Acker's *Great Expectations* recycles some of the concerns of *Blood and Guts*, particularly the 'big question' of the novel, which, as she stated, is 'my mother's suicide'.[83] The focus in *Blood and Guts* on parental abandonment is thus exchanged for a narrative about orphanhood, which is what she draws from Dickens's *Great Expectations* (1861). Acker stated that she saw Dickens as a 'golden light' for the way he presents a 'plurality of voices',[84] and his *Great Expectations* certainly does that through its character and narrator, Pip, who tells of his journey from penurious orphanhood to middle-class adult prosperity. Reflecting back on his own life, Pip's 'I' splits between past and present, while the formation of his character is attributed to a range of social determinants, including family, work, class, and the fortune his mysterious benefactor bequeaths him. Suffering from a fever at one point, Pip fancies himself trapped in greater structures:

---

[81] Kathy Acker, 'Peter Gordon: Ambiguity', 18.
[82] Ibid.
[83] Acker, 'Kathy Acker Interviewed...', 277.
[84] Kathy Acker, 'A Radical American Abroad', interview with Tony Dunn, *Drama* 160 (1986), 17.

that I was a brick in the house-wall, and yet entreating to be released from the giddy place where the builders had set me; that I was a steel beam of a vast engine, clashing and whirling over a gulf, and yet that I implored in my own person to have the engine stopped, and my part in it hammered off [...] I know of my remembrance, and did in some sort know at the time.[85]

Dickens thus turns social determinism into a matter of literary naturalism, which is particularly apposite for Acker's own interest in social control. With the added irony that Dickens had lobbied to strengthen copyright laws, Acker plagiarizes sporadically from his *Great Expectations*, building her own with textual bricks from it, some of which are retained unmodified.[86] Supplementing these appropriations with borrowings from other authors—notably Pierre Guyotat, Pauline Réage, John Keats, and Sextus Propertius—Acker highlights her indebtedness in inventing another Pip.

While the character of Dickens's Pip changes in the course of his novel, Acker's adopts various identities, including that of herself in a section that sets autobiography against the context of power mergers. Having switched to third-person narration, the section tells of how 'Kathy', 'the female artist', was abandoned by both parents as a child.[87] Her father is head of a 'North-Eastern power coalition' that, along with 'top-ranking military' and 'Southern oil producers', is controlling the American government.[88] Acker thereby draws on the sorts of power triangulations that were occurring at the time and prepares a ravelling of plot akin to that of Mr Spitz's UNUN organization in *Rip-Off Red*. In this section of *Great Expectations*, though, not only does the convolution comprise a more disparate set of powers, it also features a more incestuous confusion of the 'domestic' in terms of biopolitics and family. Kathy's lover Peter, we're told, slept with her mother, who is killed by her father on learning of it. Peter then marries Kathy to revenge himself, and so is absorbed into her family and her father's coalition:

Now the husband loves her because he's part of the North-Eastern Reagan group and wants to use her to do her father in.

The female artist still thinks art is the only purity. The North-Eastern art patron group videotapes and even stage-manages every bedroom and intimate scene they can for info and blackmail purposes. The porn tapes they have no (more) use for they sell as high art. One very famous artist in New York City is

---

[85] Charles Dickens, *Great Expectations* (London: Penguin, 1996), 462.
[86] On Dickens' copyright concerns, see John Feather, *Publishing, Piracy, and Politics: An Historical Study of Copyright in Britain* (London: Mansell, 1994), Ch. 6.
[87] Kathy Acker, *Great Expectations* (New York: Grove, 1982), 81, 82.
[88] Ibid. 82.

very fond of privately commissioning and buying these snuff films. The female artist learns her father murdered her mother.[89]

With Peter's marriage indicating how power and family are in bed with each other, Kathy's vision of art as purity is sullied by the fact that the 'North-Eastern Reagan group' is also patronizing the art scene while turning it into a pornography market. This might seem an historical counter-factual; it was the report published in 1970 by Nixon's 'Commission on Obscenity and Pornography' which paved the way to *easing* legal restrictions on pornography, and by 1977 'blue movie' videotapes were beginning to be widely available.[90] By the mid-eighties, Reagan's concerns over the spread of pornography prompted him to commission an inquiry into it, and the resultant 'Meese Report' (1986) detailed, in part, how the porn industry had links to organized crime. Yet a large part of the industry's growth was indicative of the conglomerate culture that Reagan's administration encouraged. Suffering from the recession at the start of the eighties, Hollywood's increased production of X-rated films was symptomatic of the mergers that film companies like United Artists and MGM underwent at the hands of their conglomerate owners. Acker picks up on this satirically in the passage above which suggests that the amalgamations of power taking place were undoing differences between sexuality, politics, art, and the market. Alluding to the burgeoning commercialization of art, particularly in New York at the time, the passage also suggests that sexuality is caught in a biopolitical fusion of spheres, as the production of 'snuff films'—in which someone, usually a woman, is killed during sex—segues into the father's murder of Kathy's mother.

Acker pursues this fusion of sex and power further in her next novel, *My Death My Life by Pier Paolo Pasolini* (1984). Her attraction to Pasolini, the Italian dramatist, film-maker, and poet is unsurprising on a number of counts. An openly homosexual communist, he shared Acker's enthusiasm for adapting texts, which he did notably in films such as *Oedipus Rex* (1967), *The Canterbury Tales* (1972), and *Salò or the 120 Days of Sodom* (1975). The latter is particularly focused on alliances of power and sexuality, and presents a reprise of de Sade's novel *120 Days of Sodom*, setting it in Salò, the short-lived Fascist Republic that Benito Mussolini established in Northern Italy in 1943. With its characters based on those in de Sade's novel, the film depicts how a set of corrupt Fascist officials detain a group of young men and women in a country house. Forcing

---

[89] Acker, *Great Expectations*, 82–3.
[90] See John Ehrman, *The Eighties; America in the Age of Reagan* (New Haven: Yale University Press, 2005), 177.

them to perform numerous sexual acts, including coprophagia and rape, the film ends with scenes of some of the youths torturing their peers to death. Sadism is thus converted into political allegory. On one hand, this includes a corruption of biopolitics, as when the Fascist Duke declares that the enforced acts of 'sodomy' harbour 'the death of the human species' for being non-reproductive.[91] On the other hand, such control is imagined as sovereignty, as when he declares that 'Power is true Anarchy' and 'Whoever serves it leads himself'.[92] (That's to say; a subject becomes sovereign through subjection to power—the paradox is one that Foucault also identifies in de Sade's work.) As I've stated, with his 'repressive hypothesis' Foucault argues that laws and power establish desire for the very things they prohibit. The writings of de Sade show this relation from the reverse perspective: sexuality's 'nature' is delimited by the 'Law' of social discourse, and there's no transgression that doesn't confirm a limit of law. Accordingly, argues Foucault, language in de Sade's work is constantly 'seeking the limits of the possible'.[93]

Having pondered 'laws of possibility' while writing *Great Expectations*, Acker pursues them further in *My Death My Life*. The novel opens with Pasolini as narrator discussing his life and stating that he will 'solve my murder by denying the principle of causation'.[94] Subsequently, the novel splits into two parts featuring disparate appropriations from a range of writers, including Shakespeare, James Joyce, Alain Robbe-Grillet, and Emily Brontë. In Part 1 a resetting of Shakespeare's *Hamlet* continues the anti-Reaganism of *Great Expectations* when Hamlet declares: 'I will represent the poverty of spirit that the powers behind Reagan endorse. Economic poverty. Social poverty. Political poverty. Emotional poverty. Ideational poverty' (*MDML*, 195). Hamlet's plight is thus attributed both to his father's death and to wider 'powers', and later in Part 1 his inability to act is further evinced in the narrator's 'feeling that everything is uncertain and there are decreasing possibilities unlike an opera overture in which everything is false. I am catatonic' (*MDML*, 225). Correlating possibilities and operatic falsity suggests the two might be linked through role-playing and imagination, which is precisely what we're presented with in Part 2 when the narrative switches to an epistolary exchange between Emily Brontë and her sister, Charlotte. One of Emily's letters becomes a flight of fancy addressing Japan's relations with America:

---

[91] Pier Paolo Pasolini (dir.), *Salò or the 120 Days of Sodom* (United Artists, 1975).
[92] Ibid.
[93] Michel Foucault, 'Language to Infinity', in Donald F. Bouchard (ed.), *Language, Counter-Memory, Practice* (Ithaca, NY: Cornell University Press, 1977), 61.
[94] Kathy Acker, *My Death My Life by Pier Paolo Pasolini* in *Literal Madness: Three Novels* (New York: Grove, 1987), 183, hereafter cited in the text as *MDML*.

The yellow men have captured Reagan. They bow to him and say, 'We are not original. We take what is given such as American know-how, do it better, then send the products—such as clothes, machines—back to America. We adopt everything. We adapt everything. We adapted Hiroshima. (Bowing.) Hiroshima was the way we adapted to your non-adaptable civilization. Now we give Hiroshima as a reality back to you. (Bowing.)' Reagan's head appears stuck on a white pole yellow with dog piss. (*MDML*, 321)

This deceptively crude satire offers rich engagement with historical context. While America borrowed huge amounts of funds from Japan in the eighties, there was also widespread concern about the Japanese electrical goods and cars that flooded the American market, usually undercutting the domestic equivalents in price. Acker makes this a matter of plagiarism with the statements about Japanese cultural 'adoption' and 'adaption'. Emily also suggests that such plagiarism amounts to turning atomic war into cultural-economic war: in other words, Japanese adaptions are fallout fed back from Hiroshima. Imagining this as a decapitation of Reagan picks up on the extent to which Reagan's body was repeatedly made a matter of state throughout his two terms in office. As Kenneth Dean and Brian Massumi have written, 'The Reagan presidency reintroduced the body of the leader as an effective mechanism in US politics.'[95] Draping himself in the stars-and-stripes on numerous public occasions, Reagan in his autobiography *Where's the Rest of Me?* (1965) claimed he was an embodiment of America from birth: 'My face was blue from screaming, my bottom was red from whacking, and my father claimed afterward that he was white.'[96] During his presidency his body became a source of national interest largely because of the various ailments from which he suffered. From the 1981 assassination attempt on him to hand surgery, prostate problems, and speculation about his Alzheimer's, Reagan's health was repeatedly linked to the well-being of the body politic. And if being born into his family meant being born into the fabric of America, Reagan also frequently used anecdotes about families to drive his political speeches home. For Dean and Massumi, all this meant that Reagan's presidency showed how 'Body, family, country share a common substance'—one that largely consists of 'TV'.[97] In other words, the sense of Reagan as a personification of the body politic was sustained by the media's beaming his image into households nationwide. But as Acker's Emily suggests, the common substance

---

[95] Kenneth Dean and Brian Massumi, *First and Last Emperors: The Absolute State and the Body of the Despot* (New York: Autonomedia, 1992), 88.
[96] Ronald Reagan with Richard B. Hubler, *Where's the Rest of Me?* (1965, repr.; New York: Karz, 1981), 3.
[97] Dean and Massumi, *First and Last Emperors*, 90, 94.

of such domestic drama was also open to foreign bodies. Reagan might have escaped assassination, but his head was frequently captured across the nation by Japanese television sets.

The imagined fiction of Emily's and Charlotte's correspondence clearly differs from the 'self-writing' that Foucault attributed to that of the Stoics. But if fiction and falsity are part of what make the letters allobiographical, that's not to say that they're less about life. As the narrator states earlier, 'nonsense isn't only nonsense' and 'writing isn't just writing': 'it's a meeting of writing and living the way existence is the meeting of mental and material or language of idea and sign. It is how we live' (*MDML*, 246). Fiction, no less than the Stoics' 'self-writing', can thus provide an aesthetics of existence because life and language join in a monistic substance that includes the interlacing of bodies, families, images, and country. But if that substance is porous, just how open to foreign bodies is it? This matter is raised near the end of Part 2 when Acker turns Shakespeare's *Macbeth* into a play about the Irish Republican Army (IRA) and terrorism. In Act II, the 'Play's Writer' muses on writing and the world more generally:

A definition, my first, of this world's AIDS. AIDS' the breakdown of the body's immunity system: the body becomes allergic to itself. [. . .]

What's AIDS? A virus. A virus seemingly unknowable who gets identity by preying on an entity, a cell. Writers whose identities depend on written language're viruses. I'm trying to break down the social immune system. Even this sentence's false. (*MDML*, 362)

From writing self as other (*allos*), allobiography is viewed as producing allergic reactions in the 'social immune system'. By comparing writers to AIDS, Acker presents a disturbing twist to Burroughs's idea of literature as virus. At the time she wrote the passage, HIV had only just been identified as the micro-organism that causes AIDS. In the year that the novel was published Foucault died of an AIDS-related illness, and by the end of the decade many of Acker's friends had, too. Consequently, although she proceeds to correlate writing and bodies in subsequent novels, she drops the analogy between authors and AIDS to highlight instead what she raises at the end of the passage above: writing as form of falsification, which she also associates with forging alternative bodily potentials.

Acker's disillusionment with America in the early eighties played a large part in her decision to move to London. But as her comments linking Thatcher to Reagan testify, Britain held its own problems for her, and by the end of the decade she returned to San Francisco. The state of America continued to prey on her mind while she was out of the country, though, as is evident from her *Don Quixote*. In appropriating Miguel de

Cervantes's *Don Quixote de la Mancha* (1605, 1615) Acker signals that she is further exploring relations between fiction and the world. In Cervantes's text, those relations are questioned partly in terms of authorship; the novel is presented as drawing on a 'history' written by a Moor, Cid Hamet Benengeli.[98] Don Quixote has already lost touch with reality at the start of the book by virtue of having lost himself in the worlds of chivalric romance he reads. Deciding to become a knight he sets out with his henchman Sancho Panza in quest of adventures, all of which involve Don Quixote replacing everyday reality with his fanciful delusions. To some extent, Cervantes's novel thus presents a predicament that is the reverse of what Acker portrays up until the mid-eighties. In writing herself other, Acker frequently questions the fictionality of her allobiographies by tempering her creativity with plagiarism. Rather than simply willing wholesale belief in her fictional world, then, she often suspends the fictionality in order to consider how the writing relates to contexts of power. And as we've seen, those contexts are often viewed as undermining powers of fiction and imagination, as with Janey's Persian poems or the 'decreasing possibilities' of *Great Expectations*.

Don Quixote continues in a similar vein, and opens with 'Kathy' having an abortion. Acker's return to this issue was no doubt partly prompted by the fact that it continued to be a highly controversial one in America. By the mid-eighties, Reagan was proving to be the most ardent anti-abortion president to date. In 1984 he likened the battle against abortion to the 'war' fought for civil rights, and in the year that Acker's *Don Quixote* was published his Solicitor General, Charles Fried, called for the *Roe* v. *Wade* decision to be overturned.[99] That didn't happen, but Reagan was successful in further stemming funds for abortions.[100] Understandably, then, for Acker's Kathy in *Don Quixote*, far from being a matter of quixotic fantasy, abortion presents her with a reality-check: 'this's no world for idealism. Example: the green paper would tear as soon as the abortion began.'[101] Yet the reality of the experience is what engenders her desire to escape from it, which is why she promptly renames herself Don Quixote and sets herself the task of 'saving the world' (*DQ*, 11). What proceeds mostly follows Cervantes's novel only obliquely. Acker's Don Quixote also has a henchman, Saint Simeon, but the episodic structure of the novel draws on texts

---

[98] Miguel de Cervantes's *Don Quixote de la Mancha*, trans. Charles Jarvis (Oxford: Oxford University Press, 1998), 68.
[99] Barbara Hinkson Craig and David M. O'Brien, *Abortion and American Politics* (Chatham, NJ: Chatham House, 1993), 171, 186.
[100] Ibid. 188.
[101] Kathy Acker, *Don Quixote* (New York: Grove, 1986), 9, hereafter cited in the text as *DQ*.

by a range of other authors—notably Frank Wedekind, Georges Bataille, and Giuseppe di Lampedusa—and includes lengthy lampoons of President Nixon as well as pilfered meditations on US history.

The switching between literature and history relates to the dual nature of Don Quixote's quest; on one hand, it centres on her search for love with Saint Simeon; on the other hand, their chances of finding love are dependent on defeating 'Evil enchanters such as Ronald Reagan and certain feminists, like Andrea Dworkin, who control the nexuses of government and culture [...] and will continue to persecute us' (*DQ*, 102). In Cervantes's novel the 'evil enchanter' is one of Sancho Panza's fabulations that Don Quixote believes in, but in Acker's text the enchanters are 'evil' for exerting real 'control' over people's lives. To figure Dworkin as biopolitical partner to Reagan is a satirical exaggeration— and an irony, given the links Acker made in *Great Expectations* between pornography and Reaganomics. In *Pornography: Men Possessing Women* (1981) Dworkin presents a hard-line feminism, suggesting that pornography and male sexual penetration of women essentially serve to render women objects rather than subjects. Satirizing Dworkin is also ironic for the fact that Acker's Don Quixote earlier espouses very similar views about being a woman to Saint Simeon: 'I'm your desire's object, dog, because I can't be the subject' (*DQ*, 28). Her response to this predicament seems to be a promising return to Acker's earlier aesthetics of drag: 'She had to become a knight, for she could solve this problem only by becoming partly male' (*DQ*, 29). Indeed, Don Quixote subsequently has a number of visions and fantasies, the use of which is brought into question in Part 2 in a conversation between several 'girls'. As one of them comments: 'fantasizing allows me to understand. Every possibility doesn't become actual fact. So knowing is separate from acting in the common world' (*DQ*, 54). Again, then, fictional possibilities are seen as coming up against limits of the world, which is why in Part 3 the quest becomes one of defeating the 'evil enchanters' in the form of Nixon. When this is achieved, though, the struggle simply shifts to another level:

Don Quixote realized that defeating Nixon isn't defeating America and that to defeat America she had to learn who America is. What is the myth of America, for economic and political war or control now is taking place at the level of language or myth. (*DQ*, 117)

Searching for America's identity results in a continued juxtaposition of Don Quixote's story with lengthy passages from a variety of historical sources on Puritanism, Nixon, and his Secretary of State, Henry Kissinger. As I've quoted Acker acknowledging, the novel thus turns into the kind of endeavour she'd previously been intent on: 'looking at context' in terms of passages 'with a lot of political meaning' to see 'what society meant'. By the end of the novel there is no evidence of either a myth of contemporary America or its defeat. Yet the forays back into drag, dreams, and fantasy do renew some faith in fashioning alternative alliances, and the novel closes with Don Quixote fantasizing about bands of pirates through dreams and song: 'Language is community. Dogs, I'm now inventing a community for you and me' (*DQ*, 191).

EMPIRE OF THE SENSELESS: CYBERDRAG AND 'LANGUAGES OF THE BODY'

In 1989 Acker stated that when she began writing *Empire of the Senseless* she thought to herself: 'You can't change society. You know this.'[102] If writing that felt like admitting defeat it also helped her to see how she needed to change the focus of her work. Like Burroughs, rather than try to 'defeat America' she started to explore more how writing could combat power's effects on oneself. In *Empire*, then, she launches a different approach to her writing. Instead of subordinating fiction to social analyses she begins to build 'myth' as an alternative world of bodily affect. This has a number of consequences: dream-work is foregrounded again; the narrative is less interrupted with slabs of autobiography and historical source material; consequently, the fictional frame is reinforced. Burroughs's return in the 1980s to narrative more generally and to pirates in particular was clearly an influence on Acker, for much of the myth she wrote from *Empire* onwards involves piracy. But her pirate myths differ markedly from Burroughs's interests; while he presents his later fictions as means of escaping the body, Acker presents her piracy as a way of refiguring corporeality. As she stated on several occasions, from the late eighties onwards her interest in things corporeal ranged from getting tattooed to maintaining a strict regime of body-building.[103]

She also drew inspiration from others' work on the body, including that of Jeanette Winterson, Monique Wittig, Luce Irigaray, and Judith Butler. What's clear from a number of Acker's essays is that this turn to writing bodies is largely a matter of incorporating fictive 'possibilities'. In 'Seeing Gender', for example, Acker discusses Lewis Carroll's *Alice through the Looking Glass* and states:

---

[102] Kathy Acker, 'A Few Notes on Two of My Books', in *Bodies of Work*, 11.
[103] See, for example, 'Bodies of Work' (1993), in *Bodies of Work*, 143–50.

Is it possible that the girl can find her actual body, and so what gender might be, in language? [...] Like Alice, I suspect that the body, as [Judith] Butler argues, might not be co-equivalent with materiality, that my body might be deeply connected to, if not be, language.[104]

This bears on the argument I cited earlier from Butler in terms of drag: gender roles and discourse don't simply express bodied sexuality, they also construct it. For Acker, this is a reason to develop '*languages of the body*', which she outlines more fully in two other essays. There are, in her view, a range of such languages; some of them are produced directly by the body—'laughter, silence, screaming'—while others liberate corporeality by undoing any fixed sense of self or meaning.[105] Examples of the latter include 'Languages which contradict themselves' and 'languages of flux' and of 'wonder' in which 'the "I" (eye) constantly changes'.[106] Relating these to sexuality, Acker asserts that such linguistic transformations are 'the most metaphorical'; by 'continually slipping into falsity' they also 'represent the breadth and depth or possibilities of the sexual world'.[107] As 'dangerous possibilities' these powers of falsifying flux are what Acker's pirate myths explore, and in 'Seeing Gender' she explains how they act on the body when she compares them to dream-work: 'When I dream, my body is the site, not only of the dream, but also of the dreaming and the dreamer.'[108] If the body becomes the site of the text, this implicates the reader, too, as Acker states elsewhere: 'It's the body, it's the real body, which is language, the text. The actual words, that's real. Then there's the reality of the reader reading it ... the reality of the writer writing it. It's a triangular situation, a text is not a dead thing.'[109] With this *ménage à trois*, Acker prepares a triangulated aesthetics of existence to countermand the triangulated powers of biopolitics, discipline, and sovereignty that she'd previously depicted. When Janey in *Blood and Guts in High School* declared that 'politics don't disappear but take place inside my body' it was because she felt her body to be so subordinate to politics and discourse. Having used her writings to analyse social power, Acker turns to presenting her own literary potentialism in which fiction makes different states of body possible. In that respect, and despite the generic differences, her potentialism becomes similar to Ginsberg's. If it makes

---

[104] Kathy Acker, 'Seeing Gender' (n.d.), in *Bodies of Work*, 166.
[105] Kathy Acker, 'The Languages of the Body' (1991), in The Kathy Acker Papers, Duke University Library (Box 4, Folder: 'For Ariane, 1990–1 Writings'): 1.
[106] Ibid.
[107] Kathy Acker, 'The Language of Sex, The Sex of Language' (1990), in The Kathy Acker Papers, Duke University Library (Box 4, Folder: 'For Ariane, 1990–1 Writings'): 2.
[108] Acker, 'Seeing Gender', 166.
[109] Acker, 'Kathy Acker Interviewed...', 280.

the body feel real it's on the basis of liberating it from autopathy by prising dreams, wonder, and what is 'most metaphorical' into experience.

Another important influence in Acker's turn to bodies was the thinking on cyborgs being undertaken in the eighties by intellectuals such as Donna Haraway. In 'A Cyborg Manifesto' (1985) Haraway defines a cyborg as 'a hybrid of machine and organism' and argues that this hybridity is already prevalent in society—medicine, war, and modern production being three areas in which syntheses of bodies and machines are particularly prevalent.[110] For Haraway, such syntheses testify to human bodies being fluid 'constructs' composed of various social relations, and this means their hybridity incorporates not only inorganic matter but also discourse. As social subjects we are all cyborgs, she avers; 'a condensed image of both imagination and material reality'.[111] Drawing the figure of cyborg from science fiction, Haraway also suggests that the 'fiction' of the 'cyborg myth' is materially present in the world as the *fabrication* of lived life.[112] Including as this does relations between humans, animals, machines, and the environment, Haraway declares that 'Foucault's biopolitics is a flaccid premonition of cyborg politics, a very open field'.[113] In 'Biopolitics of Postmodern Bodies' (1988), she also discusses how biotechnology and computers provide a more tangible instance of how that 'open field' compounds life as 'code'. Giving the human genome project as an example, she argues that the plan to 'sequence' the body's genetic make-up in a vast database 'library' amounts to a synthesis of genetic and computer codes that will facilitate investment in corporeal engineering.[114] Mapping the body as coded genetic text, the project constructs a model of 'man' as '"subject" of science'.[115] This genome coding is thus intimately bound to potentials for biopolitical regulation. But because the project effectively turns man as bodied subject into a 'heterogeneous construct' of the 'organic, textual, and technical', Haraway sees it as further evidence of the human as fabricated cyborg, one that harbours the potential for new 'constructs' of human life.[116] Consequently, cyborg politics also calls for 'Anthropologists of possible selves'.[117]

---

[110] Donna Haraway, 'A Cyborg Manifesto', in *Simians, Cyborgs, and Women* (London: Free Association, 1991), 149–50.
[111] Ibid. 150.
[112] Ibid. 181.
[113] Ibid. 150.
[114] Donna Haraway, 'Biopolitics of Postmodern Bodies', in *Simians, Cyborgs, and Women*, 211.
[115] Ibid. 215.
[116] Ibid. 212.
[117] Ibid. 230.

That's a good description of the main protagonists in *Empire of the Senseless*, for Thivai continually dreams up pirate adventures for herself, and her 'partner' Abhor is 'part robot, and part black'.[118] If 'constructs' are intrinsic to both drag (Butler) and cyborgs (Haraway), then it makes sense to write cyberdrag, which is what *Empire* can be read as engendering. Acker's previous concerns about robotization turn into a mix of cyborg politics and fabricated sexuality, which becomes clearer after the narrative presents a reprise of an episode from William Gibson's science-fiction novel, *Neuromancer* (1984). In Gibson's text, Case, a cowboy cyborg, is charged with stealing the 'construct' of a dead cyborg from Sense/Net, a media corporation that has a whole library of such constructs. Aided by the 'Panther Moderns', a group of Anarchist computer hackers, Case is able to retrieve the construct when the Moderns create a diversion with an attack on Sense/Net's command system.[119] In *Empire*, this plot is re-fashioned into one of biopolitics. With the help of the 'Moderns', a terrorist group, Thivai and Abhor break into the CIA 'Library' called 'MAINLINE', which is a 'central control network' that contains 'its memory, what constituted its perception and understanding' (*ES*, 36). Their search for a biological 'construct' named 'Kathy' is also a search for its 'code', which turns out to be the following statement: 'GET RID OF MEANING. YOUR MIND IS A NIGHTMARE THAT HAS BEEN EATING YOU: NOW EAT YOUR MIND' (*ES*, 38). Just as Haraway views the genome library as a blending of genetic and computational codes, so Acker turns Gibson's Sense/Net library into one that controls biopolitical coding. And if for Haraway genetic 'constructs' harbour the possibility of alternative fabrications, that's what Kathy as 'construct' reveals, for her 'code' effectively calls for the mind to be overthrown by ingesting it. In other words, breaking Kathy's code means using her languages of the body.

Those languages are employed in sections of the novel that depict Abhor and Thivai getting caught up in the revolutionary capture of Paris by Algerians. Switching between Abhor and Thivai as narrator, Acker employs her languages of 'flux' and 'wonder' not only to keep changing the I and eye, but also to break open taboo dreamscapes. A scene in which Abhor has sex with her father provides a good example:

Let's fuck on top of this fountain. Splashing the waters of hydro-chloric acid into my nostrils. Daddy. Pull off my fingernails. My back has been carved into roses.

---

[118] Kathy Acker, *Empire of the Senseless* (London: Picador, 1988), 3, hereafter cited in the text as *ES*.
[119] William Gibson, *Neuromancer* (New York: Ace, 2000), 61.

You scream that it's not only by you. As if you're alive or as if I'm not dreaming. As if I really possessed you and you really possessed me, we tore off each other's head and ate out the contents, then pecked out the remaining eyes, pulled out the shark's teeth and sucked opium out of the gums, my vagina was bleeding. And I said to my father, the sailor, 'Let's not be possessed'. (*ES*, 84)

As with the incest scenes in *Rip-Off Red*, undoing the Oedipal ban through dreaming involves dislimning the body; the implied dissolution in 'hydro-chloric acid' is thus followed by Abhor and her father tearing each other apart. But in turning visceral the passage also registers that body and text are both fabrications. The repetition of 'As if...' shows that the dream works through a subjunctive mood, while the bodies are described as composites including 'rose carvings', 'shark's teeth', and 'opium'. As an Oedipal exorcism, the passage anaesthetizes and bites simultaneously, for it presents traumatic taboo while recasting it cathartically *as fictional construction*. Vanquishing her father and his possession of her as a consequence, Abhor realizes that her 'carved' body can also be refigured, which is why she goes in search of a tattooist.

Later in the novel Abhor draws tattooing and the writing of taboo into propinquity:

Language [...] constitutes a set of codes and social and historical agreements. Nonsense doesn't per se break down the codes; speaking precisely that which the codes forbid breaks the codes.
This new way of tattooing consisted of raising defined parts of the flesh up with a knife. The tattooer draws a string through the raised points of flesh. Various coloration methods can be used on the living points. (*ES*, 134)

Breaking discursive 'code' segues into altering 'defined' flesh. This metaphor works on the same basis as Acker's comparison of dream-work with her languages of the body. If in acts of reading or writing the body becomes a site of the text, then those acts are inscriptions *of* the body. Similarly, as Elizabeth Grosz argues, the 'incisions' and 'markings' of tattoos 'create not a map of the body but the body as a map. They constitute some regions on that surface as more intensified, more significant, than others.'[120] For Acker, writing and reading taboo are also ways of incorporating 'languages of intensity' such that fiction's metaphors and falsifying become affective powers.[121] That is how writing turns into a kind of performative drag.

---

[120] Elizabeth Grosz, 'The Body as Inscriptive Surface', in *Volatile Bodies: Toward a Corporeal Feminism* (Sydney: Allen and Unwin, 1994), 139.
[121] Acker, 'The Languages of the Body', 1.

How this relates to history is a point with which Acker continued to struggle. Commenting on *Empire* in 1989 she links its break with Oedipal taboo to the status of Algerians as Western 'other'. Far from being a country of sexual liberation, though, Algeria at this time had recently passed a 'Family Code' based on Sharia law.[122] As Martin Evans and John Phillips have argued, one consequence of this was that women 'did not exist as individuals in their own right' but were patriarchally coded as 'daughters of', 'mothers of', and 'wives of' men.[123] But the importance of the Algerian revolution in *Empire* is precisely that it *is* a blatant falsification of history. Whereas in *Don Quixote* lengthy passages from historical texts break the fictional frame, in *Empire* Acker incorporates smaller rewritten passages into Abhor's and Thivai's narrations. Some of this plagiarized material is from Pierre Guyotat's fictionalized accounts of fighting in the Algerian war, while passages on the Algerian leaders Mackandal and Toussaint L'Ouverture are in fact based on the eighteenth-century Haitian revolutionaries of the same names, and are appropriated from C. L. R. James's book on them, *The Black Jacobins* (1938). For Brian McHale, this would probably be an example of Acker's rewrites having, as he puts it, 'no discernible purpose aside from that of producing the "sampling" effect itself'.[124] Yet Acker herself suggests that using the plagiarized material did elicit a critical outlook:

As I put these texts together, I realized, as I did years ago, that the hippies had been mistaken: they had thought that they could successfully oppose American post-capitalism by a lie, by creating a utopian society. But the body is real: if one, anyone, lives in hell, one is hell.[125]

The point is that the kinds of uprising that took place in eighteenth-century Haiti and the Algerian war of independence (1954–62) *could not work* in the context of a contemporary Western city, and that's what Acker portrays in the novel when the Paris revolution is overthrown by the CIA. This bears on her realization that she could not 'change society'. Writing fictions about revolution will not automatically catalyse revolution in the world. But fiction and the 'languages of the body' can refigure how one is affected by the world, and in doing so they also rewrite one's capacities for feeling and action. As Acker intimates above, the 'real' site of the text she wrote was not in society but in the writing body.

---

[122] Martin Evans and John Phillips, *Algeria: Anger of the Dispossessed* (New Haven: Yale University Press, 2007), 126.
[123] Ibid.
[124] Brian McHale, *Constructing Postmodernism* (London: Routledge, 1992), 234.
[125] Acker, 'A Few Notes on Two of My Books', 12.

In Part 2 of *Empire*, such uses of fiction are put to the test by Thivai when she's thrown in gaol by the CIA. Deciding that the 'motto of sailors' is 'ANY PLACE BUT HERE' (*ES*, 156), Thivai fantasizes a series of escapist adventures with the Persian hero Sinbad the Sailor. That she remains in prison is a fact she begrudgingly acknowledges: 'I've just been pretending I'm a pirate and mean and an Arab terrorist and have no morals. [. . .] Then I almost started to cry' (*ES*, 175). She nevertheless persists in her flights of fancy because her incarcerated 'me' is, as she states earlier, also a 'fiction' (*ES*, 147) and therefore open to fabrication: 'They [. . .] say that a child who's in prison either makes himself or dies. What is true is that the child erects himself stone after stone without any tools' (*ES*, 154). Placed in solitary confinement as a 'juvenile', Thivai's imprisonment can be related to Foucault's discussion of juvenile incarceration in *Discipline and Punish* (1975). For Foucault the juvenile delinquent in France was legally formalized as a social character in 1840 with the opening of the first prison, Mettray, that was specifically built to punish such individuals. Drawing on various models of socialization—including the army, family, and school—Mettray, argues Foucault, thus 'produced' the character of juvenile delinquent at the same time as punishing individuals for possessing it.[126] For Thivai, although her flights of fancy cannot dismantle her concrete cell, the prison makes her aware of the 'construct' she is in there, which is why she continues to rewrite herself other with fictive 'stone after stone'. Aided by Abhor she later escapes, and the two of them continue as pirates and sailors in episodes Acker appropriates from Mark Twain's *Adventures of Huckleberry Finn* (1884). Like her plagiarism of Dickens, her use of Twain is also ironic given Twain's copyright campaign against literary piracy.[127]

By the end of the novel, though, the narrative swerves back to cyborgism and the code. Already part machine, Abhor learns to ride a motorcycle with *The Highway Code* but soon decides to disobey its rules. Listening instead to her 'own heart' means taking her bike and life in her own hands, and with that in mind she decides that rather than join a male biker gang, she will ride alone (*ES*, 227). The close of the novel is thus something of an anti-climax, and if Abhor leaves us with the joys of death-driving it hardly seems to support Acker's suggestion that the narrative ends 'with the hints of a possibility [. . .] the beginning of a movement from no to

---

[126] Michel Foucault, *Discipline and Punish*, trans. Alan Sheridan (Harmondsworth: Penguin, 1991), 301.

[127] On Twain's copyright campaigning see Siva Vaidhyanathan, *Copyrights and Copywrongs: The Rise of Intellectual Property and How it Threatens Creativity* (New York: New York University Press, 2001), Ch. 2.

yes, from nihilism to myth'.[128] That beginning is evident earlier in the novel, though, in the sections where Acker links her languages of the body to myth as fiction. Her final novels of the nineties develop that link further by exploring pirate myths in terms of alternative communities. In the next section I'll discuss how that project comes to fruition in her last novel, *Pussy, King of the Pirates* (1996). Before turning to it we need to consider briefly the biopolitical developments that continued to interest her.

PUSSY, KING OF THE PIRATES: FILTHY MYTH AND THE 'LANGUAGE OF ABJECTION'

In 'The Meaning of the Eighties' (1990) Acker presents a short epistolary exchange between two characters, Zoozoo and Linda. The latter is based on herself, and in a letter written from London dated 1989 Linda expresses the sentiments Acker had formed about living in Thatcherite Britain: 'I've watched a country go to hell in four years. [...] I've seen how, when a political-economic structure turns from civilized social welfare to a poor imitation of American postcapitalism, every single person's life radically changes.'[129] Returning to San Francisco, Acker was under no illusion that her birth nation had suddenly renounced its 'political-economic structure'. Indeed, over the next eight years up until her death many of the triangulations of power Reagan had nurtured continued to evolve despite the Republicans losing office when Bill Clinton acceded to the presidency in 1993. While *Empire*'s passages on incarceration were topical considering the increase in the prison population under Reagan, that growth was subsequently augmented by the Clinton administration's policies on law enforcement and gaol sentences, all of which helped boost prisoner numbers by almost 80 per cent by the end of the decade.[130] The AIDS epidemic was another growing concern, and its effects on Acker are evident in the letter from Linda cited above: 'I've seen about half of our friends go out on drugs or die from AIDS.'[131] Having compared herself as writer to AIDS in *My Death My Life*, her novel *In Memoriam to Identity* (1990) portrays the syndrome in a different light. Recasting relations between the French symbolist poets Paul Verlaine and Arthur Rimbaud, the fact that Verlaine's 'foul habits'

---

[128] Acker, 'A Few Notes on Two of My Books', 13.
[129] Kathy Acker, 'The Meaning of the Eighties', in *Bodies of Work*, 142.
[130] See Haynes Johnson, *The Best of Times: America in the Clinton Years* (New York: Harcourt, 2001), 464.
[131] Acker, 'The Meaning of the Eighties', 142.

might have given his wife HIV is evidence of his chauvinistic indifference to her.[132] Far from being associated with a turn from 'nihilism to myth', AIDS is also what Acker depicts a suicidal Rimbaud craving when he asks for it 'to suffocate me in mucus then in blood'.[133] When Rimbaud later claims that his 'Words touch the senses [...] for the word is blood', it is clear that poetic language is his vital fluid rather than a viral suffocation.[134]

Abortion was another biopolitical issue that continued to haunt Acker, as is evident from her novel *My Mother: Demonology* (1993). Part 1 marks something of a return to the familial allobiography of earlier works like *Blood and Guts* before it switches in Part 2 to refiguring relations between the French surrealist Georges Bataille and his lover, Laure, rewriting extracts from their texts in the process. Written while George H. Bush was president, Acker was clearly incensed by his stand on abortion. Bush had called for it to be criminalized in his 1988 election campaign, and during his presidency he courted pro-life supporters and sought unsuccessfully to ban abortion counselling by health organizations that received federal funding.[135] In a section titled 'Bush on Abortion' Acker presents the president seeking control over female bodies to such a degree that he desires to kill his own daughter, yet because of his anti-abortion stance he also wants her to 'become pregnant' when she's dead.[136] Associating this with Bush's defence of the death penalty (*MMD*, 181), the implication is that sovereignty (as power to take life) and biopolitics (as power to make live) are absurdly fused. Gruesome though it is as a satire, the passage also draws attention to what Dean and Massumi educe in terms of Reagan being imaged as body-politic: 'In State societies, the body of the leader plays a major role in the limitation of corporeal potential.'[137] The dissemination of leader as biopolitical image means that s/he is also circulated as a figure of 'the social dynamics supporting the circuits of circulation his image has entered'.[138] Similarly, Acker has Bush claim that 'a state is just a mask that secretes and shelters the power relations behind it', which he knows because '*I* am talking about *MYSELF*' (*MMD*, 181). The antipathy and fantasy that Acker levels against Bush is therefore intended to parody and combat the circulation of his speaking image as a regulating biopolitical power.

---

[132] Kathy Acker, *In Memoriam to Identity* (London: Pandora, 1990), 55.
[133] Ibid. 80.
[134] Ibid. 90.
[135] See Craig and O'Brien, *Abortion and American Politics*, 191.
[136] Kathy Acker, *My Mother: Demonology* (New York: Grove, 1993), 173–4, hereafter cited in the text as *MMD*.
[137] Dean and Massumi, *First and Last Emperors*, 137.
[138] Ibid. 138.

Under Bill Clinton's presidency some of the biopolitial 'social dynamics' subtending his position were changed through legislation. Although he, like Bush, supported the death penalty, he also defended abortion rights for women.[139] What changed most dramatically, though, during Clinton's two terms in office were the 'circuits of circulation' through which life and power were networked. In part, this transformation involved taking advantage of the Cold War's demise and extending America's market liberalism internationally. As Clinton's National Security Council director Anthony Lake stated the case, America had entered 'a moment of immense democratic and entrepreneurial opportunity' in which Cold War containment policies should be abandoned in favour of enlarging 'the world's free community of market democracies'.[140] In light of that, the negotiation of new free trade agreements was bolstered by further deregulation of domestic financial services, and these in turn profited hugely from the spread of the Internet. Growing into a global 'web' the Internet has proven to be one of the most important factors in fusing institutions, networked communication, and individuals into a common biopolitical substance. With most of its technology having been developed by the US Department of Defense between the sixties and eighties, the growth of the Internet in the nineties for commercial and public use led to the 'dot.com boom' of online companies whose wealth accumulation was largely generated by investments in their shares.[141] Rooted though it was in the kinds of capitalism Acker had previously attacked, she saw in the fledgling online networks untold opportunity to establish alternative communities and to share texts. In a 1994 interview, for example, she commented that with the aid of the World Wide Web 'People are forming into tribes' with 'their own little communities' and 'different languages'.[142] The result, she argued, is like a spread of 'piracy', for not only does the technology allow people to roam and link virtually around the world, it also enables a freer exchange of writing. On this point Acker was prescient on two scores: first, for suggesting that such exchange would lead to a crossing of genres such that there will be 'a lot more visual mixed with verbal'; and second, for predicting that it would undermine

---

[139] See Craig and O'Brien, *Abortion and American Politics*, 358.
[140] Quoted in Walter LaFeber, *America, Russia, and the Cold War, 1945–2006* (New York: McGraw-Hill, 2006), 374.
[141] See James Gillies and Robert Cailliau, *How the Web was Born: The Story of the World Wide Web* (Oxford: Oxford University Press, 2000); also Johnson, *The Best of Times*, 19–37.
[142] Quoted in Chris Miller, 'Acker: A Contemporary Fiction Exploration', *The Argonaut* (4 October 1993), 3.

publishing and copyright regulations.[143] Having distributed photocopied work informally among friends ever since she began writing, even in its nascent form the Internet enhanced dramatically her ability to share writings as friendship.

In *Pussy, King of the Pirates*, Acker presents her most developed picture of how such piratical camaraderie could be forged into literary myth. Part 1 of the novel treads some familiar ground; drawing its main character and occasional narrator 'O' from Pauline Réage's erotic novel *The Story of O* (1954), the bulk of the narrative focuses on O's high school friendship with another girl, Pussycat. Interspersed with dream sequences and drawings by Acker, the episodic narrative also features a series of creation myths. Rather than establishing a distant past as stable origin, though, these myths tell of origins only to unravel them. For example, a section titled 'The Beginning of the World of Pirates' examines patriarchy as creation myth and overturns its order by suggesting that a father's primal status is born through the birth of his child. In other words, the man's child bears his paternity. And as the father desires a child to establish his own patriarchal status, it's not him so much as 'Incest [that] begins the beginning of this world'.[144] The myth of paternal law arises again when O compares herself to Ariadne, the daughter of Minos and half-sister of the Minotaur that was hidden in a labyrinth at Minos's behest (*PKP*, 150). The myth of the Minotaur's birth is also the subject of one of Acker's last essays, 'Moving into Wonder' (1995). As a story about 'the origin of art', Acker argues that it tells of the repression of female sexuality and creativity.[145] Recounted in various classical texts—including Plutarch's *Life of Theseus* and Ovid's *Metamorphoses* and *Heroides*—the myth describes how Pasiphaë, the wife of Minos, fell in love with a splendid white bull that the sea-god Poseidon had given to Minos to sacrifice. Persuading the inventor Daedalus to construct a fake hollow cow, Pasiphaë hides in it, entices the bull to have sex with her, and subsequently gives birth to the Minotaur, a hybrid 'monster' who has a human body and bull's head. As Acker points out, '*Monster* comes from the Latin word *monstrum* or wonder' (other meanings include 'divine omen' and 'miracle').[146] In her view, Minos's decision to get Daedalus to build a labyrinth in which to incarcerate the Minotaur is thus a concealment not only of transgressive female desire but also of female creation of wonder. After Ariadne gives

---

[143] Quoted in Miller, 'Acker', *The Argonaut*, 3.
[144] Kathy Acker, *Pussy, King of the Pirates* (New York: Grove, 1996), 68, hereafter cited in the text as *PKP*.
[145] Kathy Acker, 'Moving into Wonder', in *Bodies of Work*, 93.
[146] Ibid. 95.

Theseus thread to navigate his way through the labyrinth, his slaying of the Minotaur becomes Ariadne's complicity in 'the destruction of wonder'.[147]

In *Pussy*, the adventures of O and her fellow pirates are effectively aimed at undoing that destruction; they must search for the 'buried treasure' 'hidden in caves at the centers of labyrinths' (*PKP*, 206) not to destroy its monstrous wonder but to salvage it. As the narrative makes clear, this quest is inherently one of looting a language of abjection. Acker stated in a 1989 interview that her interest in abjection was indebted to Julia Kristeva's *Powers of Horror* (1982) in which Kristeva links the abject to liminal matter that undoes the distinction between subject and object.[148] For example, body fluids, excrement, and corpses are experienced as abject in showing a subject how its bodily properties can turn into objective alterity. With *monstrum* also being an etymon of 'demonstration', the abject monsters the subject with what it shows—a point Kristeva emphasizes in the following sentences: 'refuse and corpses *show me* [*me montrent*] what I permanently thrust aside in order to live. These bodily fluids, this defilement, this shit are what life withstands, hardly and with difficulty.'[149] Abjection is thus part of one's existence, but a subject's sense of its properties as its own depends on the ultimately lost battle of staying clean (in French *propre* can be either 'clean' or 'own'). Some of that cleansing is policed through the order words of language, which, as Deleuze and Guattari point out, semiotically divides subjects, objects, and other things into neat binary relations. So, for Kristeva, an individual's absorption of linguistic order is a main factor in building selfhood on the basis of banning abject liminality from one's life. As a result,

> The abjection of self would be the culminating form of that experience of the subject to which it is revealed that all its objects are based merely on the inaugural *loss* that laid the foundations of its own being. [...] all abjection is in fact recognition of the *want* on which any being, meaning, language, or desire is founded.[150]

Kristeva finds the subject *wanting* (desiring and lacking) in terms of the abjection it rejects in the name of 'self'. For Acker, writing pirate myths thus means excavating the abject as monstrous treasure in order to reject the strictures of selfhood. To do this through language entails doing what

---

[147] Ibid.
[148] See Kathy Acker, 'Kathy Acker with Angela McRobbie' [filmed interview] (London: Institute of Contemporary Art, 1989).
[149] Julia Kristeva, *Powers of Horror: An Essay on Abjection*, trans. Leon S. Roudiez (1980; New York: Columbia University Press, 1982), 3.
[150] Ibid. 5, Kristeva's emphases.

Deleuze and Guattari view to be the task of writers: drawing from order words a 'power of variation' as 'potentiality'. That's what Acker's abject piracy performs by blending languages of the body and fictive worlds into filthy myth.

One example of this in *Pussy* is a dream O has in which the ghost of Pussycat recounts a conversation about the origins of creation with a 'corpse' in hell. Asking what existed before the distinction of 'good and evil', the corpse replies: 'Amniotic fluid. In other words, inside was outside and is outside, and no inside, no outside, and vice versa' (*PKP*, 155). The womb is thus imagined as one of those 'caves' from which abject liminality is recovered—the contortions of syntax being an index of the distinctions undone. A dirtier example involves pirate sexuality:

> Pirates are hot to puncture through. After they've done this, they need to piss or shoot into another person. This is why this, my body, is the beginning of pirate sex.
>
> All of us girls have been dead for so long. But we're not going to be anymore. (*PKP*, 115)

Like her use of taboo, Acker here plunders some of the things Kristeva names—corpses, bodily fluids—in order for the writing to perform an abject experience. The result is a communion of writing and corporeality, which Acker intimates through the deictic slipperiness of the 'this' that could denote both 'my body' and the text itself. The use of abjection to open the body to otherness also blends with the fiction as other world of possibility. In that way, Acker's pirate myth opens new linguistic potentials while using a language of abjection to ensure that those potentials become affective corporeal powers. Like her cyberdrag, her literary piracy writes not just one's self but one's body other.

As this piracy is presented in *Pussy* as unlocking transgressive worlds of female creativity and sexuality, it is not regarded benevolently by the friend of O's father, Robert Frost. A fictive appropriation of the modern American poet of the same name, Frost is transformed by Acker into a crazed patriarch who believes that girls are inherently abject and so must be exterminated:

> 'My life has one purpose. I must decapitate all those girls. They're all too beautiful. [...]
>
> All their main organs are tongues, tongues which move in ways that break through the limits of the human imagination. After a girl has licked out a skull that's full of maggots [...] she places that organ between her girlfriend's lips.' (*PKP*, 134)

With the pun on 'tongues' as both organs and languages, Frost also sees the girls' abjection as a fluid fusion of the two which transgresses both corporeal organization and 'limits' of 'imagination'. When O's father also becomes enthusiastic about Frost's 'purpose', O and Pussycat escape before the decapitation plans can be put into action. In Part 2 of the novel their piracy expands to include a group of other girls. Including more of Acker's illustrations and sporadic appropriations from Robert Louis Stevenson's *Treasure Island* (1883), Part 2 relates in three ways to the 'piracy' Acker saw harboured in the Internet. First, her use of images exemplifies the genre-crossing she thought would arise from online textual sharing. Second, the occasional rewriting of Stevenson's novel combines narrative form and content into a piracy that questions the propriety of authorial copyright. Third, the group piracy portrayed is a novelistic equivalent of the Internet 'tribe' formation Acker praised. That this tribal life is not a means to an end is what the pirate Silver realizes when they discover a chest of money at the close of the narrative: 'If me and my girls take all this treasure, the reign of piracy will stop, and I wouldn't have that happen' (*PKP*, 276). When Silver and her girls walk away, O and Ange regard them with 'awe' and take what they can. Silver's rejection of the money testifies to what O has suggested all along; the real pirate booty lies elsewhere, in the wonders of abjection. And although O and Ange plunder the lucre, their commitment to shared otherness is evident in their rowing away together.

By the end of her life, Acker had thus made considerable advances on the main issues of biopolitics and self-governance that I said would be the foci of this chapter. Whereas Foucault largely leaves aside the role played by communications in biopolitics, Acker's novels consistently link the regulation of sexuality, desire, and affects to linguistic orders—from syntax and genre to institutional and media discourses. For Hardt and Negri, the intimacy of biopolitics and communications is why we should ask 'How can we discover and direct the performative lines of linguistic sets and communicative networks that create the fabric of life and production?'[151] As I've shown, the trajectory of Acker's work moves from discovering to directing. After the anarchic experiments with textual drag in her early work, Acker trammels her fiction by repeatedly breaking its frame when considering biopolitical context. Her subordination of fiction to that context is blamed by her on biopolitics itself. From *Empire* onwards, though, she affirms fictionalization of context more, and by directing it into alternative possible words she also develops performative powers for them through her languages of the body and abjection. Her exploration of what Foucault terms the 'unity of power' and human

---

[151] Hardt and Negri, *Empire*, 404.

'potentials' also amounts to connecting two forms of practice, biopolitics and the government of self, that Foucault outlined without adequately addressing their relations. Having argued that the Stoics' 'self-writing' was a form of governance, he doesn't consider how this might work in a contemporary context, nor does he consider how it might be changed to accommodate his suggestion that 'the target nowadays is not to discover what we are but to refuse what we are'. Acker does both; for example, by figuring presidential power in terms of biopolitical issues such as abortion and AIDS, while simultaneously using allobiography to write oneself other. In doing so she also shows how an aesthetics of existence can become a contemporary literary endeavour.

When Foucault talks of the 'capacities' and 'potentials' bound up in the unity of power, he states that this is a matter of managing 'possible actions'. As Acker suggests, though, such actions depend on possibilities of affect and desire, which is why she sets out to counter autopathy through her languages of abjection and the body. That refiguring one's capacity to be affected by power also means modulating one's ability to exercise it is what she argues in 1995: 'potentialities' provide 'Models and paradigms for action', which is why 'Potentiality is kin, and I am talking politically, kin to the imagination.'[152] It's on that basis that Acker builds her own literary potentialism. Its performativity, as I've acknowledged, doesn't mean that writing about revolution makes revolution materialize instantaneously in the world. Rather, because the body becomes the site of fiction in the act of writing or reading it, one incorporates different affective potentials. Whether those potentials are embraced and acted on psychologically and physically depends on the writer and reader. That Acker's languages of the body couldn't ward off the cancer that killed her might be taken as an instance of their limited power. Then again, if one believes that her bodily desire and affects take on another life through these languages, then so does she in the acts of us reading her texts.

---

[152] Acker, 'Writing, Identity, and Copyright in the Net Age', 99.

5

Making a Person Possible

Lyn Hejinian and Language Poetry

LANGUAGE GROUP BEGINNINGS: 'THE 1960s BY OTHER MEANS'?

In the previous chapters I've shown how Ginsberg, Baraka, and Burroughs saw the sixties in America as heralding new aesthetic and social potentials, and I examined how the authors sought to foster those potentials in subsequent decades. Addressing transitions from the sixties has also been a concern of the Language poets, the last major literary avant-garde movement to emerge in America. Since their formation as a group in the early seventies they've maintained a prolific output of critical and theoretical writing in addition to poetry. A substantial amount of that critical writing has framed their poetry explicitly in terms of aesthetic and political possibilities, and that in turn has led to a good deal of thinking about how conditions for poetry and politics have changed since the sixties. In examining the group's statements on these matters, one of my aims is to compare them to the potentialist stances of the other writers I've discussed and so present this chapter as a prelude to my Conclusion. That task is made easier by the fact that all of the writers I've previously examined are addressed in essays by Language poets. I shan't just offer retrospective in this chapter, though. There's been dissent within the Language group over how poetic possibilities bear on the agency of writers and readers in terms of social power more generally. After considering the different positions, I'll dedicate most of the chapter to tracing how they are negotiated in Lyn Hejinian's poetry which develops a concept of a 'person' as the performance of potential, and presents it in the form of poetic 'happenings'. Before I introduce some tenets of Language writing in more detail, though, I'll first examine the group's discussions about the context of its emergence, for the discussions bear on relations between the sixties and the group's views on poetic possibilities.

In recent years Barrett Watten has been one of the Language poets most concerned with providing a 'cultural poetics' of the group's emergence. In 'The Turn to Language and the 1960s' (2002), for example, he argues that Language poetry arose largely to continue 'the politics of the 1960s by other means'.[1] As various critics and Language writers have noted, another inspiration for the group was sixties New Poetry, which Watten praises for using 'forms and possibilities of poetry' to address the social nature of discourse.[2] Ginsberg's mantra were a prime example, he argues, in pitting their counter-cultural potential against the mainstream social 'system'. For Watten, the mantra are also emblematic of a sixties counter-culture that increasingly had to invoke utopia because real political change seemed as improbable as attaining a real position '*outside* the system'.[3] Ginsberg, he argues, thus testifies to a more general 'politics of impossibility', the main benefit of which was to offer a critical purchase on the system by presenting 'logics of negativity' in opposition to it.[4] How the New Poetry's 'poetic strands of possibility' could be turned into something more politically constructive is, for Watten, a challenge that became a defining concern for the Language poets as a group:

When these strands [...] were combined and rearranged in the following decade, the context of the 1960s, within and against which they were articulated, still survived as an agonistic demand for a democratic polity, measured by its impossible representation. The language-centered poetics of the 1970s permitted the recovery of a totalized *outside* that was a casualty of the conflict between expression and representation in the 1960s. Language derived from the failure of poetic subjectivity in its confrontation with the historical present could now be returned to constructivist ends, in confirmation of a politics.[5]

There are a number of problems with this argument, particularly in relation to Ginsberg. As I argued in Chapter 1, it's true that Ginsberg wanted his poetry to produce alternative states of thinking, as when he called for the use of 'imagination' to produce 'an unmistakable statement OUTSIDE the war psychology'.[6] But that outside, for him, didn't

---

[1] Barrett Watten, 'The Turn to Language and the 1960s', *Critical Inquiry* 29 (Autumn 2002), 139.
[2] Ibid. 140. See also: Peter Middleton, '1973', in Michel Delville and Christine Pagnoulle (eds), *The Mechanics of the Mirage: Postwar American Poetry* (Liège: Liège Language and Literature, 2000), 49–51; and Jerome McGann, 'Contemporary Poetry, Alternate Routes', in Robert von Hallberg (ed.), *Politics and Poetic Value* (Chicago: University of Chicago Press, 1987), 254–6; and Jed Rasula, *Syncopations: The Stress of Innovation in Contemporary American Poetry* (Tuscaloosa: University of Alabama Press, 2004), 15–21.
[3] Watten, 'The Turn to Language and the 1960s', 174, Watten's emphasis.
[4] Ibid.
[5] Ibid. 183.
[6] Allen Ginsberg, 'Demonstration or Spectacle as Example, as Communication; or, How to Make a March/Spectacle' (November 1965), in *Deliberate Prose: Selected Essays, 1952–95*, ed. Bill Morgan (New York: HarperCollins, 2000), 10.

amount to the utopic impossibility that Watten intimates, and that Yippies like Abbie Hoffman toyed with in using slogans like 'Be Realistic: Demand the Impossible'. Instead, Ginsberg presented his poetry as turning possibility into individual bodies of feeling, and practical 'particularities'. Appealing, in the process, to America as democracy, Ginsberg, like other counter-culturalists, didn't simply insist on radically separating an imagined 'outside' from America's 'central mind machine'; instead, he sought ways of nurturing alternative potentials—aesthetic and social—*within* the social machinery. From a Marxist perspective like Watten's, the inability to turn potentialism into wholesale political change clearly bears on what he views to be the sixties' 'failure of poetic subjectivity'. As I've argued, though, Ginsberg from the late sixties declared he was more intent on offering 'tiny particularities' with which individuals could combat the effects of power on themselves rather than overturn structures of power, and Burroughs and Acker ultimately adopted similar positions.

Baraka is a different case, one that better suits Watten's arguments. Opposing a radical African American 'outside' to a white system was certainly at the heart of Baraka's Black Arts aesthetics, and his subsequent turn to Third-World Socialism around the time of the Language poets' emergence was symptomatic of his desire to invest more in the sort of politics of a 'totalized *outside*' that Watten invokes. As I showed, though, with the Socialist Realism that Baraka pursued, aesthetic form was made subordinate to material contexts. Ironically, addressing those contexts in terms of a totality meant frequent recourse in his poetry to generalized abstractions like 'history', 'the social system', 'reality', or 'the whole structure that will change the century'. And while many of the Language poets were similarly interested in drawing on Marxism to build their 'confrontation with the historical present', as Watten puts it, they also took a very different approach to Baraka by developing that confrontation primarily through a politics of poetic form.

How that politics of form was rooted in historical context is an issue that Watten also takes up in *The Constructivist Moment* (2003): 'About 1975, new conditions for the social reproduction of nonnarrative forms emerged—during a period of national crisis about the time of the Fall of Saigon—in the Language School and elsewhere.'[7] Other Language poets, including Charles Bernstein, Bob Perelman, and Ron Silliman have discussed how their antipathy towards the war galvanized them as a group.[8]

---

[7] Barrett Watten, *The Constructivist Moment: From Material Text to Cultural Poetics* (Middletown, CT: Wesleyan University Press, 2003), 198.
[8] See, for example, Bob Perelman, *The Marginalization of Poetry: Language Writing and Literary History* (Princeton, NJ: Princeton University Press, 1996), Ch. 7; and Ron Silli-

As Hejinian has stated, all of the poets had been 'involved in some degree of political activism' protesting the war.[9] In the wake of the conflict the sense of the group as a community continued to be of great importance. For Hejinian, it was 'a space of (or space for) appearance being constructed in a world of disappearances'; in short, an experiment in building an alternative 'polis'.[10] For Watten, the end of the war turned into a poetics of loss for the Language group:

> The nonnarrative of this event—an incremental sequence of losses rather than a narrative sense of an ending such as 'the North Vietnamese won, thus ending the war'—[...] has had a major impact on historical self-consciousness since the war. A poetics of loss that is at the same time a coming into consciousness [...]. This effect is evident in writing from the mid-1970s in a genre of poetic prose that Ron Silliman has called the New Sentence, in which series of discrete statements organized 'at the level of the sentence' generate a poetic matrix without any overarching narrative form.[11]

The problems with this analysis relate to Watten's points about the sixties' 'politics of impossibility'. As I argued in Chapter 1, both the loss of the war and the Watergate scandal were seen by counter-culture proponents like Ginsberg as the 'unravelling' of the war effort's 'mass hallucination' and 'Myth rationalization'—a mythic narrative that had led media organizations, the Pentagon, and government administrations to think that the conflict could be plotted with information and statistics through initiatives like the Hamlet Evaluation System and the electronic battlefield. The loss of that myth, the loss of belief in the American military–industrial complex as something capable of securing a national grand narrative, those losses were precisely what Ginsberg and others had been fighting for! Which isn't to say that they celebrated American loss of life or the Vietnamese victory; rather, they welcomed the undoing of national myth because it helped bring the war to an end, and they felt vindicated in having stood by the new forms of political activism and parody they'd practised—including, on Ginsberg's part, lyrical counter-feedback, performance protest, and mantric poetics. That vindication included an awareness that the blow to the war's grand narrative was a setback for

---

man, 'VI', in Bob Perelman, Steve Benson, Tom Mandel, Kit Robinson, Rae Armantrout, Barrett Watten, Carla Harryman, Ron Silliman, Lyn Hejinian, and Ted Pearson, *The Grand Piano*, Part 1: *An Experiment in Collective Autobiography, San Francisco 1975–1980* (Detroit: Mode A, 2007), 47–51.

[9] Lyn Hejinian, 'Materials' (1990), in *The Language of Inquiry* (Berkeley, CA: University of California Press, 2000), 171–2.

[10] Lyn Hejinian, 'IX', in Perelman, Benson, Mandel, Robinson, Armantrout, Watten, Harryman, Silliman, Hejinian, and Pearson, *The Grand Piano*, Part 1, 71.

[11] Watten, *The Constructivist Moment*, 231.

the politics of totalization. It's curious, then, that Watten tries to recover totality by positing a wholesale sense of narrative 'loss' and identifying the Language group's 'poetic prose' as formal evidence of it. If that's the case, then the Language politics of form cannot have arisen 'outside' the historical 'nonnarrative' and must have emerged more as a 'coming into consciousness' of its own predicament. Consequently, Watten effectively aligns the group's poetics with the problematic 'politics of impossibility' he ascribes to New Poetry, for if the group's stance is so symptomatic of historical context then it's hard to see how it can amount to a 'confrontation with the historical present' or a 'confirmation of a politics' that entails 'becoming outside'. For that reason, he also renders the poetry vulnerable to the response Fredric Jameson accorded the group's New Sentence when he argued that its 'schizophrenic fragmentation' was basically symptomatic of late-capitalist culture.[12]

Watten's account of Language poetry's emergence is, however, not representative of his fellow poets' view as a whole. In stating that the group built its space of 'appearance' in a 'world of disappearance', Hejinian suggests different grounds for seeing their poetry as confronting context and instituting an alternative 'polis'. Similarly, the Language poet Bob Perelman stated that because of the war in Vietnam the group sought 'to construct or enact some *sort of person in poetry* who would be of political consequence'.[13] I'll return to Hejinian and this matter of the poetic 'person' shortly, but for now I want to continue to follow the grain of Watten's arguments on the politics of form, for they lead to the issue of poetic potential that the group has debated. Here's an example of Silliman's New Sentence writing that Watten invoked above:

Forty-three percent of the world's paper is produced in North America. A 12 year old patrols the street with a loaded submachinegun. Helicopters buzz about the accident, flies at a carcass. The mayor views it all thru a pair of field glasses. Opera of demoralization. These are our baby pictures. I help you lift off your blouse. In America's 213 manufacturing industries, the top 4 companies in each field control an average of 42% of the market.[14]

This extract is from the end of *Tjanting* (1981), the long prose-poem that Silliman wrote between 1977 and 1980 using the Fibonacci sequence to determine the number of sentences for the poem's nineteen paragraphs—1, 1, 2, 3, 5, 8, 13, 21, 34, 55, 89, 144, 233, 377, 610, 987,

---

[12] Fredric Jameson, *Postmodernism, or The Cultural Logic of Late Capitalism* (London: Verso, 1991), 28.
[13] Perelman, *The Marginalization of Poetry*, 109, Perelman's emphasis.
[14] Ron Silliman, *Tjanting* (Cambridge: Salt, 2002), 204. See also Silliman's essay 'The New Sentence', in *The New Sentence* (New York: Roof, 1995), 63–93.

1597, 2584, 4181, respectively. While the text has a distinct ramifying form, Watten is right in asserting that such a 'matrix' is not an 'overarching narrative'. As the extract shows, the parataxis of Silliman's sentences repeatedly calls into question the identity of the poem's subjects, voices, and contexts. Do we read the armed '12 year old' as being situated in the previous sentence's 'North America', or is it a reference to a young Vietcong soldier? Do the 'Helicopters' as subject flow metaphorically into 'flies', or is this a juxtaposition of two distinct events? Is the 'field' of the Mayor's vision (not to mention the poem) related to the 'field control' of America's 'manufacturing industries', or is it abstracted through opera glasses of 'demoralization'? It's undecidable, repeatedly so, for the poem works against unifying reference and meaning at the level of both sentence and paragraph—which is why the 'all' that the Mayor sees can be partial and multiple but not total. As Charles Bernstein has commented in a different context, 'The parts are greater than the sum of the whole.'[15]

In his Introduction to *Tjanting*, Watten acknowledges that the poem doesn't readily accommodate his own ideas on 'the totality of poetic form'.[16] Silliman's parataxis valorizes 'The gaps between words and things', he writes, 'rather than the positive existence of either'.[17] This change of tack brings Watten closer to Hejinian's assertion that Language poetry began by building a space of appearance *out of joint* with the world. Indeed, elsewhere he implicitly concedes that in opening a 'space' 'between things and language' Silliman's New Sentence writing *doesn't* reflect historical context so much as build alternative possibilities; it 'explores the constructive potential of a deformed chronicle', he argues, 'seeking to qualify self-consciousness of historical narrative by means of multiple and conflicting perspectives'.[18] Having thereby qualified his own approach to form, this 'constructive potential' Watten arrives at is also what he identifies elsewhere in *The Constructivist Moment* as being a principal problem for Language poetry.

I've stated that Silliman's New Sentence hands its possibilities of meaning over to the reader, and that making readers co-producers of poems has been a principal aim of Language practice. Rather than present language as an inert, transparent system subordinate to the things and concepts it refers to, Language poetry stresses how meaning and reference depend on the variability of material signifiers. Reading occasions labour-

---

[15] Charles Bernstein, 'The Revenge of the Poet-Critic, or The Parts Are Greater Than the Sum of the Whole' (1996), in *My Way: Speeches and Poems* (Chicago: University of Chicago Press, 1999), 9.
[16] Barrett Watten, 'Introduction', in Silliman, *Tjanting*, 4.
[17] Ibid. 5.
[18] Watten, *The Constructivist Moment*, 232.

ing with possibility, and for Watten that risks turning the politics of poetry to general abstraction:

> foregrounding the mode of signification depends on a politics of the reader's construction of meaning that is always only a potential effect. This resulting lowercase formalism has led [...] to a poetics of mere possibility—that to say what writing can effect is the same as to do it; that to describe literary possibility is to represent a form of agency, in a circular fashion, as a critique of representation. It is, thus, claims for the possibility of form rather than specific forms; [...] or the possibility of difference rather than a specific difference, that characterizes the aporia of our dialogic, site-specific and time-valued, manifold poetics.[19]

I quote this passage at length because I imagine some readers might think its contentions are applicable to the potentialisms I've outlined in my previous chapters. The difference is that Watten here casts poetic possibility as abstract, passive, and wholly dependent on the 'reader's construction'. With each previous potentialism, though, I've shown how it involves a writer composing specific literary forms of possibility that are intended *to act performatively as affective forces on readers in particular ways*. That holds for Ginsberg's auto-poems, Baraka's Black Arts writings, Burroughs's cut-ups and viruses, and Acker's abject piracy. Such forms are variously intended to shape, enact, or educe capacities of feeling, thinking, and acting in readers precisely in order to make a 'specific difference'.[20] As I argued in relation to Acker, that literary performativity is not Pavlovian; its effects will vary according to how much a reader wishes to embrace or resist them. But that only confirms the extent to which social and cultural diversity prevails over totalizing regulation.

Rather than address how literary possibility might turn into performative force, Watten reiterates that Language group politics can be recovered by linking it to the 'historical and cultural conditions that produced it'.[21] The result is that he compares the group's collective production of texts to the assembly lines of car production:

> The analogy between the paratactic unit structures of postmodern cultural forms and the assembly line, however provisional, suggests how works of art may be socially produced through multiauthored processes rather than single-authored invention.
> [...]
> the particular motivations that would lead to subsequent breakthroughs of poetic technique, of course, could never be anticipated by their forms (either lyric or

---

[19] Ibid. 108.
[20] Charles Bernstein discusses how affectively nimble some of Baraka's poetry readings were in 'Close Listening', in *My Way*, 283–4.
[21] Watten, *The Constructivist Moment*, 109.

paratactic). The mode of production, in this sense, exceeds any particular author, continuing with a will of its own.[22]

This repeats the dilemma I identified earlier: aside from the problem of pinioning literary production to *material* factory conditions by *analogy*, if the poetry is so symptomatic of postmodern assembly lines, then how do the poems' lines have a distinct agency? And what agency, what hand, does the individual poet or reader have in this 'mode of production' if the latter 'exceeds' the individual with 'a will of its own'?

Some of these difficulties Watten has in negotiating a politics of form derive from his adherence to aspects of Russian Formalism, which has been a major influence on Language poetics more generally. As Russian Formalism split into two strands—the Moscow Linguistic Circle and the St Petersburg OPOYAZ group—over the course of the 1910s and 1920s, it produced a variegated body of poetics. As Peter Steiner has pointed out, though, one of its main tendencies was to relate the generation of literary form to industry.[23] Like Watten, Formalists such as Viktor Shklovskii also compared literary writing to car production. As Steiner argues, their mechanistic approach links to another Formalist tendency to view literary writing in terms of a 'system'.[24] For example, taking inspiration from Ferdinand de Saussure's distinction between language as synchronic system (*langue*) and its use by individuals in acts of speech (*parole*), Formalists like Yuri Tynianov sought to outline a system of literary forms with which to circumscribe individual texts. Whereas Saussure ultimately strove to subordinate *parole* to *langue*, Tynianov and fellow Formalists proposed a more dialectical relation between the two. Yet as Steiner writes, the investment in a literary system often meant that 'an author's individuality' in Formalist writings 'figures only as an accident'.[25]

'Helicopters buzz about the accident, flies at a carcass.' There are ways of seeing the particularity of Silliman's line, and the act of writing it, not as an accident on the assembly line but as literary sabotage of systematized production. One way is through the Formalist notion of 'defamiliarization' or 'estrangement' (*ostranenie*), which Watten also cites as being at the heart of Language poetry's labours, and which provides a better way of assessing them than his analogies with car production.[26] As Shklovskii argues in 'Art as Technique' (1917), 'as perception becomes habitual, it

---

[22] Watten, *The Constructivist Moment*, 135, 139.
[23] Peter Steiner, *Russian Formalism: A Metapoetics* (Ithaca, NY: Cornell University Press, 1984), 18–21.
[24] Ibid. 68–9.
[25] Ibid. 135.
[26] See Watten, *The Constructivist Moment*, 108.

becomes automatic'; the function of art is thus to 'recover the sensation of life; it exists to make one feel things, to make the stone *stony*'.[27] And writers and artists do that, he argues, by producing novel, difficult artistic forms to render things 'unfamiliar'.[28] That is clearly closer to the construction of the 'space of appearance' Hejinian invoked, or the 'constructive potential' that Watten ascribed to Silliman's *Tjanting*. But it brings us back to the still-unresolved question of how a Language poetics of possibility acts in relation to readers and real contexts. For the rest of this chapter I'll argue that one resolution to this matter lies in Hejinian's poetry that combines a constructivism of the 'person' with Formalist estrangement and notions of the poem as event and encounter. Before I turn to Hejinian's work, though, it's important to consider the debate about realism that she initiated within the Language group at the start of the eighties, for it shows how the group were linking poetry and possibility at the time.

'ONESELF IS POSSIBLE': *MY LIFE*

Having taken shape mostly in the San Francisco Bay Area and New York City, the Language community built itself up by establishing various forums for its appearance. Little magazines like Silliman's *Tottel's* (1970–81), Watten's and Robert Grenier's *This* (1971–82), and Perelman's *Hills* (1973–81) provided for the distribution of the group's poetry, as did presses like Hejinian's Tuumba, Geoff Young's The Figures, Watten's This Press, and James Sherry's Roof Press. Two other journals, Bernstein's and Bruce Andrews's *L=A=N=G=U=A=G=E* (1978–81) and Watten's and Hejinian's *Poetics Journal* (1981–98) were dedicated to developing poetics in terms of a range of theory—predominantly Marxist, Formalist, and post-structuralist. All of those ventures were further supplemented by frequent readings and discussions in venues like The Grand Piano café in San Francisco. As Perelman has noted, the group thus established 'something of a complete literary environment' for itself.[29] While the environment enabled the poets to take shape as a new literary movement, that's not to say that it was free from differences of opinion and approach.

---

[27] Viktor Shklovskii, 'Art as Technique', in Paul A. Olson (ed.), *Russian Formalist Criticism*, trans. Lee T. Lemon and Marion J. Reis (Lincoln, NE: University of Nebraska Press, 1965), 11, 12.
[28] Ibid. 12.
[29] Perelman, *The Marginalization of Poetry*, 16. See also George Hartley, *Textual Politics and the Language Poets* (Bloomington and Indianapolis: Indiana University Press, 1989), 'Preface' and Ch. 1.

Poets such as Clark Coolidge and Susan Howe, for example, weren't interested in identifying their work with the kind of Marxist theory that Silliman and Watten were advocating, and correspondence between Hejinian and Bernstein shows that not everyone felt Silliman's New Sentence to be representative of the group's writing. The very value of a 'GROUP MIND' was something Hejinian expressed reservations about in a 1977 letter to Bernstein: 'it exerts a psychic force on one's consciousness', she wrote; 'Prblm with things like "us" is that the world has gotten too big to think of anything but our separateness.'[30] That 'us' and its 'separateness' (both in terms of each other and the world) are what Hejinian probed further when in 1980 she wrote to group members asking them what 'relevance' and 'validity' realism had for their writing.

The question bears on Watten's recent attempts to root Language poetry in historical context, and the various responses it prompted at the time are testament to the group's manifold perspectives. Bruce Andrews, Bill Berkson, Rae Armantrout, and Susan Howe all expressed reservations about the usefulness of realism.[31] Howe, for example, allied herself with Wallace Stevens in thinking it 'a corruption of reality' and stated that a 'poet's mind' must 'move towards the irrational'.[32] Perelman also queried the use of trying to reflect reality in writing: 'The real, if it's a question, is a moral question: Who or what is running the show?' As an issue of 'power', he argued, exploring that moral question in writing means contesting the real, like 'Pound trying to stop WWII'.[33] Similarly, Silliman wrote that the only realism that attracted him was 'a critical stance toward reportage', and he went on to cite Ginsberg's 'Wichita Vortex Sutra' as a prime example.[34] The strongest statement advocating poetry as an alternative realism came from Bernstein: 'I am interested in writing as the PRODUCTION of the real [...] for me writing is a place of production for its own sake [...] which means that it has a utopian content *un*realized in the world.'[35] The position is one that both he and Andrews had already

---

[30] Lyn Hejinian, letter to Charles Bernstein (21 July 1977), in Lyn Hejinian Archive, Mandeville Special Collections Library, University of California, San Diego (MSS 74, Box 2, Folder 10). All subsequent references to materials from this archive will be cited as 'Hejinian Archive, UCSD' with box and folder numbers followed by page number.

[31] Their various responses are in Hejinian Archive, UCSD (Box 44, Folders, 3, 4, 6, and 18).

[32] Susan Howe, letter to Hejinian (27 May 1981), in Hejinian Archive, UCSD (Box 44, Folder 18): 1.

[33] Bob Perelman, letter to Hejinian (15 August 1981), in Hejinian Archive, UCSD (Box 44, Folder 24): 1.

[34] Ron Silliman, letter to Hejinian (12 May 1981), in Hejinian Archive, UCSD (Box 44, Folder 29): 1.

[35] Charles Bernstein, letter to Hejinian (27 May 1981), in Hejinian Archive, UCSD (Box 44, Folder 8): 1.

advanced in several articles in $L=A=N=G=U=A=G=E$, and, as I'll discuss, Bernstein's subsequent development of it is what Watten aims at when criticizing the 'poetics of mere possibility'. Rather than uphold possibility as inert abstraction, though, the early $L=A=N=G=U=A=G=E$ articles by Andrews and Bernstein show they were thinking more along the lines of exploring possibility as forms of aesthetic force. In 'The Dollar Value of Poetry', for example, Bernstein advocates poetry that builds an '"other" world *made* from whatever materials are ready to hand [...] structuring, in this way, possibilities otherwise not allowed for'.[36] In another essay he also discusses the poetic formation of 'possible worlds' and asserts that 'What pulses, pushes [the poetry] is energy, spirit, anima, dream, fantasy: coming out always in form, as shape: these particulars'.[37] This view is closer to the previous kinds of affective potentialism that I've discussed—particularly Baraka's—and it clearly influenced Hejinian's own conclusions about the efficacy of realism. In a 1981 paper, for example, she responded to the statements on realism that the group members had sent her. Her own statement is akin to Bernstein's: 'Rather than write about the world, the work writes the world and determines the range in which reality is possible. [...] the poem is a dynamic force rather than a static fact.'[38]

How that relates to particular formal techniques is clearer from two other essays of this period, Bernstein's 'Semblance' (1981) and Hejinian's 'The Rejection of Closure' (1983). In the former, Bernstein rails against texts adhering to conventional syntax—'each word narrowing down the possibilities of each other'.[39] In contrast, he writes, Language poetry's parataxis (like Silliman's) generates 'a perceptual vividness' because it 'induces a greater desire to savor the tangibility of each sentence before it is lost to the next'.[40] The result is that the text resists the unification of its 'field' and so remains open to being composed of the interpretations it prompts in readers. Hejinian offers a similar argument in her essay. Asking whether form can generate 'potency, opening uncertainty to curiosity, incompleteness to speculation', she answers 'yes' and argues that 'Writing's forms are not merely shapes but forces; formal questions are about

---

[36] Charles Bernstein, 'The Dollar Value of Poetry', in Bruce Andrews and Charles Bernstein (eds), *The L=A=N=G=U=A=G=E Book* (Carbondale: Southern Illinois University Press, 1984), 139, Bernstein's emphasis.

[37] Charles Bernstein, 'Stray Straws and Straw Men', in Andrews and Bernstein (eds), *The L=A=N=G=U=A=G=E Book*, 39, 44.

[38] Lyn Hejinian, untitled talk on realism, in Hejinian Archive, UCSD (Box 44, Folder 1): 4.

[39] Charles Bernstein, 'Semblance', in Andrews and Bernstein (eds), *The L=A=N=G=U=A=G=E Book*, 116.

[40] Ibid. 116–17.

dynamics—how, where and why the writing moves'.[41] Like Bernstein, she advocates a form of 'open text' that extends itself to the world and readers through its paratactic interstices. Contrary to Watten's view of the poetics of possibility, the one that Bernstein and Hejinian propose doesn't involve a division of labour whereby the poem's potential is general, inert, and wholly dependent on the reader's labour of interpretation. Instead, the poetry is intended to 'generate' and 'induce' particular forms of perception, speculation, and curiosity, as well as 'a desire to create the subject by saying'.[42] But if the poem's openness is such that it doesn't form a unified field, to what extent can it gather possibilities into a view of a 'world', whether real or utopic? And if its parataxis makes such varied leaps, how can Hejinian's 'open text' turn possibility into the consistency of a tangible person? I'll consider these questions in relation to her poem *My Life* (1980, 1987).

As the title implies, *My Life* is an autobiographical work—though it's far from being conventional in that respect. Like the Fibonacci proceduralism of Silliman's *Tjanting* it employs numerical sequencing as a matrix for its form; the first edition was published when Hejinian was 37 and accordingly comprises 37 paragraphs each made up of 37 sentences of varying length. The revised edition of the book follows suit; published when Hejinian was 45, she inserted eight new paragraphs of 45 sentences and added eight new sentences to each of the previous edition's paragraphs. Formal matrix is thus presented as textual form of life, and this autobiographical framing, along with the relatively straightforward syntax of many of the text's sentences, gives *My Life* an accessibility that's helped make it one of the most widely read and anthologized works by any Language poet. Partly as a result of that, Hejinian has followed it up with *My Life in the Nineties* (2003) and, subsequently, a continuing *My Life* online blog to which she often adds a new sentence on a daily basis. I'm going to focus here on the 1987 edition because it shows well how Hejinian began relating possibility to her notion of the 'person'.

The kinds of formal dynamics the poem involves are evident from the opening section:

A pause, a rose, something on paper	A moment yellow just as four years later, when my father returned home from the war, the moment of greeting him, as he stood at the bottom of the stairs, younger, thinner than when he had left, was purple

---

[41] Lyn Hejinian, 'The Rejection of Closure', in *The Language of Inquiry*, 47, 42.
[42] Ibid. 55.

—though moments are no longer so colored. Somewhere, in the background, rooms share a pattern of small roses. Pretty is as pretty does. In certain families, the meaning of necessity is at one with the sentiment of pre-necessity. The better things were gathered in a pen.[43]

As Marjorie Perloff has noted, each paragraph appears to present a montage of a particular year in Hejinian's life, and the poem's progression is thus loosely chronological.[44] The movement within paragraphs is clearly far from linear, though. For example, in the first sentence after the section's epigraph the 'just as' serves to form a comparison of simile between 'A moment yellow' and another one 'four years later', but it also suggests that the two moments become simultaneous in the process of comparing them and so bruise (purple-yellow) together. Given the stated war context, the sentences' colours are also evocative of yellow ribbons and purple hearts. Right from the outset, then, the poem signals that it's more concerned with how language, memory, and experience can be combined as a dynamic form rather than a static fact. The significance of any experience, as with any sentence, is largely a matter of the *relations* it forms, and Hejinian plays on that in writing about family relatives. After the memory of her father, for example, the next sentence draws on a memory of her grandmother that she recounts in an earlier essay: 'the small yellow roses on the yellowing paper in my grandmother's room'.[45] Even by this early stage the poem suggests that if it has a 'pattern' it lies in the process of making it, of forming relations. And just as remembering her father melds discrete moments over a gap in time, so the sentence stating it relates to others scattered throughout the text that picture various family relations, some of which are also connected through particular images such as window scenes. There's no single way of patterning the sentences' relations overall, then; one can do it in terms of objects, or subjects, or phonetic sound, or syntax. But Hejinian does induce the reader to see particular kinds of pattern in the sets of related words and phrases she scatters, as well as to make relations between those patterns. So, for example, the 'small roses' of the second sentence also reiterates the epigraph '*A pause, a rose, something on paper*'. And not only does that epigraph harbour homonymically another possible statement, '*A pause arose...*', permutations of it reappear in numerous other paragraphs in

---

[43] Lyn Hejinian, *My Life* (1987 rev. edn; repr. Los Angeles: Green Integer, 2002), 7, hereafter cited as *ML*.
[44] Marjorie Perloff, *Radical Artifice: Writing Poetry in the Age of the Media* (Chicago: University of Chicago Press, 1991), 162.
[45] Lyn Hejinian, 'Variations: A Return of Words' (1976), in Ron Silliman (ed.), *In the American Tree* (Maine: National Poetry Foundation, 1986), 507.

both *My Life* and *My Life in the Nineties*—for example: 'There is a pause, a rose, something on paper' (*ML*, 74); 'A pause, a rose, something on paper, of true organic spirals we have no lack' (*ML*, 90).

Like the linguistic variations Acker presented in novels like *Blood and Guts in High School*, Hejinian's permutations can be viewed in terms of Gilles Deleuze and Félix Guattari's assertion that language consists of 'order words' whose performative capacity to formalize relations always bears a linguistic 'power (*puissance*) of variation' as 'potentiality'.[46] That this kind of potentiality plays an intrinsic part in *My Life* is implicit from sentences like the following:

Let's say that every possibility waits. (*ML*, 7)
An other is a possibility, isn't it. (*ML*, 41)
Any work dealing with questions of possibility must lead to new work. (*ML*, 65)
What you can't discover is the limit of possibility, which must always remain to be discovered. (*ML*, 93)

Possibility is thus figured as latent—it 'waits'—rather than abstract, and the lack of its 'limit' is clearly what helps to make *My Life* an 'open text'. It also opens one to ethical relations, an other's potential, while suggesting that those relations are open to construction and 'must lead to new work'. Such work isn't about moving towards totalization (which would require the discovery of limits) but about the production of open singularities; *an* other. That becomes clearer from sentences in which Hejinian introduces her notion of a person, for example: 'I don't exactly remember my name, of a person, we'll call it Asylum, a woman who, and I've done this myself, has for some reasons renounced some point, say the window in the corner of the room, then it accepts it again' (*ML*, 97). Identity here is provisional; contingent upon performing actions like naming or renunciation. If one founds oneself as a person by reflecting on oneself, that reflection involves making oneself both subject and object, first and third person, simultaneously: 'I', 'myself', 'a woman', 'it'. The singularity of Hejinian's person is thus predicated on being relational and under construction. That also gives it an open performativity—'As persons think so are they thoughts being things' (*ML*, 158)—which makes of personhood a series of encounters and situations: 'A person is a bit of space that has gotten itself in moments' (*ML*, 163).

These statements reflect thinking that Hejinian was developing elsewhere. In 1984 she began a poem entitled 'The Person', which she intended to be a long sequence. It remains unfinished, however, and

---

[46] Gilles Deleuze and Félix Guattari, *A Thousand Plateaus*, trans. Brian Massumi (Minneapolis: University of Minnesota Press, 1991), 101, 99.

only some of its sections have been published. Those sections are largely concerned with elaborating particular moments in which a person personifies itself by reflecting on things and language, as in the following:

> People desire to believe in...
> Rain falls
> Physical reality consists of sympathetic units
> Grammar and consciousness[47]

The ellipsis of the first line suggests that what 'People desire to believe in' isn't simply subjective but subject to, interrupted by, simple events like falling rain. It's hard to take a rain check on that belief and desire by the second line, though; is 'Rain falls' a generic plural noun or an event happening now? Are rainfalls something to believe in, or do 'People' desire to believe when they are in them? The point is that if events impinge on flows of 'desire' and 'consciousness', so does 'Grammar' with its own weather of possibilities. Hence, the 'Physical reality' of a person is composed of interactions between 'units' of events, grammar, and consciousness, and those units are 'sympathetic' because one feels *with them* in forming a sense *of them*. How that involves a process of personification that incorporates possibility is clear from two of Hejinian's essays. In 'The Person and Everyday Life' (1988) she reiterates what 'The Person' implies: 'As a person, I am always a subject-object', and 'experience myself [...] discontinuously, but also as discontinuous'.[48] And in 'The Person and Description' (1991) the relation between possibility and situations of experience that *My Life* makes is also elaborated:

sense of being, of selfhood, can only be reached *after* one is in place and surrounded by possibilities. That comes first: the perceiving of something, not in parts but whole, as a situation and with a projection of possibilities. The recognition of those possibilities follows and constitutes one's first exercise *of* possibility, and on that depends one's realization that oneself is possible. It is in the exercise of *that* possibility that one inescapably acknowledges others, which have in fact already been admitted when and as one initially perceived something. And the exercise of possibilities (including that of consciousness) amid conditions and occasions constitutes a person.[49]

---

[47] Lyn Hejinian, 'The Person', in *The Cold of Poetry* (Los Angeles: Sun and Moon, 1994), 144.
[48] Lyn Hejinian, 'The Person and Everyday Life', in Hejinian Archive (Box 112, Folder 25); 5, 7.
[49] Lyn Hejinian, 'The Person and Description', in *The Language of Inquiry*, 203, Hejinian's emphases.

This passage provides the basis for a complex form of potentialism that's comparable to the others I've discussed in previous chapters. It also affords a way of considering the questions that I posed above for *My Life* regarding the nature of its world and subject. Rather than present an autobiographical field unified in terms of themes or objects, the poem is a textual place in which the reader is 'surrounded by possibilities'. Recognizing and relating those possibilities amounts to exercising them and thereby constructing the poem's field and oneself simultaneously *as a set of 'occasions'*. The poem thus calls for the reader to become a 'person' in the encounter with the text. Any attempt to totalize the encounter will founder on the openness of the text. If one experiences oneself 'discontinuously' that doesn't discount the need to perceive things 'not in parts but whole', but that whole is plural and open: 'a situation [...] with a projection of possibilities'.

Is one only a person occasionally, then? Is the world a discontinuous series of situations? By reiterating sets of related words and single sentences in permutation, *My Life* has more threads of continuity running through it than many other Language texts, but like other poems that Hejinian has written it also refuses to compose a unified 'whole' more than most of the texts I've discussed in previous chapters. Ginsberg's auto-poems fragment at points, for example, but their 'speech acting' also sustains a lyric 'I' in opposition to structures of power while appealing to America as democracy. Baraka's Black Arts writing also appeals to political institutions while presenting images for individuals to identify with in terms of racial identity. In contrast, Acker's allobiographies do experiment with more fragmented voices, but these are sometimes linked to generalized structures of power, myth, and taboo. And while some of Burroughs's early cut-ups are more randomly fragmented than *My Life*, at the point when the Language poets begin experimenting with 'nonnarrative' he returned to narrative to portray the potential of his novels' worlds and characters more in terms of synthesized hybridity than open dispersal. As I'll show, there's also a larger horizon that Hejinian engages in assembling her poetics of the person; namely, US–Soviet relations in the final stages of the Cold War. But her emphasis is on drawing series of aesthetic and ethical situations from that horizon rather than on subordinating those instances to a generic political ideology.[50] Such a stance diverges from the

---

[50] For that reason, I agree with Peter Nicholls when he states that 'any future readings which give serious consideration to [Hejinian's] stated intentions will have to situate themselves somewhere on the "border" between ethics and aesthetics' ('Phenomenal Poetics: Reading Lyn Hejinian', in Delville and Pagnoulle (eds), *The Mechanics of the Mirage*, 251).

political role some other Language poets were claiming for the group, so before discussing Hejinian's trips to Soviet Russia and the poetry she wrote about them, I'll first discuss other statements about politics and community that she and other Language poets were making around the time.

THE CONSPIRACY OF 'US': 1980s LANGUAGE POLITICS

In a prefatory note that Hejinian later added to her 1983 paper, 'Who Is Speaking?', she writes that this question—taken from Foucault's article 'What is an Author?'—was first posed by the San Francisco Language group as a topic for discussion in 1980.[51] The group's desire to think about language with regard to social discourse and power is one reason why, from the mid-eighties, university critics began taking more notice of Language poetry as a movement. Maintaining a prodigious production of both poetry and critical theory in their various journals, the group also gained attention around this time with the publication of anthologies such as Bernstein's and Andrews's *The L=A=N=G=U=A=G=E Book* (1984), Perelman's *Writing/Talks* (1985), Silliman's *In the American Tree* (1986), and critical monographs like Watten's *Total Syntax* (1985) and Bernstein's *Content's Dream* (1986). But if these publications provided a more accessible body of writing with which to approach the group's poetry, they also led to negative responses from some critics who argued that the aspirations stated in the theory weren't fulfilled by the poetic practice. The criticisms are understandable if one considers some of the group's statements on politics. The main political stance continued to be revolutionary socialism, and the publication of *The L=A=N=G=U= A=G=E Book*—which gathered a selection of articles first published in the L=A=N=G=U=A=G=E journal—presented numerous statements translating such socialism into Language poetics. Discussing how the poetry could combat capitalism's commodity fetishism is a particularly common line in the anthology, and Steve McCaffery's 'From the Notebooks' is a good example. 'The Capitalist rationale', he wrote, works on the basis of making everything consumable and exchangeable in the name of profit. This rationale is also evident in work written for easy consumption; writing in which signifiers are readily exchangeable for signified meaning. Such ready-to-read meaning is produced and consumed as

---

[51] Lyn Hejinian, 'Who Is Speaking?', in *The Language of Inquiry*, 30–1.

'surplus value' and 'profit rate', argues McCaffery, and is intended to agglomerate into larger units of meaning: 'the chapter, the book, the collected works'.[52] In contrast, Language poetry, with its parataxis and rejection of unified fields, opposes the ready consumption of texts and calls for participatory production from readers: 'it diminishes the profit rate and lowers investment drives just as a productive need is increased'.[53] The aspiration to turn that opposition into class action was summed up by Silliman when he reprised the French Symbolists' call of *épater le bourgeoisie*: 'Let us undermine the bourgeoisie.'[54]

There are several objections one can make in response to those arguments, and some of them relate to Watten's assertions about a politics of totalization. As Rod Mengham stated in a 1989 review, the argument equating the dynamic of 'normative grammar' to 'profit structure' is too sweeping.[55] It depends on too general a notion of conventional writing, and cannot account for different economies of literary exchanges like 'gifts and counter-gifts'[56]—to which I'd add other forms of readerly exchange, like the compound becoming that Burroughs's hybrid characters require, or the lyrical counter-feedback of Ginsberg's auto-poems. As other Language poets have admitted, it's reductive to argue that all hypotactic flows of meaning are inherently conventional.[57] Whether refusing to subordinate sentences to larger units of meaning (paragraphs and chapters) necessarily translates into a concrete politics of production is also questionable. As Mengham argued, the fragmented difficulty of much Language poetry can also render it virtually 'impenetrable' such that it alienates readers rather than encouraging their participation in it.[58] Similarly, critic Charles Altieri in a 1987 article argued that by focusing on serried instances of linguistic opacity the group's poetry frequently 'reifies' language and so detaches it from the agency of individuals.[59] It's important, of course, not to generalize about Language poetry's dynamics—the

---

[52] Steve McCaffery, 'From the Notebooks', in Andrews and Bernstein (eds), *The L=A=N=G=U=A=G=E Book*, 160.
[53] Ibid. 161.
[54] Ron Silliman, 'If By "Writing" We Mean Literature (if by "literature" we mean poetry (if…))…', in Andrews and Bernstein (eds), *The L=A=N=G=U=A=G=E Book*, 168.
[55] Rod Mengham, untitled review of writing by Clark Coolidge, Steve McCaffery, Charles Bernstein, and Barrett Watten, *Textual Practice* 3:1 (Spring 1989), 119.
[56] Ibid. 120.
[57] See, for example, Bernstein, 'The Revenge of the Poet-Critic, or The Parts Are Greater Than the Sum of the Whole', 6.
[58] Mengham, untitled review, 121. Charles Bernstein extols the virtues of 'antiabsorptive' poetry in 'Artifice of Absorption', *A Poetics* (Cambridge, MA: Harvard University Press, 1992), 9–89.
[59] Charles Altieri, 'Without Consequences is No Politics: A Response to Jerome McGann', in von Hallberg (ed.), *Politics and Poetic Value*, 305.

different forms and subjects that I'll follow in Hejinian's work provide just one example of the variety in approach that Language poets have valued. Altieri and Mengham were right to take issue with the group, though, to the extent that its theoretical stance on class politics wasn't adequately borne out in its poetry, which was more intent on atomization.

That inconsistency is also evident in statements the poets made reflecting on their group as community. For example, the misgivings that Bernstein had already expressed about group identity were evident in his essay 'The Conspiracy of "US"', which was included in *The L=A=N=G=U=A=G=E Book*: 'I don't believe in group formation', he stated, 'I don't like group formation.'[60] But in an another essay republished in *Content's Dream* Bernstein wrote that 'The essential aspect of writing centered on its language is its possibilities for relationship, *viz*, it is the body of "us" ness, in which *we* are'.[61] He also affirmed the power of 'us' by stating a commitment to 'political struggle': 'to making the factories & the schools & the hospitals cooperative, to finding a democracy that allows for the participatory authority of each one to the extent of the responsibility we place on her or him'.[62] That sounds more like the kind of political activism that Ginsberg or Baraka pursued, but the aspirations never turned into Language practice, which only lends weight to Mengham's accusation that, given the group's theoretical stance, their poetry 'seems doomed to sustain a myth of activism'.[63] Behind the scenes, poets like Hejinian continued to question the group's solidarity. In a 1984 letter to Steve Benson, for example, she wrote that the group's 'scene' in San Francisco is 'over for us'; 'fewer and fewer of us appear at readings, and the domestic or occupational demands appear to control social access'.[64] Like most of the other Language poets, though, in public she continued to defend the group as a communitarian movement, most notably in the manifesto 'Aesthetic Tendency and the Politics of Poetry' that she, Silliman, Benson, Perelman, Watten, and Carla Harryman co-published in the journal *Social Text* in 1988.

Situating themselves in relation to 'avant-garde tradition', the manifesto's co-authors defended themselves against some of their critics' accusations by stating that the 'first principle' of the group was neither the 'self-sufficiency'

---

[60] Charles Bernstein, 'The Conspiracy of "US"', in Andrews and Bernstein (eds), *The L=A=N=G=U=A=G=E Book*, 185.
[61] Charles Bernstein, 'Three or Four Things I Know About Him', in *Content's Dream: Essays 1975–1985* (Evanston, IL: Northwestern University Press, 2001), 31.
[62] Ibid. 30.
[63] Mengham, untitled review, 122.
[64] Lyn Hejinian letter to Steve Benson (October 1984), in Hejinian Archive, UCSD (Box 2, Folder 7): 1.

nor 'materiality' of language, but *the reciprocity of practice implied by a community of writers who read each other's work*.[65] The manifesto is thus aimed at reinforcing the group's literary endeavour as a form of social work that eschews 'institutional norms' in order to build an alternative community as 'a group of individuals'.[66] Far from envisaging a politics of totalization, this stance aligned the group more with the small-scale alternative community built by sixties counter-culture groups. Indeed, the move towards a more individuated social stance is evident in other Language publications like *The Politics of Poetic Form* (1990) in which Bernstein assembles various talks given by Language poets in the late eighties on the issue of the book's title. In his own contribution he acknowledges the 'lack of mass audience' that any poet faces, but cites sociologist Erving Goffman in contending that 'every interpersonal interaction should be read as an institutional and ideological event'.[67] In that respect the 'political power of poetry' requires a 'microcosmic view', he argues: 'you affect the public sphere with each reader'.[68] These two statements come close to the assertion that Acker made in her essay 'Postmodernism' (part of which was published in the 1987 issue of *Poetics Journal* edited by Hejinian and Watten): 'All aspects of language are [...] politically, economically, and morally coded', which is why 'when I use words [...] I am always taking part in the constructing of the political, economic, and moral community'.[69] Similarly, Andrews's contribution to Bernstein's volume argues for such constructivism in terms of potentialization: showing in poetry *'possibilities* of sense & meaning being constructed' is aimed at 'widen[ing] the realm of social possibility'.[70] Taking a 'microcosmic view' of that constructivism also entails a realization similar to the one that Acker underwent after writing *Don Quixote* (1986): if as a literary writer one cannot change social institutions of power—make 'factories' and 'hospitals cooperative', for example—one can combat the effects of power on oneself and, to varying degrees, on 'each reader'. In that sense, the engagement with the 'public sphere' that Bernstein and Andrews propose is more akin to the building of 'pirate' commu-

---

[65] Ron Silliman, Carla Harryman, Lyn Hejinian, Steve Benson, Bob Perelman, and Barrett Watten, 'Aesthetic Tendency and the Politics of Poetry: A Manifesto', *Social Text* (Autumn 1988), 271, authors' emphasis.
[66] Ibid.
[67] Charles Bernstein, 'Comedy and the Poetics of Political Form', in Bernstein (ed.), *The Politics of Poetic Form* (New York: Roof, 1998), 241.
[68] Ibid. 242.
[69] Kathy Acker, 'Postmodernism', in *Bodies of Work: Essays* (London: Serpent's Tail, 1997), 4. This statement forms part of the untitled section she published in *Poetics Journal* 7 (September 1987), 117.
[70] Bruce Andrews, 'Poetry as Explanation, Poetry as Praxis', in Bernstein (ed.), *The Politics of Poetic Form*, 28, 31, Andrews's emphasis.

nities that Burroughs and Acker sought to foster. Again, I'm not suggesting that Bernstein's and Andrews's views should be taken as representative of the Language group as a whole—their position, as I've stated, is intrinsic to the 'poetics of possibility' that Watten later criticizes. But such divergence in opinion shows the extent to which the Language movement itself has developed along various individual lines.

For Hejinian's part she continued to speak of the group as a collective, and in a 1990 essay she modified the view she put her name to in the *Social Text* manifesto, declaring that

the Language community has less in common with modernist avant-garde movements than with aesthetic tendencies grounded in marginalized cultural communities—the cultures, for example, of the so-called (racial) 'minorities' and of gay and lesbian communities.[71]

Aligning the Language community with forms of minoritarian identity politics is highly questionable, though, particularly considering that it had not engaged in the kind of concerted 'political struggle' that Bernstein and others had earlier invoked. Although the group had faced some harsh critics, it had by no means had to fight for collective rights and status like gays and lesbians or the Black Power movement. Nor was Hejinian's poetry presenting subjectivity in terms of such group identity, which is a point that Juliana Spahr makes when criticizing *My Life* for not dealing with race.[72] If her poetry does engage matters of the polis, it does so primarily through her figure of the person. That figure emerges partly from the wider horizon of Soviet–American relations that Hejinian experienced in her trips to the USSR. As I'll show, though, the poetry she wrote about the trips also arrives at the person by combining aesthetics and ethics with the kind of 'microcosmic view' that Bernstein espoused.

RUSSIA, ESTRANGEMENT, AND THE 'COLD OF POETRY'

In a 1986 letter to Bernstein, Hejinian wrote that the main '"breakthrough" for me in the past few years' was a visit to Russia the previous summer which 'confirmed [. . .] my desire to speak of [Language] writing in terms of "ethical" aspirations and metaphysical constructs'.[73] That

---

[71] Hejinian, 'Materials', 171.
[72] Juliana Spahr, *Everybody's Autonomy: Connective Reading and Collective Identity* (Tuscaloosa: University of Alabama Press, 2001), 81.
[73] Lyn Hejinian letter to Charles Bernstein (7 February 1986), in Hejinian Archive, UCSD (Box 12, Folder 13): 3.

trip was one of many that she made over a ten-year period up to the formal end of the Cold War, her other visits being in 1983, 1987, 1989 (twice), 1990, and 1992.[74] As that period includes 'Star Wars', the Soviet Union's collapse, and the rise of biopolitical conservatism in America that I discussed in the last chapter, the Soviet trips made by Hejinian and some other Language poets clearly afforded them concrete experiences of cultural and political estrangement with which to develop their poetry. As Hejinian has stated, the poets' common interest in Russian Formalism was a primary reason for making the trips.[75] Fascination with alternatives to capitalism and liberal democracy was another reason, and the social upheavals in the Soviet Union during this period certainly provided plenty of occasion for comparing the relative merits of the two countries. During the 1983 visit, Yuri Andropov was Soviet president and the Communist Party was still rigorously regulating writers. Hejinian met a number of underground intellectuals and writers, including the poet Arkadii Dragomoshchenko with whom she subsequently collaborated in writing several poetic works in addition to translating some of his writings.[76] The Soviet cultural situation changed dramatically, though, after Mikhail Gorbachev's accession to the presidency in 1985, the year of Hejinian's 'breakthrough'. Intent on relaxing the Communist Party's policies of regulation, Gorbachev launched 'perestroika', a policy of widespread economic restructuring, and 'glasnost', a policy that involved publicizing 'political openness' to 'individual initiative'.[77] The two strategies converged in a number of liberalizing initiatives, such as permitting the establishment of private business cooperatives, which were previously unheard of under Soviet Communism. Glasnost had a variety of other consequences; it inadvertently encouraged regions of ethnic minorities within the USSR to seek independence from Soviet rule, and, as Svetlana Boym has pointed

---

[74] For more background to these trips and Hejinian's interest in Russia see Jacob Edmond's 'Lyn Hejinian and Russian Estrangement', *Poetics Today* 27:1 (Spring 2006), 97–123.

[75] Lyn Hejinian, 'An Introduction', in Michael Davidson, Lyn Hejinian, Ron Silliman, and Barrett Watten, *Leningrad: American Writers in the Soviet Union* (San Francisco: Mercury House, 1991), 2–3.

[76] For detailed discussion of their collaborations, see Jacob Edmond, '"A Meaning Alliance": Arkadii Dragomoshchenko and Lyn Hejinian's Poetics of Translation', *Slavic and East European Journal* 46:3 (2002), 551–64; also Stephanie Sandler, 'Arkadii Dragomoshchenko, Lyn Hejinian and the Persistence of Romanticism', *Contemporary Literature* 46:1 (2005), 18–45.

[77] See Walter LaFeber, *America, Russia, and the Cold War, 1945–2006* (New York: McGraw-Hill, 2006), 338.

out, it also enabled underground writers to gain a wider public voice as a result of censorship being lifted.[78]

Gorbachev's policies thus precipitated challenges to Soviet identity, not only at the national level but also at an individual one. As Boym has argued, the Communist faith in collective social life had for decades been bolstered by communal apartments, which provided an objective correlative for the fact that there's no word in Russian equivalent to 'privacy' in English; the closest 'concept', as she points out, is '*chastnaia zhizn*'— literally: 'particular (partial) life'.[79] More important is the 'inner life' of the 'Russian soul', writes Boym, but that inner life belongs to a realm of spiritual being (*bytie*) that remains transcendent to everyday existence (*byt*).[80] This higher inner life is therefore not an object of daily lived existence, which is why the Russian experience of being a person remains mired in a collective *byt*—the word also having connotations of routine and drudgery. The Russian divergence from Western notions of selfhood is also one that Hejinian cites Dragomoshchenko as mentioning: 'Subjectivity is not the basis for being a Russian person. Our independent separate singularity can hardly be spoken of, but Arkadii said, "many people wish it".'[81] As Hejinian makes clear, the Russian basis for being a person is also what she explored in order to pose her own figure of the person as an alternative to all that is implied by the English world 'self'.[82] That exploration of Russian personhood, and the growing desire in Russia for a more Western subjectivity, is what she presents in her two booklength poems, *The Cell* (1992) and *Oxota: A Short Russian Novel* (1991).

Written before *Oxota* between October 1986 and January 1989, *The Cell* comprises a series of 150 poems of varying length, most of which are dated to a single day. Unlike *My Life*, which frequently goes into the past tense to frame memory, the emphasis in *The Cell* is on daily observations in the present. In that sense, the form of the poem bears on Hejinian's assertion that a person occasions itself in situated acts of reflection, and in a later interview she suggests that such occasions in *The Cell* include its scenes of writing: 'The writing precedes the thought—the writing performs the thinking and also begins at the very moment of writing.'[83]

---

[78] Svetlana Boym, *Common Places: Mythologies of Everyday Life in Russia* (Cambridge, MA: Harvard University Press, 1994), 205.
[79] Ibid. 73.
[80] Ibid. 84.
[81] Hejinian, untitled entry, in Davidson, Hejinian, Silliman, and Watten, *Leningrad*, 34.
[82] Hejinian, 'The Person and Description', 201–2.
[83] Lyn Hejinian, transcript of untitled interview with Laura Hinton (December 1994–February 1995), in Hejinian Archive, UCSD (Box 97, Folder 15): 12.

If, as Hejinian claimed in *My Life*, 'persons are thoughts being things', then the instances of thinking that *The Cell* performs are also constructions of personhood. Indeed, that correlation between writing and person is evident in poems that figure 'cells' in terms of the body, a room, and units of description, as in the poem dated 'January 14, 1987':

> Do you patrol? outside the
> self? around a body and
> the follicle in which it
> stands?
> Or cell?[84]

These lines follow on from the 'subject–object' personhood of *My Life*. Whether 'you patrol' bears on how you isolate and guard 'the self'. And as that surveillance necessitates standing 'outside' self or 'around a body' in order to reflect on it as object, then 'you' emerge as already split and dispossessed of self—hence the absence of possessive pronouns in relation to the nouns. Forced to be inside *and* outside, the kind of 'cell' one 'stands' in can thus be situated in both a room and a 'follicle'. Stable subjectivity gives way to a bodily situation, and one's bearing in that situation also involves orders of language; or, as Hejinian puts it, 'cell[s] of description' (*TC*, 55):

> The cell in shifts
> Cells in drifts
> So we're feeling a loss
>   but not a conclusion
> The smallest unit of imagination
>   in time, a retrospection
> A unit of space so
>   small it seems to be
>   going backwards (*TC*, 56)

As in all of *The Cell*'s poems the start of each line is marked with a capital letter, and the hypotaxis and enjambement of the five closing lines here are also representative of the volume in general. Not a single full-stop appears in any of its poems, and *The Cell* thus stands as a pointed departure from *My Life*'s sentences. Hejinian's refusal to accept the New Sentence as basic unit of Language writing is evident from a short note she published in 1988 in which she stated that for her the poetic *line* is 'the standard (however variable) of meaning in the poem, the primary

---

[84] Lyn Hejinian, *The Cell* (San Francisco: Sun and Moon, 1992), 55, hereafter cited as *TC*.

unit of observation, and the measure of felt thought'.[85] Relating that to the lines above, we can see that the poem's initial staging of self-reflection now includes meta-textual reflection. The sense of 'cell' as body and room 'shifts' syntactically in 'drifts' of meaning with each new 'cell of description', and in that way Hejinian composes the presence of her person with lines that can act as units of 'imagination' as well as of 'space' and 'time'. The use of rhyme also emphasizes how the lines hark 'backwards' while progressing—which is why they can involve 'feeling a loss' of stable presence as much as a loss of self. Such poetic 'shift' work can thus amount to *selling-out* the self in poetic cells, but that loss is recompensed because the person continues to drift without 'conclusion' and so remains open to construction.

Those references to labour and economics are clearly metaphorical to some degree, but that's because figurative language and ambiguity are frequently employed to draw linguistic agency out of a particular situation. In poems like the one dated 'February 7 & 10, 1987' that agency forms as a distinct struggle:

> An orientated person writing appears
>   to face north, so going
>   from the west (but creating
>   an accumulation)
> A midday glare, an avant-garde
> Very abstract (*TC*, 71)

Just as the cells 'of description' hark back to each other in moving on, so the orientation of the 'person' here accumulates 'from the west' in 'going' away from it, and the 'midday glare' is suddenly seen in terms of 'an avant-garde' lineage. In other words, being open to the moment through open-form poetry means being indebted to a literary tradition, one that abstracts the person from the situation's immediacy. This bears on the belief of Formalists like Tynianov that a writer's work must be viewed primarily in terms of a synchronic system of literature akin to Saussure's notion of *langue*. But when Hejinian considers the 'causes' of her material, she effectively rejects the possibility that any such single, unified system could be their prime mover:

> There's no dogma out of this predicament
> It might have turned up
>   out of anywhere

---

[85] Lyn Hejinian, 'Line', in *The Language of Inquiry*, 133. In a letter to Robert Grenier (21 May 1988) Hejinian made it clear that she had gone off writing sentences: 'I don't like sentences', in Hejinian Archive, UCSD (Box 19, Folder 4): 1.

> All the nameable causes of
> my material
> Even *glasnost*
> The poem can make me
> a public discussion of my
> causes (*TC*, 71)

As *glasnost* involved a public policy of individual initiatives, the reference to it here again points the orientation of a person in the direction of systems. But the sheer multiplicity of 'causes' that might lie behind any situation or moment makes it impossible to fix or limit their relations, which is why the poem's 'material' and person remain open to further construction—'The poem can make me'—and 'public discussion'. Sensing that causality is illimitable might produce an acute anxiety to accompany the 'loss' previously noted, but it also means that a person is composed of potential. As the final poem in the volume puts it:

> A person's character is in
> the realm of possibility
> This means hysteria (*TC*, 216)

Such 'hysteria' manifested itself as '*globus hystericus*' in Hejinian; the 'sensation of a lump in the throat', which she first developed after the death of her father from cancer that spread to his throat.[86] That the *possibility* of becoming ill with cancer can become a bodily symptom of imagined futurity is all the more reason to train oneself for the eventuality of hazards and fatality—which, as we'll see, is precisely what she does later with her collections *Happily* (2000) and *The Fatalist* (2003).

In a 1987 letter to Michael Molnar, Hejinian wrote that there had been times during her visit to the USSR that year in which she had 'felt completely isolated, and thought maybe I was losing personality and would become no one'.[87] If for the Russian Formalists attaining defamiliarization was a principal aim for a writer, then the estrangement from home and personality that Hejinian explored in *The Cell* would clearly have piqued their interest. By 1989, though, the year that Hejinian finished writing the volume, wider forms of political estrangement were afoot in the Eastern bloc. In July that year Gorbachev overturned the Brezhnev Doctrine and accepted the right of other Eastern bloc countries

---

[86] Lyn Hejinian, letter to Rae Armantrout (29 July 1991), in Hejinian Archive, UCSD (Box 11, Folder 1): 1. Hejinian did have cancer in 1996 but unlike Kathy Acker she was cured of it.

[87] Quoted in Edmond, 'Lyn Hejinian and Russian Estrangement', 112.

to hold democratic elections.[88] Consequently, by the end of the year Communist governments had lost power in Poland, Hungary, Czechoslovakia, Bulgaria, and Romania, and in November the Berlin Wall was taken down. It was the beginning of the Cold War's end, and was soon followed by the Soviet Union's collapse. In August 1991 Gorbachev signed a treaty allowing for nine of the fifteen Soviet republics to be given sovereign autonomy. Angered at the Union's demise the Soviet military attempted a *coup d'état* but were defeated by Boris Yeltsin, head of the Russian Federation, and his supporters. With the Soviet economy in a parlous state, Yeltsin's Federation refused to pay the president's bills, and in December 1991 Gorbachev resigned and was replaced by Yeltsin. Subsequently, the Cold War was officially declared to be over and Yeltsin began encouraging free markets and further privatization. As Boym wrote after a 1991 visit to Russia, embracing Western capitalism also meant importing its terms: 'The fashionable word of the 1991 season was "stock market"'; 'The newspapers have sections labeled "stock market of news" [...] or a "stock market of ideas".'[89]

Engaging with the import of Soviet upheavals was what Hejinian and other Language poets sought to do in their group trips to Russia in 1989 and 1990. In August 1989, for example, with Watten, Silliman, and Michael Davidson, she participated in a six-day colloquium in Leningrad entitled 'Language—Consciousness—Society'. The aim of the event was primarily to stage discussions between the Language poets and their Russian counterparts, including Dragomoshchenko and members of the Moscow Conceptualists like Dmitrii Prigov.[90] One of its outcomes was *Leningrad* (1991), a co-authored work in which Hejinian and her fellow Language participants wrote a series of short prose accounts about the context and their experience of the event. That much of the colloquium entailed exchanging views on cultural defamiliarization is evident from the poets' responses. Davidson, for example, wrote that the fears of their hosts about the upheavals in the Soviet Union were more directed at consequences of pursuing 'Western economic goals'.[91] Watten, in contrast, stated that he'd 'never experienced the irrelevance of money more immediately' than in Russia,[92] while Hejinian noted that to establish 'a passage between Russian and American experiences, one negotiates vast fields of

---

[88] See LaFeber, *America, Russia, and the Cold War*, 356–7.
[89] Boym, *Common Places*, 230.
[90] Both Dragomoshchenko and Prigov had already contributed articles to issue 8 (June 1989) of Watten's and Hejinian's *Poetics Journal*.
[91] Michael Davidson, untitled entry, in Davidson, Hejinian, Silliman, and Watten, *Leningrad*, 20.
[92] Barrett Watten, untitled entry, ibid. 123.

vertiginous shimmering'.[93] The group visit she made in 1990 with Clark Coolidge, Jean Day, Michael Palmer, and Kit Robinson showed the poets how those fields were very much a matter of wider political machinations. Sponsored by the United States Information Agency (USIA)—which had been instrumental in driving a Cold War policy of advancing US art and culture overseas—the group first travelled to Helsinki. Not only was there a summit taking place there between Gorbachev and President George Bush (to discuss the crisis taking place between Iraq and Kuwait), staff from the US embassy in Moscow had recently been posted there because the embassy had been bugged.[94]

Written between December 1989 and February 1991, Hejinian's *Oxota* makes numerous gestures towards the shimmerings and changes occurring in wider political fields, but it focuses more on turning the Formalist notion of estrangement into an exploration of particular things and situations. The importance of developing that practice was outlined by her in an essay, 'Strangeness' (1989), in which she argued that what she wanted to produce was 'the strangeness that results from the description of the world given in the terms "there it is", "there it is", "there it is", that restores realness to things in the world and separates things from ideology'.[95] In that sense, the estrangement she aims at builds on the Language group's earlier discussions about realism and also draws on her 1981 statement about potentiating the real: 'the work writes the world and determines the range in which reality is possible'. The dynamic form Hejinian uses to explore that range in *Oxota* is inspired by Alexander Pushkin's verse novel *Eugene Onegin* (1833), which was written as a series of sonnets. *Oxota*, which means 'the hunt' in Russian, is also made up of sonnets; 271 in total, which comprise the volume's 270 'chapters' and 'coda'. Unlike the sonnets in Pushkin's work, Hejinian's have no fixed metre or rhyme scheme and thereby stand as instances of 'open text'. Undated, each poem nevertheless occasions a particular set of reflections, many of which involve the kinds of cultural estrangement that were discussed at the Leningrad colloquium. In 'Chapter 112: Counting for One', for example, Hejinian links anaphorically a series of disorienting exchanges:

> It's the man with the dancing collie, Zina whispered
> My god, said Arkadii, and I can't forget how the girl in the

---

[93] Lyn Hejinian, untitled entry, ibid. 54.
[94] See Lyn Hejinian letter to Dennis Wolf, USIA (9 October 1990), in Hejinian Archive, UCSD (Box 48, Folder 4): 1–4; also her letter to Clark Coolidge, Jean Day, Michael Palmer, and Kit Robinson (28 March 1990), in Hejinian Archive, UCSD (Box 48, Folder 4): 1–4.
[95] Lyn Hejinian, 'Strangeness', in *The Language of Inquiry*, 158.

>   hard currency shop smiled
> It's *glasnost*!
> It crowds our pages
> It's a bell off to the left[96]

Writing the world of a single encounter doesn't preclude the effects of ideology like glasnost, then, but the poem again works against identifying it as a stable cause or structure by diffusing what 'It' is and does—'It's the man'; 'It crowds our pages'; 'It's a bell'. Just as *langue* remains open to *parole*, so ideology is not transcendent to particular scenes of exchange but is made singular and unfamiliar through them.

That making is what the poems are engaged in, and throughout *Oxota* establishing a thing's 'realness' in terms of a range of possibility means opening it to disjunction and permutation both within and between poems. The opening poems, for example, do that with snow. In 'Chapter One' we're told that 'The old thaw is inert, everything set again in snow | At insomnia, at apathy' (*O*, 11). The first line's 'thaw' can be read in terms of the state of the weather and the Cold War, both of which blend into a state of mind in the second line. The gathering sense of snow as objective correlative for a range of relations is then reiterated in 'Chapter Nine':

> Snow was falling in the yard around a hard currency hospital
>   of the same colour
> The rubles too as thick as snowflakes (*O*, 19)

By this point the snow lines are accumulating meaning like the 'shifts' and 'drifts' of Hejinian's cells. If the snow sets the hospital against the previous state of Cold War weather, it also does so in terms of the economy. And if it prompts reflection on the solidity of a hospital run on 'hard currency', it also intimates that the ruble's consistency is as indeterminate and unstable as the drifts of particular relations that the poetry is accumulating. Consequently, in 'Chapter Eleven' we find both snow and money being called to account:

> But a whistling man is luckless in money
>   What then if snow is the substance of an accounting
> No objects of metonymy, of economy (*O*, 21)

The well-being of the man—and doubtless his ability to weather the winter—depends on the economy and his ability to work, just as weather and the work of such individuals affects the economy. The fungibility of such relations is what makes it hard to identify a solid identity of objects,

---

[96] Lyn Hejinian, *Oxota: A Short Russian Novel* (Great Barrington, MA: The Figures, 1991), 127, hereafter cited as *O*.

whether of language or 'economy', which is precisely why the poems' accounting of this has fallen back on snow's ephemeral solidity.

The 'strangeness' that Hejinian produces thus results from her delineating the movement between particular situations and wider systems—whether political or economic. What she doesn't do is suggest that the situations, and the poem's reflection on them, are overdetermined by those systems. That is why *Oxota* presents neither the totalizations that Watten pursues, nor the sweeping view of textual economics that McCaffery theorizes. Instead it suggests that social and economic structures are composed of people, things, and situations whose identity is the relations—including possible ones—they can enter into. As identity is therefore mutable, open to alienation and estranging exchanges, so are the structures. The poem as 'open text' composes possibilities of those relations and exchanges as its own set of situations. Or, as Hejinian puts it, 'The weather is syntax | Thus we can speak of a cold of poetry' (*O*, 133). The correlation between description and alienation, scene and poem, is clearer from 'Chapter 212':

> But alienation insists that this life is something you yourself
>   haven't experienced
> Or anything rushes into the eyes whenever it's given a chance,
>   freeing anything from everything, isolating the minutest fact
> So between phrases it's essential that other phrases be
>   inserted, and that they intercede logically, so the world
>   will gain stability and the writer won't seem like an idiot (*O*, 230)

The 'alienation' mentioned here can result from the poetry itself, as in the instance of the poem I discussed from *The Cell* in which the tradition of 'an avant garde' is felt to alienate the 'person' from the immediacy of the 'midday glare' that's experienced. As the extract above suggests, though, a person's experience *is* a process of alienation if 'anything' that 'rushes into the eyes' can free up 'anything from everything' and so give 'the minutest fact' new significance. That's why the poem is required to 'intercede' in the flux of this estrangement by shaping it with 'phrases'. But that intercession is also made 'between' its own 'phrases', which is why the estrangement is doubled by the writing; the poem incorporates 'inserted' lines like the eye incorporates what comes between 'anything' and 'everything'. As the opening line suggests, then, 'Alienation is a condition of utmost duality' for it forms *between* experience and writing *as the poem*. In light of that, when in 'Chapter 109' the poem ends with the statement 'I think now of the truly startling antiquity of the sensation that | *this is happening*' (*O*, 124, Hejinian's emphasis), the deixis of '*this*' points both to the description of an experience *and* the poem's performance of it.

HAPPILY: FROM *AMOR FATI* TO *AMOR POSSIBILIS*

I mentioned earlier that Hejinian shows how a poetics of possibility exerts a performative force when she combines a constructivism of the person with Formalist estrangement and a notion of the poem as event. The foundations for that combination are what *The Cell* and *Oxota* provide. In doing so, the volumes mark an advance in relation to other issues that I've cited as being problematic for the Language group. They engage with wider political and economic structures while suggesting that these are forged microcosmically in the daily exchanges between things and people. They show how in composing the 'range of possibility' for a thing or situation, a poem also composes the person's experience of reality into an affective form of 'strangeness'. Each poem thus relates an agency of language and the person as the dynamic form of the poem.

All of that is significant in respect of the criticisms that have continued to be levelled at the Language group by some critics. In the 1989 review by Mengham that I previously cited, one of his charges was that the difficulty in extracting a sense of poetic agency from the group's writing lay in the 'depersonalized' nature of the language used, along with the lack of coherent 'matrix' or 'frame' for the poems.[97] Hejinian's Russian volumes answer such a charge by presenting specific frames of situated reference, and by constructing her figure of a person in relation to them. Developments like these have led Altieri to modify his previous criticisms of the group. In an article of 1996 he continued to question the practice of Language poetry, asking how it could offer 'effective resistance to aspects of the dominant culture' if it doesn't construct more coherent 'hypothetical countermodels', nor offer the poems as objects of 'will' rather than of intellectual 'free play'.[98] Discussing Hejinian's *The Cell*, he does concede that 'its indeterminacies take on affective force', but 'only if we do not stop with the specific uncertainty but try to motivate it by understanding how for the author certain pressures within the thinking seem to require letting several possibilities float'.[99] In my view that doesn't adequately account for the affective importance Hejinian places in both *The Cell* and *Oxota* on estrangement, nor does it account for the performative force she ascribes to the poems—'the writing performs the thinking'—nor does it answer to her potentialist argument that 'the exercise of possibilities [. . .] amid

---
[97] Mengham, untitled review, 121, 123.
[98] Charles Altieri, 'Some Problems about Agency in the Theories of Radical Poetics', *Contemporary Literature* 37:2 (1996), 213.
[99] Ibid. 217.

conditions and occasions constitutes a person'. Adhering to his position on the floating nature of Language poetry's possibilities and agency, Altieri in a 1999 article developed it into further criticism of the group's politics: 'it is questionable whether they deserve to be called political since they do not directly affect any of the agendas we pursue in public life or the specific commitments we make to actual political communities'.[100]

Such matters also continued to be debated by the group. It's true that throughout the nineties the group came no closer to fighting the concerted 'political struggle' that Bernstein and others had earlier advocated, nor had it grown into the sort of cultural minority that Hejinian had compared it to, nor the kind of political community that Altieri saw it not to be. If anything the group members were more dispersed—partly because of the diverse approaches they were taking with their writing, and partly because they were now more scattered around the country in teaching positions at universities. A number of critics have discussed whether those institutional affiliations have compromised the group's status as avant-garde.[101] Whereas Donald Allen in *New American Poetry* (1960) declared that what united the anthology's poets was 'a total rejection of all those qualities typical of academic verse',[102] Language poetry since the nineties has thrived in academe. To the extent that it has become academic, though, it's nothing like the relatively conservative New-Criticism-inspired 'verse' to which Allen was referring. Indeed, the group's academic positions have also aided its avant-gardism: they've freed the poets from staking their livelihood on mainstream literary markets, and have enabled them to think of community-building partly in terms of teaching. Such affiliations have also not prevented poets like Silliman and Bernstein from speaking out against the conformism that is evident in some US creative writing programmes. For Silliman, the freedom to criticize the academy from inside it shows that 'the university is not a monolith, but rather an ensemble of competing historically specific discourses and practices'.[103] In line with his own 'microcosmic view', Bernstein has argued along similar lines. Railing against the uniformity of tone and style in most academic

---

[100] Charles Altieri, 'The Transformations of Objectivism: An Afterword', in Rachel Blau DuPlessis and Peter Quartermain (eds), *The Objectivist Nexus: Essays in Cultural Poetics* (Tuscaloosa: University of Alabama Press, 1999), 313.

[101] See, for example, Rasula, *Syncopations*, Chs 1 and 7; Geoff Ward, *Language Poetry and the American Avant-Garde* (Keele: British Association of American Studies, 1993), 34–5; and Linda Reinfeld, *Language Poetry: Writing as Rescue* (Baton Rouge: Louisiana State University Press, 1992), Ch. 5.

[102] Donald Allen, 'Preface', *The New American Poetry, 1945–1960* (Berkeley, CA: University of California Press, 1999), xi.

[103] Ron Silliman, 'Canons for Institutions: New Hope for the Disappeared', in Bernstein, *The Politics of Poetic Form*, 165.

writing, he's stated that he teaches 'poetry-as-a-second-language',[104] which, for him, has also meant defending a new concept of language writing as 'ideolect'.

Bernstein outlines that concept in a 1996 essay, 'Poetics of the Americas', and discusses it in terms of an 'impossible poetics' that Watten later criticizes. There is 'no one America', argues Bernstein, because it's not a unified totality or conglomerate: 'The U.S. is less a melting pot than a simultaneity of inconsolable coexistences.'[105] In light of that, the 'impossible poetics' he describes is one that recognizes the impossibility of America being a totality, and that 'insists that our commonness is in our partiality and disregard for the norm, [...] the overarching, the universal'.[106] This is also what 'ideolectical' poetry does. Defining the latter as 'ideologically informed nonstandard language practice', Bernstein declares that whereas 'dialect poetry seems to foster group identifications, ideolect poetry may seem to foster the opposite: a rejection or troubling of identity structures, group or individual'.[107] That clearly has implications for the Language group as a community, and there certainly continued to be differences of opinion within the group about the question of its unity. For example, whereas Watten and others were lauding the benefits of the Internet for building the group as a networked community, Bernstein called for an 'uncommunity': 'Echoing W.C. Fields's famous repost to being corrected about his insistence that Jews were running the Studio—Catholics, worst kind of Jews—might we say: Virtual communities, worst kind of communities!?'[108] In Watten's opinion, though, by refusing any kind of cultural 'identity structures' what Bernstein envisages is itself a 'virtual community' of a different kind; one that consists of floating, indeterminate possibilities: 'the possibility of form rather than specific forms [...] or the possibility of difference rather than a specific difference'.[109]

---

[104] Charles Bernstein, 'What's Art Got to Do with It?: The Status of the Subject of the Humanities in an Age of Cultural Studies' (1992), in *My Way*, 50. See also his 'Warning—Poetry Area: Publics under Construction' (1996), in *My Way*, 304–11.

[105] Charles Bernstein, 'Poetics of the Americas', in *My Way*, 114. Asserting the impossibility of *America* as totality doesn't discount poetic possibilities, and the potentialism that Bernstein and Andrews had earlier proposed was given a further boost with the publication of Andrews's *Paradise and Method: Poetics and Praxis* (Evanston, IL: Northwestern University Press, 1996); see, in particular, 39–41, 45–7, and 113–15.

[106] Ibid. 115.

[107] Ibid. 117, 134.

[108] Charles Bernstein, 'Community and the Individual Talent', *Diacritics* 26, 3/4 (Autumn–Winter 1996), 178.

[109] Watten, *The Constructivist Moment*, 108.

Such criticism clearly gave Hejinian pause for thought. Having already formulated her own potentialism—exercising possibility is to constitute oneself as a person—she tempered her commitment to a 'poetics of possibility' with a 1998 essay that addresses the issue. Like Watten she argues that if such a poetics upholds a pluralism of possibility as 'telos' or 'absolute' then it may fall short of 'activating relationships within that plurality'.[110] As she acknowledges, though, that doesn't mean that a 'poetics of possibility is wrongheaded'.[111] Rather, it means that such a poetics must turn possibility into particular forms, which is what much of her poetry from the nineties onwards has done in terms of a performativity of affect.

I argued earlier that one of the things that characterizes the other forms of potentialism I've traced is their ability to act on readers by turning modes of literary potential into affective power. The more extreme the feeling, the more tangible and oppositional the potential; Baraka's rage and Acker's abjection being cases in point. As we've seen, Hejinian in 'The Rejection of Closure' also conceives of an affective potentialism when she discusses form as a 'potency' and 'dynamic' that can open 'uncertainty to curiosity' for a reader. Compared to the affects that writers like Baraka and Acker encourage, though, curiosity is a weak affect; indeed, if it's the main outcome of her writing then it lends support to Altieri's argument that a text like *The Cell* has 'affective force' only if the reader stops at its 'uncertainty' and tries to understand what motivated the writer to keep various possibilities afloat. Critic Oren Izenberg takes a stronger line on the issue; in his view, the fragmented discontinuity of the group's writing means that affect is something it cannot do: 'Language poetry produces the sensation that language as Language poetry imagines and manifests it has neither affect nor tone.'[112] The resistance in the group's New Sentence writing to gathering linguistic units into larger structures is perhaps part of the problem. As Gertrude Stein argued, 'Sentences are not emotional but paragraphs are,' for paragraphs, like emotions, are accumulations of what moves a person.[113] But as we've also seen, while Hejinian's *The Cell* and *Oxota* aren't written in prose paragraphs their stanzas do present accumulations of experience through the 'drifts' and 'shifts' of their long lines and enjambement. That departure from the New Sentence clearly

---

[110] Lyn Hejinian, 'Reason', in *The Language of Inquiry*, 348.
[111] Ibid.
[112] Oren Izenberg, 'Language Poetry and Collective Life', *Critical Inquiry* 30 (Autumn 2003), 135.
[113] Gertrude Stein, *How to Write* (1931, repr.; New York: Dover, 1975), 24. See also Silliman's discussion of Stein and emotional paragraphs in 'The New Sentence', 86–7.

helped prepare for her subsequent exploration of affect, which marks a distinct turn in the focus of her work.

In the mid-seventies Hejinian had declared herself to be more interested in thinking than feeling:

Feelings are common to us all, never new, stunning only to the person feeling them at the time, and foolish (or boring) to everyone else. Thoughts, however, can be affective whether one shares them at the moment or not, and they can be original.

Feelings have no potential, they can never be anything but what they are. Ideas and thoughts, however, are full of potential.[114]

This view of the relative unimportance of feeling manifests itself in much of Hejinian's earlier writing, which concentrates on relations between memory, perception, and thinking. Clearly, it's odd to value thought for having affective potential while dismissing the potential of affects as feelings. In that respect works like *The Cell* and *Oxota* show her changing her position, for the estrangement she presents in them combines forms of perception, logic, and feeling. It also involves turning feeling into the kind of hybrid 'affect' that Deleuze and Guattari theorize; a 'compound' of subject and object like those I identified in Burroughs's later writings.[115] Such an affect occurs as an interaction, which is what Hejinian explores by turning the poem as event—*'this is happening'*—into the exploration of 'happiness' as being complicit with the 'happenstance'.

Hejinian elaborates some of the ideas behind this poetry of happening in a 1994 lecture on the Objectivist poet George Oppen. At one point in it she returns to the sensation she'd described in 'Chapter 109' of *Oxota*:

To sense the antiquity of the realization that *this is happening* alerts one to the perennial presence of the immediate, an immediate in which one has always participated in anticipation of death. It is in the phrase *this is happening* that the presence of death is acknowledged.

And as a phrase it prompts another: our elated response to *this is happening* expresses itself not as *I am here*, nor even as *so I see*, but as *I can go away*. It makes way for the next, perhaps incongruous, adventure.[116]

This sense of what's happening is also a sense of one's experience being shaped in and by time passing, for the fleeting present is what ensures that experiences can pass on (as 'antiquity') and pass away (as

---

[114] Lyn Hejinian, 'Variations', 507.
[115] See Gilles Deleuze and Félix Guattari, *What is Philosophy?*, trans. Hugh Tomlinson and Graham Burchell (1991, repr.; New York: Columbia University Press, 1994), Ch. 7.
[116] Lyn Hejinian, 'The Numerous: Oppen's Affirmation' (lecture delivered 8 December 1994), in Hejinian Archive, UCSD (Box 112, Folder 22): 108–9, Hejinian's emphases.

'death') simultaneously. To phrase the fleeting becomes a sense of fleeing. As Hejinian acknowledges, her inspiration for this poetry of events is partly derived from the ideas that the philosopher Jean-François Lyotard builds around the question '*Is it happening?* [*Arrive-t-il?*]. It's a question, he states, of the '*now*' whose flux is a 'stranger' to the stable presence that 'consciousness' tries to establish.[117] As such, this 'now', for Lyotard, is also the time in which the sublime takes place as an event that forms experience by calling it into question: 'The event happens as a question mark "before" happening as a question. *It happens* is rather "in the first place" *is it happening, is this it, is it possible?*'[118] Lyotard cites Barnett Newman's paintings as a spur to these reflections, but ultimately the 'event' and 'now' that he describes appear abstract and general rather than rooted in specific situations. As Hejinian notes in her Oppen lecture, though, in *The Differend* (1983) Lyotard argues against generalized abstractions: 'there is not "language" and "Being", but occurrences'.[119] For her part, the nature of such occurrences is not a generalized temporality or questioning of experience; rather, they betoken how experience happens to be particular. In a 1995 letter to Perelman, for example, Hejinian reverses the emphasis of Lyotard's 'now' and her poetics of happening from time to particular things: 'To experience things in time is to experience the fleeting instant; to experience time in things is to experience *now*—as a recognition that *this is happening.*'[120] Those 'things' include poetic lines as well as other objects, which is why the happening of the poem composes language and experience together as 'simultaneities'. This is where her line on happiness also makes an entrance.

In a 1996 letter to Leslie Scalapino, Hejinian wrote that 'the question of "happiness"' is one that 'I continue to ponder'.[121] By the end of the decade she began turning that pondering into *Happily*, a poem of 176 lines. Preparatory notes that she made for it in 1998 show how she was conceiving the project. Drawing on Friedrich Nietzsche's *Gay Science* (1882), she wrote that 'Happiness erupts in *amor fati*—it is a term for the uproar in one's emotions in response to all that comes to one,

---

[117] Jean-François Lyotard, 'The Sublime and the Avant-Garde' (1984), in Thomas Docherty (ed.), *Postmodernism: A Reader* (London: Longman, 1993), 244, Lyotard's emphases. Lyotard also discusses the question '*Is it happening?*' in *The Differend: Phrases in Dispute*, trans. Georges Van Den Abeele (1983, repr.; Minneapolis: University of Minnesota Press, 1988), xv–xvi, 116, 131–2, 172–4.
[118] Ibid. 245, Lyotard's emphasis.
[119] Hejinian, 'The Numerous', 109.
[120] Lyn Hejinian, letter to Bob Perelman (20 August 1995), in Hejinian Archive, UCSD (Box 92, Folder 12): 1, Hejinian's emphases.
[121] Lyn Hejinian, letter to Leslie Scalapino (8 August 1996), in Hejinian Archive, UCSD (Box 97, Folder 15): 1.

good or bad.'[122] Performing this love of fate with the poem is also to explore the 'etymological link' of 'happiness' to 'happening' and 'haphazardness' so the work presents 'an accumulation responding to and/or producing the sensation that *this is happening*'.[123] And those connections are implicit right from the poem's opening lines:

> Constantly I write this happily
> Hazards that hope may break open my lips
> What I feel is taking place, a large context, long yielding, and
>   to doubt it would be a crime against it
> I sense that in stating 'this is happening'[124]

As in *Oxota* each new 'line' begins with a capital letter, and in these four opening lines Hejinian turns the 'etymological link' that she'd noted into a frame for the poem's writing and reading. That frame is also determined through the use of the present tense and reiteration of deictic 'this', which combine to suggest that happiness and hazards are combined in and as the time of the writing itself. For a reader, that time is also the present in which the writing is read; thus Hejinian compounds the 'simultaneities' of language and experience. And if 'What I feel is taking place', the 'context' is that of the writing and its reading 'yielding' to each other in the encounter. It also involves generative interaction; thus 'Hazards' are willed by the speaker so they move one to hope and speak.

In her preparatory notes to the poem Hejinian also considers how the improvisational method she used to compose its 'haphazardness' makes an event of possibility: 'By making sentences as I am—putting down sentence beginnings and sentence ends and then inserting multiple "middles" between those frames—something like "events" occur. Or eventuality(?) is implied. [...] Eventuality: a *possible* event.'[125] The importance of these improvisations is that they induce the kind of linguistic agency that Hejinian composed in *The Cell*: 'the writing performs the thinking'. Thus *Happily*'s lines don't represent experiences that occurred before the writing; rather, an experience takes shape in the process of writing and reading each line, and both line and experience become clear only in terms of a future anteriority, as what *will have been written*. Being happy for that to occur means turning *amor fati* into an *amor possibilis* such that

---

[122] Lyn Hejinian, 'Background Notes for *Happily*' (1998), in Hejinian Archive, UCSD (Box 110, Folder 11): 1.
[123] Ibid. 2.
[124] Lyn Hejinian, *Happily* (Sausalito, CA: Post-Apollo Press, 2000), 3, hereafter cited as *H*.
[125] Hejinian, 'Background Notes for *Happily*', 3, Hejinian's emphasis.

improvised syntax is embraced as form of affective potential. If this means that Hejinian presents affect in terms of an 'eventuality' that usually expresses hypothetical possibility—'in the eventuality that x were to happen...'—she also counteracts the abstraction of such possibility by making it happen *as particular experiences* of writing. Just as she refuses the abstraction of Lyotard's 'now', so she refuses to turn potentiality into a generalized 'absolute'. Instead, possibility takes shape as lines that activate relations with the haphazardness of particular events, as in the following extract:

> The trees moving slowly upward among the going and the
>   coming sensations through the wind's blown tones
>   expressing our extension into the wind feeling such rapid
>   empathy that there is hardly time for analogy
> Unlike each detail happiness comes to no end, no good but
>   that of something like the mouth in the windblown tree-
>   tops shaping a sound and I experience the experiencing
>   effect of it as an acknowledgement is discovered to begin
>   that (*H*, 28)

The first line suggests that affects are comprised of a situation. The movement of the trees blends with the 'going and the coming' of 'sensations' and the 'wind's blown tones' so that all three combine in 'expressing' their common 'extension'. The result is a compound affect that includes the wind's excitation of 'feeling' as much as feeling for the wind; an interactive simultaneity of person and thing that forms as a kind of subject–object 'empathy' (like the 'sympathetic units' she wrote of in 'The Person'). Accepting the formation of that experience means accepting the flux in such things. And if 'happiness comes to no end' in the poem it's because it is a sense of how affects aren't engendered according to an overarching 'telos' but rather accumulate haphazardly in and as a given context. The second line of the extract thus shifts attention to 'a sound' that the 'mouth' in the tree is shaping, before reflecting on the kind of empathetic loop that the first line posed: to form an experience of the sound is to discover its effect on shaping experience. In that respect the lines construct a particular sense of affect as being composed of interactions with things. And if the lines do that for the reader by performing something of what they relate (the use of the present tense emphasizes this), they also show how affects arise from improvised syntax. Far from simply trying to excite 'curiosity' into authorial motivations, then, Hejinian presents the poem as activating *a distinct comportment for readers towards language and the world*. That comportment builds on the potentialism she outlined in 'The Person and Description'; it means being happy to turn the haphazardness of events into how one happens to be a person; it means turning possibilities of language into a capacity to experience and relate to events; it involves realizing that accumulating and exercising potential through one's interactions is what builds and 'constitutes a person'.

Happily thus stands as a complex rejoinder to accusations that Language poetry is without affect, or presents an inert plurality of possibilities that leaves a reader with no clear idea of how they amount to any kind of agency. If *Happily* frames a plurality of things, it also activates relations between them as a series of poetic events. Yet as the extracts I drew from the poem show, those events are mostly framed as a combination of aesthetics and epistemology. How the comportment of Hejinian's poetry can turn happily towards ethical and political instances is what she explores in two other book-length poems: *A Border Comedy* (2001) and *The Fatalist* (2003).

A BORDER COMEDY AND *THE FATALIST*: A CRITIQUE OF FATAL JUDGEMENT

Hejinian wrote *A Border Comedy* over the same period in which she was thinking about 'the question of happiness'. Having started it in 1994, she discusses the process of composition in the poem itself:

I would write a line or two
No more
And go away
And come back another day only to add something that would change everything
On the scales of poetry[126]

This process of accumulation echoes that of the 'inserted' 'phrases' of *Oxota* and is also similar to the composition of the *My Life* project and *Happily*. Where *A Border Comedy* differs from those works is in the way it stages Hejinian's poetics of happening as a comedy of defamiliarization. In that regard it returns to the focus on estrangement she developed in *Oxota* while reframing the comportment of *Happily* in relation to the comic. How she conceives comedy as linked to estrangement is clear from a 1994 letter to Susan Howe: 'The comedian is antinomian [...] by virtue of being a foreigner—that is, the comedian makes the familiar foreign by

---

[126] Lyn Hejinian, *A Border Comedy* (New York: Granary, 2001), 63, hereafter cited as *ABC*.

regarding it from a foreign point of view.'[127] This view is close to one that Paolo Virno has expounded at length in relation to jokes. Social mores and beliefs are also 'linguistic customs', he argues, which make up 'the *grammar* of a form of life'.[128] To the extent that jokes explore those mores to extract 'absurd and ridiculous consequences' from them, the joke becomes 'a performative example of how the grammar of a form of life can be transformed'.[129] Consequently, it also demonstrates how social situations are 'contingent', which is why jokes, for Virno, are models and performances of socially 'innovative action'.[130] Following on from *Happily*, Hejinian is certainly intent on making *A Border Comedy* perform innovative linguistic action as an affective encounter. And as she intimates in her letter to Howe, those encounters also entail experiences of becoming foreign to oneself.

Comprising fifteen short 'Books' of enjambed lines *A Border Comedy* draws on a range of poetry along with critical and philosophical works on comedy, aesthetics, and morality. Analysing jokes and laughter is a reliable way of killing mirth, and there are numerous passages in Hejinian's poem that offer flurries of aphoristic reflection on comedy and other things rather than comic affects—the various definitions of laughter listed in Book 6 are a case in point (*ABC*, 80). But the poem isn't simply playing for laughs and is focused more on relating the comic to both realizations and feelings of estrangement. Some of those instances present the kind of encounter with things that *Happily* performed, but with a comic twist:

> As Nelson Goodman says, some stories when reordered in certain ways are no
>   longer stories but studies
> Employing iambics, baubles, and a dildo to make us laugh
> And a bent horn and broken glass for inner dialogue
> And a telescope and slang sleep for wordy anecdote
> And familiarization
> Whose function is to represent the genitals (*ABC*, 120)

Such a passage presents an anarchic clowning with things through the series of haphazard relations it makes. Goodman's apothegm slips up in the line that juggles 'iambics, baubles, and a dildo'—a masturbatory rhythm-method isn't just for Christmas?—before we're presented with

---

[127] Lyn Hejinian, letter to Susan Howe (23 December 1994), in Hejinian Archive, UCSD (Box 22, Folder 13): 1.
[128] Paolo Virno, *Multitude: Between Innovation and Negation*, trans. Isabella Bertoletti, James Cascaito, and Andrea Casson (Los Angeles: Semiotext(e), 2008), 94, Virno's emphasis.
[129] Ibid.
[130] Ibid. 97.

the anaphoric lines that exchange a hazardous mess of objects (including 'broken glass') for forms of language ('inner dialogue', 'wordy anecdote') and then 'familiarization'. This is certainly breaking the usual 'syntax of events', which is what Book 13 tells us a comedian often does. The references to sex and 'sleep' also suggest that the passage is following Sigmund Freud in demonstrating that jokes, like dream-work, license access to repressed contents of the unconscious.

Freud has already made an entrance in Book 1:

> A joke, says Freud, is a contribution made to the comic by the unconscious
> That sounded promising
> And I suddenly sat up in bed laughing, remembering the acts of violence I'd committed while it was still dark
> In fact, my legs were still tied apart, so that I was off balance
> And that made me laugh all the more (*ABC*, 22)

If there is comedy here, it's a mixture of black humour and hysteria. The 'contribution' of the unconscious is manifest in the speaker waking to memories of having committed a 'violence', which becomes blurred with the 'fact' that her 'legs were still tied apart'. The 'scales of poetry' here throw each line off 'balance' as it opens to the next because they're set to perform estrangement at the same time as describing it. And that performance turns to different questions of others and violence a few lines later:

> And memory has a great desire to be understood
> As the very barbarism that this ('after Auschwitz') must be
> That the walls may be seen
> Unlike, between
> The way men stand between women
> In cross-dress and incorrigible
> Or, says the interlocutor, women between men (*ABC*, 78)

Estrangement here involves a series of transferences between things. Memory, for example, can be 'understood' as 'barbarism', to the extent that it makes the past foreign by rendering it present to the mind. But 'this' present is also barbarous if it's seen as having inherited a past that includes the atrocities of Auschwitz. In that context the shift to 'walls' triggers associations with the Berlin Wall and Iron Curtain. But the subsequent suggestion that the walls can be viewed 'Unlike, between | the way men stand between women' is more evocative of the play within Shakespeare's comedy *A Midsummer Night's Dream* in which the character Snout plays a wall through which the lovers Pyramus and Thisbe must speak.[131] Suddenly, then, we're in a different comedy of transference in which genders, and the boundaries between them, consist of their performance—the lines add to that sense by mixing masculine and feminine rhymes: 'be' and 'seen', 'between' and 'women', respectively. The move from Auschwitz to transvestism is jarringly estranging for both of those things, but the implication is that being amenable to becoming-other is precisely the stance that *wasn't* adopted by the Nazis when exterminating Jews. That is why Hejinian sees writing such a poetry of estrangement as almost an ethical imperative, as she made clear in a 1995 letter to Bob Perelman:

> I've been thinking [...] about [Theodor] Adorno's comment, that 'to write poetry after Auschwitz is barbarism' [...] but it is also probably accurate that there has to be poetry after Auschwitz precisely because it *is* a barbarism, i.e., it doesn't speak the same language—it's from another country, it's come from across the border, it's foreign, it's going to break the local laws.[132]

The barbarism of poetry is its ability to make a writer or reader experience themselves as a foreigner within their own language while breaking what Virno calls the 'grammar of life' as 'local laws'. It is also the work of Hejinian's comic, as Book 13 makes clear: 'Comedians (being foreigners) often break local laws' (*ABC*, 170).

Given the range of affects, scenes, and barbarities that *A Border Comedy* presents, it also stretches the genre of comedy to breaking point. But as Hejinian and Virno realize, comedy *is* a breaking-apart of social orders, and the laughter one breaks into as a result of comedy is the sound of those orders losing control of one's body. That the 'encounters' the poem presents are aimed at the reader's body is made explicit in Book 15:

> Just as you'll note that breathlessly though wordily I've been making microscopically libidinous movements
> Toward your nebulous rosy and always retreating body
> Which feathers at mention (*ABC*, 211)

These 'movements' are both the shifts between lines and the way these lines animate particular affects of estrangement for a person. Despite acknowledging the reader as distinct from the text and 'always retreating', the poem also moves to make the reader an unfamiliar form of person, as the mention of its 'feathers' suggests. That reference relates to Hejinian's earlier statement that 'a person is the means by which my animal occupies

---

[131] William Shakespeare, *A Midsummer Night's Dream*, in *Shakespeare: Complete Works*, ed. W. J. Craig (London: Oxford University Press, 1974), Act V, Sc. 1, 188–9.
[132] Lyn Hejinian, letter to Bob Perelman (19 January 1995), in Hejinian Archive, UCSD (Box 92, Folder 12): 1, Hejinian's emphasis.

social space. It's a politicized bird'.[133] The characterization plays with Aristotle's definition of man as 'political animal' (*zoōn politikon*) whose character arises from inhabiting a polis. For Hejinian, a poem is a textual construction of social space, which is why she stated that Language poetry, for her, meant building a polis. The poem thus provides different, unfamiliar experiences of being a political animal to the extent that one occupies oneself with the situations and encounters that the poem presents. Admitting alterity is not without hazards, though, as the instances of trauma and hysteria that appear in the poem suggest. Yet that's also how Hejinian reorients the comportment that *Happily* encouraged:

> Happiness is gratuitous, free
> A response to chance, to hazard, accident
> And hence it is itself hazardous, precarious (*ABC*, 181)

If *A Border Comedy* turns Hejinian's poetics of happening to matters of ethics and politics, its 'microscopically libidinous movements' also show that it approaches politics more in terms of the 'microcosmic view' that Bernstein proposed—one that targets the public sphere through individual readers. Comporting a 'precarious' openness to 'hazard' and the foreign, the 'happiness' of such poetry clearly faces a huge challenge when it encounters death. It's also a challenge that Hejinian explores in *The Fatalist*, an elegy that addresses, among other things, the terrorist attacks of 11 September 2001, and is dedicated to her mother who died in March 2002.

As we've seen, Hejinian's sense of '*this is happening*' already has death at its heart, for it 'alerts one to the perennial presence of the immediate, an immediate in which one has always participated in anticipation of death'. If the poetics of happiness requires *amor fati*, it also needs to reckon with fate's fatalities. Such reckoning is part of what's assembled in *The Fatalist*, which therefore combats the kind of 'hysteria' that *The Cell* related to the 'realm of possibility'. The attempt to address mortality is registered with a return to sentences with full stops, but there's also repeated enjambement between lines. The combined rhythm of stopping and starting pertains to the reflections on time and mortality the poem presents in its opening lines to signal its elegiac labours: 'Everything that works does so in time and testifies | to time's inability to stop life.'[134] Modifying Auden's elegy to Yeats, we can say that such 'inability' is also evident in works of writing

---

[133] Hejinian, 'The Person and Everyday Life', 9.
[134] Lyn Hejinian, *The Fatalist* (Richmond, CA: Omnidawn, 2003), 15, hereafter cited as *TF*.

that carry past lives and their words to the guts of the living.[135] Such transference also bears on the passage of time in events, a passage felt to be fate: 'All that happened is what is happening' (*TF*, 75); 'That's what fate is: whatever's happened | —time regained' (*TF*, 83). It's notable that what's rejected here is a notion of fate as being predetermined by something transcendent. We're not looking at a higher figure who turns the wheel of events, like Dante's Fortuna, nor is it a Miltonic paradise that's 'regained'. Instead, fate is given as time to forge relations of past and future in the present:

> [...] At one's birth
> many things have already happened. One's fate is
> what has happened to one, not what is going to happen. Think
> of the future anterior: think of what will have been. It begins
> (is beginning) right now. (*TF*, 59)

Hejinian here merges Nietzsche's concept of the 'eternal return' with her poetics of happening. If fate is what 'will have been', that future anteriority is inseparable from what's happening 'now'. As fate is what remains open to the present, it never reaches an end, whether as termination or telos. And if fate is a process of becoming, that's why the experience of it remains open to improvisation. As Hejinian argues elsewhere: 'Improvisation begins at the moment when something has just happened [...] it is always involved with the process of beginning.'[136]

That process necessitates squaring in the heat of a moment how one is affected by events with how one reacts to them. In that respect it also involves improvising reason, and as Hejinian pointed out in a 1998 talk such 'reason' combines two senses of the word: conceptual reasoning as well as the causal reasons for why something occurs.[137] The end of *The Fatalist*'s second stanza provides an example of how the poem draws the two together:

> Sure, while we seek to grasp deep sleep from which we wake
> our own reality shrinks the totality of reality (a cosmos
> from which little heroines are perpetually trying to escape)
> which is infinitely extensive. We're left with a sense
> of murky doings, whether it is possibility or impossibility that's lodged
> there is hard to say. The overblown soundtrack (and the voice-over
> narration by Tom Hanks) would suggest that everything that lies

---

[135] See W. H. Auden, 'In Memory of W. B. Yeats' (1939), in *W. H. Auden: Selected Poems*, ed. Edward Mendelson (London: Faber and Faber, 1989), 81.

[136] Lyn Hejinian, 'Planning Notes for *Slowly*', in Hejinian Archive, UCSD (Box 112, Folder 4): 2.

[137] Hejinian, 'Reason', 340–1.

between the outer infinity of the cosmos and our own brief spot
in it harbors power, freedom (they are much
the same). The ensuing show is awful. (*TF*, 16)

Seeking 'to grasp deep sleep' suggests an attempt to conceive what lies unconscious behind our wakeful states, but trying to possess 'our own reality' in this way is itself a shrinking of 'the totality of reality' and its infinitude. One's rational 'grasp' arises as *an occlusion* of the infinite causes that suffuse both reason and reality, which is why 'We're left with a sense | of murky doings'. As reason's grasp is thereby founded on its negation, it's hard to decide whether it's empowering or disempowering, just as it's 'hard to say' whether it harbours 'possibility or impossibility'. That acknowledgment of reason as partial and needing to confront the aporia it's based on is what Hejinian contrasts with the 'overblown soundtrack' and 'voice-over narration' by actor Tom Hanks. The latter is partly a reference to the voice-over that Hanks in 2000 provided for one of the video shows at the Hayden Planetarium in New York City. In suggesting that his narration is 'overblown' for equating the cosmos to 'power' and 'freedom', the lines also begin to register murkily both the 11 September attacks and the military response to them. In June 2001, Michael Bay's film *Pearl Harbor* was released. Criticized in the *New York Times* for its 'tumescent music and earnest voice-over pronouncements', the Japanese attacks on America that the film presented were subsequently invoked by various commentators struggling to contextualize the events of 11 September.[138] If an allusion to that film is also 'lodged' in the passage above through the use of the word 'harbors', the choice of 'infinity' and 'freedom' in the context of 'power' also points to America's response to the terrorist attacks. Initially launching the 'war against terror' with strikes against Afghanistan, this mobilization of force was first named 'Operation Infinite Justice', and when that appellation was condemned on the grounds that only God's justice is infinite it was replaced with 'Operation Enduring Freedom'.[139] Whether anyone can arrogate infinitude as reason to act or judge freely is also what the poem has already questioned. Admittedly, linking its lines to such political events might involve a stretch of the imagination, but explicit references to the events elsewhere in the poem provide reasons for making the connection. At one point, for

---

[138] A. O. Scott, 'War is Hell, but Very Pretty', *New York Times* (25 May 2001), Reviews Section, 5. For further discussion of the 11 September attacks and film imagery, see my *Terrorism and Modern Literature: From Joseph Conrad to Ciaran Carson* (Oxford: Oxford University Press, 2002), 1–2.

[139] See Arundhati Roy, 'The Algebra of Infinite Justice', *The Guardian*, Saturday Review (29 September 2001), 1–2.

example, we're told that 'the so-called "war on terrorism" has sapped energy from every | discussion | even those at tables sheltered from the rain' (*TF*, 54). At another point the speaker declares that 'These letters will go | into the files of visiting citizens and that defines | "terrorism"' (*TF*, 38). In light of that, if the poem enjoins us to think of fate in terms of what's happened, it also gives us cause to relate its poetics of happening to the judgement and experience of terror—or, in other words, to the sublime.

I mentioned earlier that Lyotard relates the sublime to his idea of an event that 'happens as a question mark' for a person. That's because the sublime has traditionally been figured as an experience of what exceeds the limits or boundaries of experience. In Kant's *Critique of the Power of Judgement* (1790), for example, the sublime arises from an encounter with a 'formless object' or landscape of 'rude nature', the experience of which brings a sense of infinitude. A feeling of terror ensues because one's mental faculties of perception, imagination, and the understanding are overpowered.[140] At this point, though, Kant affirms what he calls a 'subreption': the discord experienced results in the subject's faculty of reason coming to the rescue. What seemed illimitable in the experience is comprehended and absorbed by the infinitude of reason's ideas; consequently, terror is converted into a pleasurable feeling of relief and security. And once reason is felt to transcend any condition of sensible experience, it can be claimed to be 'unconditioned' and 'supersensible' (*CPJ*, 153). That's to say, reason, for Kant, is what can detach and free the subject from whatever experience has affected it. As both a quasi-divine faculty and the highest realm of judgement, the recognition of reason's power also entails feelings of 'respect' (*Achtung*) for reason's 'moral law': 'it is a law (of reason) for us and part of our vocation to estimate everything great that nature contains as an object of the senses for us as small in comparison with ideas of reason' (*CPJ*, 141). Effectively, then, Kant outlines his own philosophical war on terror: what is terrifying must be converted into rational security, just as suffering (from the faculties' initial discord) is converted into hard-won 'pleasure' (*CPJ*, 143).

As Kant acknowledges, though, the 'infinitude' he claims for reason is never actually experienced or witnessed by the individual—if it were, reason wouldn't be transcendent (*CPJ*, 156). That's why Romantic

---

[140] Immanuel Kant, *Critique of the Power of Judgement*, trans. Paul Gruyer and Eric Matthews (Cambridge: Cambridge University Press, 2000), 129–30, hereafter cited as *CPJ*. See also my 'Sacrifice and the Sublime since 11 September 2001', forthcoming in Adam Piette and Mark Rawlinson (eds), *The Edinburgh Companion to Twentieth-Century British and American War Literature* (Edinburgh: Edinburgh University Press, 2012).

poets such as Wordsworth averred that transcendence is only intimated through flights of the imagination.[141] But if transcendence can be imagined but not actually possessed, then the subject is unable to claim that its rationality is 'supersensible' or capable of being freed from the terrors fate throws its way. Relate that to 11 September and 'The ensuing show is awful.' As novelist Don DeLillo wrote in the wake of the attacks, despite all the media footage the day remained 'so unaccountable [...] we can't tilt it to the slant of our perceptions'.[142] Indeed, the media coverage doubled the events' terror, which took place both as unforeseen attacks on actual buildings and people *and* as the networked inability of the government, military, and emergency agencies to account for what was happening, or to plot a coordinated response to it *as it happened*. In opening her poetics of happening to 11 September and the war on terror, Hejinian is clearly not trying to give a more adequate account of a 'totality' of causes or effects. Rather, she responds to such terror with a critique of judgement that draws on the ethical comportment of *Happily* and *A Border Comedy*. That critique includes a fatalism that understands that at any moment a person's rational judgement is *not* detached from the affects that keep one rooted in bodily situations. Rather than try to transcend or free oneself from affective situations, one needs to realize that one's fate is to be immured in settings that nevertheless remain open to improvisation and potentiality. The openness of that potentiality combines the 'haphazardness' of events, the mutability of 'fate', and one's capacity to experiment in language with different ways of relating to things and others. Hence the importance, for Hejinian, of poetry which improvises new forms of reasoning: 'multifarious logical operations—making wild connections'.[143] That also means constructing a range of possibilities in particular situations, for 'Possibilities are probably often only intuited | —known as an instance in an instant and taken whole' (*TF*, 67). Because one's potential for affecting and being affected by situations isn't fixed or transcendent, one needs to exercise and build it while remembering that it remains partial and subject to fate. And that's what a poem like *The Fatalist* is for:

> I gather fate all at once but 'all at once' (eye open and close)
> does not mean best nor fully seen. My address is pathos

---

[141] See for example, Wordsworth's apostrophe to the imagination in lines 525–42, Book 6 of *The Prelude* (1805 edn, repr.; Oxford: Oxford University Press, 1984), 463–4.
[142] Don DeLillo, 'In the Ruins of the Future', *The Guardian* (22 December 2001), available at http://www.guardian.co.uk/books/2001/dec/22/fiction.dondelillo, accessed 10 August 2009.
[143] Lyn Hejinian, letter to Leslie Scalapino (22 July 2000), in Hejinian Archive (Box 98, Folder 8): 2.

and time (at least that much is obvious) and my goal
is to follow myself into the present
and restore to the political a capacity for ambivalence and quandary as
    sharp
(and as beneficial) as acupuncture (*TF*, 80)

Bernstein's 'microcosmic view' of poetry's political stance turns into Hejinian's Language acupuncture. Going happily under its needles means accepting a need to train oneself to face the slings and arrows that become the person one will have been. In that respect, we also need to bear in mind that by the time Hejinian finishes *The Fatalist* she's built her figure of the person in relation to a number of different 'border' experiences; from those in the USSR at the end of the Cold War to that of 11 September in the USA. Any consistency that person has as a figure is a continued openness to changing context. And if its comportment means taking a particular stance in relation to language and others, it also builds a critique of judgement in terms of *practical imagination*. How that relates to the other forms of potentialism I've traced is one of the things I'll consider in my Conclusion.

Conclusion
Potentialism and Practical Imagination

Each of the potentialisms I've discussed builds practical imagination largely through a literary performativity of affect. With Ginsberg that performativity included using mantra, for example, as poetic vehicles that would educe 'latent' anti-war sentiments. With Baraka, it involved imagining new images of blackness and a world of possibility to move people to new realizations of racial identity. For Burroughs, it entailed scrambling space-time textually with cut-ups intended to effect novel forms of experience and even 'biological potentials' for readers. Acker similarly posed alternative worlds of experiential possibility and gave these a performative bite through her 'languages of the body'. And as I've just shown, Hejinian also improvises lines of feeling that occur as events in the acts of writing and reading them. That's not to say that the slant of the performativity is identical in each instance. Although each writer's potentialism requires turning textual possibility into affective force, this has included different kinds of experiment with form and content that have been employed to various ends—even opposing ends, as is evident from the contrasts between Ginsberg's democratic humanism, Burroughs's anti-humanism, and Baraka's Black Nationalism. Those contrasts are a primary reason for my *not* arguing that the various potentialisms I've traced amount to a literary movement that hasn't previously been identified. As a concept of literary approach potentialism doesn't simply denote a common style or form or content; rather, it designates a literary or performance practice that presents experiments with form and content designed to exert an affective force to alter particular effects of social power on individuals' capacities for thinking and feeling. Accordingly, the term admits a flexibility of style and stance no less than 'avant-garde' or 'postmodernism', but it also has a clearer consistency than these two terms, whose identity and relationship have been so contested over recent decades. Having addressed questions of avant-gardism and postmodernism in my Introduction and preceding chapters, I'm not going to take them up again here. Instead, what I want to outline are some of the other ramifications that potentialism has for discussions about how language, literature, affects, and performativity can become linked, for doing so will enable a clearer idea of what's at stake in practical imagination.

Since J. L. Austin coined the term 'performative' in the William James Lectures he delivered at Harvard University in 1955, his exclusion of literature and theatre from the bounds of performativity has been debated by various critics.[1] For Austin a performative is a statement that performs a real social action (like 'I bet...', 'I promise...', or 'I declare war...'). In order for such statements to work—and so be 'felicitous' or 'happy'—he argues, particular social conditions or conventions must obtain; one needs to be head of state, for example, to declare war.[2] Ginsberg's declaration of an end to the Vietnam War would thus be seen by Austin as highly infelicitous for the same reason that he'd see the emotional enactments of Hejinian's *Happily* to be *un*happy; because poetic statements, like jokes or an actor's soliloquy, are suspended from reality and so cannot execute a 'serious' performative statement.[3] For Austin performativity is about people doing things with language, not about language doing things to people. He does, however, come close to linking performatives and affects when he proposes a distinction between 'illocution' and 'perlocution'; the former being a statement that's an action (like the performativity he'd already outlined) and the latter being a statement that produces 'feelings, thoughts or actions' as an 'oblique' consequence.[4] On that basis—and contrary to Austin's exclusion of literature and theatre—Baraka's *Slave Ship* can be seen as exerting perlocutionary emotional effects, as was evidenced when the *suffering* of slaves it gave voice to prompted riotous *rage* in a Louisiana audience. The play wasn't performing the rage that was felt as a consequence, which is why the resultant emotion was causally 'oblique'. In contrast, instances like Burroughs's spatial cut-ups, Ginsberg's mantra, Baraka's dramatic hate-speech, and Hejinian's happy-happenstance lines are more illocutionary for being aimed at shaping in readers and audiences the very emotion being performed. Such performativity may be intrinsic to the potentialisms I've discussed, but there's been very little critical and philosophical attention given to how we might think of performatives not in terms of doing things with language but in terms

---

[1] See, for example, James Loxley, *Performativity* (London: Routledge, 2007), Ch. 1, and Sandy Petrey, *Speech Acts and Literary Theory* (London: Routledge, 1990), Ch. 4.
[2] J. L. Austin, *How To Do Things With Words* (1962, repr.; Oxford: Oxford University Press, 1971), 15.
[3] Ibid. 22.
[4] Ibid. 99–101.

of doing feeling with it. And there's been even less consideration of how *literary* language might fashion performatives in that way.[5]

Denise Riley and Judith Butler are among the very few who have deliberated on performativity with regard to affect. For Riley, even though language is indifferent to those who use it, its 'very architecture' plays a formative role in building our feelings.[6] Consequently, she argues, 'only a slight amplification of the performative [...] would let us think of language as a performer',[7] for we need to see that language doesn't simply 'express feeling', rather, it 'does feeling'.[8] As Deleuze and Guattari argued, in being obliged socially to use orders of language (which range from vocabulary to syntax), when individuals do so they are always ordering things up in particular ways—which is why Deleuze and Guattari see every usage of language as illocutionary to some degree.[9] What they don't elaborate is how their notion of performative 'order words' pertains to forming affect; even when they discuss the statement 'I love you' it's more in terms of formalizing interpersonal relations as a state of affairs.[10] In contrast, Butler considers affective injuries of hate speech, while Riley considers how both vocabulary and syntax don't simply express feeling so much as shape and modulate it.[11] For example, in writing to someone whose father has died that you send 'your deepest sympathy', that stock phrase reinforces a sentimental belief that many people subscribe to: namely, that emotions are purely what one generates and possesses inside oneself. The irony is that using the phrase is hardly different from signing one's name next to it in a mass-produced card. Forming and expressing feeling thus require identifying with linguistic conventions (not to mention discourses of things like romance, revenge, and tragedy) that remain irreducible to yourself and yet provide shape for what is felt to be most 'deeply' personal.

---

[5] For a selection of fine essayings on the matter, see the special issue of *Textual Practice* I edited on 'Affects, Text, and Performativity', 25:2 (March/April 2011), with articles by Derek Attridge, Chris Nealon, Geoff Gilbert, Simon Jarvis, Jean-Jacques Lecercle, Drew Milne, Adam Piette, and Krzysztof Ziarek.
[6] Denise Riley, *The Words of Selves: Identification, Solidarity, Irony* (Stanford, CA: Stanford University Press, 2000), 3. Sue Campbell makes similar claims in *Interpreting the Personal: Expression and the Formation of Feeling* (Ithaca, NY: Cornell University Press, 1997), 12, 58, 102.
[7] Denise Riley, *Impersonal Passion: Language as Affect* (Durham, NC: Duke University Press, 2005), 4.
[8] Riley, *The Words of Selves*, 36.
[9] Gilles Deleuze and Félix Guattari, *A Thousand Plateaus*, trans. Brian Massumi (Minneapolis: University of Minnesota Press, 1987), Ch. 4.
[10] Ibid. 82.
[11] See Judith Butler, *Excitable Speech: A Politics of the Performative* (London: Routledge, 1997), 1–41, and Riley, *The Words of Selves*, 12–40.

As we saw in Chapter 3, Burroughs's response to that predicament was to view words as alien viruses and to use cut-ups to sever ossified lines of verbal association. A realization that power shapes and manages individuals' capacities largely through discursive structures is also what prompts the other writers I've considered to forge their potentialist approaches. In that respect, each of them can be seen as responding to the kind of question posed by Michael Hardt and Antonio Negri: 'How can we discover and direct the performative lines of linguistic sets and communicative networks that create the fabric of life and production?'[12] The writers I've examined seek to redirect such lines in terms of affective life, and that takes on a greater significance when one considers that literature's performative muscle has usually been considered to be non-existent or atrophied precisely because of the *suspended* nature of literary discourse. That suspension has also led various critics and philosophers to question whether affects shaped in and as literature can be incorporated into actual experience. I'll discuss those views of literature shortly; first, I want to consider how some of the possibilities that potentialism fosters might be structurally inherent to both affects and performativity.

I've been using 'feeling', 'emotion', and 'affect' interchangeably because there's no consensus about how we can make clean distinctions between the terms. I'm also following other theorists like the psychologist Silvan Tomkins in maintaining that affects are more complex than sensations like cold or pain, and comprise emotional compounds of bodily feeling and cognition, where cognition can include imagination no less than reasoning. Tomkins's work bears on my discussion for two reasons. First, because he ascribes to affects a generative dynamic that borders on performativity (though he doesn't use that term): 'It is enjoyable to enjoy. It is exciting to be excited. It is terrifying to be terrorized and angering to be angered.'[13] And second, because he asserts that affects are fundamentally relational and so have the capacity to become attached to anything.[14] As Eve Kosofsky Sedgwick has pointed out, such affective pliancy is an openness to possibility:

---

[12] Michael Hardt and Antonio Negri, *Empire* (Cambridge, MA: Harvard University Press, 2000), 404.

[13] Silvan Tomkins, *Affect Imagery Consciousness*, Vol. III (New York: Springer, 1991), 404.

[14] Silvan Tomkins, 'What Are Affects?', in Eve Kosofsky Sedgwick and Adam Frank (eds), *Shame and Its Sisters: A Silvan Tomkins Reader* (Durham, NC: Duke University Press, 1995), 54.

Affects can be, and are, attached to things, people, ideas, sensations, relations, activities, ambitions, institutions, and any number of things, including other affects. Thus, one can be excited by anger, disgusted by shame, or surprised by joy.

This freedom of affects also gives them a *structural potentiality* not enjoyed by the drive system: in contrast to the instrumentality of drives and their direct orientation toward an aim different from themselves, the affects can be autotelic.[15]

Ginsberg's anti-war auto-poems have in their sights that 'autotelic' aspect; in striving to attach feeling to war statistics he draws on the structural potential of affects, and in view of the anaesthetizations of media war-talk he sees the suscitation of affects as an end in itself. Along different lines Acker has faith in her 'languages of the body' as being capable of modulating the orientation of drives (particularly the sex drive), which Sedgwick suggests is rigidly instrumental.

As we saw in Chapter 4, some of the techniques Acker employs to do that are indebted to Burroughs's cut-ups, which correlate experiential liberation with the kind of performative potentiality that Jacques Derrida attributes to language in general. Derrida began what was to be his lengthy engagement with performatives in his essay 'Signature Event Context' (1971) in which he takes issue with Austin's exclusion of literature and theatre. If all felicitous performatives draw on linguistic conventions and scripts, argues Derrida, then drawing any rigid distinction between 'serious' and 'non-serious' instances is problematic:

> isn't it true that what Austin excludes as anomaly, exception, 'non-serious', *citation* (on stage, in a poem, or a soliloquy) is the determined modification of a general citationality—or rather a general iterability—without which there would not even be a 'successful' performative?[16]

Derrida's point is that language has a 'general citationality' or 'iterability' because *any* linguistic sign one uses already exists as a textual and vocal script. This iterability is what enables us to make a sign perform its sense in different contexts. As its sense is partly determined by the contexts in which it's used, though, iteration also allows a sign's meaning and function to become errant. For that reason its dynamic harbours a 'breaking force' (*force de rupture*), argues Derrida: 'this is the possibility on which I want to insist: the possibility of disengagement and citational graft which belongs to the structure of every mark, spoken or written'.[17] And

---

[15] Eve Kosofsky Sedgwick, *Touching Feeling: Affect, Pedagogy, Performativity* (Durham, NC: Duke University Press, 2003), my emphasis.

[16] Jacques Derrida, 'Signature Event Context', trans. Samuel Weber and Jeffrey Mehlman, in *Limited Inc* (Evanston, IL: Northwestern University Press, 1988), 17, Derrida's emphasis.

[17] Ibid. 44–5.

that general possibility of grafting not only opens signs to new meanings but also to new performative functions.

Having posited in his essay a general iterability that dislimns the difference between serious and non-serious performatives, Derrida doesn't elaborate on specific possibilities of grafting that literature and theatre might perform. For Judith Butler his view of language's 'breaking force' is too general; it doesn't take into account, for example, how linguistic meaning and performativity are policed by various social institutions.[18] Contesting that policing is a prime concern for the writers I've discussed. I've mentioned how Ginsberg, for example, draws on the structural potentiality of affects with his auto-poems. As we saw, those poems also posed alternative performative effects, as when his declaration of an end of the war was made not to enact a state of affairs so much as a state of oppositional feeling in people—one which could, in turn, force a cessation of the conflict. In other words, the pronouncement was made to be illocutionary regarding affect, with the hope of it being perlocutionary in respect of action. Such performative redirection takes advantage of literature as posing alternative worlds of possibility, but Ginsberg, like Baraka, was certainly aware that while his writing could act as an aesthetic force on individual readers and audiences, if it were to be directed at political institutions it needed to be augmented with other forms of activism.

In a 1989 interview with Derek Attridge, Derrida does develop a more literary angle to his theory of iterative potential. In the West, he argues, literature has come to be instituted as a discourse in which one can 'say anything' (*tout dire*) on the condition that what's said has its relation 'to meaning and reference' suspended.[19] Everything is possible in terms of form, content, and style, because literature is licensed to break with reality and so poses

> a force of provocation to think phenomenality, meaning, object, even being as such, a force which is at least potential, a philosophical *dunamis*—which can, however, be developed only in response, in the experience of reading, because it is not hidden in the text like a substance.[20]

The implication here is that literature's potentiality isn't purely divorced ontologically from the world, for its suspended status is in fact contractual; conditional upon social conventions. Literary suspension has also been

---

[18] Butler, *Excitable Speech*, 150.
[19] Jacques Derrida, 'This Strange Institution Called Literature' [interview with Derek Attridge], in *Acts of Literature* (London: Routledge, 1991), 49.
[20] Ibid. 46.

policed, as Foucault has pointed out, through things like copyright law and conventions around an author's function.[21] Derrida's suggestion is that literary suspension is only realized in acts of reading by individuals who acknowledge (and effectively 'countersign') its suspension, and for this reason the potentiality, identity, and meaning of literary texts are performative in being largely contingent on such acts. What Derrida doesn't consider, though, is how literature not only exerts a 'force' that provokes thinking about 'phenomenality, meaning, [and] object', but also flexes a force of affect. And on that score he's not alone, for as I've mentioned, the suspension of literature is precisely what various critics and philosophers have seen as an obstacle to its performativity and even its ability to do real feeling with words.

When critics have considered literary performatives, they've tended to examine representations *in* literature of the kinds of explicit 'speech acts' that Austin analysed (including promises, oaths, and ritual declarations). And in the few instances where the performativity of literary writing itself has been addressed, critics have been divided along lines of realism and 'irrealism'. Mary Louise Pratt defends the former position and refuses to accept that literary performativity is suspended from real life, for the 'fictive' side of literature, she argues, is also evident in 'jokes, ironic rejoinders, parables, [and] fables within political speeches'.[22] That these forms of social discourse share fictive powers doesn't mean that literary performatives are no different to any non-literary ones, though. Rather, it suggests that there are other forms of non-literary discourse that can also enact social suspension—as, for example, when a person uses the evasive statement 'I was only joking' to ironize the hurt done to someone else's feelings. Whether that evasion works is socially conditional upon the other person accepting it as a joke, just as literary suspension is contingent upon social acknowledgement of it. And doubt about that suspension is what makes it possible for a literary text to be viewed as performing libel, or hate speech, or blasphemy—a notorious case of the latter being the controversy over Salman Rushdie's *Satanic Verses*. This doesn't mean that literature can only have a performative and affective impact if one wills disbelief in its suspension. Pratt does will that disbelief, but doesn't consider how literature's social performativity might lead to it doing feeling. In contrast, Richard Ohmann is a firm believer in the suspension of literary

---

[21] See Michel Foucault, 'What is an Author?', in *Language, Counter-Memory, Practice*, trans. Donald F. Bouchard and Sherry Simon (1977, repr.; Ithaca, NY: Cornell University Press, 1988), 113–38.
[22] Mary Louise Pratt, *Toward a Speech Act Theory of Literary Discourse* (Bloomington, IN: Indiana University Press, 1977), 91.

performatives and ascribes them a 'quasi' status accordingly. Yet he doesn't view that status as precluding them from having affective consequences:

> Since the quasi-speech-acts of literature are not carrying on the world's business—describing, urging, contracting, etc.—the reader may well attend to them in a non-pragmatic way, and thus allow them to realize their emotive potential. In other words the suspension of normal illocutionary forces tends to shift a reader's attention to the locutionary acts themselves and to their perlocutionary effects.[23]

Ohmann here is taking an Austinian line; literary performatives are suspended from real social interactions, which is why he claims they're not 'carrying on the world's business' and so cannot be illocutionary but can have 'perlocutionary' emotional 'effects'. But if, as Derrida and Pratt argue, literature's suspension is a fact for being socially contractual, then its performatives are *not* simply excluded from the worldly business of 'describing, urging, contracting, etc.'; instead, they need to be seen as modifying such business by breaking it from normal conventions and forging for it different performative possibilities. And if that modification can include shifting performativity from states of affairs to 'emotive potential'—as the writers I've examined do—then that's all the more reason to consider how literature can exert *illocutionary* effects on individuals' affective capacities.

Very few critics have considered that shift. In *The Literary Speech Act* (1980) Shoshana Felman discusses Austin's *How To Do Things With Words* alongside Molière's play *Don Juan* (1665), and while her engagement with Molière mostly consists of considering how speech acts are represented *in* the play, she also suggests that the seductions of fancy with which Don Juan humours himself are scripted to seduce and humour the audience so the latter is drawn into the play's 'performative field of pleasure'.[24] The stage that Felman sets is largely replicated by other critics who broach the topic: they've tended to look at performativity in terms of literary *representations* of speech acts, and they've considered the affective side of those acts mostly with regard to desire. J. Hillis Miller's argument that literature engenders romantic passion in a reader by turning suspension into mystery is a case in point: 'a work of literature is strictly parallel to a love affair: my sense that my beloved hides an unrevealable secret, that she is unfathomably mysterious, arouses in me the passions of love and

---

[23] Richard Ohmann, 'Speech Acts and the Definition of Literature', *Philosophy and Rhetoric* 4 (1971), 17.

[24] Shoshana Felman, *The Literary Speech Act: Don Juan with J.L. Austin, or Seduction in Two Languages*, trans. Catherine Porter (1980, repr.; Ithaca, NY: Cornell University Press, 1983), 33.

desire for the beloved'.[25] But this generalizes and genders the dynamic of literary texts much too reductively and casts performativity more in terms of perlocutionary consequences. In contrast, Eve Kosofsky Sedgwick does relate illocution and affect when discussing Henry James's writings; again, though, she focuses her discussion on representations of how speech acts and desire become entangled, rather than on performative aspects of the literature itself.[26]

There have, of course, been numerous critics who don't make explicit recourse to notions of performativity but do consider the emotional effects that literature and theatre can wield. Much of that consideration has been by way of genres that have been developed to provoke particular modes of feeling.[27] Aristotle's theory of catharsis, for example, clearly recognizes that tragedy can both elicit and purge emotions for an audience, though that purgation is more perlocutionary when a spectacle of suffering inspires pity, or one of rage prompts fear. The performance becomes more illocutionary when the pity, terror, or rage portrayed is contagious for an audience, and the same holds for the infectious effects of mirth and laughter in comedy. Affective contagion is what writers of gothic fiction or pornography also aim at in describing scenes of horror or arousal that are intended, respectively (and sometimes simultaneously), to horrify or arouse. Literature of the sublime is another example, as Edmund Burke averred when affirming its capacity to instil in a reader the very feeling of sublimity being described.[28] For the most part, though, when critics have acknowledged these kinds of emotional effects they've upheld a generic view of the emotions themselves: the literature is taken to be *representing* real emotions that are viewed as being a stock subjective state, and such generic emotion is what the literature is seen to provoke in readers and audiences. In other words, the literary text is maintained as being a conduit and catalyst for emotion, but that emotional content isn't viewed

---

[25] J. Hillis Miller, *Speech Acts in Literature* (Stanford, CA: Stanford University Press, 2001), 160.
[26] See Sedgwick, *Touching Feeling*, Ch. 1.
[27] See, for example, Adrian Poole, *Tragedy: A Very Short Introduction* (Oxford: Oxford University Press, 2005); Nöel Carroll, *The Philosophy of Horror; or, Paradoxes of the Heart* (London: Routledge, 1990); Peter de Bolla, *The Discourse of the Sublime: History, Aesthetics, and the Subject* (Oxford: Blackwell, 1989); David Kennedy, *Elegy* (London: Routledge, 2007); Julius Walter Lever, *The Elizabethan Love Sonnet* (London: Methuen, 1974); Charles Altieri, *The Particulars of Rapture: An Aesthetics of the Affects* (Ithaca, NY: Cornell University Press, 2003), and Philip Fisher, *The Vehement Passions* (Princeton, NJ: Princeton University Press, 2002), 1–11.
[28] Edmund Burke, *A Philosophical Enquiry into the Origin of our Ideas of the Sublime and the Beautiful* (1757; repr.; Oxford: Oxford University Press, 1998), 158–61.

as being substantially altered, coloured, or generated by literary genre, style, or form. In contrast, the writers I've examined in the previous chapters frequently break with literary conventions and eschew emotional realism in order to produce new affective compounds that are largely shaped by experiment with form and genre.

In stating that, I'm *not* arguing that potentialist literature is the only kind that has ever turned performativity towards feeling. One could argue, for example, that the gothic and sublime do so, and that it's also been a main concern for avant-garde writing. My point is that despite such concern, critics and theorists have rarely linked affects and performativity, and when discussing the genres I've mentioned they generally overlook how formal and generic aspects of literature can fashion novel forms of feeling and aren't simply embellishments serving to represent affect more effectively. That potentialism is intended to be a kind of affective activism is all the more significant given the claims I cited in my Introduction about a 'waning of affect' being one of the symptoms of postmodernism.[29] The importance of potentialist approaches also becomes more apparent if one considers the critical debate regarding whether literary emotion is ever more than a fiction.

As with the debate about literary performativity, the one around literary emotions divides broadly between the realists and irrealists. In addition, the majority of it is focused solely on fiction. For emotional irrealists like Kendall Walton, Gregory Currie, and Jerrold Levinson, the feelings that fiction presents are not real but 'make-believe', and the emotions that a reader feels in response are also fictional.[30] As Walton states the case, such responses 'do not involve, literally, fearing, grieving for, admiring fictional characters'; instead, one *imagines* that one feels those things.[31] The question of whether the 'make-believe' involves a certain performativity, as the phrase suggests, isn't something the irrealists raise. Nor do they adequately consider how 'real' affects can be generated by imagination, fantasy, or irony. At the opposite end of the spectrum, emotional realists

---

[29] On the treatment of affect in postmodern and post-structuralist theory more generally, see Rei Terada, *Feeling in Theory: Emotion after the 'Death of the Subject'* (Cambridge, MA: Harvard University Press, 2001).

[30] See Kendall Walton, *Mimesis as Make-Believe* (Cambridge, MA: Harvard University Press, 1987); Gregory Currie, *The Nature of Fiction* (Cambridge: Cambridge University Press, 1990); and Jerrold Levinson, *The Pleasures of Aesthetics* (Ithaca, NY: Cornell University Press, 1996).

[31] Kendall Walton, 'Spelunking, Simulation, and Slime: On Being Moved by Fiction', in Mette Hjort and Sue Laver (eds), *Emotion and the Arts* (Oxford: Oxford University Press, 1997), 38, 48.

such as Derek Matravers, Berys Gaut, and Jenefer Robinson argue that fiction does convey and exact real affect.[32] In Robinson's opinion the emotions a reader forms about characters 'actually work just the same way [...] as they do when we respond to people and events in real life'.[33] But such a view occludes the fact that literary texts are acknowledged to pose suspensions of reality and alternative worlds of potential. In addressing the existence of imagined emotion Gaut similarly maintains its parity with real feeling: 'make-believe fear must keep its phenomenology the same as that of fear, because it is a truth of introspection that one can be in a state that *feels* like fear when watching a horror film'.[34] Emphasizing '*feels*' in that sentence distracts us from the following word: 'like'. If the intensity of such an affect is coupled with an awareness of simulation or simile, then are the phenomenologies of fear and the 'make-believe' exactly the 'same'? In Robinson's theory, the equivalence she upholds between literary and 'real life' emotion is also questionable when she proposes a very limited function for literary form. Formal devices, she argues, 'act as defensive strategies' for the reader to 'manage or deal with the explosive fantasies' of the text, and this management occurs 'more carefully than is possible in life'.[35] While Gaut doesn't account for how the fear one feels in watching a film might be tangibly *cinematic*—deriving, in part, from camera shots, editing, and soundtrack—Robinson doesn't account for how the 'explosive fantasies' of a literary work can be *augmented* by formal devices like metaphor or anaphora or free indirect discourse. In other words, such a view forecloses an understanding of how affect can in various ways take on a distinctly *literary* performativity and shape.

That literary sensibility is what the writers I've explored aim to advance. In the case of Ginsberg's 'Wichita Vortex Sutra', for example, one might expect that his flurry of subjunctives would detach the poem from real feeling. Along with flights of fancy, though, they voice a poignancy when they involve him desiring states of affairs that seem as though they can only be hoped for and imagined. And far from the formal aspects of his poetry acting apotropaically in relation to fantasy, the mantra and 'seed syllable' chanting are intended to give rise to 'bodily potential' and open people's sensibilities to the explosive realities of war. Acker's writing is

---

[32] See Derek Matravers, *Art and Emotion* (Oxford: Clarendon Press, 1998); Berys Gaut, *Art, Emotion, and Ethics* (Oxford: Oxford University Press, 2007); and Jenefer Robinson, *Deeper Than Reason: Emotion and Its Role in Literature, Music, and Art* (Oxford: Clarendon Press, 2005).
[33] Robinson, *Deeper than Reason*, 105.
[34] Gaut, *Art, Emotion, and Ethics*, 210.
[35] Robinson, *Deeper than Reason*, 196, 197.

similarly complex in forging distinctly literary affects by opening taboo topics while employing 'languages of the body' and drawing attention to the text's fictionality. As I argued in relation to her early writing, that combination of factors is sometimes aimed at reversing the kind of dream work that Freud theorizes: in undoing the Oedipus complex in her writing, for example, she seeks to weaken psychic defences and provoke a more fluid intensity of desire. In later novels like *Empire of the Senseless*, though, she figures taboo traumas *as fictions*, and combines subjunctivity and visceral language such that passages provide a form of anaesthetic while performing what she considers to be a kind of affective tattooing. Similarly, in novels like Burroughs's *The Soft Machine* the passages of cut-up space travel draw attention to fictive suspensions of reality while the language is nevertheless intended to have tangibly disorienting effects on readers. In short, it's a mistake to think that as soon as an emotion is mixed with subjunctivity, literary suspension, or a sheen of 'as if', that emotion is hermetically sealed from life and has no possibility of being genuinely affective. To assert as much is to overlook the affective potential that Tomkins affirmed: affect can become attached to anything.

My position is that literary suspension doesn't simply arrest the reality of emotional responses to it; rather, it can generate novel compounds of feeling. Burroughs, for example, draws attention metatextually to the suspended nature of his fictive characters, but he also presents scenes in which suspension engenders its own form of pleasure. And as we've seen, for Burroughs and Ginsberg literary suspension is also intended to suspend readers from regulated senses of discourse and so open them to new possibilities of experience. Thus, in reading Acker's scenes of taboo and abjection a person can be genuinely disgusted (as I've witnessed when teaching her novels), but those feelings are partly orchestrated *by* the literary language, and are partly feelings *for the language*. Hejinian's *Happily* also shapes a literary performance with its long unpunctuated lines that encourage readers to feel how figurative language doesn't simply describe but can also improvise affect. Such examples of synthesizing distinctly literary affect inflected with figurative language, referential suspension, and formal experiment cannot be accounted for by emotional realists and irrealists who deliberate solely on whether a reader can really empathize with the feelings of a fictional character. The potentialisms I've discussed present a more complex and adequate view in conceiving affects not as stock subjective forms but as fluid compounds that arise in interactions with any number of things—language, objects, situations, fantasies, etc. As such, those affects are doubly *of* those things; a sense of them that's shaped *with* them.

An important corollary of such interactivity is that the performative force I'm attributing to potentialism cannot be seen as guaranteed in its efficacy. It's not a form of Pavlovian literary determinism. Thus, the degree to which one of Baraka's Black Arts performances could instil the racial sentiment it figured was partly contingent on the race of those watching it. Similarly, whether Hejinian's experiments perform their feeling felicitously will depend on the willingness of the reader to embrace them. Moreover, while the writings I've discussed are certainly aimed at prompting particular sentiments, they're also designed to provide people with a critical awareness of how they're being affected. The performative slant of literary potentialism thus fosters critical abilities for interacting with it, as well as with the world. In doing so it also builds what I've been calling 'practical imagination'.

I mentioned in my Introduction that Spinoza views the singularity of a person as comprising capacities to affect and to be affected. Practical imagination enables a person to modulate those capacities on the basis that they exist not as fixed forms but as mutable potentials for both doing and not doing particular things. If that facilitates degrees of individual freedom it's not by way of the 'practical power' that I've cited Massimo de Carolis as criticizing—that power being conceived on the basis of having 'concrete possibilities' at one's disposal in proportion to one's disposable income.[36] Rather, as the writers I've discussed show, practical imagination can involve wresting some freedom over how one's capacities for thinking and feeling are regulated politically, discursively, and even by markets—as when Burroughs fashions the bizarre from the bazaar. If such imagination can be viewed as a faculty, it is no less flexible than other individual capacities; that is to say, it is built through interactions, and its practicality is contingent upon being practised. An awareness of that is what subtends the literary experiments of the writers I've examined, so that the dynamic of Hejinian's 'open text' poetry, for example, affirms that a recognition of possibility in a situation 'constitutes one's first exercise *of* possibility, and on that depends one's realization that oneself is possible'.

As with the issue of doing feeling, I'm not arguing that practical imagination is cultivated only by potentialist writing. That potentialism is specifically aimed at nurturing it by linking potentiality and capacity for individuals is significant, though, particularly given the postmodernist claim (which I cited in my Introduction) that the loss of a 'practical sense of the future' is symptomatic of individual agency being compro-

---

[36] Massimo de Carolis, 'Toward a Phenomenology of Opportunism', trans. Michael Turits, in Michael Hardt and Paolo Virno (eds), *Radical Thought in Italy: A Potential Politics* (Minneapolis: University of Minnesota Press, 1996), 38.

mised no less than the agonism of avant-gardes. Potentialism's imaginative flexings can also contribute to recent philosophical understandings of how the imagination, affect, and motivations for action become entwined. Much of the thinking on the issue draws on psychological research along with the debate around fiction and emotional realism. As Timothy Schroeder and Carl Matheson state, 'the commonalities between the neural effects of fictional and non-fictional stimuli are known to be so great in the brain's representational and emotional systems that scientists experiment upon human subjects using fictions to elicit feelings.'[37] Nevertheless, Schroeder and Matheson, like Jonathan Weinberg and Aaron Meskin, also contend that the feelings elicited by fiction are controlled by one's belief about the irreality of the state of affairs that one is imagining; thus 'beliefs about genre may play a role in the direction of our imagination, as can the beliefs about stars in the context of theatrical and/or cinematic works'.[38] My view is that such beliefs don't simply suppress or control the feelings that literature provokes; rather, interactions between the two can engender new compounds of feeling that bring an awareness of how the imagination turns potentiality into experience. This potentiality bears on one's other interactions in the world, as when planning or improvising a course of action requires imagination in weighing up various possibilities of comportment, affect, and outcome. In other words, if we're capable of bringing imagination and feeling under a reality principle of belief, the beliefs we settle on regarding real situations also derive from having exercised imagination to view those situations as harbouring various potentials.[39]

If the imagination has practical benefits, then, it's because it negotiates reality with a potentiality principle. I mentioned in my Introduction that Doreen Maitre outlines a refreshing alternative to most theorists' view of fiction's possible worlds when she affirms that they 'extend the range of one's experience'.[40] Susan L. Feagin takes a similar position in viewing fiction as building the kind of practical imagination that I've described. In

---

[37] Timothy Schroeder and Carl Matheson, 'Imagination and Emotion', in Shaun Nichols (ed.), *The Architecture of the Imagination: New Essays on Pretence, Possibility, and Fiction* (Oxford: Oxford University Press, 2009), 28–9.
[38] Jonathan M. Weinberg and Aaron Meskin, 'Puzzling over the Imagination: Philosophical Problems, Architectural Solutions', in Nichols (ed.), *The Architecture of the Imagination*, 179.
[39] See Ruth M. J. Byrne, *The Rational Imagination: How People Create Alternatives to Reality* (Cambridge, MA: Massachusetts Institute of Technology Press, 2005).
[40] Doreen Maitre, *Literature and Possible Worlds* (London: Middlesex Polytechnic Press, 1983), 54.

presenting a reader with alternative worlds of feeling, she argues, fiction enhances a 'capacity' for 'affective flexibility': 'it expands our imaginative potential with respect to generating affects, so that it's possible to *imagine* a wider variety of possibilities, for instance, what it is like to *do* this or that....'.[41] Pragmatic and affective pliancy are thus conjoined: 'Without that flexibility, one is not able to respond differently from the way one does. That is a handicap—a limitation on one's power over one's affective life.'[42] Such thinking verges on a notion of potentialism, and the affective power that Feagin describes is certainly what the writers I've examined are keen to develop. Again, that doesn't mean that potentialism is the only literary means to affective power any more than it is to emotional performativity or practical imagination. There's also no reason to think that those three things are pertinent to fiction more than to other literary genres or to theatrical performance. My position is simply that potentialism has been particularly inclined towards drawing the three things together, and that's been done with affective experiments that engage particular effects of social power.

Taken together, the characteristics of potentialism that I've outlined also provide parameters for ascribing the term to the work of writers other than those I've discussed. The emphasis on affectivity and political engagement, for example, is a reason why I wouldn't attribute potentialism to the procedurally constrained work of novelists such as Raymond Queneau and Georges Perec, who were associated with *Ouvroir de Littérature Potentielle* (OuLiPo). It's also why potentialism isn't reducible to the kinds of formal 'possibility' that some other literary scholars have focused on.[43] As I've argued, potentialism is not simply a style but a complex approach to using literature and performance to engage with social issues, and the works I've examined each do that by registering something of how potentiality itself gained currency in debates about individuality and social evolution in America over a particular period. If the concept is to be used in relation to writers in other contexts, then it should help to emphasize rather than submerge particularities of individual approaches. One could make a case, for example, for drawing potentialism out of Antonin Artaud's *To Have Done with the Judgement of God*

---

[41] Susan L. Feagin, *Reading with Feeling: The Aesthetics of Appreciation* (Ithaca, NY: Cornell University Press, 1996), 248, Feagin's emphases.
[42] Ibid. 254.
[43] See, for example, Michael Edwards, *Poetry and Possibility: A Study in the Power and Mystery of Words* (Basingstoke: Macmillan, 1988), and David Caplan, *Questions of Possibility: Contemporary Poetry and Poetic Form* (Oxford: Oxford University Press, 2005).

(1947), Ezra Pound's *Pisan Cantos* (1948), and Samuel Beckett's *How It Is* (1964), but it would mean identifying in each instance differing characteristics of experiment, affective force, and engagements with power.[44] In other words, critical flexibility is required to match the varying potentialisms of these and future writers so that we can continue to ask sanguinely of criticism and theory as much as of literature: who knows what is yet to come?

[44] Regarding potentiality in Pound's *Pisan Cantos*, see my *Terrorism and Modern Literature: From Joseph Conrad to Ciaran Carson* (Oxford: Oxford University Press, 2002), 159–72. For Beckett's novel, see my '"Various Infinitudes": Narration, Embodiment, and Ontology in Beckett's *How It Is* and Spinoza's *Ethics*', in Martin McQuillan, Graeme MacDonald, Robin Purves, and Stephen Thomson (eds), *Post-Theory: New Directions in Criticism* (Edinburgh: Edinburgh University Press, 1999), 176–87.

Bibliography

Acker, Kathy, 'A Radical American Abroad' [interview with Tony Dunn], *Drama* 160 (1986), 15–23.
—— 'Kathy Acker Interviewed by Rebecca Deaton', *Textual Practice* 6:2 (February 1991), 271–82.
—— 'Kathy Acker with Angela McRobbie' [filmed interview] (London: Institute of Contemporary Art, 1989).
—— 'On Narrative' (1993), in The Kathy Acker Papers, Duke University Library (Box 4, Folder: 'Reading the Lack of the Body').
—— 'Opening Speech for the Lahti Writers' Reunion' (1990), in The Kathy Acker Papers, Duke University Library (Box 4, Folder: 'Magazine Articles').
—— 'Peter Gordon: Ambiguity' (1981), in The Kathy Acker Papers, Duke University Library (Box 4, Folder: 'Peter Gordon: Ambiguity').
—— 'The Language of Sex, The Sex of Language' (1990), in The Kathy Acker Papers, Duke University Library (Box 4, Folder: 'For Ariane, 1990–1 Writings').
—— 'The Languages of the Body' (1991), in The Kathy Acker Papers, Duke University Library (Box 4, Folder: 'For Ariane, 1990–1 Writings').
—— 'William Burroughs' (1997), in The Kathy Acker Papers, Duke University Library (Box 4, Folder: 'William Burroughs/J. G. Ballard').
—— *Blood and Guts in High School* (New York: Grove, 1984).
—— *Bodies of Work: Essays* (London: Serpent's Tail, 1997).
—— *Don Quixote* (New York: Grove, 1986).
—— *Empire of the Senseless* (London: Picador, 1988).
—— *Eurydice in the Underworld* (London: Arcadia, 1997).
—— *Great Expectations* (New York: Grove, 1982).
—— *Hannibal Lecter, My Father* (New York: Semiotext(e), 1991).
—— *In Memoriam to Identity* (London: Pandora, 1990).
—— *My Death My Life by Pier Paolo Pasolini* in *Literal Madness: Three Novels* (New York: Grove, 1987).
—— *My Mother: Demonology* (New York: Grove, 1993).
—— *Portrait of an Eye: Three Novels: The Childlike Life of the Black Tarantula by the Black Tarantula; I Dreamt I was a Nymphomaniac: Imagining; The Adult Life of Toulouse Lautrec by Henri Toulouse Lautrec* (New York: Grove, 2000).
—— *Pussy, King of the Pirates* (New York: Grove, 1996).
—— *Rip-Off Red, Girl Detective and The Burning Bombing of America* (New York: Grove, 2002).
Agamben, Giorgio, 'Form-of-Life', trans. Cesare Cesarino, in Hardt and Virno (eds), *Radical Thought in Italy*, 150–6.
—— *Potentialities: Collected Essays in Philosophy*, trans. Daniel Heller-Roazen (Stanford, CA: Stanford University Press, 1999).

Allen, Donald (ed.), *The New American Poetry, 1945–1960* (Berkeley, CA: University of California Press, 1999).
Allen, Robert L., *A Guide to Black Power in America: An Historical Analysis* (New York: Victor Gollancz, 1970).
Alliez, Éric, and Antonio Negri, 'Peace and War', *Theory, Culture & Society* 20:2 (2003), 109–18.
Altieri, Charles, 'Some Problems about Agency in the Theories of Radical Poetics', *Contemporary Literature* 37:2 (1996), 207–36.
—— 'The Transformations of Objectivism: An Afterword', in Blau DuPlessis and Quartermain (eds), *The Objectivist Nexus*, 301–17.
—— 'Without Consequences is No Politics: A Response to Jerome McGann', in von Hallberg (ed.), *Politics and Poetic Value*, 301–8.
—— *The Particulars of Rapture: An Aesthetics of the Affects* (Ithaca, NY: Cornell University Press, 2003).
American Express [website], available at http://www.AmericanExpress.com/Potential, accessed 4 September 2010.
Anadolu-Okur, Nilgun, *Contemporary African American Theater: Afrocentricity in the Works of Larry Neal, Amiri Baraka, and Charles Fuller* (New York: Garland, 1997).
Andrews, Bruce, 'Poetry as Explanation, Poetry as Praxis', in Bernstein (ed.), *The Politics of Poetic Form*, 23–43.
—— *Paradise and Method: Poetics and Praxis* (Evanston, IL: Northwestern University Press, 1996).
—— and Charles Bernstein (eds), *The L=A=N=G=U=A=G=E Book* (Carbondale: Southern Illinois University Press, 1984).
Arendt, Hannah, 'Man's Conquest of Space', *American Scholar* 32 (Autumn 1963), 527–40.
—— *The Human Condition* (1958; repr. Chicago: University of Chicago Press, 1998).
Aristotle, *Metaphysics, I–IX*, trans. Hugh Tredennick (Cambridge, MA: Harvard University Press, 1980).
Aronson, Arnold, *American Avant-Garde Theatre: A History* (London: Routledge, 2000).
Arthur, Abby, and Ronald Maberry Johnson, *Propaganda and Aesthetics: The Literary Politics of Afro-American Magazines in the Twentieth Century* (Amherst: University of Massachusetts Press, 1979).
Atwill, William D., *Fire and Power: The American Space Program as Postmodern Narrative* (Athens: University of Georgia Press, 1994).
Auden, W. H., 'In Memory of W. B. Yeats' (1939), in *W. H. Auden: Selected Poems*, ed. Edward Mendelson (London: Faber and Faber, 1989), 81.
Austin, J. L., *How To Do Things With Words* (1962; repr. Oxford: Oxford University Press, 1971).
Baldwin, Peter, *Disease and Democracy: The Industrialized World Faces AIDS* (Berkeley, CA: University of California Press, 2005).

Baraka, Amiri [LeRoi Jones], 'AM/TRAK', in Paul Hoover (ed.), *Postmodern American Poetry: A Norton Anthology* (New York: Norton, 1994), 269–72.

—— 'Book of Life' [book outline] (December 1966), in Amiri Baraka Archive, Howard University Library (Box 26, Folder: '*Book of Life*').

—— 'Creation is Evolution' (1966), in Amiri Baraka Archive, Howard University Library (Box 16, Folder: '*Book of Life*').

—— 'Creativity Workshop Report and Resolution' (September 1968), in Amiri Baraka Archive, Howard University Library (Box 20, Folder: 'Black Power Conference, 1968').

—— *Black Magic* (New York: Bobbs-Merrill, 1969).

—— *Four Black Revolutionary Plays: Experimental Death Unit; A Black Mass; Madheart; Great Goodness of Life* (New York: Marion Boyars, 1998).

—— *Hard Facts* (Newark, NJ: CAP, 1975).

—— *Home: Social Essays* (1966; repr. Hopewell, NJ: Ecco Press, 1998).

—— *It's Nation Time* (Chicago: Third World Press, 1970).

—— *Raise Race Rays Raze: Essays since 1965* (1971; repr. New York: Vintage, 1972).

—— *Selected Plays and Prose of Amiri Baraka/LeRoi Jones* (New York: William Morrow, 1979).

—— *Somebody Blew Up America, and Other Poems* (2001; repr. Philipsburg: House of Nehesi, 2007).

—— *Spirit Reach* (Newark, NJ: Jihad, 1972).

—— *Strategy and Tactics of a Pan-African Nationalist Party* (Newark, NJ: CFUN, 1971).

—— *The Autobiography of LeRoi Jones/Amiri Baraka* (New York: Freundlich, 1984).

—— *The LeRoi Jones/Amiri Baraka Reader*, ed. William J. Harris (New York: Thunder's Mouth Press, 2000).

—— *The Motion of History and Other Plays* (New York: William Morrow, 1978).

—— *Transbluesency: The Selected Poems of Amiri Baraka/LeRoi Jones (1961–1995)*, ed. Paul Vangelisti (New York: Marsilio, 1995).

—— and Billy Abernathy, *In Our Terribleness: Some Elements and Meaning in Black Style* (New York: Bobbs-Merrill, 1970).

—— and Larry Neal (eds), *Black Fire: An Anthology of Afro-American Writing* (1968; repr. New York: William Morrow, 1973).

Barnes, Clive, 'The Theater: New LeRoi Jones Play', *New York Times* (22 November 1969), A2, 22.

Barnes, Elizabeth, *States of Sympathy: Seduction and Democracy in the American Novel* (New York: Columbia University Press, 1997).

Baudrillard, Jean, *Fatal Strategies*, trans. Philip Beitchman and W. G. J. Niesluchowski (1983; repr. London: Pluto, 1990).

Beach, Christopher, *Poetic Culture: Contemporary American Poetry between Community and Institution* (Evanston, IL: Northwestern University Press, 1999).

Benston, Kimberley, 'Amiri Baraka: an Interview' (1977), *boundary 2* 6:2 (Winter 1978), 303–16.
Berghaus, Günther, *Avant-garde Performance: Live Events and Electronic Technologies* (Basingstoke: Palgrave Macmillan, 2005).
Bernstein, Charles, 'Community and the Individual Talent', *Diacritics* 26 (Autumn–Winter 1996), 176–95.
—— Letter to Hejinian (27 May 1981), in Lyn Hejinian Archive, Mandeville Special Collections Library, University of California, San Diego (Box 44, Folder 8).
—— 'Semblance', in Andrews and Bernstein (eds), *The L=A=N=G=U=A=G=E Book*, 115–18.
—— 'Stray Straws and Straw Men', in Andrews and Bernstein (eds), *The L=A=N=G=U=A=G=E Book*, 39–45.
—— 'The Conspiracy of "US"', in Andrews and Bernstein (eds), *The L=A=N=G=U=A=G=E Book*, 185–8.
—— 'The Dollar Value of Poetry', in Andrews and Bernstein (eds), *The L=A=N=G=U=A=G=E Book*, 138–40.
—— *A Poetics* (Cambridge, MA: Harvard University Press, 1992).
—— *Content's Dream: Essays 1975–1985* (Evanston, IL: Northwestern University Press, 2001).
—— *My Way: Speeches and Poems* (Chicago: University of Chicago Press, 1999).
—— (ed.), *The Politics of Poetic Form* (1990; repr. New York: Roof, 1998).
Bibby, Michael, *Hearts and Minds: Bodies, Poetry, and Resistance in the Vietnam Era* (New Brunswick: Rutgers University Press, 1996).
Bigsby, C. W. E., *A Critical Introduction to Twentieth-Century American Drama*, Vol. 3: *Beyond Broadway* (Cambridge: Cambridge University Press, 1985).
Blau DuPlessis, Rachel, and Peter Quartermain (eds), *The Objectivist Nexus: Essays in Cultural Poetics* (Tuscaloosa: University of Alabama Press, 1999).
Bly, Robert (ed.), *Forty Poems Touching on Recent American History* (Boston: Beacon Press, 1970).
Bockris, Victor, *With William Burroughs: Private Conversations with a Modern Genius* (London: Fourth Estate, 1996).
Boym, Svetlana, *Common Places: Mythologies of Everyday Life in Russia* (Cambridge MA: Harvard University Press, 1994).
Brown, Scot, *Fighting for US: Maulana Karenga, the US Organization, and Black Cultural Nationalism* (New York: New York University Press, 2003).
Buckminster Fuller, R., *Utopia or Oblivion: The Prospects for Humanity* (1969; repr. London: Penguin, 1970).
Bürger, Peter, *Theory of the Avant-Garde*, trans. Michael Shaw (Minneapolis: University of Minnesota Press, 1984).
Burke, Edmund, *A Philosophical Enquiry into the Origin of our Ideas of the Sublime and the Beautiful* (1757; repr. Oxford: Oxford University Press, 1998).
Burroughs, William S., 'Afterword: My Purpose is to Write for the Space Age', in Skerl and Lydenberg (eds), *William S. Burroughs at the Front*, 265–70.

Bibliography

—— 'Rencontre Avec William Burroughs' (1964) [interview with Eric Mottram], in Allen Hibberd (ed.), *Conversations with William S. Burroughs* (Jackson, MS: University Press of Mississippi, 1999), 11–15.
—— *Burroughs Live: The Collected Interviews of William S. Burroughs, 1960–97*, ed. Sylvère Lotringer (New York: Semiotext(e), 2001).
—— *Cities of the Red Night* (London: Picador, 1981).
—— *Exterminator!* (1966; repr. London: Calder, 1984).
—— *Naked Lunch* (1959; repr. New York: Grove Weidenfeld, 1990).
—— *Nova Express* (1964; repr. New York: Grove, 1992).
—— *The Four Horsemen of the Apocalypse* (Bonn: Expanded Media Editions, 1984).
—— *The Place of Dead Roads* (1983; repr. London: Flamingo, 2001).
—— *The Soft Machine* (1961; repr. London: Flamingo, 1995),
—— *The Ticket that Exploded* (1966 rev. edn; New York: Grove, 1967).
—— *The Western Lands* (1987; repr. London: Picador, 1988).
—— *The Wild Boys: A Book of the Dead* (New York: Grove, 1971).
—— and Brion Gysin, *The Third Mind* (1976; repr. London: Calder, 1979).
—— and Daniel Odier, *The Job* (rev. edn; London: Calder, 1984).
Butler, Judith, *Excitable Speech: A Politics of the Performative* (London: Routledge, 1997).
—— *Gender Trouble* (1990; repr. London: Routledge, 2008).
Byrne, Ruth M. J., *The Rational Imagination: How People Create Alternatives to Reality* (Cambridge, MA: Massachusetts Institute of Technology Press, 2005).
Calinescu, Matei, *Five Faces of Modernity: Modernism, Avant-Garde, Decadence, Kitsch, Postmodernism* (Durham, NC: Duke University, 1987).
Campbell, Sue, *Interpreting the Personal: Expression and the Formation of Feeling* (Ithaca, NY: Cornell University Press, 1997).
Caplan, David, *Questions of Possibility: Contemporary Poetry and Poetic Form* (Oxford: Oxford University Press, 2005).
Carroll, Nöel, *The Philosophy of Horror; or, Paradoxes of the Heart* (London: Routledge, 1990).
Carter, Dale, *The Final Frontier: The Rise and Fall of the American Rocket State* (London: Verso, 1988).
Cervantes, Miguel de, *Don Quixote de la Mancha*, trans. Charles Jarvis (1605, 1615; repr. Oxford: Oxford University Press, 1998).
Chafe, William H., *The Unfinished Journey: America Since World War II* (Oxford: Oxford University Press, 1991).
Chattarji, Subarno, *Memories of a Lost War: American Poetic Responses to the Vietnam War* (Oxford: Clarendon, 2001).
Copeland, Rita, *Rhetorics, Hermeneutics, and Translation in the Middle Ages: Academic Traditions and Vernacular Texts* (Cambridge: Cambridge University Press, 1991).
Cornis-Pope, Marcel, *Narrative Innovation and Cultural Rewriting in the Cold War and After* (Basingstoke: Palgrave, 2001).
Cruse, Harold, *Rebellion or Revolution?* (New York: William Morris, 1968).

Cruse, Harold, *The Crisis of the Negro Intellectual: A Historical Analysis of the Failure of Black Leadership* (1967; repr. New York: New York Review of Books, 2005).
Currie, Gregory, *The Nature of Fiction* (Cambridge: Cambridge University Press, 1990).
Davidson, Michael, Lyn Hejinian, Ron Silliman, and Barrett Watten, *Leningrad: American Writers in the Soviet Union* (San Francisco: Mercury House, 1991).
Davidson, Phillip B., *Vietnam at War: The History, 1946–1975* (Oxford: Oxford University Press, 1988).
Dean, Jodi, *Aliens in America: Conspiracy Cultures from Outerspace to Cyberspace* (Ithaca, NY: Cornell University Press, 1998).
Dean, Kenneth, and Brian Massumi, *First and Last Emperors: The Absolute State and the Body of the Despot* (New York: Autonomedia, 1992).
de Bolla, Peter, *The Discourse of the Sublime: History, Aesthetics, and the Subject* (Oxford: Blackwell, 1989).
de Carolis, Massimo, 'Toward a Phenomenology of Opportunism', trans. Michael Turits, in Hardt and Virno (eds), *Radical Thought in Italy*, 36–50.
De la Durantaye, Leland, *Giorgio Agamben: A Critical Introduction* (Stanford, CA: Stanford University Press, 2009).
Deleuze, Gilles, *Spinoza: Practical Philosophy*, trans. Robert Hurley (San Francisco: City Lights, 1988).
——and Félix Guattari, *A Thousand Plateaus: Capitalism and Schizophrenia*, trans. Brian Massumi (Minneapolis: University of Minnesota Press, 1987).
—— *What is Philosophy?*, trans. Hugh Tomlinson and Graham Burchell (New York: Columbia University Press, 1994).
DeLillo, Don, 'In the Ruins of the Future', *The Guardian* [website] (22 December 2001), available at http://www.guardian.co.uk/books/2001/dec/22/fiction.dondelillo, accessed 10 August 2009.
Delville, Michel, and Christine Pagnoulle (eds), *The Mechanics of the Mirage: Postwar American Poetry* (Liège: Liège Language and Literature, 2000).
Depero, Fortunato (ed.), *Numero Unico Futurista Campari 1931* (1931; repr. Paris: Éditions Jean-Michel Place, 1979).
Derrida, Jacques, 'Signature Event Context', trans. Samuel Weber and Jeffrey Mehlman, in *Limited Inc* (Evanston, IL: Northwestern University Press, 1988), 1–23.
—— 'This Strange Institution Called Literature' [interview with Derek Attridge], in *Acts of Literature* (London: Routledge, 1991), 33–75.
Dickens, Charles, *Great Expectations* (1861; repr. London: Penguin, 1996).
di Prima, Diane, *Recollections of My Life as a Woman: The New York Years* (New York: Viking, 2001).
—— *War Poems* (New York: The Poets' Press, 1968).
Docherty, Thomas (ed.), *Postmodernism: A Reader* (London: Longman, 1993).
Doležel, Lubomir, *Heterocosmica: Fiction and Possible Worlds* (Baltimore: Johns Hopkins University Press, 1998).
Du Bois, W. E. B., *The Souls of Black Folk* (1903; repr. Oxford: Oxford University Press, 2008).

Duncan, Robert, *Bending the Bow* (1968; repr. London: Jonathan Cape, 1971).
Edmond, Jacob, '"A Meaning Alliance": Arkadii Dragomoshchenko and Lyn Hejinian's Poetics of Translation', *Slavic and East European Journal* 46:3 (2002), 551–64.
—— 'Lyn Hejinian and Russian Estrangement', *Poetics Today* 27:1 (Spring 2006), 97–123.
Edwards, Michael, *Poetry and Possibility: A Study in the Power and Mystery of Words* (Basingstoke: Macmillan, 1988).
Effiong, Philip Uko, *In Search of a Model for African-American Drama: A Study of Selected Plays by Lorraine Hansberry, Amiri Baraka, and Ntozake Shange* (New York: University Press of America, 2000).
Ehrman, John, *The Eighties; America in the Age of Reagan* (New Haven: Yale University Press, 2005).
Elam, Harry J., *Taking It to the Streets: The Social Protest Theater of Luis Valdez and Amiri Baraka* (1997; repr. Ann Arbor: University of Michigan Press, 2001).
Evans, Martin, and John Phillips, *Algeria: Anger of the Dispossessed* (New Haven: Yale University Press, 2007).
Faas, Ekbert (ed.), *Towards a New American Poetics: Essays and Interviews* (Santa Barbara: Black Sparrow Press, 1978).
FBI (Newark) File (17 June 1968), in Amiri Baraka Archive, Howard University Library (Box 9, Folder: 'FBI Files').
FBI File (25 July 1966), in Amiri Baraka Archive, Howard University Library (Box 9, Folder: 'FBI Files').
FBI Special Agent (Baltimore, MD) Report (21 March 1968), in Amiri Baraka Archive, Howard University Library (Box 9, Folder: 'FBI Files').
FBI Special Agent (Tampa, FL) Report (7 February 1969), in Amiri Baraka Archive, Howard University Library (Box 9, Folder: 'FBI Files').
FBI Special Agent Memo (25 March 1969), in Amiri Baraka Archive, Howard University Library (Box 9, Folder: 'FBI Files').
—— (27 February 1969), in Amiri Baraka Archive, Howard University Library (Box 9, Folder: 'FBI Files').
Feagin, Susan L., *Reading with Feeling: The Aesthetics of Appreciation* (Ithaca, NY: Cornell University Press, 1996).
Feather, John, *Publishing, Piracy, and Politics: An Historical Study of Copyright in Britain* (London: Mansell, 1994).
Federman, Raymond, *The Twofold Vibration* (Bloomington, IN: Indiana University Press, 1982).
Felman, Shoshana, *The Literary Speech Act: Don Juan with J.L. Austin, or Seduction in Two Languages*, trans. Catherine Porter (1980; repr. Ithaca, NY: Cornell University Press, 1983).
Finney, Ben R., and Eric M. Jones (eds), *Interstellar Migration and the Human Experience* (Berkeley, CA: University of California Press, 1985).
Fisher, Charles, *The Vehement Passions* (Princeton, NJ: Princeton University Press, 2002).

Flowers, Sandra Hollin, *African American Nationalist Literature of the 1960s: Pens of Fire* (New York: Garland, 1996).

Foley, Michael, 'Presidential Leadership and the Presidency', in *The Reagan Years: The Record in Presidential Leadership* (Manchester: Manchester University Press, 1990), 23–53.

Fortune, Dion, *Psychic Self-Defence: A Study in Occult Pathology and Criminality* (London: Aquarian, 1952).

Foucault, Michel, *Discipline and Punish*, trans. Alan Sheridan (Harmondsworth: Penguin, 1991).

—— *Essential Works of Foucault, 1954–84*, Vol. 1: *Ethics, Subjectivity and Truth*, ed. Paul Rabinow, trans. Robert Hurley et al. (London: Penguin, 2000).

—— *Essential Works of Foucault, 1954–84*, Vol. 3: *Power*, ed. James Faubion, trans. Robert Hurley et al. (London: Penguin, 2002).

—— *Foucault Live: Collected Interviews, 1961–84*, ed. Sylvère Lotringer, trans. Lysa Hochroth and John Johnston (New York: Semiotext(e), 1989).

—— *Language, Counter-Memory, Practice*, ed. Donald F. Bouchard, trans. Donald F. Bouchard et al. (1977; repr. Ithaca, NY: Cornell University Press, 1988).

—— *'Society Must Be Defended': Lectures at the Collège de France, 1975–76*, eds Mauro Bertani and Alessandro Fontana, trans. David Macey (London: Allen Lane, 2003).

—— *The Birth of Biopolitics: Lectures at the Collège de France, 1978–79*, ed. Michel Senellart, trans. Graham Burchell (London: Palgrave Macmillan, 2008).

—— *The History of Sexuality*, Vol. 1: *An Introduction*, trans. Robert Hurley (1976; repr. London: Vintage, 1990).

—— *The Use of Pleasure: The History of Sexuality*, Vol. 2, trans. Robert Hurley (1984; repr. London: Penguin, 1992).

Freud, Sigmund, *The Interpretation of Dreams*, trans. Joyce Crick (1900; repr. Oxford: Oxford University Press, 1999).

Gaut, Berys, *Art, Emotion, and Ethics* (Oxford: Oxford University Press, 2007).

Gibson, William, *Neuromancer* (New York: Ace, 2000).

Gillies, James, and Robert Cailliau, *How the Web was Born: The Story of the World Wide Web* (Oxford: Oxford University Press, 2000).

Ginsberg, Allen, 'Vietnam War / 1972 Election Note & Copybook', in Allen Ginsberg Papers (M0733), Department of Special Collections, Stanford University Libraries, Series 2 (Box 24, Folder 16).

—— *Allen Verbatim: Lectures on Poetry, Politics, Consciousness by Allen Ginsberg*, ed. Gordon Ball (New York: McGraw-Hill, 1974).

—— *Collected Poems* (1984; repr. London: Penguin, 1987).

—— *Composed on the Tongue*, ed. Donald Allen (Bolinas, CA: Grey Fox Press, 1980).

—— *Deliberate Prose: Selected Essays, 1952–95*, ed. Bill Morgan (New York: HarperCollins, 2000).

—— *Spontaneous Mind: Selected Interviews, 1958–96*, ed. David Carter (2001; repr. New York: Perennial, 2002).

Gitlin, Todd, *The Whole World is Watching: Mass Media in the Making and Unmaking of the New Left* (Berkeley, CA: University of California Press, 1980).
Glück, Robert, 'The Greatness of Kathy Acker', in Scholder, Harryman, and Ronell (eds), *Lust for Life*, 45–57.
Griffiths, Philip Jones, *Vietnam Inc.* (New York: Collier, 1971).
Grosz, Elizabeth, *Volatile Bodies: Toward a Corporeal Feminism* (Sydney: Allen and Unwin, 1994).
Gysin, Brion, 'Cut-Ups: A Project for Disastrous Success', in Burroughs and Gysin, *The Third Mind*, 42–51.
Hammond, William M., *Reporting Vietnam: Media and Military at War* (Lawrence: University Press of Kansas, 1998).
Haraway, Donna, *Simians, Cyborgs, and Women* (London: Free Association, 1991).
Hardt, Michael, and Antonio Negri, *Empire* (Cambridge, MA: Harvard University Press, 2000).
—— and Paolo Virno (eds), *Radical Thought in Italy: A Potential Politics* (Minneapolis: University of Minnesota Press, 1996).
Harris, Oliver, 'Cut-Up Closure: The Return to Narrative', in Skerl and Lydenberg (eds), *William S. Burroughs at the Front*, 251–62.
—— 'Cutting Up Politics', in Davis Schneiderman and Philip Walsh (eds), *Retaking the Universe: William S. Burroughs in the Age of Globalization* (London: Pluto, 2004), 175–200.
Harris, William J., *The Poetry and Poetics of Amiri Baraka: The Jazz Aesthetic* (Columbia, MO: University of Missouri Press, 1985).
Hartley, George, *Textual Politics and the Language Poets* (Bloomington and Indianapolis: Indiana University Press, 1989).
Hawkins, Susan E., 'All in the Family: Kathy Acker's *Blood and Guts in High School*', *Contemporary Literature* 45:4 (2004), 637–58.
Hawthorne, Nathaniel *The Scarlet Letter* (1850; repr. Oxford: Oxford University Press, 2007).
Heidegger, Martin, *Nietzsche*, Vol. II: *The Eternal Recurrence of the Same*, trans. David Farrell Krell (San Francisco: Harper and Row, 1984).
Hejinian, Lyn, 'Background Notes for *Happily*' (1998), in Lyn Hejinian Archive, Mandeville Special Collections Library, University of California, San Diego (Box 110, Folder 11).
—— Letter to Bob Perelman (20 August 1995), in Lyn Hejinian Archive, Mandeville Special Collections Library, University of California, San Diego (Box 92, Folder 12).
—— Letter to Bob Perelman (19 January 1995), in Lyn Hejinian Archive, Mandeville Special Collections Library, University of California, San Diego (Box 92, Folder 12).
—— Letter to Charles Bernstein (21 July 1977), in Lyn Hejinian Archive, Mandeville Special Collections Library, University of California, San Diego (Box 2, Folder 10).

Hejinian, Lyn, Letter to Charles Bernstein (7 February 1986), in Lyn Hejinian Archive, Mandeville Special Collections Library, University of California, San Diego (Box 12, Folder 13).

——Letter to Clark Coolidge, Jean Day, Michael Palmer, and Kit Robinson (28 March 1990), in Lyn Hejinian Archive, Mandeville Special Collections Library, University of California, San Diego (Box 48, Folder 4).

——Letter to Dennis Wolf, USIA (9 October 1990), in Lyn Hejinian Archive, Mandeville Special Collections Library, University of California, San Diego (Box 48, Folder 4).

——Letter to Leslie Scalapino (22 July 2000), in Lyn Hejinian Archive, Mandeville Special Collections Library, University of California, San Diego (Box 98, Folder 8).

——Letter to Leslie Scalapino (8 August 1996) in Lyn Hejinian Archive, Mandeville Special Collections Library, University of California, San Diego (Box 97, Folder 15).

——Letter to Rae Armantrout (29 July 1991), in Lyn Hejinian Archive, Mandeville Special Collections Library, University of California, San Diego (Box 11, Folder 1).

——Letter to Robert Grenier (21 May 1988), in Lyn Hejinian Archive, Mandeville Special Collections Library, University of California, San Diego (Box 19, Folder 4).

——Letter to Steve Benson (October 1984), in Lyn Hejinian Archive, Mandeville Special Collections Library, University of California, San Diego (Box 2, Folder 7).

——Letter to Susan Howe (23 December 1994), in Lyn Hejinian Archive, Mandeville Special Collections Library, University of California, San Diego (Box 22, Folder 13).

——'Planning Notes for *Slowly*', in Lyn Hejinian Archive, Mandeville Special Collections Library, University of California, San Diego (Box 112, Folder 4).

——'The Numerous: Oppen's Affirmation' [lecture delivered 8 December 1994], in Lyn Hejinian Archive, Mandeville Special Collections Library, University of California, San Diego (Box 112, Folder 22).

——'The Person and Everyday Life', in Lyn Hejinian Archive, Mandeville Special Collections Library, University of California, San Diego (Box 112, Folder 25).

——Transcript of interview [untitled] with Laura Hinton (December 1994–February 1995), in Lyn Hejinian Archive, Mandeville Special Collections Library, University of California, San Diego (Box 97, Folder 15).

——'Variations: A Return of Words' (1976), in Ron Silliman (ed.), *In the American Tree* (Maine: National Poetry Foundation, 1986), 503–9.

——*A Border Comedy* (New York: Granary, 2001).

——*Happily* (2000; repr. Sausalito, CA: Post-Apollo Press, 2000).

——*My Life* (1987 rev. edn; repr. Los Angeles: Green Integer, 2002).

——*Oxota: A Short Russian Novel* (Great Barrington, MA: The Figures, 1991).

——Talk on realism [untitled], in Lyn Hejinian Archive, Mandeville Special Collections Library, University of California, San Diego (Box 44, Folder 1).
—— *The Cell* (San Francisco: Sun and Moon, 1992).
—— *The Cold of Poetry* (Los Angeles: Sun and Moon, 1994).
—— *The Fatalist* (Richmond, CA: Omnidawn, 2003).
—— *The Language of Inquiry* (Berkeley, CA: University of California Press, 2000).
Hernton, Calvin C., 'Dynamite Growing out of Their Skulls', in Baraka and Neal (eds), *Black Fire*, 78–104.
Hinkson Craig, Barbara, and David M. O'Brien, *Abortion and American Politics* (Chatham, NJ: Chatham House, 1993).
Hjort, Mette, and Sue Laver (eds), *Emotion and the Arts* (Oxford: Oxford University Press, 1997).
Hobbs, Stuart D., *The End of the American Avant-Garde* (New York: New York University Press, 1997).
hooks, bell, *Ain't I a Woman: Black Women and Feminism* (1981; repr. London: Pluto Press, 1982).
Hoover, Paul (ed.), *Postmodern American Poetry: A Norton Anthology* (New York: Norton, 1994).
Houen, Alex, 'Introduction: Affecting Words', *Textual Practice* 25:2 (March/April 2011), 215–32.
——'Sacrifice and the Sublime since 11 September 2001', forthcoming in Adam Piette and Mark Rawlinson (eds), *The Edinburgh Companion to Twentieth-Century British and American War Literature* (Edinburgh: Edinburgh University Press, 2012).
——'"Various Infinitudes": Narration, Embodiment, and Ontology in Beckett's *How It Is* and Spinoza's *Ethics*', in Martin McQuillan, Graeme MacDonald, Robin Purves, and Stephen Thomson (eds), *Post-Theory: New Directions in Criticism* (Edinburgh: Edinburgh University Press, 1999), 176–87.
—— *Terrorism and Modern Literature: from Joseph Conrad to Ciaran Carson* (Oxford: Oxford University Press, 2002).
Howe, Susan, Letter to Hejinian (27 May 1981), in Lyn Hejinian Archive, Mandeville Special Collections Library, University of California, San Diego (Box 44, Folder 18).
Hudson, Theodore R., 'The Trial of LeRoi Jones' (1973), in Kimberley W. Benston (ed.), *Imamu Amiri Baraka (LeRoi Jones): A Collection of Critical Essays* (Englewood Cliffs, NJ: Prentice-Hall, 1978), 49–53.
Hume, Kathryn, 'William S. Burroughs's Phantasmic Geography', in *Contemporary Literature*: 40:1 (1999), 111–35.
Huyssen, Andreas, *After the Great Divide: Modernism, Mass Culture, and Postmodernism* (Bloomington, IN: Indiana University Press, 1986).
Hyman, Arthur, 'Aristotle, Algazali, and Avicenna on Necessity, Potentiality, and Possibility', in Karl-Ludwig Selig and Robert Somerville (eds), *Florilegium Columbianum: Essays in Honor of Paul Oskar Kristeller* (New York: Italica, 1987), 73–82.

Isserman, Maurice, and Michael Kazin, *America Divided: The Civil War of the 1960s* (Oxford: Oxford University Press, 2000).

Izenberg, Oren, 'Language Poetry and Collective Life', *Critical Inquiry* 30 (Autumn 2003), 132–59.

Jameson, Fredric, 'Periodizing the 60s', in Sohnya Sayres, Anders Stephenson, Stanley Aronowitz, and Fredric Jameson (eds), *The 60s Without Apology* (Minneapolis: University of Minnesota Press, 1984), 178–209.

——*Postmodernism, or The Cultural Logic of Late Capitalism* (London: Verso, 1991).

Johnson, Haynes, *The Best of Times: America in the Clinton Years* (New York: Harcourt, 2001).

Kant, Immanuel, *Critique of the Power of Judgement*, trans. Paul Gruyer and Eric Matthews (1790; repr. Cambridge: Cambridge University Press, 2000).

Kennedy, David, *Elegy* (London: Routledge, 2007).

Kinnard, Douglas, *The War Managers* (Hanover, NH: University of Vermont Press, 1977).

Kristeva, Julia, *Powers of Horror: An Essay on Abjection*, trans. Leon S. Roudiez (1980; repr. New York: Columbia University Press, 1982).

LaFeber, Walter, *America, Russia, and the Cold War, 1945–2006* (New York: McGraw-Hill, 2006).

Lahr, John, 'On-stage', *The Village Voice* (6 December 1969), 45.

Lemaire, Gérard-Georges, '23 Stitches Taken by Gérard-Georges Lemaire and 2 Points of Order by Brion Gysin', in Burroughs and Gysin, *The Third Mind*, 9–28.

Lever, Julius Walter, *The Elizabethan Love Sonnet* (London: Methuen, 1974).

Levertov, Denise, *1968 Peace Calendar & Appointment Book: Out of the War Shadow* (New York: War Resisters' League, 1967).

Levine, Arthur L., *The Future of the U.S. Space Program* (New York: Praeger, 1975).

Levinson, Jerrold, *The Pleasures of Aesthetics* (Ithaca, NY: Cornell University Press, 1996).

Lichty, Lawrence, 'Comments on the Influence of Television on Public Opinion', in Peter Braestrup (ed.), *Vietnam as History* (Washington, DC: Woodrow Wilson International Center for Scholars, 1984), 158–64.

Lowenfels, Walter, *Where is Vietnam?: American Poets Respond* (New York: Doubleday, 1967).

Loxley, James, *Performativity* (London: Routledge, 2007).

Lukács, György, *The Meaning of Contemporary Realism*, trans. John Mander and Necke Mander (1957; repr. London: Merlin, 1969).

Lyotard, Jean-François, 'The Sublime and the Avant-Garde' (1984), in Thomas Docherty (ed.), *Postmodernism: A Reader* (London: Longman, 1993), 244–57.

——*The Differend: Phrases in Dispute*, trans. Georges Van Den Abeele (1983; repr. Minneapolis: University of Minnesota Press, 1988).

——*The Postmodern Condition: A Report on Knowledge*, trans. Geoffrey Bennington and Brian Massumi (Minneapolis: Minneapolis University Press, 1984).

McCaffery, Steve, 'From the Notebooks', in Andrews and Bernstein (eds), *The L=A=N=G=U=A=G=E Book*, 159–62.
McDougall, Walter A., *The Heavens and the Earth: A Political History of the Space Age* (Baltimore: Johns Hopkins University Press, 1985).
McGann, Jerome, 'Contemporary Poetry, Alternate Routes', in Robert von Hallberg (ed.), *Politics and Poetic Value* (Chicago: University of Chicago Press, 1987), 254–72.
McHale, Brian, *Constructing Postmodernism* (London: Routledge, 1992).
—— *Postmodernist Fiction* (London: Methuen, 1987).
Macfarlane, Robert, *Plagiarism and Originality in Nineteenth-Century Literature* (Oxford: Oxford University Press, 2006).
Mackey, Nathaniel, 'The Changing Same: Black Music in the Poetry of Amiri Baraka', *boundary 2* 6:2 (Winter 1978), 355–86.
—— *Discrepant Engagement: Dissonance, Cross-Culturality, and Experimental Writing* (Cambridge: Cambridge University Press, 1993).
McQuaid, Kim, *The Anxious Years: America in the Vietnam–Watergate Era* (London: HarperCollins, 1989).
Mailer, Norman, *Armies of the Night: History as a Novel, The Novel as History* (1968; repr. London: Harmondsworth, 1971).
—— *Of a Fire on the Moon* (Boston: Little, Brown, 1970).
Maitre, Doreen, *Literature and Possible Worlds* (London: Middlesex Polytechnic Press, 1983).
Marcuse, Herbert, *Eros and Civilization* (1955; repr. London: Sphere, 1970).
—— *One Dimensional Man: Studies in the Ideology of Advanced Industrial Society* (1964; repr. London: Routledge, 2002).
Marinetti, Filippo Tommaso, *Let's Murder the Moonshine: Selected Writings*, ed. R. W. Flint, trans. Arthur A. Copatelli (Los Angeles: Sun and Moon, 1991).
Marx, Karl, *Capital: A Critique of Political Economy*, Vol. 1: *The Process of Capitalist Production*, trans. Ben Fowkes (1867; repr. London: Penguin, 1990).
Matravers, Derek, *Art and Emotion* (Oxford: Clarendon Press, 1998).
Matusow, Allen, *The Unravelling of America: A History of Liberalism in the 1960s* (New York: Harper, 1984).
Melville, Herman, 'Bartleby, the Scrivener' (1853), in *Billy Budd, Sailor, and Selected Tales*, ed. Robert Milder (Oxford: Oxford University Press, 2009), 3–41.
Mengham, Rod, Review [untitled] of writing by Clark Coolidge, Steve McCaffery, Charles Bernstein, and Barrett Watten, *Textual Practice* 3:1 (Spring 1989), 115–24.
Mersmann, James J., *Out of the Vietnam Vortex: A Study of Poets and Poetry against the War* (Lawrence: University of Kansas Press, 1974).
Middleton, Peter, '1973', in Delville and Pagnoulle (eds), *The Mechanics of the Mirage*, 49–66.
Miles, Barry, *Ginsberg: A Biography* (1989; repr. London: Virgin, 2000).
—— *William Burroughs: El Hombre Invisible* (1992; London: Virgin, 2002).

Miller, Chris, 'Acker: A Contemporary Fiction Exploration', *The Argonaut* (4 October 1993), 3.
Miller, J. Hillis, *Speech Acts in Literature* (Stanford, CA: Stanford University Press, 2001).
Miller, Stephen Paul, *The Seventies Now: Culture as Surveillance* (Durham, NC: Duke University Press, 1999).
Mitchell, David, *Pirates* (London: Thames and Hudson, 1976).
Monroe, Robert A., *Journeys Out of the Body* (London: Corgi, 1974).
Morgan, Ted, *Literary Outlaw: The Life and Times of William S. Burroughs* (1988; repr. London: Pimlico, 2002).
Mottram, Eric, *William Burroughs: The Algebra of Need* (London: Boyars, 1977).
Mumford, Lewis, *The Myth of the Machine: The Pentagon of Power* (1970; repr. London: Secker and Warburg, 1971).
Murphy, Gardner, *Human Potentialities* (New York: Basic Books, 1958).
Murphy, Timothy S., *Wising Up the Marks: The Amodern William Burroughs* (Berkeley: University of California Press, 1997).
Neal, Larry, 'And Shine Swam On', in Baraka and Neal (eds), *Black Fire*, 638–56.
—— 'The Black Arts Movement' (1968), in Addison Gayle, Jr (ed.), *The Black Aesthetic* (New York: Doubleday, 1971), 272–90.
Nel, Philip, *The Avant-Garde and American Postmodernity: Small Incisive Shocks* (Jackson, MS: University Press of Mississippi, 2002).
Newfield, Jack, 'LeRoi Jones at Arms: Blues for Mr Whitey', *Village Voice* (17 December 1964), 1, 12.
Newman, Edwin, 'NBC 11th Hour News' [transcript] (19 November 1969), in Amiri Baraka Archive, Howard University Library (Box 39, Folder: '*Slave Ship*').
Nicholls, Peter, 'Phenomenal Poetics: Reading Lyn Hejinian', in Delville and Pagnoulle (eds), *The Mechanics of the Mirage*, 241–52.
Nichols, Shaun (ed.), *The Architecture of the Imagination: New Essays on Pretence, Possibility, and Fiction* (Oxford: Oxford University Press, 2009).
Ohmann, Richard, 'Speech Acts and the Definition of Literature', *Philosophy and Rhetoric* 4 (1971), 1–19.
Olson, Charles, 'Projective Verse' (1950), in Paul Hoover (ed.), *Postmodern American Poetry: A Norton Anthology* (New York: Norton, 1994), 613–21.
Olson, Paul A. (ed.), *Russian Formalist Criticism*, trans. Lee T. Lemon and Marion J. Reis (Lincoln: University of Nebraska Press, 1965).
Ostrander, Sheila, and Lynn Schroeder, *Psychic Discoveries behind the Iron Curtain* (London: Souvenir, 1997).
Parenti, Christian, *Lockdown America: Police and Prisons in the Age of Crisis* (New York: Verso, 2000).
Pasolini, Pier Paolo (dir.), *Salò or the 120 Days of Sodom* (United Artists, 1975) [film].
Perelman, Bob, Letter to Hejinian (15 August 1981), in Lyn Hejinian Archive, Mandeville Special Collections Library, University of California, San Diego (Box 44, Folder 24).

—— *The Marginalization of Poetry: Language Writing and Literary History* (Princeton, NJ: Princeton University Press, 1996).

—— Steve Benson, Tom Mandel, Kit Robinson, Rae Armantrout, Barrett Watten, Carla Harryman, Ron Silliman, Lyn Hejinian, and Ted Pearson, *The Grand Piano*, Part 1: *An Experiment in Collective Autobiography, San Francisco 1975–1980* (Detroit: Mode A, 2007).

Perloff, Marjorie, *21st-Century Modernism: The 'New' Poetics* (Oxford: Blackwell, 2002).

—— *Poetry On and Off the Page: Essays for Emergent Occasions* (Evanston, IL: Northwestern University Press, 1998).

—— *Radical Artifice: Writing Poetry in the Age of Media* (Chicago: University of Chicago Press, 1991).

Petrey, Sandy, *Speech Acts and Literary Theory* (London: Routledge, 1990).

Pinkney, Alphonso, *Red, Black, and Green: Black Nationalism in the United States* (Cambridge: Cambridge University Press, 1976).

Poggioli, Renato, *The Theory of the Avant-Garde*, trans. Gerald Fitzgerald (Cambridge, MA: Harvard University Press, 1968).

Poole, Adrian, *Tragedy: A Very Short Introduction* (Oxford: Oxford University Press, 2005).

Portugés, Paul, *The Visionary Poetics of Allen Ginsberg* (Santa Barbara: Ross-Erikson, 1978).

Pound, Ezra, *The Cantos of Ezra Pound* (London: Faber and Faber, 1994).

Pratt, Mary Louise, *Toward a Speech Act Theory of Literary Discourse* (Bloomington, IN: Indiana University Press, 1977).

Raskin, Jonah, *For the Hell of It: The Life and Times of Abbie Hoffman* (1996; repr. Berkeley, CA: University of California Press, 1998).

Rasula, Jed, *Syncopations: The Stress of Innovation in Contemporary American Poetry* (Tuscaloosa: University of Alabama Press, 2004).

Reagan, Ronald, with Richard B. Hubler, *Where's the Rest of Me?* (1965; repr. New York: Karz, 1981).

Rediker, Marcus, 'Hydrarchy and Libertalia: The Utopian Dimensions of Atlantic Piracy in the Early Eighteenth Century', in David J. Starkey, E. S. van Eyck van Heslinga, and J. A. de Moor (eds), *Pirates and Privateers: New Perspectives on the War on Trade in the Eighteenth and Nineteenth Centuries* (Exeter: University of Exeter Press, 1997), 29–46.

Reilly, Charlie (ed.), *Conversations with Amiri Baraka* (Jackson, MS: University Press of Mississippi, 1994).

Reinfeld, Linda, *Language Poetry: Writing as Rescue* (Baton Rouge: Louisiana State University Press, 1992).

Reiss, Edward, *The Strategic Defense Initiative* (Cambridge: Cambridge University Press, 1992).

Republic of New Africa, 'The Freedom Corps: For Service in the Revolution' (1969), in Amiri Baraka Archive, Howard University Library (Box 16, Folder: 'Republic of New Africa').

Republic of New Africa, 'Working Papers: Projection of Problems and Solutions for Ocean Hill-Brownsville as Independent State' (7–8 December 1968), in Amiri Baraka Archive, Howard University Library (Box 16, Folder: 'Republic of New Africa').

Republic of New Africa Security Forces, 'Directive No. 2' (6 May 1970), in Amiri Baraka Archive, Howard University Library (Box 16, Folder: 'Republic of New Africa').

Riley, Denise, *Impersonal Passion: Language as Affect* (Durham, NC: Duke University Press, 2005).

—— *The Words of Selves: Identification, Solidarity, Irony* (Stanford, CA: Stanford University Press, 2000).

Robinson, Jenefer, *Deeper Than Reason: Emotion and Its Role in Literature, Music, and Art* (Oxford: Clarendon Press, 2005).

Ronen, Ruth, *Possible Worlds in Literary Theory* (Cambridge: Cambridge University Press, 1994).

Rorvik, David M., *As Man Becomes Machine: Evolution of the Cyborg* (London: Sphere, 1979).

Rose, Nikolas, *Governing the Soul: The Shaping of the Private Self* (London: Routledge, 1989).

Roszak, Theodore, *The Making of a Counter Culture: Reflections on the Technocratic Society and its Youthful Opposition* (1968; repr. Berkeley, CA: University of California Press, 1995).

Roy, Arundhati, 'The Algebra of Infinite Justice', *The Guardian* (29 September 2001), Saturday Review section, 1–2.

Russell, Charles, *Poets, Prophets, and Revolutionaries: The Literary Avant-Garde from Rimbaud through Postmodernism* (Oxford: Oxford University Press, 1985).

Russell, Jamie, *Queer Burroughs* (London: Palgrave, 2001).

Sagan, Carl, *The Cosmic Connection: An Extraterrestrial Perspective* (London: Hodder, 1975).

Sandford, Mariellen (ed.), *Happenings and Other Acts* (London: Routledge, 1995).

Sandler, Stephanie, 'Arkadii Dragomoshchenko, Lyn Hejinian and the Persistence of Romanticism' *Contemporary Literature* 46:1 (2005), 18–45.

Sayre, Henry M., *The Object of Performance: The American Avant-Garde since 1970* (Chicago: University of Chicago Press, 1989).

Scheffler, Israel, *Of Human Potential: An Essay in the Philosophy of Education* (London: Routledge and Kegan Paul, 1985).

Scholder, Amy, Carla Harryman, and Avital Ronell (eds), *Lust for Life: On the Writings of Kathy Acker* (New York: Verso, 2006).

Schroeder, Timothy, and Carl Matheson, 'Imagination and Emotion', in Nichols (ed.), *The Architecture of the Imagination*, 19–39.

Schulman, Bruce J., *The Seventies: The Great Shift in American Culture, Society, and Politics* (Cambridge, MA: Da Capo, 2002).

Schulzinger, Robert D., 'Richard Nixon, Congress, and the War in Vietnam, 1969–74', in Randall B. Woods (ed.), *Vietnam and the American Political*

Tradition: The Politics of Dissent (Cambridge: Cambridge University Press, 2003), 282–300.

Schumacher, Michael, *Dharma Lion: A Biography of Allen Ginsberg* (1992; repr. New York: St Martin's Press, 1994).

Scott, A. O., 'War is Hell, but Very Pretty', *New York Times* (25 May 2001), Reviews Section, 5.

Sedgwick, Eve Kosofsky. *Touching Feeling: Affect, Pedagogy, Performativity* (Durham, NC: Duke University Press, 2003).

—— and Adam Frank (eds), *Shame and Its Sisters: A Silvan Tomkins Reader* (Durham, NC: Duke University Press, 1995).

Shakespeare, William, *A Midsummer Night's Dream*, in *Shakespeare: Complete Works*, ed. W. J. Craig (London: Oxford University Press, 1974).

Shklovskii, Viktor, 'Art as Technique', in Paul A. Olson (ed.), *Russian Formalist Criticism*, trans. Lee T. Lemon and Marion J. Reis (Lincoln, NE: University of Nebraska Press, 1965), 3–24.

Siegel, Carol, 'The Madness Outside Gender: Travels with Don Quixote and Saint Foucault', *rhizomes* [online journal] 1 (Fall 2000), available at http://www.rhizomes.net/issue1/mad/quixote.html, accessed 5 August 2009.

Silliman, Ron, 'Canons for Institutions: New Hope for the Disappeared', in Bernstein (ed.), *The Politics of Poetic Form*, 149–74.

—— 'If By "Writing" We Mean Literature (if by "literature" we mean poetry (*if...*))...', in Andrews and Bernstein (eds), *The L=A=N=G=U=A=G=E Book*, 167–8.

—— Letter to Hejinian (12 May 1981), in Lyn Hejinian Archive, Mandeville Special Collections Library, University of California, San Diego (Box 44, Folder 29).

—— *The New Sentence* (New York: Roof, 1995).

—— *Tjanting* (1981; repr. Cambridge: Salt, 2002).

—— and Carla Harryman, Lyn Hejinian, Steve Benson, Bob Perelman, and Barrett Watten, 'Aesthetic Tendency and the Politics of Poetry: A Manifesto', *Social Text* (Autumn 1988), 261–75.

Skerl, Jennie, *William S. Burroughs* (Boston: Twayne, 1985).

—— and Robin Lydenberg (eds), *William S. Burroughs at the Front: Critical Reception, 1959–89* (Carbondale: Southern Illinois Press, 1991).

Slocum-Schaffer, Stephanie, *America in the Seventies* (Syracuse, NY: Syracuse University Press, 2003).

Sollors, Werner, *Amiri Baraka/LeRoi Jones: The Quest for a 'Populist Modernism'* (New York: Columbia University Press, 1978).

Spahr, Juliana, *Everybody's Autonomy: Connective Reading and Collective Identity* (Tuscaloosa: University of Alabama Press, 2001).

Stein, Gertrude, *How to Write* (1931; repr. New York: Dover, 1975).

Steiner, Peter, *Russian Formalism: A Metapoetics* (Ithaca, NY: Cornell University Press, 1984), 18–21.

Stephens, Julie, *Anti-Disciplinary Protest: Sixties Radicalism and Postmodernism* (Cambridge: Cambridge University Press, 1998).

Stewart, Brand (ed.), *Space Colonies* (Harmondsworth: Penguin, 1977).
Sukenick, Ronald, *Blown Away* (Los Angeles: Sun and Moon Press, 1986).
Tallmer, Jerry, 'LeRoi Jones Strikes Again', *New York Post* (24 March 1964), 64.
Tauberman, Howard, 'The Theater: *Dutchman*', *New York Times* (25 March 1964), Arts section, 3.
Terada, Rei, *Feeling in Theory: Emotion after the 'Death of the Subject'* (Cambridge, MA: Harvard University Press, 2001).
Tomkins, Silvan, 'What Are Affects?', in Eve Kosofsky Sedgwick and Adam Frank (eds), *Shame and Its Sisters: A Silvan Tomkins Reader* (Durham, NC: Duke University Press, 1995).
——*Affect Imagery Consciousness*, Vol. III (New York: Springer, 1991).
Troy, Gil, *Morning in America: How Ronald Reagan Invented the 1980s* (Princeton: Princeton University Press, 2005).
Vaidhyanathan, Siva, *Copyrights and Copywrongs: The Rise of Intellectual Property and How it Threatens Creativity* (New York: New York University Press, 2001).
Vanderborg, Susan, *Paratextual Communities: American Avant-Garde Poetry since 1950* (Carbondale and Edwardsville: Southern Illinois University Press, 2001).
Virilio, Paul, 'Critical Space' (1984), in *The Virilio Reader*, ed. and trans. James Der Derian (Oxford: Blackwell, 1998), 58–72.
——*Pure War*, trans. Mark Polizzotti and Brian O'Keefe (New York: Semiotext(e), 1997).
Virno, Paolo, *A Grammar of the Multitude*, trans. Isabella Bertoletti, James Cascaito, and Andrea Casson (New York: Semiotext(e), 2004).
——*Multitude: Between Innovation and Negation*, trans. Isabella Bertoletti, James Cascaito, and Andrea Casson (Los Angeles: Semiotext(e), 2008).
von Hallberg, Robert (ed.), *Politics and Poetic Value* (Chicago: University of Chicago Press, 1987).
Wallace, Michelle, *Black Macho and the Myth of the Superwoman* (1978; repr. New York: Verso, 1999).
Wallis Budge, E. A., *The Egyptian Book of the Dead: The Papyrus of Ani—Egyptian Text, Transliteration and Translation* (1895; repr. New York: Seager, 1967).
Walsh, Richard, *Novel Arguments: Reading Innovative American Fiction* (Cambridge: Cambridge University Press, 1995).
Walton, Kendall, 'Spelunking, Simulation, and Slime: On Being Moved by Fiction', in Mette Hjort and Sue Laver (eds), *Emotion and the Arts* (Oxford: Oxford University Press, 1997), 37–49.
——*Mimesis as Make-Believe* (Cambridge, MA: Harvard University Press, 1987).
Ward, Geoff, *Language Poetry and the American Avant-Garde* (Keele: British Association of American Studies, 1993).
Watten, Barrett, 'Foucault Reads Acker and Rewrites the History of the Novel', in Scholder, Harryman, and Ronell (eds), *Lust for Life*, 58–77.
——'The Turn to Language and the 1960s', *Critical Inquiry* 29 (Autumn 2002), 139–83.
——*The Constructivist Moment: From Material Text to Cultural Poetics* (Middletown, CT: Wesleyan University Press, 2003).

Watts, Jerry Gafio, *Amiri Baraka: The Politics and Art of a Black Intellectual* (New York: New York University Press, 2001).
Weber, Ronald, *Seeing Earth: Literary Responses to Space Exploration* (Athens, OH: Ohio University Press, 1985).
Weinberg, Jonathan M., and Aaron Meskin, 'Puzzling over the Imagination: Philosophical Problems, Architectural Solutions', in Nichols (ed.), *The Architecture of the Imagination*, 175–202.
Weiss, Paul, 'The Dunamis', *Review of Metaphysics* 40:4 (June 1987), 657–74.
Wescott, Roger W., *The Divine Animal: An Exploration of Human Potentiality* (New York: Funk and Wagnalls, 1969).
Wirbel, Loring, *Star Wars: US Tools of Space Supremacy* (London: Pluto, 2004).
Witt, Charlotte, *Ways of Being: Potentiality and Actuality in Aristotle's* Metaphysics (Ithaca, NY: Cornell University Press, 2003).
Wolfe, Tom, *Electric Kool-Aid Acid Test* (1968; repr. New York: Bantam, 1999).
—— *The Right Stuff* (1979; repr. London: Picador, 1990).
Woodard, Komozi, *A Nation within a Nation: Amiri Baraka/LeRoi Jones and Black Power Politics* (Chapel Hill, NC: University of North Carolina Press, 1999).
Woolf, Cecil, and John Bagguley (eds), *Authors Take Sides on Vietnam* (London: Peter Owen, 1967).
Wordsworth, William, *The Prelude* (1805 ed.; repr. Oxford: Oxford University Press, 1984).
Zaroulis, Nancy, and Gerald Sullivan, *Who Spoke Up?: American Protest against the War in Vietnam, 1963–1975* (New York: Doubleday, 1984).
Zweig, Paul, 'A Music of Angels', *The Nation* (10 March 1969), 313.

Index

11 September 2001 attacks 102, 237–9, 240
1960s 11, 22–5, 48, 58–61, 193–7
1970s 7, 58–9, 120–1, 165–6
1980s 175–6, 185–6, 209–13
1990s 187, 224–5

abortion 160–1, 176, 186
Abstract Expressionism 23
Acker, Kathy
   The Childlike Life of the Black Tarantula 152–4
   I Dreamt I was a Nymphomaniac Imagining 154–6
   Rip-Off Red, Girl Detective 156–9
   Blood and Guts in High School 160–5, 169, 170
   Great Expectations 169–72
   My Death My Life by Pier Paolo Pasolini 172–5
   Don Quixote 176–8
   Empire of the Senseless 178–85
   In Memoriam to Identity 185–6
   My Mother: Demonology 186–7
   Pussy, King of the Pirates 188–91
Adorno, Theodor 234
aesthetics 10, 82, 87, 89, 99, 148, 151, 192
   Black Cultural Nationalist 82, 87, 89, 99
   of existence 148–9, 151
affects 10, 36–7, 93, 143–4, 155–6, 192, 226–31, 234–5, 241–5, 250–5
   see also happiness; hatred; shame; sympathy; terror
Agamben, Giorgio 2–4
Allen, Donald 224
Altieri, Charles 210–11, 223–4, 226
Andrews, Bruce 203, 212–13
Antin, David 13
Arendt, Hannah 42, 108, 111, 121
Aristotle 3, 8, 149, 235, 249
Artaud, Antonin 84, 91, 255
Ashbery, John 82
Auden, W. H. 235
audio-tape recording 17, 31, 48, 114–15, 118–19
Auschwitz 233–4
Austin, J. L. 242, 245, 247–8
   see also performativity

autobiography 31–2, 44, 152–5, 204–5, 208
avant-garde 11, 13–16, 23–4, 38, 84, 224–5, 241
   see also Beat movement; Dadaism; Futurism; Language poetry; Vorticism
Avicenna 8

Baraka, Amiri (LeRoi Jones)
   and *Floating Bear* 65–6
   and *Yugen* 65–6
   Preface to a Twenty Volume Suicide Note 67
   Dutchman 74–6
   The Slave 76–7
   Black Magic 83–4
   Great Goodness of Life 85–6
   A Black Mass 86–7
   Madheart 87
   Slave Ship 91–4, 242
   In Our Terribleness 94–5
   It's Nation Time 95–6
   Hard Facts 100–1
   Spirit Reach 99–101
   What was the Relationship between the Lone Ranger and the Means of Production? 68, 102
   see also Black Arts Movement; Black Cultural Nationalism; Maulana Karenga; US Organization
Bataille, Georges 186
Baudrillard, Jean 136–8, 143
Beat movement 24–6, 30–1, 63–4, 67, 69, 109
Beckett, Samuel 256
Beiles, Sinclair 109
Benson, Steve 211
Bernstein, Charles 12–13, 198, 202–4, 209, 211–13, 224–5, 240
Berry, Wendell 135
biopolitics 7, 147–50, 154, 159–62, 165–8, 186, 191–2
   see also Michel Foucault
Black Arts Movement 71, 77–94
   see also Larry Neal
Black Cultural Nationalism 18, 63–6, 79–82, 90, 96–7, 101
Black Panther Party 63, 79, 88, 90, 97, 117
   see also Huey P. Newton

Index

Black Power 62–4, 87
  see also Malcolm X
Black Revolutionary Nationalism 63–4, 90
  see also Black Panther Party
Blake, William 27, 55, 59
Bly, Robert 24, 37
bodies 27–8, 36, 46–7, 131–3, 178–83, 234–5
  astral 131–3, 140–1
body politic 22, 39, 44, 64, 114, 174, 186
  see also democracy
Boym, Svetlana 214–15
Brown, Earl 109
Bullins, Ed 87
Bürger, Peter 15
Burroughs, William S.
  Naked Lunch 103–5, 117–18
  Exterminator! 109, 127
  The Soft Machine 109, 112, 252
  The Ticket that Exploded 113–15
  Nova Express 112–13, 115
  The Wild Boys 116, 125, 132
  The Third Mind 110–11
  The Job 117, 119, 125
  Cities of the Red Night 125–31
  The Place of Dead Roads 132–5
  The Western Lands 138–43
Bush, President George H. 146, 186, 220
Butler, Judith 154, 179, 243, 246

Cage, John 11, 13, 20, 91, 109
Calinescu, Matei 11
capitalism 1–3, 50, 102, 197, 209–10
Carroll, Lewis 178
Carter, President Jimmy 120
Carver, Raymond 14
Cassady, Neal 30
Civil Rights movement 62–3, 73–4
  see also Martin Luther King
Clinton, President Bill 185, 187
Cold War 5, 8, 28–9, 42–4, 112–14, 136, 219–21
  and Vietnam War 42–44
  and Strategic Arms Limitation Treaties (SALT) 54, 136
  and space race 106–9, 120–4, 136
Coleman, Ornette 70, 71
Coltrane, John 70, 99, 102
comedy 231–5, 239, 249
Communism 36–7, 54, 124, 214–15, 218–20
  see also Cold War
Congress of Afrikan People (CAP) 97–9
consumerism 11–12, 15, 60
Coolidge, Clark 202

Corso, Gregory 31, 42, 82, 109
counter-culture 22–6, 29–30, 42–50, 117–18, 126, 194–7
  and 1967 March on the Pentagon 42–4
  and 1968 Democrat's Convention in Chicago 45–7
  see also Diggers; Merry Pranksters; Students for a Democratic Society; Yippies
Creeley, Robert 38, 65, 82
Cruse, Harold 62–3, 66–7
cut-ups 26, 109–18, 125, 146, 243

Dadaism 71, 109
Davidson, Michael 219
de Carolis, Massimo 2, 4, 12–13, 253
de Cervantes, Miguel *Don Quixote de la Mancha* 176
de Sade, Marquis 153
de Saussure, Ferdinand 200, 217
death 32, 74–5, 114, 138–9, 173, 235–6
  see also immortality
Defoe, Daniel *A General History of the Pyrates* 126
Deleuze, Gilles, and Félix Guattari 8, 143, 163–4, 190, 206, 227, 243
DeLillo, Don 239
democracy 35–6, 56–7, 62–4, 159, 208, 211
Derrida, Jacques 245–8
di Prima, Diane 24, 65,
Dickens, Charles *Great Expectations* 170–1
Diggers 49–50
Doležel, Lubomir 9
drag 154, 162, 177, 181–3
Dragomoshchenko, Arkadii 214, 215
dreams 131–2, 142, 154–9, 165–6, 181–2
  see also Sigmund Freud
drugs 25, 49, 167–8
Duncan, Robert 24, 37
Dworkin, Andrea 177

Eisenhower, President Dwight D. 107
Eliot, T. S. 104, 105, 110, 110
ethnicity 62–3, 95–7, 101–2, 156
  see also race
experimental writing 14, 17–20, 241–2, 253, 255

Federal Bureau of Investigation (FBI) 84, 88–90
Felman, Shoshana 248
fictionality 9–10, 130–1, 176–7, 252–3
  see also possible worlds

Fitzgerald, F. Scott 68, 142
Ford, President Gerald 161
Foucault, Michel 3–4, 145–50, 162–3, 168–9, 173, 184, 191–2
Free Southern Theater 79, 87, 94
Freud, Sigmund *The Interpretation of Dreams* 155–6, 165, 233, 252
Fulbright, Senator William 40–1
Futurism 11, 15, 38

Gagarin, Yuri 107, 113
gender 154, 156–7, 178–9, 234
Genet, Jean 117, 164
Gibson, William 14, 181
Ginsberg, Allen
 Howl and Other Poems 25, 69
 'Wichita Vortex Sutra' 31–40
 The Fall of America 31, 57–9
 'Friday the Thirteenth' 52
 'Grant Park' 47, 52
 'Iron Horse' 39–40
 'Pentagon Exorcism' 43–4
 Planet News 31, 48
 'These States' 55–6
 'Public Statement Signed by Poet Friends' 56–7
 'September on Jessore Road' 59
 'Plutonian Ode' 60
Glück, Robert 155
Gorbachev, President Mikhail 214–15, 218–20
Gysin, Brion 26, 109–10, 121, 127

Happenings 91, 194
 see also Antonin Artaud; John Cage
happiness 151, 227–31, 235–6
Haraway, Donna 180–1
Hardt, Michael, and Antonio Negri 148–9, 191, 244
hatred 71–6, 86–7, 118, 243
Hawthorne, Nathaniel *The Scarlet Letter* 159, 161–3
Heidegger, Martin 4
Hejinian, Lyn *My Life* 201–9, 213, 216
 My Life in the Nineties 204, 206
 The Cell 215–18, 223, 226
 Oxota 220–3, 227, 231
 Happily 223–32, 235, 242, 252
 A Border Comedy 231–5, 239
 The Fatalist 235–40
Hippies 5, 24, 42–3, 117, 119, 183
HIV/AIDS 7, 167–8, 175, 185–6
Hoffman, Abbie 42, 43, 45, 195
Howe, Susan 202, 231–2
Huyssen, Andreas 11, 13

hybridity 59, 104–6, 140–1, 180, 208

imagination 18, 35, 77, 146, 151, 190–1, 216–17, 238–9, 253–5
immortality 134, 136, 138–42
Internet 187–8, 191, 225

Jameson, Fredric 1–2, 11–13, 15, 23, 48, 104–5, 143, 197
 see also Marxism
Jazz 68–72, 78, 84, 93
 see also Ornette Coleman; John Coltrane
Johnson, President Lyndon Baines 29, 35, 40, 45, 78
Jones, LeRoi
 see Amiri Baraka
Joyce, James 119, 142, 173

Kafka, Franz 84, 115
Kant, Immanuel 238–9
Karenga, Maulana 80, 82, 90, 96–7
 see also Kawaida; US Organization
Kawaida 80–1, 89, 94
Kennedy, President John F. 28, 29, 107
Kerouac, Jack 25, 60, 151
Kesey, Ken 30, 49, 135
King, Martin Luther 62, 73, 90
Kissinger, Henry 53, 177
Kripke, Saul 9
Kristeva, Julia 189–90

labour 2–3, 147–8, 151, 166–7, 198–9, 204, 217
Language poetry 193–204, 209–13, 223–6, 253
Leary, Timothy 25, 42, 135–6
Lemaire, Gérard-Georges 109–10, 112
 see also cut-ups
Levertov, Denise 24, 37–8, 82
Lewis, Wyndham 38
 see also Vorticism
liberation
 political 158
 racial 77, 97
 sexual 151, 179
 and 1960s 7, 22–3, 47, 50, 114
Lukács, György *The Meaning of Contemporary Realism* 8–9, 14, 64–5, 67, 94
Lumumba, Patrice 66, 85
Lyotard, Jean-François 13, 115, 228, 230, 238
lyric poetry 26, 31–2, 34–6, 38–40, 67, 199–200, 210

McCaffery, Steve 209–10, 222
  see also Language poetry
McCarthy, Mary 103, 105, 144
McClure, Michael 135
  see also Beat movement
Mailer, Norman 43–5, 56, 103–4, 117, 122
Malcolm X (Malcolm Little) 63, 69, 73, 77, 80, 85
Marcuse, Herbert 5, 42, 151, 154, 165–6
Marinetti, Filippo Tommaso 38, 84
  see also Futurism
Marxism 2–3, 23, 50, 61, 79, 195, 202
mass media 24, 51–4, 80, 84, 107–8, 174–5, 186, 196
  see also radio; television
Melville, Herman 3, 159
Mengham, Rod 210–11, 223
Merry Pranksters 30, 49
  see also Ken Kesey
Miller, Henry 103
modernism 8, 13–16, 105, 213
  see also avant-garde
Mumford, Lewis 6, 42, 121, 123, 134–5
Murphy, Gardner 5

Nabokov, Vladimir 157
NASA 105–9, 119–24
National Black Theater 79, 87, 101
Neal, Larry 64, 78, 86–7, 101
  see also Black Arts Movement
New Journalism 43–4, 122
  see also Norman Mailer; Tom Wolfe
New Left 5–6, 23–4, 42, 49, 117, 194–7
  see also counter-culture
Newton, Huey P. 63
  see also Black Panther Party
Nietzsche, Friedrich 228, 236
Nixon, President Richard 48, 50–3, 56–8, 118, 121, 125, 165, 177
  see also Watergate scandal

O'Hara, Frank 65, 74
obscenity 25, 117–18, 160, 172
Olson, Charles 65–6, 70–2, 82, 151
Oppen, George 227–8
order words 164, 170, 189–90, 206, 243
Orlovsky, Peter 26, 27, 31
OuLiPo 255
Ovid 188

Pan-Africanism 94–101
  see also Congress of Afrikan People
Pasolini, Pier Paolo 172–3
Perelman, Bob 197, 201, 202

performativity 32–6, 71–4, 162–4, 191, 199, 206–7, 241–55
  see also order words
Perloff, Marjorie 13, 205
piracy: maritime 125–9;
  literary 129–30, 178–81, 184–5, 188–91, 212
  see also plagiarism
plagiarism 129, 151–3, 161, 169–71, 174, 183–4
Poggioli, Renato 11, 15
Pop Art 11
possibility 2–5, 16–20, 22–5, 32, 62–5, 77, 173, 180, 198–9, 206–8, 229–30
possible worlds 9–11, 16–17, 32–5, 86, 132–3, 203, 254–5
postmodernism 1–2, 11–16, 23–4, 50, 104–8, 115–6, 143–4, 180–1, 212
potentialism 16–21, 241–2, 253–6
  and Allen Ginsberg 24, 36–7, 40, 45–6, 199, 242
  and Amiri Baraka 71–2, 77–8, 195, 199, 242, 253
  and William S. Burroughs 104–6, 115–16, 133–4, 140–1, 199, 252–3;
  and Kathy Acker 179–80, 191–2, 199, 208, 226, 241
  and Lyn Hejinian 207–8, 223–7, 230, 241–2, 252–3
potentiality 1–10, 16–17, 104–5, 245–9, 253–6
  as capacity 2–5, 8–10, 12–13, 64–5, 192, 206, 239–40, 255
  as *dunamis* 3, 246
  as force 16, 19, 70, 77, 99, 138, 199, 203, 223, 241–2, 253
  as latency 1, 3, 16, 36, 106, 116, 140, 143, 156, 206, 241
  abstract 8–9, 36, 64–5, 67, 70, 88, 94, 199, 206, 230
  concrete 2, 8–9, 64–5, 67, 70, 77, 88, 94, 102, 104, 253
  see also possibility
Pound, Ezra 33, 104, 256
power 3–8, 146–50, 168–70, 184–8, 191–8
  as practical power 2–4, 12–13, 253
  as labour-power 2–3
  and sovereignty 3, 146–7, 167–8, 173, 186
  and discipline 168, 179
  and governmentality 148–9, 168
  see also Black Power; biopolitics
Prigov, Dmitrii 219

Index

Pushkin, Alexander 220
Pynchon, Thomas 11

race 63–5, 69–85, 94–102, 104, 213
radio 26, 29, 33–4, 54,
Rasula, Jed 14
rationality 41–2, 44, 57, 61, 69, 196, 238–9
Reagan, Ronald 136, 166–9, 171–7, 185–6
realism
  emotional 250–4;
  literary 8–9, 14, 202–3, 220
  and performativity 247–9
Republic of New Africa 89–90
revolution 61, 63–5, 76–80, 87–8, 99–101, 117–18, 125, 158, 183–4, 192
  see also Marxism
Riley, Denise 243
Rimbaud, Arthur 185–6
Ronen, Ruth 10
Roszak, Theodore 5, 23, 64
Rubin, Jerry 42, 45, 56,
Rushdie, Salman 247
Russian Formalism 200–1, 214, 217–18, 220, 223

sacrifice 34, 68–9, 73–6, 85, 188
Sagan, Carl 122–3, 134, 135,
Sanders, Ed 42, 43
Sayre, Henry 13
Scalapino, Leslie 228
Schechner, Richard 91
Seale, Bobby 63
Sedgwick, Eve Kosofksy 244–5, 249
Seneca 150
  see also Stoics
sexuality 46, 131, 151–65, 172–3, 179, 181–2, 190
  see also gender
Shakespeare, William 173, 175, 233
shame 162, 245
Shklovskii, Viktor 200–1
  see also Russian Formalism
Silliman, Ron 195, 197–8, 200–4, 210, 219, 224
Snyder, Gary 25, 42, 135
  see also Beat movement
Somerville, Ian 114
Soviet Union 112, 213–15, 218–20
  and space programmes 106–9, 120, 123–4, 135–7
  and US relations 112, 123–4, 213–15

space 103–6, 196, 206, 216–7, 235
  literary 104–6, 110–13, 142–3, 252
  and space programmes 106–9, 112–13, 119–24, 133, 135–8
Spinoza 8–9, 253
spirituality 25–7, 34–5, 37, 71–2, 80–3, 86, 94–100, 143, 203, 215
Stein, Gertrude 226
strikes 2–3
Students for a Democratic Society (SDS) 5, 23, 30, 50, 64, 146,
sublime 238–9, 250
Sukenick, Ronald 14
sympathy 10, 41, 159–62, 207, 230, 243
syntax 115, 163, 203, 222, 230, 243
  see also order words

Teer, Barbara Ann 87, 101
  see also National Black Theater
television 26, 39, 41, 108
  see also mass media
terror 238–9, 244, 249
terrorism 52, 82, 102, 175, 181, 184, 237–8
  see also terror
Thatcher, Prime Minister Margaret 146, 175, 185
Third-World Socialism 100–2
  see also Marxism
time 103–5, 110–11, 132–3, 142, 227–31, 235–7
tragedy 243, 249
Trocchi, Alexander 152
Twain, Mark 184
Tynianov, Yuri 200, 217
  see also Russian Formalism
Tzara, Tristan 109
  see also Dadaism

United Nations (UN) 66, 82, 120, 158
US Organization 80–1, 90, 97
  see also Kawaida; Maulana Karenga
utopianism 12, 89–90, 98, 126, 183, 194, 202–3
  see also counter-culture; Republic of New Africa

Verlaine, Paul 185–6
Vietnam War 24–61, 117, 196–7
  and *Authors Take Sides on Vietnam* 41–2
  and CIA 51–2
  and 'electronic battlefield' 42, 56–7, 196
  and 'Operation Rolling Thunder' 29

Vietnam War (*cont.*)
   and Senator George Aiken 33–4
   and 'Tet Offensive' 45, 48, 51
   and 'Tonkin Gulf Resolution' 29
Virilio, Paul 136–7, 143
Virno, Paolo 2, 4, 232, 234
von Braun, Werner 122, 130
Vorticism 15, 38

war against terror 237–9
   see also 11 September 2001 attacks
Watergate scandal 48, 57–8, 117–8, 158, 196

Watten, Barett 193–204, 212–3, 225
Welch, Denton 132
Wescott, Roger 6
Westmoreland, General William 42, 43–4, 51
Whalen, Philip 65
Wolfe, Tom 49, 122, 130

X, Malcolm
   see Malcolm X

Yeats, W. B. 72, 152–4, 235
Yippies 43, 45–50, 117, 195